D0687005

YOUNG
FASHION
DESIGNERS AMERICAS

Introduction   4

INTRODUCTION

Art into Objects of Fashion

Fashion has emerged as a simple functional necessity into a badge of class and status, and in the turn of the twentieth century, evolved into an art form and applied science dedicated to lifestyle. Fashion is derived from the cultural and social influences of a specific place, where individuality and tastes are manifested in the design of the clothing. Where fashion designers were traditionally the primary conveyors of the general trends of the society in which they live, today's current fashions can be seen as a rebellious message against set traditions, or the practice of alternative lifestyles. A new breed of visually aware designers has taken hold of this evolution. These rising stars of the fashion world create wearable decorative art by linking material culture with their national identity, and use clothing as a canvas to spread their personal vision.

Coco Chanel once said that fashion "does not exist in dresses only, but in the sky, the street, and fashion has everything to do with ideas, the way we live, and what is happening". Wearable objects of style are a mediator between the individual and current social climate. Fashion has become a way for designers to openly display the progress and development of the collective conscious of the society in which they live. The fashion in these pages reflect a variety of styles born from the inspirations derived from the environment and the identity of the designer, and is an example of how clothing is used to reflect culture in the American continents through the use of design.

During the past few decades of rapid globalization, the unique styles from the American continents began to be adopted all over the world and have a profound impact on fashion today. North American fashion designers create clothing that concentrates on the multitude of subcultures in their society, such as the casual, clean-cut styles of the conservative mainstream, the street fashions of city-dwellers, or the sporty lifestyle of the health-conscious set. Latin American fashions exemplify the culture rich in symbolism and history as their other art forms.

Through a visual journey of the emotion evoking designs of today's trendsetters and the clothing from fashion's emerging talents, one can get a general view of the material world in the American continents. These up-and-coming designers have the individual skills and talents needed to predict fashion trends, and the power to use tools to revolutionize the fashion industry itself. The young fashion designers featured in these beautifully illustrated pages provide inspiration for others to break the molds of fashion as they use fabrics, textiles, thread, and dye to convey their story.

Kunst mutiert zu Modeobjekten

Früher war Mode eher eine simple, zweckmäßige Notwendigkeit. Mittlerweile repräsentiert Mode Klasse und Status. Sie entwickelte sich zur Wende des zwanzigsten Jahrhunderts zu einer Kunstart und angewandten Wissenschaft, die sich dem Lebensstil verschrieben hatte. Mode wird aus den kulturellen und sozialen Einflüssen eines bestimmten Ortes abgeleitet, wo sich Individualität und Geschmack im Design der Kleidung widerspiegeln. Während Modedesigner traditionell die ersten Förderer der allgemeinen Trends der Gesellschaft waren, in der sie lebten, können die heutigen Modetrends als eine gegen festgelegte Traditionen rebellierende Botschaft betrachtet werden, beziehungsweise als das Praktizieren alternativer Lebensstile. Eine neue Generation visuell orientierter Designer hat sich diese Entwicklung zu Nutzen gemacht. Jene aufstrebenden Sterne der Modewelt kreieren tragbare, dekorative Kunst, indem sie Materialkultur mit ihrer nationalen Identität verknüpfen und benutzen Kleidung als Kanvas, um ihre eigene Vision zu verbreiten.

Coco Chanel sagte einmal, dass Mode „nicht nur in Kleidern lebt, sondern im Himmel, auf der Straße, und dass Mode mit Ideen zu tun hat, der Art wie wir leben und was geschieht". Tragbare Stilobjekte fungieren als Mediator zwischen dem individuellen und aktuellen sozialen Klima. Mode ermöglicht es den Designern offen den Fortschritt und die Entwicklung des kollektiven Bewusstseins der Gesellschaft, in der sie leben, zu demonstrieren. Die Mode auf diesen Seiten reflektiert verschiedene Stilrichtungen, die inspiriert wurden von der Umgebung und der Identität des Designers. Sie zeigt beispielhaft wie Kleidung genutzt wird, um Kultur mittels Design auf dem amerikanischen Kontinent zu reflektieren.

Während der letzten Jahrzehnte der zügigen Globalisierung begann die weltweite Akzeptanz des einzigartigen Stils des amerikanischen Kontinents, der die heutige Mode nachhaltig beeinflusst. Nordamerikanische Modedesigner kreieren Kleidung, die sich auf eine Vielzahl von Subkulturen ihrer Gesellschaft konzentriert, wie die lässigen, geradlinigen Modelle des konservativen Mainstream, die Straßenmode der Städter oder der sportliche Lebensstil der Gesundheitsbewussten. Lateinamerikanische Mode veranschaulicht die Kultur, die, genau wie ihre anderen Kunstformen, reich an Symbolik und Geschichte ist.

Eine visuelle Reise der Emotionen, die das Design der heutigen Trendsetter sowie die Kleidung der jungen Talente der Modewelt prägt, ermöglicht einen allgemeinen Überblick der Materialwelt des amerikanischen Kontinents. Diese aufstrebenden Designer besitzen die notwendigen individuellen Fähigkeiten und Talente, um Modetrends vorauszusagen sowie die Macht, Instrumente einzusetzen, um die Modeindustrie selbst zu revolutionieren. Jene Modedesigner, die auf diesen wunderschön illustrierten Seiten die Hauptrolle spielen, schaffen Inspirationen für andere, um die Modeformen zu sprengen, indem sie Stoffe, Textilien, Faden und Färbemittel verwenden, die es ihnen ermöglichen, ihre Geschichte zu kommunizieren.

Objetos de Arte en la Moda

La moda se ha transformado, emergiendo de simple necesidad funcional a insignia de clase y estatus social, evolucionando a la vuelta del siglo XX en una forma de arte y de ciencia aplicada dedicada al estilo de vida. La moda procede de las influencias culturales y sociales de un lugar específico, donde individualidades y gustos se manifiestan en el diseño de las prendas. Aún si los diseñadores de moda se han tradicionalmente considerado como vehículos primarios de transmisión de las tendencias generales de la sociedad donde viven, las modas corrientes de hoy pueden verse como un mensaje de rebelión hacía las tradiciones establecidas, o bien como la práctica de estilos de vida alternativos. Una nueva generación de diseñadores, conscientes de los aspectos visuales, se ha encargado de esta evolución. Estas estrellas nacientes en el mundo de la moda crean arte decorativa para vestir, entrelazando la cultura material y su propia identidad nacional, y utilizan la ropa al igual que un pintor utiliza una tela para difundir su visión personal.

Coco Chanel dijo una vez que la moda "no existe tan sólo en la ropa, sino también en el cielo, en la calle, y la moda tiene totalmente que ver con ideas, con nuestra manera de vivir, y con lo que pasa". Los objetos de estilo para llevar hacen de mediadores entre el individuo y el clima social corriente. A través de la moda los diseñadores demuestran abiertamente el progreso y el desarrollo de la conciencia colectiva de la sociedad en la que viven. La moda en estas páginas refleja una variedad de estilos nacidos de la inspiración derivada del ambiente y de la identidad del diseñador y es un ejemplo de como la ropa es utilizada para reflejar la cultura en el continente americano a través del diseño.

En las últimas décadas de rápida globalización, los estilos únicos procedentes del continente americano han empezado a adoptarse en todo el mundo y ejercen un profundo impacto en la moda de hoy. Los diseñadores de moda norteamericanos crean prendas que se concentran en la multitud de subculturas existentes en su sociedad, como por ejemplo los estilos despreocupados y limpios de la mayoría conservadora, la moda de la calle de los habitantes de las ciudades, o el estilo de vida deportivo de los que son muy conscientes de la importancia de su salud. Las modas latinoamericanas ejemplifican la cultura rica en simbolismos y en historia de aquel continente, de la misma manera que las otras formas artísticas.

Por medio de un viaje visual a través de los diseños producidos por los trendsetters de hoy, con las emociones que nos evocan, y de las prendas creadas por los talentos emergentes de la moda, podemos echar un vistazo general al mundo material en el continente americano. Estos sobresalientes diseñadores poseen tanto las habilidades individuales y los talentos necesarios para prever las tendencias, como el poder de utilizar los instrumentos apropiados para revolucionar la misma industria de la moda. Los jóvenes diseñadores de moda presentados en estas páginas espléndidamente ilustradas proporcionan inspiración para otros, para romper los moldes de la moda utilizando tejidos, hilos y tintas para transmitir su historia.

L'Art changé en Objets de Mode

De simple nécessité fonctionnelle, la mode est devenue un symbole de classe et de statut, et au tournant du vingtième siècle, elle a évolué pour devenir une forme d'art et une science appliquée consacrées au style de vie. La mode émane des influences sociales et culturelles d'un lieu spécifique, où l'individualité et les gouts se manifestent dans le dessin des vêtements. Alors que traditionnellement les stylistes étaient les premiers à transmettre les tendances générales de la société dans laquelle ils évoluaient, les modes actuelles peuvent être considérées comme un message de rébellion contre les traditions établies, ou comme la mise en pratique d'un style de vie alternatif. Une nouvelle génération de créateurs, conscients de l'importance du visuel, ont su s'emparer de cette évolution. Ces étoiles montantes du monde de la mode créent un art décoratif mettable en unissant la culture des matières avec leur identité nationale, et utilisent le vêtement comme une toile pour propager leur vision personnelle.

Coco Chanel a dit un jour que la mode « ce n'est pas que des vêtements, la mode est dans l'air. Elle a quelque chose à voir avec les idées, notre mode de vie, avec ce qui se passe autour de nous. » Les vêtements-objets de style sont un médiateur entre l'individu et le climat social actuel. La mode est devenue une manière pour les stylistes d'afficher ouvertement les progrès et développements de la conscience collective de la société dans laquelle ils vivent. La mode présentée dans ces pages montre une variété de styles nés des inspirations issues de l'environnement et de l'identité du styliste, et est un exemple de la manière dont le vêtement, grâce au stylisme, est utilisé pour refléter la culture sur les continents américains.

Pendant ces dernières décennies de mondialisation rapide, les styles singuliers des continents américains ont été progressivement adoptés par le monde entier, et ils exercent une influence profonde sur la mode d'aujourd'hui. Les stylistes nord-américains créent des vêtements qui condensent la multitude de sous-cultures de leur société, comme le style décontracté, aux coupes simples, de la majorité conservatrice, la mode streetwear des citadins, ou le style de vie sportif adopté par la partie de la population la plus soucieuse de sa santé. En Amérique Latine, la mode représente, au même titre que les autres formes d'art, cette culture riche de symbolisme et d'histoire.

A travers un voyage visuel dans les créations palpitantes des faiseurs de tendances d'aujourd'hui et les vêtements des nouveaux talents de la mode, on peut se faire une idée générale du monde matériel des Amériques. Ces stylistes émergents ont à la fois les compétences individuelles et le talent nécessaires pour prévoir les tendances, et le pouvoir d'utiliser de nouveaux outils pour révolutionner l'industrie de la mode elle-même. Les jeunes créateurs de mode présentés dans ces pages richement illustrées inspirent les autres pour briser les moules de la mode : ils utilisent les tissus, les textiles, les fils et la teinture pour communiquer leur histoire.

L'Arte negli oggetti di Moda

Nata come risposta ad una semplice necessità funzionale, la moda si è elevata al rango di simbolo di classe e di condizione sociale, e si è convertita verso la fine del ventesimo secolo in una forma d'arte e di scienza applicata al lifestyle. La moda scaturisce dalle influenze culturali e sociali di un luogo specifico, dove individualità e gusti si manifestano nel design. Mentre tradizionalmente gli stilisti erano ambasciatori delle tendenze della società in cui vivevano, la moda di oggi può essere interpretata come un messaggio di ribellione contro le tradizioni consolidate, oppure come la scelta di stili di vita alternativi. Una nuova generazione di stilisti con uno spiccato orientamento visuale è promotrice di questa evoluzione. Queste stelle nascenti del mondo della moda creano arte decorativa da indossare, unendo la cultura degli oggetti con la propria identità nazionale. Usano i vestiti come tele su cui dipingere e diffondere la propria visione personale.

Coco Chanel un giorno disse che la moda "non esiste solo nei vestiti, ma anche in cielo ed in strada, ed è tutto ciò che è legato alle idee, al modo in cui viviamo, a ciò che accade". Gli oggetti da indossare costituiscono un elemento mediatore tra l'individuo ed il clima sociale contemporaneo. La moda è diventata per gli stilisti un modo di dimostrare apertamente il progresso e lo sviluppo della coscienza collettiva della società in cui vivono. La moda presentata in queste pagine riflette una varietà di stili nati dalle ispirazioni derivate dall'ambiente e dall'identità dello stilista, ed è un esempio di come l'abbigliamento sia usato per riflettere la cultura del continente americano tramite l'uso del design.

Nel corso degli ultimi decenni, caratterizzati da una rapida globalizzazione, gli stili peculiari del continente americano sono stati poco alla volta adottati nel mondo intero, esercitando un profondo impatto sulla moda attuale. Gli stilisti nordamericani creano abbigliamento che concentra la moltitudine di culture presenti nella loro società, come lo stile casual e dai tagli puliti della massa conservatrice, lo streetwear di chi abita in città, o lo stile sportivo di chi è consapevole dell'importanza della propria salute. Le mode latino americane esemplificano invece una cultura ricca di simbolismi e di storia, così come le altre forme d'arte di quelle terre.

Attraverso un viaggio visuale tra le emozioni evocate dal disegno dei trendsetters di oggi e dall'abbigliamento proposto dai talenti emergenti della moda, è possibile avere una visione d'insieme del mondo materiale nel continente americano. Tutti questi stilisti rampanti possiedono l'abilità ed il talento individuali necessari ad anticipare le tendenze; ed il potere di usare gli strumenti adatti per rivoluzionare l'industria stessa della moda. I giovani stilisti presentati in queste pagine magnificamente illustrate sono fonte di ispirazione per altri, per rompere gli schemi della moda, usando stoffe, tessuti, fili e tinte per trasmettere il proprio messaggio.

BLOKE | LOS ANGELES (CA), USA
Jerell Scott

Once again, necessity proved the mother of invention when style visionary Jerell Scott began reconstructing his own clothes in order to create something different from the masses. Inspired by fine art, jewelry, and furniture, his current collection is meant to stimulate wearers as well as onlookers. Scott continues to create bold, new designs that ultimately define fashion.

Photos: Michael Dar (1), Eddie Wolfe (portrait, 2)

BOMBSHELL INDUSTRIES | MEXICO CITY, MEXICO
Deborah Stockder, Benjamín Estrada

Bombshell Industries accomplishes a synergy between silhouettes, textiles, and graphics to create a contemporary fashion statement with modern Mexican influences. Designed by textile designer Stockder and complemented with graphics from her partner Estrada, this fashion line was launched in 2005.

www.bombshellind.com

Photos: Héctor Ramírez

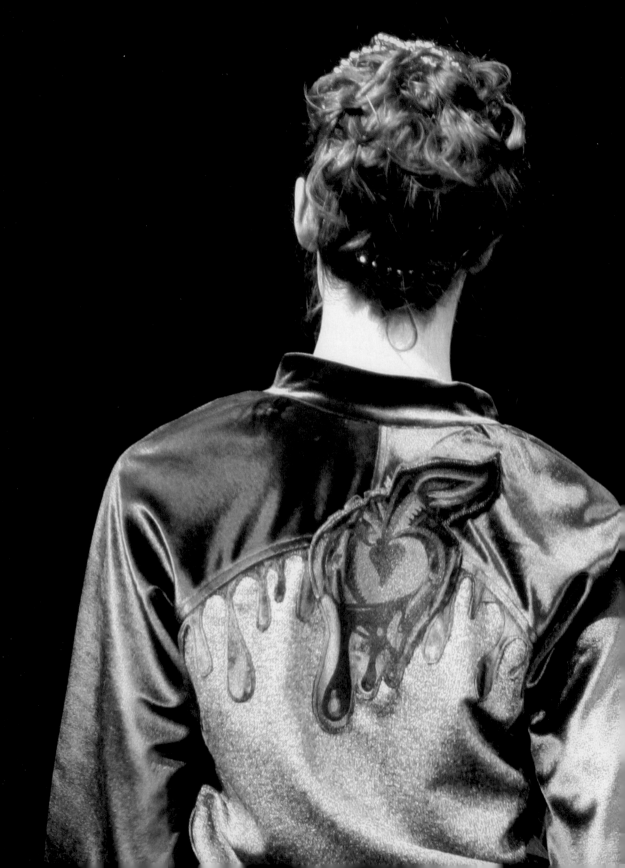

IZZY CAMILLERI | TORONTO (ON), CANADA
Izzy Camilleri

With the launch of her signature collection of ready-to-wear women's clothing, Camilleri is putting out her vision of a fresh, forward look for the internationally minded woman. She uses couture techniques of sleek skin in combination with fur, suede, and other well appointed textiles in order to create a modern luxe collection that is both smart and sophisticated.

www.izzycamilleri.com

Photos: Chris Chapman

VANESSA CARREÑO | HERMOSILLO, MEXICO
Vanessa Carreño

Mexican-born designer Carreño trained in Milan and Los Angeles. Her signature style of metal hardware and distressed leather combined with lace and silk pays homage to the female soldiers of her country's revolution. Carreño's designs reflect a struggle for balance between the rough and the feminine.

www.vanessacarreno.com

Photos: Waldy Duarte

BENJAMIN CHO | NEW YORK (NY), USA
Benjamin Cho

Cho has formed a reputation for his daring creativity displaying his remarkable talents and completely original view. He has translated this aesthetic reverence into a decidedly American arena: modern, unique and sexy. Cho's collections have a pointedly post-modern air, but remain organic, artfully organized, and idiosyncratic.

Photos: Dan Lecca

KAREN DAHER | ASUNCIÓN, PARAGUAY
Karen Daher

Paraguay-born Karen Daher launched her own brand in 2005 at the age of 23. After studying fashion design in Milan, she presented her first Prêt-a-Porter collection at the 2006 Asunción Fashion Week. Her line is characterized by exclusive contemporary designs that concentrates on dressing the extroverted woman and the self-confident man.

www.karendaher.com.py

Photos: Abdala Oviedo

DALLIN CHASE | NEW YORK (NY), USA
Jason Cauchi

While attending the Parsons School of Design, Cauchi interned at Calvin Klein. Later, while attending the Fashion Institute of Technology, he began working for Alice Roi and later left school to become her design director. He launched Dallin Chase for pre-spring in 2006, with the concept of creating casual dresses with a refreshing spin. The line is named after his children.

www.dallinchase.com

Photos: Mike Benigno (portrait), Marija Saric
Model: Jenna Danneberger/Elite New York

LAURA DAWSON | NEW YORK (NY), USA
Laura Dawson

Laura Dawson graduated from the College of Design, Architecture, Art and Planning at the University of Cincinnati. Before starting her own company, she worked for Donna Karan and Three as Four. This New York-based designer also works as a stylist with the likes of Moby and Scissor Sisters.

www.lauradawson.com

Photos: Alex Norden (portrait),
Andrew Stinson (1), Jessica Miller (2)

FABRIZIO DE CASTRO | BARRANQUILLA, COLOMBIA
Fabrizio de Castro

De Castro's artistic inclinations led him to study theatre and fine arts before he attended the prestigious ESMOD school of design in Paris. He opened his own store after two years in the fashion scene. The mix of colors and textures in his designs are authentic and elegant, and aspire to attract attention. He has been the leading designer at Vitalina, and at the 2006 Miami Fashion Week won the coveted Prêt-à-Porter Style Award.

Photos: José Gabriel Maxiaz

NICOLAS FELIZOLA | MIAMI (FL), USA
Nicolas Felizola

As a photographer for the most prestigious fashion designers, Venezuelan-born Felizola became inspired to bring his
unique perspective to the world of Haute Couture. His style
is renowned for its understated elegance and glamour, having conquered the Latin American and Hispanic markets, as
well as being a featured designer for several years at Miami
Fashion Week.

www.nicolasfelizola.com

Photos: Johnny Arraiz (portrait), Nicolas Felizola

ERIN FETHERSTON | NEW YORK (NY), USA
Erin Fetherston

After earning a BA from the University of California in 2002, Fetherston moved to France where she pursued post-graduate studies at Parsons School of Design. After completing her studies in 2004, she immediately created her own label. Shortly thereafter, Fetherston presented her debut collection of feminine and whimsical clothing in Paris in 2005 and her ready-to-wear collection was debuted in fall 2006.

www.erinfetherston.com

Photos: Dan Lecca

TONI FRANCESC | MEXICO CITY, MEXICO
Toni Francesc

Francesc started his fashion career by designing exclusive dresses. A few years after presenting his collections in a Prêt-a-Porter runway collection in Paris, Francesc launched his own fashion line in 2006. He has been featured in Bread & Butter, Fashion Week México, and is a favorite among Hong Kong's fashionable set.

www.tonifrancesc.es

Photos: Stephane Papegay (1)
Runway photos courtesy of Héctor Ramírez,
Alfonso Garcia and Gonzalo Fuentes
(Mexican Fashion Week)

1

H FREDRIKSSON | NEW YORK (NY), USA
Helena Fredriksson

Inspired by art, film, literature, and history with a special closeness to nature, Swedish designer Fredriksson has created her own unique aesthetics. She uses her own photography to create custom-made prints for her silk fabrics, screens and graphics. The modern yet organic abstract prints have become the identity and staple for her entire line.

www.hfredriksson.com

Photos: Kurt Mangum (1), Andy Eaton (2)

1

2

GEREN FORD | LOS ANGELES (CA), USA
Geren Lockhart

Lockhart was raised by artist parents between Northern California and New York City. Following a 12-year career in advertising, this 34-year-old left her job to start her own label. Inspirations that form the collections are derived directly from her life and travels, as well as her passion for art, film, music and architecture. Lockart studied fashion design at Parsons in New York and Otis in Los Angeles.

www.gerenford.com

Photos: Michael Powers

GHITA | LOS ANGELES (CA), USA
Alexis West

West received her degree in fashion design from the Fashion Institute of Design and Merchandising in Los Angeles. Her passion stems from a vision to create garments that inspire women to feel their lively feminine power. Her collection consists of unique and special one-of-a-kind pieces such as stylish dresses that maintain a classic sense of elegance while paying tribute to a more modern sense of design.

www.ghitafashion.com

Photos: Karuna Tillman James

BRUNO GRIZZO | NEW YORK (NY), USA
Bruno Grizzo

The semblance of simplicity in Grizzo's designs floats on a sea of fastidious details: hand-sewn hems, grosgrain ribbon set into collars, street influenced hardware and corsetry techniques. By draping and cutting garments himself, he delicately cuts and tailors his garments in such a way that eliminates seams. Grizzo marked the launch of his eponymous collection by winning two coveted GenArt style awards.

www.brunogrizzo.com

Photos: IOULEX (1), Alexander Berg (2)

2

CORA GROPPO | BUENOS AIRES, ARGENTINA
Cora Groppo

Argentinean-born Groppo has proudly participated 13 times as a designer at the Buenos Aires Fashion Week, has presented her collections three times at London Fashion Week, and participated in Cibeles representing the Argentinean fashion designers. Her clothing is characterized by asymmetry, monochrome, and deconstruction giving a unique perception on how one wears a garment.

www.coragroppo.com

Photos: Candelaria Gil

SARI GUERON | NEW YORK (NY), USA
Sari Gueron

Israeli-born Gueron grew up between Connecticut and Tel Aviv, where she was constantly inspired by her own life and the lives of the successful, artistic women working in creative fields. The manipulation of fabric is a constant source of her inspiration as she expands her label, bringing the same subtle cool but consummate attention to detail to jackets, skirts, tops, and her signature dresses.

www.sarigueron.com

Photos: Nevil Dwek (portrait), Dan Lecca

GUY BAXTER | LOS ANGELES (CA), USA
Turya Nations

Nations got her introduction to fashion while running her own vintage clothing store in Nashville, Tennessee. After moving to Los Angeles, she launched her first collection in spring 2006 with her husband Braxton. The heart of Guy Baxter is an ageless classic enthusiasm, spontaneous textile and trims, and perfectly fitted pieces that carry an elegant yet comfortable excitement.

www.guybaxter.com

Photos: Daniel Discala

HABITUAL | LOS ANGELES (CA), USA
Dena Mooney

American designer Mooney, who studied costume design at the University of Hartford, shares her artful design direction, technical expertise, great love and appreciation of denim as the design director of Habitual. Mooney culminated her design experience in New York City at several fashion labels. She now divides her time between New York and Los Angeles bringing both coasts' sensibility to the line.

www.habitual.com

Photos: Dan Martensen

PAUL HARDY | CALGARY (AB), CANADA
Paul Hardy

Canadian-born Hardy evolved from design school graduate to personal shopper to an acclaimed fashion designer that *Elle* listed as one of the top 10 Canadian designers in 2006. He officially began his design career in 2002 with an opening show at Toronto Fashion Week where his first collection received a host of rave reviews. Hardy is currently in the process of working on a concept for a men's line.

www.paulhardydesign.com

Photos: Phil Crozier (portrait), Chad Johnston
Model: Cierra Jonasson/Mode Models

CATHERINE HOLSTEIN | NEW YORK (NY), USA
Catherine Holstein

New York native Holstein left the prestigious Parsons School of Design something akin to a fashion fairy tale. Her first nautical-inspired collection was picked up by Barneys while she was still completing her last semester. Shortly thereafter, she became the subject of marquee profiles from fashion authorities like *The New York Times*, *Teen Vogue*, and *Elle* at the tender age of 22 years old.

Photos: Alex Hawgood (portrait), David Ransone

ISHII | NEW YORK (NY), USA
Tamae Ishii

Tokyo-born Ishii is a graduate of Parsons School of Design in New York. She has apprenticed with master couturier Valentino in Italy as well as other leading fashion houses including Jean Paul Gaultier, Calvin Klein, and Zac Posen. Her design aesthetic is most influenced by her love for all things French and Italian as well as her affinity for the refined elegance found in the traditional Japanese gardens of Kyoto.

www.ishiinyc.com

Photos: Jon Abeyta (portrait), Michael Creagh (1), Zack Seckler (2)

2

ISSHŌ | LOS ANGELES (CA), USA
Neely Shearer, Gordon Morikawa

isshō, which means 'together' in Japanese, is a joint collaboration between two designers who together own the Los Angeles boutique Xin. Their collection is designed for the woman who embraces fashion, but whose independent spirit does not allow her to take herself too seriously. Their design projects are fun, colorful, and casual, yet sophisticated with expert tailoring and quality construction.

www.xinboutique.com/issho

Photos: Courtney Hansen (portrait), June Choi (1),
Scott Miller (2)

2

KARA JANX | NEW YORK (NY), USA
Kara Janx

Behind the camera of Bravo's Project Runway, former architect Janx demonstrated her keen eye for color and quirky sportswear sensibility by creating clean, chic and effortless clothing for the modern woman. Janx's designs echo a self confident ease with quiet details infused with interesting juxtapositions: colorful and energetic yet minimal and clean, tailored yet organic, and timeless yet youthful.

www.karajanx.com

Photos: Studio Flash (portrait), Andrew McLeod (1), Jennifer Graylock (2)

2

MACARIO JIMÉNEZ | MEXICO CITY, MEXICO
Macario Jiménez

Jiménez studied Fashion Design at The Marangoni Fashion School in Milan and was the first international designer featured at the Museum of Art in Puerto Rico. His entire collection is synonymous with fluency and elegance. Inspired by women that are essentially looking for a sensual experience combined with sophistication, his impeccable designs and feminine silhouettes can be summarized in one word: Air.

www.macariojimenez.com

Photos: Pedro Flores/Acervo IASA (portrait),
Alejandro Pay (1), Dimithry Calderón (runway photos)

JOVOVICH-HAWK | LOS ANGELES (CA), USA
Milla Jovovich, Carmen Hawk

Jovovich and Hawk, who have been friends for over 10 years, created this line with the common view that clothes have to be wearable, but should never make a spectacle of the wearer. Their design strategy encompasses the belief of 'feel good, look great, feel bad, look great'. This line is relevant to the lives of independent, hardworking women who are creative and funny, yet elegant and romantic.

www.jovovich-hawk.com

Photos: Carmen Hawk (1), Bogden Teslar Kwiatkowski (2)

1

2

JULIA Y RENATA | GUADALAJARA, MEXICO
Julia Franco, Renata Franco

Mexican-born Julia and Renata have created a unique fashion line with the philosophy based on the study of the female anatomy through their own research and experimentation. They find inspiration in the slight imperfections in nature and use it as an outlet for creative and stylistic possibilities. Their collections are sold in Mexico, New York and Los Angeles.

www.juliayrenata.com

Photos: Walter Shintani (portrait), Marc Powell (1)
Art Direction: Omelette and Gustavo García
Runway photos courtesy of SIMM

1

JESSE KAMM | LOS ANGELES (CA), USA
Jesse Kamm

This collection was first presented in spring 2006 at Colette, Paris with rave reviews. Kamm draws all of her original textile designs by hand in her California studio. She strives to create moving works of art with her beautiful limited edition pieces.

www.jessekamm.com

Photos: Guillaume Saint Michel (1),
Lucas Brower (portrait, 2)

2

KATE & KASS | LOS ANGELES (CA), USA
Anya Teresse

Teresse's love for fashion began at the age of 12, when she began collecting vintage clothing with her lunch money. She is an avid film lover and worked as an assistant costume designer for six years on movies that include Art School Confidential and Friends with Money. Teresse studied fashion design at Parsons School of Design in Paris and Otis College of Art and Design in Los Angeles.

www.kateandkass.com

Photos: Patrick Hoelck (portrait), Frankie Batista

JENNI KAYNE | LOS ANGELES (CA), USA
Jenni Kayne

Kayne designs her fashion line with a core value that embodies an ageless collection for the woman that lives in
her clothing but still likes to bend the rules that fashion
dictates. Whether sequins for breakfast, crystals for lunch,
white for winter, or fur for everyday, Kayne creates unique
concepts that challenge the norms of the fashion industry.

www.jennikayne.com

Photos: courtesy of Jenni Kayne

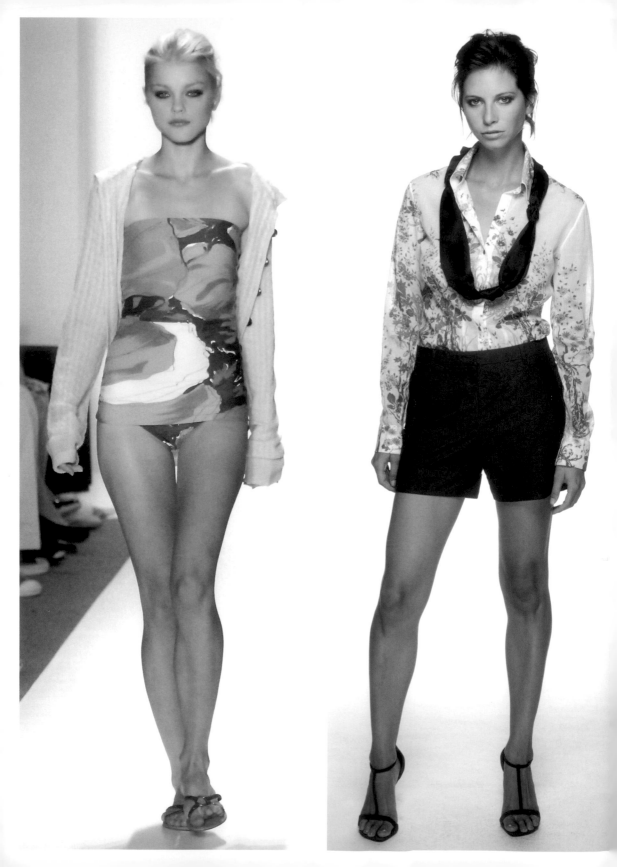

ADAM KIMMEL | NEW YORK (NY), USA
Adam Kimmel

Adam Kimmel believes that men's wear is about pushing towards a new sensibility while retaining wearability. He plays with uncommon fabrics and unique proportions as he maintains a simple yet masculine silhouette. His personal vision is to elevate the industry by infusing it with a relaxed elegance. Kimmel's designs exude an overall feeling of New York City, the atmosphere that he knows and loves best.

www.adamkimmel.com

Photos: Kate Schafer (portrait), Alexei Hay

JEREMY LAING | TORONTO (ON), CA
Jeremy Laing

Toronto-based designer Jeremy Laing creates collections that often stem from his elaborations on simple principles of construction and form, drawing simultaneously from couture and tailoring traditions. His self-taught method combines organic and geometric approaches to pattern making, demonstrating his strength in innovative garment construction and use of textile to create unique shapes.

www.jeremylaing.com

Photos: Thomas Kletecka

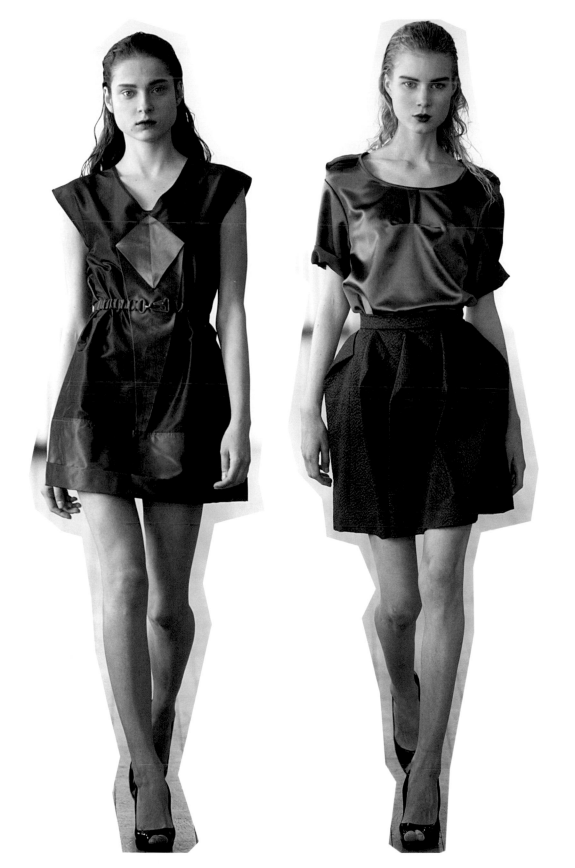

LEWIS CHO | NEW YORK (NY), USA
Annie Lewis, Helen Cho

The two designers behind Lewis Cho met while working for Anna Sui and soon became friends as they quickly discovered they shared a similar vision for fashion: a stylish and versatile collection that is also timeless in design. Their new collection was launched in 2005, and in that same year they were selected by GenArt to debut their fashion line in the Fresh Faces in Fashion runway show for New York Fashion Week.

www.lewischo.com

Photos: Jeffrey Swart (portrait), Jody Kivort
Illustration: Aelfie Starr Tuff

LOST ART | NEW YORK (NY), USA
Jordan Betten, Nikhil Sharma

This unique collection, which has been exhibited at the Metropolitan Museum of Art, combines various materials such as leather, suede, alligator, crocodile, python, and furs garnished with beads, feathers, teeth, stones, and crystals. Each piece is made entirely by hand in their New York City studio with rich materials that are often combined with art that is either hand painted or burned into the skins.

www.lostart.com

Photos: Marco Guerra (Betten portrait, 1),
Mallory Culbert (Sharma portrait), Tom Kletecka (2),
Sam Norval (3)
Illustration: Jordan Betten

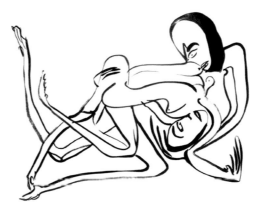

MACKAGE | MONTREAL (QC), CA
Elisa Dahan, Eran Elfassy

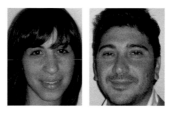

Mackage co-designers Elisa Dahan and Eran Elfassy are lifelong friends who attended fashion college together. They were discovered in 1999 by word-of-mouth marketing through the city's most fashionable set when the designers were just 20 years old. These Montreal-based designers have captured a huge following due to their vision of sexy and glamorous wool and leather outerwear.

www.mackage.com

Photos: Patrick Seguin (1), Mario Miotti (2),
Blais & Bilinski (3)

BULL ET BILL
Prop.: Centre Hippique
Montérégie

MALAFACHA | MEXICO CITY, MEXICO
Francisco Saldaña, Victor Hernal

Saldaña studied fashion design at the Instituto Jannette Klein in Mexico City. Hernal earned a creative visualization degree before launching Malafacha together with Saldaña. Both have achieved incredible accomplishments in the world of fashion with their completely different creative knowledge. Their line has achieved success by merging their talents rather than taking their own individual fashion design approach.

www.malafacha.blogspot.com

Photos: Erika Zavala (portrait), Ivan Aguirre (1),
Dimithry Calderón (2)

1

2

ARTHUR MENDONÇA | TORONTO (ON), CANADA
Arthur Mendonça

Born in Toronto and raised in Portugal, Mendonça received his fashion design degree from Ryerson University. Since launching his line in 2003, Mendonça's highly acclaimed collections have been presented in Los Angeles, Montréal, New York, São Paulo and Toronto. Fans such as singer Nelly Furtado appreciate his cutting-edge and dramatic designs with bold colors and cuts that reveal the feminine silhouette.

www.mendonca.ca

Photos: Arlene Malakian (1), Geoff Barrenger (2), Jason Wills (3)

3

MIKE & CHRIS | LOS ANGELES (CA), USA
Mike Gonzalez, Christine Park-Gonzalez

This husband and wife design duo has managed to meld chic and street, resulting in a line that is both laid back yet put together. After embarking on their much sought after "hoodie" line, these designers have created collections that reflect the art and sub-culture of their roots. Born in Queens, New York, Christine has always been inspired by the arts while Mike pursued a career in fashion photography.

www.mikeandchris.com

Photos: Mike Gonzalez

RENATA MORALES | MONTREAL (QC), CANADA
Renata Morales

This handcrafted collection reflects a mix of imaginative inspirations, handled with great attention to detail, technical expertise, sense of humor, and has an innate rebellious nature. Morales is primarily an artist, adapting techniques of the canvas onto her garments, infusing them with a personalized and exceptional feel. She creates clothing that can only be described as a feast for the senses.

www.renatamorales.com

Photos: Renata Morales (1), George Fok (2),
Jimmy Hammelin (3), Wire Image (4),
Phoebe Greenberg (5), Serge Pare (6)

3

4

5

OELTJENBRUNS | NEW YORK (NY), USA
Jurgen Oeltjenbruns

Oeltjenbruns is a trained tailor with a master's degree in menswear from the Royal College of Art. For four years he was design director at Versace in Milan, and most recently senior design director at Donna Karan in New York. Specializing in tailored, hand-finished menswear with an acute eye for detail, Oeltjenbruns launched his first solo line in fall 2006 with a well-designed yet wearable line.

www.oeltjenbrunsinc.com

Photos: Minh Ngo

PEPA POMBO | BOGOTÁ, COLOMBIA
Mónica Holguín

Born in Bogotá, Colombia, textile designer Holguín has developed the Pepa Pombo brand by integrating mixtures of color and knitted textures into shapes that offer different stylistic and esthetic possibilities. In the last five years, Holguin's intuition for the needs of the contemporary woman and spontaneous humor formed the foundation of her unique and versatile conceptual style.

www.pepapombo.com

Photos: Camilo Echeverri
(courtesy of IN Fashion Magazine)

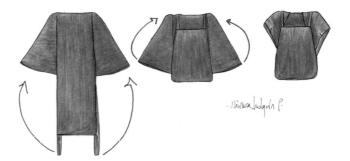

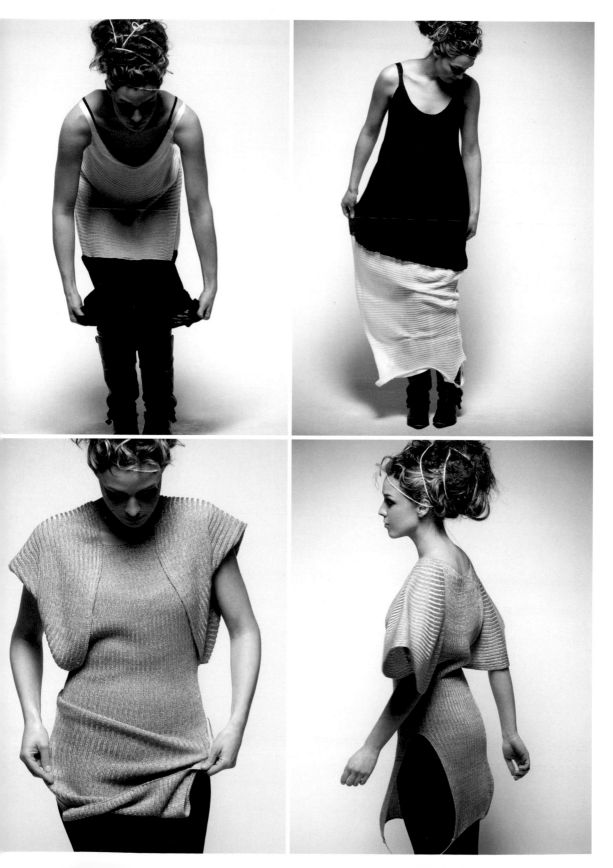

OCTAVIO PIZARRO | SANTIAGO, CHILE
Octavio Pizarro

Born in Chile and trained in Paris, Pizarro presented his first collection when he was just 18 years old. After some years working as creative director and stylist at some of the world's most renowned fashion houses in France, he created a new line with forms that are less structured with a sporty chic spirit, starting a new adventure that mixes his South American roots with his experiences with French luxury.

www.octaviopizarro.com

Photos: Mikael Beauplet (portrait), Adrian Parfene

SAMANTHA PLEET | BROOKLYN (NY), USA
Samantha Pleet

Pleet established her Brooklyn-based design studio in spring 2005 and has been charming everyone since her debut collection in fall 2006. This Pratt alumna has been inspired by her world travels in search of beauty and the mystery in foreign environments. Pleet brings her fantasies into reality with mini dresses, tunics, and dandy-inspired tailored jackets with matching rompers.

www.samanthapleet.com

Photos: Jessica Skiles (portrait), Nadav Benjamin

PORTS 1961 | NEW YORK (NY), USA
Tia Cibani

Tia Cibani, the global soul with an urban spirit, is quickly becoming known as the creative force behind the luxury label Ports 1961. Cibani divides her time between international cities in Europe, Asia and the United States. Her unique vision and multi-cultural experiences have influenced every aspect of the global identity of Ports 1961 today.

www.ports1961.com

Photos: Martin Laporte (1), Geoff Barrenger (2)

ALEJANDRA QUESADA | MEXICO CITY, MEXICO
Alejandra Quesada

Mexican-born Quesada attended several fashion design schools (ESMOD/Paris, IESMODA/Mexico City, Central Saint Martins/London) and has worked at notable fashion houses such as Alexander McQueen before launching her own line in 2006. Quesada's innocent and feminine style is influenced by her Mexican heritage combined with a timeless fantasy world. Her clothing is available in Mexico, Japan, England, France and Dubai.

www.alejandraquesada.com

Photos: Ximena Romero (1), Rodrigo Cassou (2),
Rene de la Rosa (3)

PABLO RAMÍREZ | BUENOS AIRES, ARGENTINA
Pablo Ramírez

Ramírez studied apparel design at the University of Buenos Aires and worked as a designer for several fashion companies in Argentina before starting his own fashion line in 2000. He is also a respected and well-known wardrobe designer for opera, ballet and theatre, and was elected as one of the "100 Designers" in the book *Samples* (Phaidon).

www.pabloramirez.com.ar

Photos: Gabriel Rocca

CHARLOTTE RONSON | NEW YORK (NY), USA
Charlotte Ronson

Born in London into an artistic family and raised in New York, Ronson followed the tradition by developing her own unique style at an early age. Friends took notice of the distinctive style of her own customized vintage tees and tanks, and asked her to create pieces for them. Shortly after creating her own line in 2005, she joined forces with Japanese apparel giant Sanei International.

www.charlotteronson.com

Photos: Pamela Hanson (1)
Runway photos courtesy of Dan Lecca

ALANA SAVOIR | MEXICO CITY, MEXICO
Alana Savoir

Mexican-born Savoir has created unique fashion concepts that are elegant, practical and comfortable. The full range of clothing featured in her collection includes casual clothing and ready-to-wear to elegant upscale clothing with cocktail and wedding dresses. Her internationally recognized collection can be found in London, Barcelona and Dubai.

www.alanasavoir.com

Photos: Dafna de Niño (1), Fabien Tijou (2),
Ivan Berastegui (3)
Models: Contempo Models (2)

RUBIN SINGER | NEW YORK (NY), USA
Rubin Singer

Vienna-born Rubin Singer comes from a dynasty of Russian fashion designers. He attended the prestigious Central Saint Martin's in London and has designed for Oscar de la Renta and Bill Blass. Living between Los Angeles and New York, Singer successfully created four collections for Kai Milla before leaving the company to launch his own line that bears his name.

www.rubinsinger.com

Photos: Barry Salzman (1), Dahlen Wee (2)

1   2

CHARLOTTE SOLNICKI | BUENOS AIRES, ARGENTINA
Melina Solnicki, Jessica Solnicki

In 2002, the Solnicki sisters arrived in the United States from Buenos Aires with a few samples of their contemporary collection, which became an instant success with popular New York City boutiques. Within a few years, their fashion line evolved into a complete ready-to-wear collection including exotic furs and satin dresses while maintaining the classic styles that propelled their success.

www.charlottesolnicki.com

Photos: Nacho Ricci

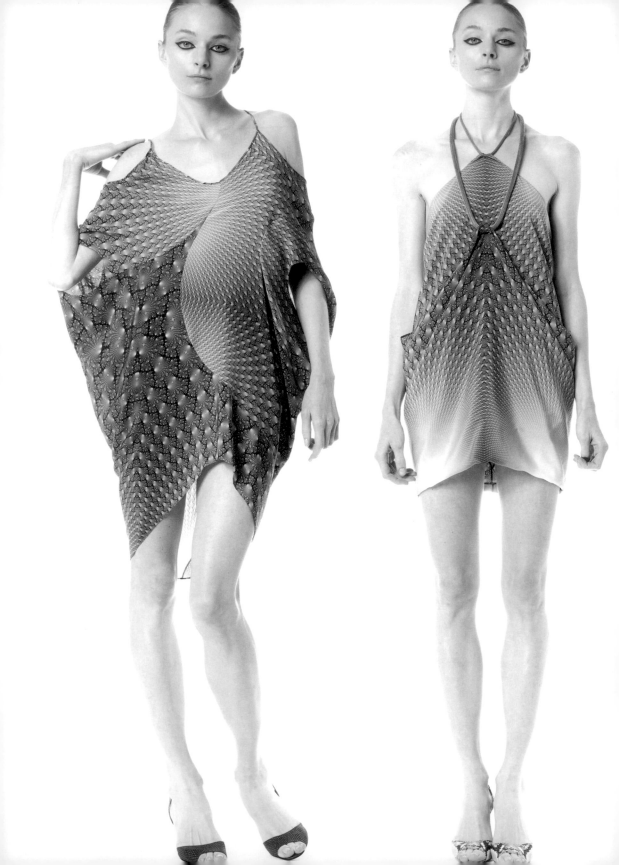

THREE AS FOUR | NEW YORK (NY), USA
Adi Gil, Gabriel Asfour, Angela Donhauser

This international collective based in New York City is the brainchild of three designers of Israeli, Russian, and Palestinian descent who aim to soften the boundaries between fashion and art. Primarily known for their curvilinear design and multimedia fashion shows, their work has been exhibited in some of the world's most prestigious museums and galleries, such as The Metropolitan Museum of Art.

www.threeasfour.com

Photos: Erez Sabag

MARIANO TOLEDO | BUENOS AIRES, ARGENTINA
Mariano Toledo

Toledo studied architecture before creating this glamorous and internationally recognized brand. His designs are characterized for their innovation in silhouettes with exaggerated, voluminous shapes, and textile development in a range of tangy colors. His flirty collections are easy-to-wear and are influenced by pop culture.

www.marianotoledo.com

Photos: Claudio Divella
Art Direction: Malcom Pozzi

XIMENA VALERO | MEXICO CITY, MEXICO
Ximena Valero

Mexican-born Valero studied at FIDM in Los Angeles and worked as a designer for Victoria's Secret in New York. She has been featured at New York Fashion Week and Asunción Fashion Week, as well as the DFashion event in Mexico. She has been awarded Best Designer of the Year for gala dresses at the 2006 Miami Fashion Week. Her creations are sold in Mexico, New York, Los Angeles, Miami, St. Kitts and Japan.

www.ximenavalero.info

Photos: Josue Peña (1), Seth Sabal (2), James Warick (3)

2

3

2

2

2

VENA CAVA | BROOKLYN (NY), USA
Lisa Mayock, Sophie Buhai

These Brooklyn-based designers have been designing together since their graduation from Parsons in 2003. Their
inspiration comes from their own vast vintage collection,
unique personal style, and natural objects. They prefer simple designs enhanced by subtle details and elegant fabrics.
The designers and their collection have been featured in
Vogue, *Harpers Bazaar*, and Style.com.

www.venacavanyc.com

Photos: Georgia Nerheim

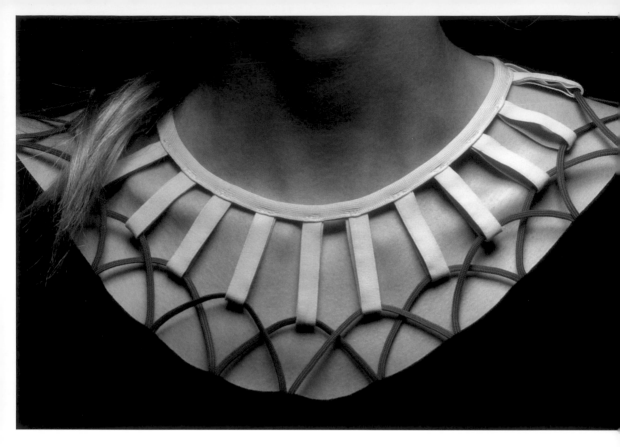

VIRIDIS LUXE | LOS ANGELES (CA), USA
Hala Bahmet, Amadea West

These Los Angeles-based designers and longtime friends felt compelled to start a company that provides consumers with a chance to buy beautiful, stylish, and fashion forward clothing that also contributes to a healthy environment for the world's children. As a result of their vision for an organic clothing line, they launched this eco-friendly luxury collection made from sustainable fibers in spring 2007.

www.viridisluxe.com

Photos: Andreea Radutoiu

ALEXANDER WANG | NEW YORK (NY), USA
Alexander Wang

When Alexander Wang began his line in 2005, he took cashmere to another level by modernizing the classics and bringing an element of hip rarely seen. Now at the age of 23, Wang has created a full ready-to-wear line that has a street edge matched with a sense of ease.

www.alexanderwang.com

Photos: Dan Martensen (1), Miko Lim (2)

WAYNE HADLY | LOS ANGELES (CA), USA
Wayne Joffe

Designer and owner Wayne Joffe was born in South Africa and grew up in Los Angeles. Before starting his own line, he had no prior fashion education or experience. Joffe's designs are the pure product of his exposure to different cultures and his eye for detail, which can be seen by the unique fabric and color combinations as they epitomize his fundamental belief in fit, fabric, and quality.

www.waynehadly.com

Photos: Tyler Shields

JEAN YU | NEW YORK (NY), USA
Jean Yu

Yu's signature collection of refined dresses and separates deliberately departs from constricting form and superfluous bulk, and is distinguished by its modern aesthetics and old world construction. Sculptural, sensual and sublime, her silk lingerie collection elevates the concept of the sexy woman and reckons the sensual pleasure of wearing the garment that glorifies the body.

www.jeanyu.com

Photos: Trent McGill (1), Kenny Jossick (2),
Matthew Lee (3)

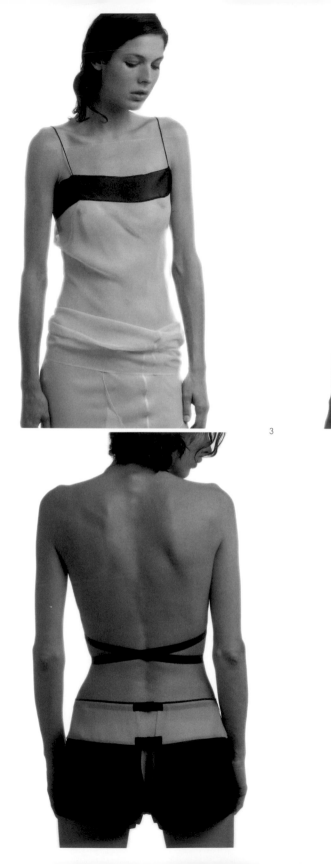

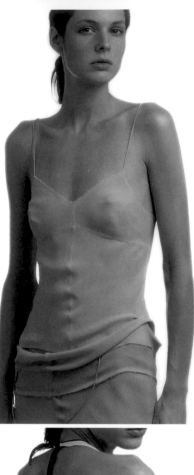

3

1

ZERO+MARIA CORNEJO | NEW YORK (NY), USA
Maria Cornejo

The fashion line Zero is a deceptively simple collection of sculptural garments based on volume and circular shapes that are often cut from a single piece of cloth. Each season, Chilean-born Cornejo subtly refines her technique to develop a modern way of imagining dynamic and intelligent clothing for women.

www.zeromariacornejo.com

Photos: Monica Feudi

INDEX

© 2007 daab
cologne   london   new york

published and distributed worldwide by
daab gmbh
friesenstr. 50
d-50670 köln

p + 49 - 221 - 913 927 0
f + 49 - 221 - 913 927 20

mail@daab-online.com
www.daab-online.com

publisher ralf daab
rdaab@daab-online.com

creative director feyyaz
mail@feyyaz.com

© 2007 edited and produced by fusion publishing gmbh stuttgart . los angeles
www.fusion-publishing.com
team: patrice farameh (editor, introduction, layout), dana goldenberg, michelle galindo (coordination,
bios), martin herterich (imaging & pre-press)

special thanks to carly willis (satin/los angeles) and nathalia rojas (asunción fashion week) for their
expert advice

photo credits
coverphoto arelene malakian, backcover renata morales
introduction page 7 sam norval, page 9 nacho ricci, page 11 dan martensen, page 13 renata morales,
page 15 adrian parfene

printed in italy
www.zanardi.it

isbn 978-3-86654-015-6

all rights reserved.
no part of this publication may be reproduced in any manner.

1/2012

D0687028

WITHDRAWN

The ASTD
Leadership Handbook

Elaine Biech, Editor

Alexandria, Virginia

Berrett–Koehler Publishers, Inc.
San Francisco
a BK Business book

© 2010 the American Society for Training & Development

All rights reserved. Printed in the United States of America.

14 13 12 11 10   1 2 3 4 5 6 7 8

No part of this publication may be reproduced, distributed, or transmitted in any form or by any means, including photocopying, recording, or other electronic or mechanical methods, without the prior written permission of the publisher, except in the case of brief quotations embodied in critical reviews and certain other noncommercial uses permitted by copyright law. For permission requests, please go to www.copyright.com, or contact Copyright Clearance Center (CCC), 222 Rosewood Drive, Danvers, MA 01923 (telephone: 978.750.8400, fax: 978.646.8600).

ASTD Press is an internationally renowned source of insightful and practical information on workplace learning and performance topics, including training basics, evaluation and return-on-investment, instructional systems development, e-learning, leadership, and career development.

Ordering information: Books published by ASTD Press can be purchased by visiting ASTD's website at store.astd.org or by calling 800.628.2783 or 703.683.8100.

Library of Congress Control Number: 2009935136

ISBN-10: 1-56286-716-4
ISBN-13: 978-1-56286-716-4

ASTD Press Editorial Staff:

Director: Adam Chesler
Manager, ASTD Press: Jacqueline Edlund-Braun
Senior Associate Editor: Tora Estep
Associate Editor: Victoria DeVaux

Copyeditors: Tora Estep and Alfred Imhoff
Indexing: April Michelle Davis
Proofreader: Kris Patenaude
Interior Design and Production: Kathleen Schaner
Cover Design: Ana Ilieva Foreman

Printed by Sheridan Books, Inc. Ann Arbor, MI, www.sheridanbooks.com

✒ Contents

❧ Foreword

The *ASTD Leadership Handbook* is the third of its kind in a series of handbooks published by the American Society for Training & Development. With 33 chapters written by 48 renowned leaders in leadership and carefully edited by Elaine Biech—an accomplished expert in training—this book provides you with tremendous content. I can't think of many publications that give readers as much expertise—more than 2,000 years!—all in one place.

In addition to a wealth of knowledge, this publication covers the entire scope of leadership. From the competencies that are necessary for success, to developing leaders and the attributes of those who are successful, to challenges faced by today's leaders, and finally to how we broaden the leadership discussion in the future—the *Handbook* takes the most comprehensive look at all aspects of leadership from those who understand it best.

As we hope this book will quickly become part of your library for many years to come, we also want to ensure that you can easily implement the concepts discussed in the book. Included in the appendix and on the companion website (www.astd.org/LeadershipHandbook) are free tools that will help you put into practice the research and models that you read about in each chapter.

Many thanks go to Cindy McCauley and the staff from the Center for Creative Leadership for partnering with us on this project and to Elaine Biech for taking on the heavy lifting of editing the *Handbook* and providing direction and guidance to all of the authors who contributed tremendous content and expertise. We are grateful to you for helping all of us champion more effective leadership in our organizations.

Tony Bingham
President and CEO, ASTD
July 2010

❧ Introduction

The *ASTD Leadership Handbook* brings together the work of many of the most respected thought leaders in the field. Thirty-three inspiring chapters present the wisdom of these legends, who share their insights about leadership today and in the future. As a reader who decides to invest in a handbook, you have high expectations, and we believe we have met them, giving you a handbook that is authoritative, complete, and useful—as a book like this must be.

The *ASTD Leadership Handbook* Is Authoritative

Of all collected works, a handbook strives to be the most definitive. Its name alone implies that it has been written by respected authorities—authors whose work you implicitly and totally trust. When you pick up *The ASTD Leadership Handbook,* you hold almost 2,000 years worth of experience in your hands. You know the authors. You've read their work and have depended on their theories and concepts for years.

How did we select these authors? How do you start a project of this magnitude? Do you select the authors first? Or the topics first? This is one of those chicken-and-egg questions. We realized that the process needed to be not an "or" but an "and." That is, we implemented an iterative yet creative process that considered both author and topic at the same time and wove back and forth, constantly remaining open to other input.

For example, when contemplating the topic of leadership, several influential and respected names immediately come to mind: Jim Kouzes and Barry Posner, Jack Zenger, Bill Byham, Ken Blanchard, Bill George, and Frances Hesselbein. In addition, several topics immediately come to mind: building a team, strategic planning, ethics, leading change, getting results, leadership development, coaching, authenticity, global savviness, and women in leadership.

When comparing these two lists, you can see some immediate matches: Bill Byham and leadership development, Ken Blanchard and ethics, and Bill George and authenticity. But who can best address the other topics? Only one person can be considered for leading change: John Kotter. Similarly, for getting results, Dave Ulrich and Norm Smallwood are the only options, while coaching equals Marshall Goldsmith. Now other leadership experts are left without a topic. Why not invite Jim Kouzes and Barry Posner to write about what they know best: the practices of exemplary leaders? And why not likewise invite Jack Zenger to write about the engaging and inspiring leader, and Frances Hesselbein to write about leading the workforce of the future?

We also needed someone to establish the foundation for the handbook. Who better than Cindy McCauley, a senior fellow at the Center for Creative Leadership (CCL), and coeditor of *The Center for Creative Leadership Handbook of Leadership Development*?

As the table of contents took shape, we realized that other topics are also essential. For each one, we tried to identify the best and most experienced author available. For example, Leonard Goodstein has been writing about strategic planning for almost 50 years, and hasn't Patrick Lencioni written a couple of great books about leadership and teams? And the staff of CCL, which has done marvelous work for dozens of years, helped us organize the handbook's structure. Nine CCL authors wrote seven of the chapters.

Well, you get the picture. This is how the contents for *The ASTD Leadership Handbook* came together. The end result is 33 chapters by 48 extraordinary authors.

The ASTD Leadership Handbook Is Complete

"Complete"—what does this word mean? In this context, it means that a handbook must cover all the fundamental topics of the field. Readers expect a handbook to be a systematic collection of chapters that are related, yet unique in content. As a reader, you must believe that you will be able to turn to this handbook to find the most accurate and useful answers to the full spectrum of questions about leadership. To achieve this comprehensiveness, *The ASTD Leadership Handbook* consists of five sections:

- Leadership Competencies
- Leadership Development
- Attributes of Successful Leaders
- Contemporary Leadership Challenges
- Broadening the Leadership Discussion.

Each section offers five to nine chapters on pertinent topics. We tried to squeeze in as much as possible, and in the end we were only limited by the physical restrictions of bookmaking.

The ASTD Leadership Handbook Is Useful

The very nature of a handbook is to be written by gurus who have conducted research, identified theories, and produced exhaustive volumes of findings on a narrow subtopic. Yet most of you are too busy to delve into the full complexity of this research. You want the nuggets of information, the how-tos, and the go-do advice. You want distilled yet pithy answers to questions and practical, implementable ideas.

In preparing this handbook, we considered how we could make the content most useful and easily implementable in day-to-day work. So we asked each author to contribute a tool that you can use to better understand the content they offer, to apply the content in working with others, or to adapt the content for different situations. Thus the handbook is supported by about three dozen tools, such as

- John Kotter's Eight-Stage Process
- Bill Gentry's Checklist for Avoiding Leader Derailment
- Marshall Goldsmith's Coaching Minisurvey
- Patrick Lencioni's Team Assessment
- Beverly Kaye and Sharon Jordan-Evan's Jerk Checklist
- Leonard Goodstein's Strategic Planning Analysis Questionnaire.

These tools will help you implement the leadership concepts you will read about in the handbook. You can find a list of the tools in the appendix of this book. But here's the best part: You will also find the tools available for downloading at a companion website: www .astd.org/LeadershipHandbook. As long as you maintain the copyright information and the "used with permission" designation on the tool, you will be able to use it for your daily work. Free tools—now that's exciting! You'll find the website useful in other ways, too. We've invited the authors to update their chapters on the website and to share new ideas or answer questions.

In addition to the tools, most authors have given ideas for further reading, which you'll find at the end of their chapters. These articles and books will enable you to follow a particular point of interest, in many cases through the author's own work, beyond the space limitations of the handbook.

Thanks for a Special Opportunity

What's it like to work with the gurus of the profession? Heady? Exhilarating? Humbling? Daunting? It's all these. In the end, editing this handbook was exciting—one of the highlights of my career. I am honored and delighted to have had such an exhilarating opportunity. And, of course, *The ASTD Leadership Handbook* would not have been possible without the

- Authors: How can we thank you enough? You have more important things to do than to write a chapter for this handbook. Thank you for sharing content based on your lifework. It will surely be useful for years to come.
- Center for Creative Leadership staff: Thanks for your encouragement and for helping to set the standard for excellent planning and collaboration. The result is a carefully organized handbook with seven informative chapters by CCL authors.
- Editors: Tora Estep and Alfred Imhoff, we all appreciate your eagle eyes and your sharp pencils as you perfect our prepositions and validate our verbs.
- ASTD staff: Thanks for your vision of this handbook, a resource for workplace learning and performance professionals who work with leaders in all capacities. And thanks for the opportunity to be a part of this exciting project.

Elaine Biech
June 2010

☞ Chapter 1

Concepts of Leadership

Cynthia D. McCauley

In This Chapter

■ The common elements in current conceptualizations of leadership.

■ Some pitfalls to avoid in your conceptualization of leadership.

■ Emerging concepts of leadership.

Given the attention that people give to the topic of leadership, the multiple disciplines that contribute to the understanding of leadership, and the plethora of models put forth to improve the practice of leadership, you might expect the field to be fragmented and full of disparate ideas. On the surface, you can find plenty of evidence to support this view: multiple competing leadership models, research studies that use different criteria to identify effective leaders, and no widely accepted general theory of leadership. But dig a little deeper and you'll find some common elements: the conceptualization of leadership as an influence process, a focus on the characteristics of individuals identified as leaders, and a recognition that the context or setting affects how leadership is enacted.

This introductory chapter primarily seeks to highlight the common elements found in current conceptualizations of leadership. Armed with these elements, you'll be better able to compare, contrast, and integrate the various topics, models, and frameworks offered in this handbook (and elsewhere). The chapter also points out several potential pitfalls associated with these common elements—difficulties associated with the concept of leadership that you'll need to decide how to navigate. Finally, the chapter explains how the concept of leadership is continuing to evolve—that there are emerging conceptualizations worth exploring.

Common Elements in Concepts of Leadership

Think about leadership as a social tool—a device, so to speak—that humans have crafted, refined, and learned to use over time. Leadership is a tool designed to help with a particular human dilemma: how to get individuals to work together effectively to produce collective outcomes. Whether it's a team working to produce a new product, a community working to keep neighborhoods safe, or a large organization working to increase shareholder value, success is more likely if everyone is headed in the same direction, coordinating work, and motivated to put the group above self. Leadership is a means for generating the shared direction, alignment, and commitment these groups need.

Exactly what this tool looks like in action varies somewhat, depending on what leadership model you consider or what stream of research you follow. However, these various conceptualizations of leadership do have three common elements:

- influence as the primary social process used in leadership
- characteristics of the leader as the main leverage point for enhancing leadership
- context as an important caveat for leadership.

Let's briefly consider each element.

Influence as the Primary Social Process Used in Leadership

Most leadership theories take for granted that leadership is an influence process (Antonakis, Cianciolo, and Sternberg 2004; Chemers 1997). Those individuals who exert more influence in a group are identified as the leaders. Those being influenced are the followers. This is not to say that followers don't also have influence. It's just that leaders influence more than followers—and this asymmetrical influence process is often considered the defining feature of leadership. After reviewing the many definitions and models of leadership that have been offered in the literature, Bass (1990, 14) concluded that "defining effective leadership as successful influence by the leader that results in the attainment of goals by the influenced followers . . . is particularly useful."

One can see why influence is at the core of many current definitions of leadership. Deciding on a shared direction and coordinating work so that people are aligned is facilitated by an influence process—in which people are willing to exert influence and be influenced by others. At the same time, there are many forms of influence—such as rational persuasion, inspirational appeals, and mutual exchange—which is one reason why particular leadership models can vary from one another, because they may make different assumptions about which forms of influence are best.

Characteristics of the Leader as the Main Leverage Point for Enhancing Leadership

Perhaps the most frequently examined question in leadership research is "What are the characteristics of effective leaders?" With knowledge about what distinguishes effective leaders from ineffective ones, you can more readily identify potential leaders and will know what characteristics to develop and encourage in individuals so they are better equipped to lead.

The characteristics that researchers have examined in trying to understand what differentiates effective and ineffective leaders cover a broad range of human capabilities, including personal attributes, actions or behaviors, competencies, expertise, and experience. Let's briefly consider each one.

Personal Attributes

Personal attributes include stable dispositional traits (for example, extroversion) and abilities (for example, cognitive ability), as well as personal qualities that can change over time, such as motivation and integrity. Personal attributes are constructs that explain consistent patterns of behavior across situations. Cognitive ability and personality are two of the most frequently studied types of leader attributes (Zaccaro, Kemp, and Bader 2004). More recently, scholars have encouraged more research on the motivation to lead (Chan and Drasgow 2001) and the leader's maturity level or developmental stage (McCauley and others 2006).

Actions or Behaviors

Rather than examining underlying personal attributes, other researchers have examined the observable actions or behaviors of leaders. A wide variety of methodologies have been used, including observations, diaries, interviews, behavior description questionnaires, and laboratory and field experiments. This approach yields taxonomies of behaviors used by leaders. Many of these taxonomies can be organized around three major concerns of leaders: task efficiency (for example, accomplishing tasks and maintaining orderly operations), human relations (building relationships and enhancing teamwork), and adaptive change (recognizing and supporting innovation and improving processes and systems).

Competencies

Describing effective leadership in terms of competencies is a more recent approach, but one that organizations have quickly adopted—many organizations now have developed their own leadership competency models. A competency is an interrelated set of knowledge, skills, and perspectives that can manifest itself in many forms of behavior or a wide variety of actions. For example, a leader with a high "developing others" competency would know strategies for developing others, would be skilled at coaching and mentoring, and would believe that developing others is an important aspect of his or her role.

Expertise

The knowledge or expertise that leaders possess is another potential differentiator of more and less effective leaders. Leadership scholars (Lord and Hall 2005; McCall and Hollenbeck 2008) have drawn from research and theories about the development of expertise in other domains to describe the process of moving from a novice to an intermediate to a master leader. An important concept here is leaders' tacit knowledge—experienced-based knowledge that increases leaders' sensitivity to important information in a given situation and their understanding of what action to take in response to that information (Cianciolo, Antonakis, and Sternberg 2004).

Experience

Finally, leaders can be characterized in terms of their leadership experiences. One can argue that these experiences enable leaders to learn the behaviors, competencies, and expertise needed to be effective; thus, experience is the key leverage point in enhancing leadership (McCall 2010). From this perspective, understanding the key experiences that differentiate more and less effective leaders (for example, boundary-spanning roles and leading change assignments) is as important as understanding leadership attributes or competencies.

Context as an Important Caveat for Leadership

Leadership happens in many different settings, and the leadership field recognizes that the context makes a difference when it comes to effective leadership. Influencing individual followers is different from building commitment on a team or galvanizing people in support of a vision for a social movement. And the characteristics admired in leaders vary from country to country around the globe.

One important distinction is between formal and informal leaders. Formal leaders have positional power (for example, a manager or an elected official), and informal leaders take on leadership roles without any formal authority. Leaders in positions of authority have access to different resources and use different influence strategies than those who lead without being in positions of authority (Heifetz 1994). Thus, effective leadership can be understood quite differently in settings where leadership is shaped by formal leaders as compared with those where it is shaped by informal leaders.

Within formal organizations, leader effectiveness is studied at every organizational level from first-line supervisory and project team leaders to chief executive officers and governing boards. Clearly, the demands of leadership vary by organizational level. For example, leaders at higher organizational levels tend to create rather than carry out organizational strategies and must integrate work across multiple groups and functions. At lower levels, leaders tend to emphasize motivating employees and building effective teams. These differences in demands on leaders across organizational levels call for different leadership practices.

Globalization has increased interactions among leaders from various parts of the world and the likelihood of individuals from one country leading others from different countries, making societal culture another important contextual feature of the leadership process. Although there are similarities across countries in what is expected of leaders, societies also differ in their expectations. For example, in some cultures being a risk taker is highly valued in leaders but in other cultures being cautious is highly valued; this difference is likely tied to whether a society tends to embrace or avoid uncertainty (Den Hartog and Dickson 2004).

Summing Up

These common elements in conceptualizations of leadership provide a shared foundation for understanding it as a phenomenon. They also provide a means for making sense of the wide range of leadership literature. When evaluating the value of any leadership model or theory for your own purposes, it is useful to ask these questions:

- What assumptions about social influence processes is the model built upon? Will these assumptions make sense to the people who will be using the model?
- What kinds of leader characteristics does the model focus on? Are these the kinds of characteristics you want to focus on to enhance leader effectiveness?
- For what contexts is the model most relevant? Are these contexts similar to the ones in which you'll be using the model?

Potential Pitfalls in Concepts of Leadership

Current conceptualizations of leadership aren't without their difficulties. Here are four of the most common ones:

- Assuming a leader is a leader is a leader.
- Confusing authority and influence.

- Expecting too much of leaders.
- Overemphasizing individual leaders.

Let's briefly examine each one.

Assuming a Leader Is a Leader Is a Leader

Despite recognition that context plays a role in leadership effectiveness, focusing primarily on the characteristics of effective leaders can bolster the notion that someone who is an effective leader in one context will be effective in other contexts. This assumption is particularly problematic when promoting individuals who have been successful leaders at lower organizational levels. Thus, individuals who continue to rely on the more tactical methods and behaviors that served them well as team or frontline leaders at a lower level can be derailed at higher levels of leadership responsibility where they are expected to be more strategic, build coalitions with diverse groups, and lead from a distance. Effectively taking on more complex leadership challenges requires continuous learning, growth, and change.

Taken to an extreme, the "once a leader, always a leader" perspective supports a view of the world as simply made up of leaders and nonleaders. In reality, individuals possess an array of characteristics that make them more and less effective in different leadership situations. Categorizing people as either "leaders" or "nonleaders" can create a static view of a dynamic social process and lead to the underutilization of leadership talent.

Confusing Authority and Influence

Management hierarchies are authority structures, not leadership structures. Just because someone is authorized to make certain decisions in an organization and others with less authority willingly carry out those decisions doesn't mean that the less powerful have been influenced. They may simply be complying with authority or concerned about fitting into the organizational system—with no sense of shared direction or commitment to the organization.

Certainly managers in today's organizations are expected to be more than wielders of authority; they also are expected to lead—which is why they are increasingly rewarded for engaging and developing employees and collaborating with peers. However, the practice of referring to those in the management hierarchy as "organizational leaders" simply because of the positions they occupy muddies the concept of leadership. Managers may not be generating direction, alignment, and commitment in the organization—and thus not be leading—not to mention that others outside the management ranks may be doing as much or more to generate leadership.

Strangely enough, those who often refer to managers as organizational leaders are often the same people who go out of their way to make a big distinction between management and leadership. They either describe management in more task-oriented terms (for example, planning and monitoring) and leadership in more people-oriented terms (motivating others and charismatic), or they describe managers as maintaining the status quo and leaders as creating change. Those who work in organizations know that such distinctions break down in real life. For example, the right strategic planning process can generate shared enthusiasm for the organization's goals, and the manager who supports meaningful organizational traditions is often enhancing employee commitment.

One solution to this confusion is to recognize that a manager is identified by his or her position and responsibilities in an organization and a leader is identified by his or her role in producing the direction, alignment, and commitment needed in collective work.

Expecting Too Much of Leaders

Look at any organization's leadership competency model, and you'll see that leaders are expected to display a wide range of competencies, from strategic thinking and developing employees to learning agility and fostering innovation. What these competency models often do not point out is that every leader has a mixture of strengths and weaknesses, and that there are many routes to effective leadership. Although expecting individuals to continue improving and broadening their leadership skills is certainly realistic, it is unrealistic to expect them to be high performers in all dimensions of leadership. Such expectations can lead to the underutilization of other strategies for effective leadership, such as matching leaders with tasks at which they are particularly good, putting together teams with complementary skills, and shared or co-leadership arrangements.

Those who write about and teach leadership also can create high expectations when many of their examples come from the ranks of extraordinary or heroic leaders. Certainly, Gandhi, Martin Luther King, Jr., and Eleanor Roosevelt are inspirational examples, but effective leadership rarely requires incredible self-sacrifice, charismatic oratory, or even a sense of duty. If we want the vast majority of people taking on leadership roles to enhance their "everyday" leadership, we must share stories of how "ordinary" people like them can become influential and encourage people to work together to achieve collective goals.

Overemphasizing Individual Leaders

Perhaps the biggest criticism of current concepts of leadership is their failure to fully depict leadership as a social process happening in a social system. Because of their focus on the individual leader, they tend to oversimplify the leadership process. One might assume in examining popular models of leadership that followers play a more passive role, waiting to be influenced or motivated. Practicing leaders know that this is far from reality. Even in theories where followers are more explicitly a part of the equation (for example, leader-member exchange), the dynamic interplay between leaders and followers is rarely closely examined.

In practice, leadership is also rarely an individual activity. Many leaders in organizations are influencing their coworkers in many different directions. In conceiving leadership as an influence process in which leaders are the individuals exerting more influence, figuring out who should be labeled leaders becomes quite difficult in many modern organizations. At any point in time, many people are both leading and following. The danger of only paying attention to people who are labeled "leaders" in the system (particularly when this label is primarily associated with certain management positions) is that it will lead to a failure to leverage other systemic aspects to enhance leadership, such as relationships and networks or the members' collective beliefs and values (that is, the organization's culture).

Emerging Conceptualizations of Leadership

The limitations of existing conceptualizations of leadership and the increased prevalence of particularly challenging leadership settings (for example, leading in a globally competitive marketplace, leading across cultural boundaries, and leading a partnership among multiple organizations) are pushing concepts of leadership in new directions. These emerging conceptualizations do not negate but rather broaden the perspectives typically used to understand leadership and improve its practice.

One developing aspect of leadership theory in recent years is the conceptualization of shared or distributed leadership (Pearce and Conger 2003). The concept of shared leadership has deepened the understanding of how teams are able to lead themselves—not by relying on a formal team leader but through a collaborative, emergent process of group interaction. Shared leadership is not conceived as the parsing out or alternation of leader-based influence, where the leader role passes from one individual to another, but as a qualitatively different social process of group interaction and negotiation of shared understanding. This is a social process that requires its own competencies, such as accepting responsibility for providing and responding to lateral influence and developing skills as both leader and follower (Pearce and Sims 2000).

Another emerging approach is the application of complexity science to leadership theory (Schneider and Somers 2006; Uhl-Bien, Marion, and McKelvey 2007). From the holistic perspective of complexity science, leaders and followers do not add up to leadership; that is, the behavior of leaders and the response of followers to that behavior do not predict with any certainty the collective outputs of a leadership system. A complexity leadership framework focuses not just on leaders and followers but also on the whole system of interacting "agents" and the top-down and bottom-up leadership processes these interactions produce.

At one leading organization in the field, the Center for Creative Leadership, the understanding of leadership has broadened from a strong focus on individual leaders as the target for leadership development efforts to seeing an organization's collective leadership beliefs and practices (that is, its leadership culture) as the target (Drath and others 2008; McCauley, Van Velsor, and Ruderman 2010; McGuire and Rhodes 2009). From this perspective, leadership development includes individual development, relationship development, team development, organization development, changes in patterns of behavior in the organization, and changes in organizational processes. Leadership development has thus become much more of a process in which the whole organization engages.

Conclusion

Leadership is a broad and evolving concept. At its most basic, leadership can be understood as a social process for generating the direction, alignment, and commitment needed for individuals to work together productively toward collective outcomes. Researchers and theorists have examined leadership through different lenses in a wide variety of settings, resulting in numerous models and theories of leadership.

These models and theories have common elements that represent areas of deep knowledge in the field: leadership as an influence process, the characteristics of effective leaders, and how context affects leadership practices. At the same time, these concepts can be relied on too much, leading to oversimplification of and confusion about leadership. To address these limitations and the increased complexity of leadership in practice, emerging leadership concepts balance the current intense focus on the individual leader with a broader exploration of how leadership is produced in social systems.

Further Reading

American Psychologist, "Special Issue: Leadership," vol. 62, no. 1, January 2007.
John Antonakis, Anna T. Cianciolo, and Robert J. Sternberg, *The Nature of Leadership.* Thousand Oaks, CA: Sage, 2004.
Wilfred Drath, *The Deep Blue Sea: Rethinking the Source of Leadership.* San Francisco: Jossey-Bass, 2001.

Ellen Van Velsor, Cynthia D. McCauley, and Marian N. Ruderman, eds., *The Center for Creative Leadership Handbook of Leadership Development,* 3rd ed. San Francisco: Jossey-Bass, 2010.

Gary Yukl, *Leadership in Organizations,* 7th ed. Upper Saddle River, NJ: Prentice Hall, 2009.

References

Antonakis, J., A. T. Cianciolo, and R. J. Sternberg. 2004. Leadership: Past, Present, and Future. In *The Nature of Leadership,* ed. J. Antonakis, A. T. Cianciolo, and R. J. Sternberg. Thousand Oaks, CA: Sage.

Bass, B. M. 1990. *Bass and Stodgill's Handbook of Leadership: Theory, Research, and Managerial Applications.* New York: Free Press.

Chan, K., and F. Drasgow. 2001. Toward a Theory of Individual Differences and Leadership: Understanding the Motivation to Lead. *Journal of Applied Psychology* 86, no. 3: 481–498.

Chemers, M. M. 1997. *An Integrative Theory of Leadership.* Mahwah, NJ: Lawrence Erlbaum.

Cianciolo, A. T., J. Antonakis, and R. J. Sternberg. 2004. Practical Intelligence and Leadership: Using Experience as a "Mentor." In *Leadership Development for Transforming Organizations: Growing Leaders for Tomorrow,* ed. D. V. Day, S. J. Zaccaro, and S. M. Halpin. Mahwah, NJ: Lawrence Erlbaum.

Den Hartog, D. N., and M. W. Dickson. Leadership and Culture. 2004. In *The Nature of Leadership,* ed. J. Antonakis, A. T. Cianciolo, and R. J. Sternberg. Thousand Oaks, CA: Sage.

Drath, W. H., C. D. McCauley, C. J. Palus, E. Van Velsor, P. M. G. O'Connor, and J. B. McGuire. 2008. Direction, Alignment, Commitment: Toward a More Integrative Ontology of Leadership. *Leadership Quarterly* 19, no. 6: 635–653.

Heifetz, R. A. 1994. *Leadership Without Easy Answers.* Cambridge, MA: Harvard University Press.

Lord, R. G., and R. J. Hall. 2005. Identity, Deep Structure, and the Development of Leadership Skills. *Leadership Quarterly* 16, no. 4: 591–615.

McCall, M. W. 2010. Recasting Leadership Development. *Industrial and Organizational Psychology: Perspectives on Science and Practice* 3, no. 1: 3–19.

McCall, M. W., and G. P. Hollenbeck. 2008. Developing the Expert Leader. *People & Strategy* 31, no. 1: 20–28.

McCauley, C. D., W. H. Drath, C. J. Palus, P. M. G. O'Connor, and R. Baker. 2006. The Use of Constructive-Developmental Theory to Advance the Understanding of Leadership. *Leadership Quarterly* 17, no. 6: 634–653.

McCauley, C. D., E. Van Velsor, and M. N. Ruderman. 2010. Our View of Leadership Development. In *The Center for Creative Leadership Handbook of Leadership Development,* 3rd edition, ed. E. Van Velsor, C. D. McCauley, and M. N. Ruderman. San Francisco: Jossey-Bass.

McGuire, J. B., and G. B. Rhodes. 2009. *Transforming Your Leadership Culture.* San Francisco: Jossey-Bass.

Pearce, C. L., and J. A. Conger. 2003. *Shared Leadership: Reframing the Hows and Whys of Leadership.* Thousand Oaks, CA: Sage.

Pearce, C. L., and H. P. Sims. 2000. Shared Leadership: Toward a Multi-Level Theory of Leadership. In *Advances in Interdisciplinary Studies of Work Teams*, ed. M. M. Beyerlei, D. A. Johnson, and S. T. Beyerlein. Greenwich, CT: JAI Press.

Schneider, M., and M. Somers. 2006. Organizations as Complex Adaptive Systems: Implications of Complexity Theory for Leadership Research. *Leadership Quarterly* 17, no. 4: 351–365.

Uhl-Bien, M., R. Marion, and B. McKelvey. 2007. Complexity Leadership Theory: Shifting Leadership from the Industrial Age to the Knowledge Age. *Leadership Quarterly* 18, no. 4: 298–318.

Zaccaro, S. J., C. Kemp, and P. Bader. 2004. Leader Traits and Attributes. In *The Nature of Leadership*, ed. J. Antonakis, A. T. Cianciolo, and R. J. Sternberg. Thousand Oaks, CA: Sage.

About the Author

Cynthia D. McCauley is a senior fellow at the Center for Creative Leadership, where she has been involved in research, product development, program evaluation, coaching, and management. Her work has focused on methods of leadership development, including 360-degree feedback, job assignments, developmental relationships, formal programs, and action learning. She has written extensively for both scholarly and practitioner readerships and is coeditor of *The Center for Creative Leadership Handbook of Leadership Development* (2010).

✎ Section I

Leadership Competencies

What key competencies do leaders need? At times, the extraordinary challenges that organizations face today exceed individuals' and organizational capacity to be quickly resolved. What knowledge and skills do leaders need to ensure they are prepared for what lies ahead for them and their organizations?

Competencies are the skills and knowledge that ensure a leader is equipped to lead—that constitute leadership effectiveness. This section addresses the "what" of leadership—what leaders need to know. This is by far the longest section in the book, encompassing nine chapters, and it could have been even longer. As our world becomes more complex, the competencies required of today's leaders likewise become more complex. It becomes more and more difficult to identify the most "important" competencies, because they both multiply and become more complicated. Competencies grow in breadth as well as depth.

Organizations can select a model like the one developed by Kouzes and Posner, which opens this section in chapter 2, or they can begin to look at the multitude of skills and knowledge required by leaders. Of course, we could not cover all the competencies, so in addition to presenting the Kouzes-Posner model, we also selected those skills that seemed most critical (in our minds—only your organization will know what applies to you): team building, strategic planning, communicating, influencing, leading change, managing talent, getting results, and engaging and retaining talent.

Here's how our authors present these competencies. In chapter 2, "The Five Practices of Exemplary Leadership," James Kouzes and Barry Posner not only share these practices but also provide examples of how leaders use the practices in their work.

In chapter 3, "Leading to Build the Team," Patrick Lencioni tackles a competency that is difficult not because leaders do not believe in teamwork but because, though they firmly believe it is important, they often proceed to do the opposite. This paves the way for Lencioni to present a list of questions leaders should ask themselves before making a decision about becoming a team.

In chapter 4, "Strategic Planning: A Leadership Imperative," Leonard Goodstein—who has been firmly entrenched in strategic planning for almost 50 years—presents a time-tested facilitated approach to strategic planning and identifies the competencies that support it.

Communication is critical for good leadership. In chapter 5, "Five Critical Communication Skills for Leaders of the Future," Dianna Booher—seen by many as America's communication expert—presents what she believes are the essential communication competencies required of leaders—to listen, consult, involve, praise, and explain why as well as what needs to be done.

In chapter 6, "Influence Tactics for Leaders," Gary Yukl presents tactics leaders can use to influence those who report directly to a manager, peers, and supervisors in a variety of situations.

In chapter 7, "Leading Change: A Conversation with John P. Kotter," I had the honor to interview Kotter about his views on leadership and change, as well as change in a changing world.

Although talent management is a relatively new phenomenon, organizations are taking advantage of new research, techniques, and technology to improve the concept. In chapter 8, "Managing Talent," Kevin Oakes, Holly Tompson, and Lorrie Lykins explore the importance, common elements, and best practices of talent management.

In chapter 9, "Getting Results: Our Journey to Turn Leadership Competencies into Outcomes," Dave Ulrich and Norm Smallwood share their path to demonstrate that leadership competencies lead to results and outcomes.

In chapter 10, "Engaging and Retaining Talented People in Any Economy," Beverly Kaye and Sharon Jordan-Evans discuss strategies for how leaders can best initiate an engagement and retention process.

 **Chapter 2**

The Five Practices
of Exemplary Leadership

James M. Kouzes and Barry Z. Posner

In This Chapter

- The Five Practices of Exemplary Leadership.

- Examples of how leaders use these practices in their work.

- The 10 Commitments of Leadership.

L eadership is ultimately about creating a way for people to contribute to making something extraordinary happen," states Alan Keith of Genentech. There are no shortages
of challenging opportunities, and in these extraordinary times the challenges only seem
to be increasing. All generations confront their own serious threats and receive their own
favorable circumstances. That's not the issue. It's how we respond that matters. Through
our responses to these challenges, we have the potential to seriously worsen or profoundly
improve the world in which we live and work. There are countless opportunities to make a
difference—opportunities to

- restore hope and create a deeper sense of meaning in our lives
- rebuild economies and put people back to work

This chapter is adapted from *The Leadership Challenge,* 4th edition, by James M. Kouzes and Barry
Z. Posner. Copyright © 2007 by John Wiley & Sons, Inc. All rights reserved. Used with permission.

- bring peace to a world tired of war
- rebuild a sense of community and increase understanding among diverse peoples
- turn information into knowledge and improve the collective standard of living
- apply knowledge to products and services, creating extraordinary value for the customer
- weave the innocence and wisdom of different generations into our workplaces and into our products and services
- use the tools of technology to weave a web of human connection
- tap the wealth of scientific knowledge to create a safer, more sustainable world
- find a better balance in our always-on, 24/7/365 lives
- provide direction and support during uncertain times.

More than ever, people need to seize these opportunities to lead others to greatness. For more than three decades, we've had the privilege of listening to thousands of leaders tell us their stories of how they did just that—of how they did their best as leaders in times of adversity and change. In this chapter, you'll meet a few of them and hear what they have to say about bringing forth the best from themselves and others.

We begin with the stories of two leaders who faced dramatically different circumstances but exhibited surprisingly similar actions to get extraordinary things done. (Unless otherwise noted, all quotations are taken from personal interviews or from personal-best leadership case studies written by the respondent leaders. The titles and affiliations of the leaders may be different today from what they were at the time of their case study or publication of this volume. We expect that many have moved on to other leadership adventures while we were writing, or will do so by the time you read this.)

From Retired Executive to Passionate Employee Advocate

"When I walked in the door on my first day," Dick Nettell told us, "we had 400 people working really, really hard, but they weren't winning. We had people who were walking around looking like they ran over their dogs on the way to work. It was very, very sad." As the new site executive for Bank of America's Customer Call Center in Concord, California, Dick found "rep scores" (the key performance measure) 21 percentage points behind the top-performing call center and 18 points behind the next-lowest performer. Fifty-five percent of the employees felt they were working in an environment where they couldn't speak their minds, and 50 percent believed nothing would happen if they did.

It's Dick's firm belief that "everybody wants to win. Everybody wants to be successful. Everybody comes to work trying to make a difference." But the call center employees suffered from "management whiplash." The constant turnover in leadership and changes in priorities had been sending them down the path of poor performance. Dick said that when he started asking about the comparisons with other call centers, "all I heard were the reasons why we couldn't do this or that. If there were an Olympic excuse-making team, we would be gold medalists. People were very disempowered." So he set out to change all that.

Dick set aside three entire days just for talking with and listening to people. He gathered as much data as he could from these interviews and elsewhere. "If you keep your eyes open and periodically actually shut your mouth, and you have the courage to turn the mirror around on yourself," he said, "it's amazing what you can learn and how you can change things."

After the interviews, Dick met with the call center's senior managers and support staff in a large basement conference room and presented his findings. Then he handed out a stack of notepads and asked the group to write down five adjectives that described the call center at that time. He repeated this process two more times, asking them to write down five adjectives that described how they thought their peers would describe the center and what they thought the associates, or customer service representatives, would say. Each time, their responses were written on an easel. It was a bleak picture, with the lists filled with words like

- demotivated
- volatile
- imprecise
- failing
- disorganized
- frustrating
- not fun
- constantly changing priorities
- lack of appreciation
- too many changes
- not enough coaching.

Even so, there were some positive comments about the people, such as dedicated, energetic, and supportive.

Then Dick asked them to go through the process once more, this time describing how they would like the call center to look in the future. "If you could wave a magic wand," he asked the group, "in three to five years how would you like the call center to be described?" The language they used to express their hopes, dreams, and aspirations painted a dramatically different picture from the one Dick found when he came aboard:

- amazing results
- world class
- a model for others to follow

- a unique place to work
- partnership
- opportunities to learn and grow
- a true passion for our customers.

Armed with this list of aspirations, Dick and the management team began to craft a vision, mission, and set of values, which they called commitments. The resulting vision and mission is given in the sidebar.

Over the next six weeks, Dick held 22 state-of-the-center meetings, each lasting about 45 minutes, with every team in the call center. "Here's our vision, here's what we're committed to," he would say to begin raising awareness of the issues. And then he'd ask, "Does this make sense to you? Is there something we need to change?" Then he told them about his own beginnings at the Bank of America. He told them about how he'd started as a garage helper, worked his way up to be an automobile fleet manager, and eventually found his way into senior management. He told them, "I'm here at the call center because I want to be here," and then related the story of how he had retired as the bank's corporate services executive and decided to come back.

Dick recounted how he'd woken up early one morning and realized something was missing in his life: "At four in the morning, you can't lie to yourself. I realized that I'm really passionate about working with folks to get them to think differently about themselves. What was missing in my life was the ability to make a difference in people's lives. It may sound corny, but I love to be able to work with people so that they can be the best they can be." So he reached out to an executive he admired at the bank and asked about the chance of coming back. He got his wish when the opportunity to take on the Concord Call Center came along. And when they heard his story, everyone in those state-of-the-center meetings realized they

---

Our Vision of the Future . . .

- We will be seen as a world-class call center and the standard against which others are measured—one with a true passion for our customers.
- We will be acknowledged across the franchise as a model to follow, where every associate truly feels like a partner, has an equal opportunity to learn and grow, and understands his or her personal impact on our overall success.
- We will be viewed as a unique place to work, an organization that drives amazing results while having fun along the way.

Our Mission Is . . .

. . . to provide an experience that consistently "delights" our customers every single minute of every single day.

---

had a champion on their side, a genuine leader who would enable them to realize their aspirations. They understood that Dick was there because he wanted to be there, not because the call center was on some career path to a higher position.

At those meetings, Dick challenged everyone to take the initiative to make their new vision a reality: "You've lost the right to suffer in silence. If you have an issue, open your mouth. I want you to talk to your managers, talk to my communications person, talk to me, or visit AskDick.com. Think about sitting in my chair. Give me ideas and proposals that I have the authority to approve." He made it clear that from then on, changing the call center was everybody's business: "You have to be a part of this. You want to be like a partner, then you've signed up for some responsibility in the process." His challenge made it clear that things were going to change and that the associates were empowered to act. "Everybody should have that equal opportunity to succeed and learn and know what it feels like to win," he said, and "once you've done that—you've got people well positioned—get the hell out of their way and watch them rock and roll."

To maintain the momentum, Dick began holding monthly "town hall" meetings. But to make these meetings happen, he had to challenge the way things are normally done—it's tough to pull call center people off the phone, even once a month. So they do two half-hour town halls each month, with half the call center attending one and the other half coming to the other. At each one, Dick constantly reiterates the mission, commitments, and vision— that's a ritual with him. He gives a "you said, we did" report. Then there's a discussion of current initiatives. For example, the month that we visited Dick, the topics of discussion were the new-hire onboarding process, the upcoming associate survey, and clothing guidelines. After the initiative discussion comes a report on the month's performance. Then each town hall concludes with "Celebrating Heroes," when individuals who've made significant contributions to the center are publicly recognized. And it's not just Dick and his managers doing the recognizing. Associates also get time on the agenda to celebrate peers for living the values of the bank and keeping the commitments they've made to each other.

Recognition and celebration are a big deal to Dick. When he arrived at the Concord Call Center, very little of either was going on, so he put them on the agenda. Every Wednesday, for example, is "Pride Day," when people wear company logo merchandise and you see a lot of red, blue, and white bank shirts. Although Pride Day was started before Dick arrived, he added new dimensions to the ritual. For starters, there's the 15-minute spirit huddle; once a month, every team manager has to bring at least one associate with him or her, and in the huddles the managers recognize their local heroes. You'll also see people wearing gold, blue, and green spirit beads. Dick came up with the idea because he wanted something really visible yet inexpensive enough so they could do a lot of it. The beads come in different colors, but on every string hangs a medallion with the same word: *Pride.*

Pride is Dick's motto—for him, its letters stand for *personal responsibility in delivering excellence*. That medallion suspended from the beads symbolizes what the values, vision, and mission are about for Dick. They're about taking pride in what you do. And when he conducts quarterly coaching sessions with the people who report directly to him, they talk about *Pride*, and mission, and vision, and values. Another thing they talk about is how other people see them as leaders. "When we turn that mirror around," he asks, "is there a match to what we are saying? How do we spend our time every day? Do our goals match our commitments?" It's in these discussions that Dick gets down to aligning actions with the values of the call center.

Despite the tremendous progress they've made in becoming a model call center and toward keeping the commitments that they've made to each other, Dick still believes that "every day is opening day." As he says, "It doesn't matter what you did yesterday. Each and every decision and action is a moment of truth. You say something and what do people see? The two have to be aligned. It's all about the video matching the audio."

And for Dick, the challenge continues, because he knows that every day will present him and the organization with some wonderful chance to try something new: "In today's environment, if you want to be successful, doing things the same way just won't get it done, period. Expectations continue to be raised by our shareholders, by our managers, and by our customers. And if we're not willing to be innovative and do things differently, we're going to have the competition pass us like we're sitting still on the freeway."

Dick demonstrates exemplary leadership skills, and he shows us how leaders can seize the opportunities to bring out the best in others and guide them on the journey to accomplishing exceptionally challenging goals. He serves as a role model for leaders who want to get extraordinary things done in organizations.

Leadership Opportunities Are Everywhere

Leadership can happen anywhere, at any time. It can happen in a huge business or a small one. It can happen in the public, private, or social sector. It can happen in any function. It can happen at home, at school, or in the community. The call to lead can come at four o'clock in the morning, or it can come late at night. The energy and motivation to lead can come in ways you'd never expect. While Dick Nettell's most recent personal-best leadership grew out of a need to challenge himself again, Claire Owen's leadership best grew out of necessity.

Claire Owen is founder and leader of Vision & Values of the SG Group in London, England, a 110-person firm that's a collection of four businesses designed to meet the marketing and human resource recruitment needs of agencies and corporations. Stopgap, the United Kingdom's first specialist freelance marketing agency and the SG Group's original business, began because the marketing agency Claire was working for at the time went into receivership. She had a four-week-old baby and a huge mortgage and wondered what was going to happen to her client, who was midway through an important promotion. Her care for her client overrode her personal concerns, so she called her contacts there, told them what was happening, and agreed on what they were going to do.

"I said to the client, 'Look, you are up you-know-where without a paddle, but don't panic. I will provide you with a stopgap.' So the account manager and I provided the client with a temporary solution and finished running the promotion. I thought at the end of that, gosh, there is something here, providing people with a temporary marketing solution. But I knew *I* didn't want to be that temporary solution. I had had enough of printers and creatives and copywriters, so I thought maybe I could find other people to do the doing and I would just put them together with the client."

When Stopgap opened its doors, no other business was out there doing what Claire proposed. "We created the marketplace that we operate in," she said. "When we started, nobody provided freelance marketers. You could get locum [temporary] doctors, teachers, lawyers, dentists, and vets. In most professions you could get a temp, interim, whatever you like, but you couldn't in marketing." The fact that no other business was like hers was fine with Claire. "I hate the predictable," she told us. "I hate doing things the way everyone else does. I like to do something different. I never wanted to be a me-too company from day one."

Claire is outspoken about her lack of respect for the traditional ways the recruitment industries have been run. "I had been a candidate myself, and I had been so mistreated by the recruitment consultancy that I wanted to challenge the rules the recruitment industry was playing by," she told us. "If I could change those practices, then I'd be proud to work in this field, and that is what I did."

For Claire, the most fundamental rules had to do with how they operated. "I wanted an open and transparent business that people could trust," she said. "Whether it was about our fee structure, or the fact that we never send a candidate to a job before telling him or her everything about the organization, we operate by the principle of total transparency. We might say to a candidate, 'This looks like a great job for your career, but the location is terrible.'"

The early days were tough. There were a lot of naysayers. Because Claire was so outspoken about her views of the industry, competitors were particularly harsh. She remembers one time when a competitor looked at her, wagged his finger, and told her she would never be a success in the business. She just laughed and said, "You don't know how wrong you are."

Success for Claire is not defined by a specific revenue amount or a specific head count. Quite simply, she said, "I wanted to run a business that had a phenomenal reputation." Her vision was that there would be Stopgaps all over the country, just as there are Reeds (the U.K. leaders in specialist recruitment, training, and human resources consulting)—an outlet on every corner, so to speak. She knew they were never going to be a center-city-type recruitment firm, but she wanted Stopgap to be everywhere and to be a company with which people wanted to do business. Claire said that she's not a dreamer, but she is living her dream every day. For her the future is now. Rather than waiting to run the business the way she thinks it should be run, she's bringing it to life every day of the week.

A clear set of values guides the daily decisions and actions that Claire and her staff make. These values came from walking in the shoes of her staff and their candidates. These wouldn't work, however, if they weren't shared values. As Claire told us, "People have said to me time and time again, 'I wouldn't work for any other recruitment consultancy. The only reason I'm sitting here is because I like these values. They're the same as mine.'"

"That's music to my ears," Claire said. "We're not everybody's cup of tea. People come and work for us because they want to make a difference to people. They want to help people. It's what they do."

"We are a very, very candidate-driven business," Claire told us. But even more important to her than the candidate is her staff. She fervently believes that if you take care of your staff members, they will take care of the candidate; if the staff takes care of the candidate, the candidate will take care of the client; and if the candidate takes care of the client, the client will return to the SG Group for more business. Claire puts her staff members first, knowing that they're the ones who ultimately determine the company's reputation.

As you'd expect, staff turnover at the SG Group is extremely low. People rarely leave the business, and if they do, they are always welcomed back if they want to return. "Friendship is the glue that keeps people here. Why would I want to leave when my best mates work with me? Someone once said to me, 'Don't take this the wrong way, Claire, but coming to work is a bit like going to a coffee morning.' I asked her what she meant, and she said, 'I am with the people I like, and we can socialize. And yes, we do the job.' I thought that was wonderful. They love coming to work because of the people who are here."

The values of helping and caring for clients and staff by no means include permission to coddle people or to allow them to do whatever they want. Claire is very clear that she expects the values to be lived, not just talked about. They are as much a discipline as any other operational values. "If you want customers to have a certain experience," she says, "you have got to have people who can deliver on that experience. It's a darn sight easier if you employ people who have the values that you want to give your customers."

Clearly the SG Group's values aren't just posters on the wall—they are the guidelines the group uses in everything they do. For example, there is the "First Tuesday of the Month" Meeting. It's actually never held on the first Tuesday, but that's what it was called when they were first held, and the name has stuck. It happens once a month, from 9:00 to 10:00 a.m., and everybody comes. They share the company's financials. Everybody learns what the business has turned over, and the profit made or loss taken. They talk about where the business has come from, so people won't forget about their important clients. They share any marketing that's going on. They share a lot of "people" things—who's joining, who's leaving, who's got an anniversary this month, and anything else that affects staff. And they always have the "grapevine"—a time when people can ask about things they might have heard about and want to know if it's really happening. And they film the meeting, so if someone has to miss it, he or she can watch it later.

Then there's the Friday Meeting. It's a look back at the week, a sharing of good things and bad things that have happened during the week. There's also the Thursday Breakfast Club, which happens every other Thursday. That's a forum for consultants to talk about candidates and clients and to share the issues with which they're dealing in depth. Notes from these meetings are often posted in the restrooms so that they are visible at all times—you never know when you might come up with a solution to someone's problem. Finally, a staff newsletter goes out every other week for more personal needs, like someone wanting details of a great Mexican restaurant, a good plumber, or someone who could share an apartment.

Being physically present is important for Claire. She asked her staff what they wanted from her, and they told her "that they just wanted to see more of me, to have time to talk to me, to see me wandering around." She radiates energy. When you're around her, you have no doubt that she cares deeply about the business and, in particular, about the people in the business. She fully understands the potency of her physical presence: "You see that I get excited about things," she pointed out to us—not that there was any doubt—"and people go, 'Well, Claire is excited about it, so I'm going to get excited about it. She believes it and she thinks it is going to be great—well I think it's going to be great.' That's really all I do."

Claire also realizes that if her enthusiasm isn't genuine, it's going to have a negative effect: "If it's an act, they'll see right through it. People really respect you for who you are, and they don't want you to be someone you are not. They prefer to see who you are, the real you."

The SG Group has a positively charged atmosphere that is fueled by numerous recognitions and celebrations. These are the informal kinds at which people toast personal successes, anniversaries, and births of babies. Every month, staff members nominate people who have gone the extra mile. Anybody can nominate anybody. All the nominations are considered, 99 percent are approved, and every winner gets a silver envelope placed on his or her desk thanking him or her for going the extra mile and presenting usually between 25 and 50 Stopgap points. Each point is worth about £1, and they can convert the points into whatever they want to spend it on. The SG Group also has a flexible benefits program called "Mind, Body, Soul." Nothing is formal, and staff members create things for themselves. The whole idea is that each person is different, and people can customize the plan to fit their needs. For some it's a gym membership, for others it's health insurance, and for others it's personal coaching. The entire program celebrates the individuality of each person.

The marketplace for freelance marketers has grown more and more competitive. But the SG Group is being recognized for the difference it is making. What began out of necessity has grown into something that others now look to for ideas that will help them grow their businesses and retain their staffs. In 2004 Stopgap was listed as number 10 on the London *Sunday Times* "50 Best Small Companies to Work For" list, and in 2005 was named number five. Claire Owen was declared the "Best for Leadership" by the *Sunday Times* two years in a row.

"You can never get complacent," Claire said. "As a business we are always, always thinking, 'What else can we do to stay ahead?'" But something that won't change is Claire's leadership philosophy: "We are human beings. We don't have employees. We don't have staff. We have people, and people have emotions, and people have needs. If you are happy, you do a better job. If you are excited about the business, and if you are excited about where it is going and what is happening in it, then there is a buzz, a physical buzz. It's my job to create that kind of place."

Distilling Practices That Epitomize Leadership

Since 1983, we've conducted research on personal-best leadership experiences, and we've discovered that there are countless examples of how leaders like Dick and Claire mobilize others to get extraordinary things done in practically every arena of organized activity. We've found them in profit-based firms and nonprofits, manufacturing and services, government and business, health care, education and entertainment, and work and community service. Leaders reside in every city and every country, in every position and every place. They're employees and volunteers, young and old, women and men. Leadership knows no racial or religious bounds, no ethnic or cultural borders. We find exemplary leadership everywhere we look.

From our analysis of thousands of personal-best leadership experiences, we've discovered that ordinary people who guide others along pioneering journeys follow rather similar paths. Though each experience we examined was unique in expression, every case followed remarkably similar patterns of action. We've distilled these common practices into a model of leadership, and we offer it here as guidance for leaders as they attempt to keep their own bearings and steer others toward peak achievements.

In developing this model, as we looked deeper into the dynamic process of leadership, through case analyses and survey questionnaires, we realized that personal-best leadership experiences reflect five common practices. When getting extraordinary things done in organizations, leaders engage in these Five Practices of Exemplary Leadership:

- Model the way.
- Inspire a shared vision.
- Challenge the process.
- Enable others to act.
- Encourage the heart.

These five practices aren't the private property of the people we studied or of a few isolated shining stars. Leadership is not about personality; it's about behavior. The five practices are available to anyone who accepts the leadership challenge. And they're also not the accident of a unique moment in history. The five practices have stood the test of time, and our most recent research confirms that they're just as relevant today as they were when we first began our investigation more than 25 years ago. Let's briefly consider each one.

Model the Way

Titles are granted, but your behavior wins you respect. As Tom Brack, with Europe's Smart-Team AG, told us, "Leading means you have to be a good example and live what you say." This sentiment was shared across all the cases we collected. Exemplary leaders know that if they want to gain commitment and achieve the highest standards, they must be models of the behavior they expect of others. *Leaders model the way.*

To effectively model the behavior they expect of others, leaders must first be clear about guiding principles. They must *clarify values.* As Lindsay Levin, chairman for Whites Group in England, explained, "You have to open up your heart and let people know what you really think and believe. This means talking about your values." Leaders must find their own voice, and then they must clearly and distinctively give voice to their values. As the personal-best stories illustrate, leaders are supposed to stand up for their beliefs, so they'd better have some beliefs for which to stand up. But it's not just the leader's values that are important. Leaders aren't just representing themselves. They speak and act on behalf of a larger organization. Leadership must forge agreement around common principles and common ideals.

Eloquent speeches about common values, however, aren't nearly enough. Leaders' deeds are far more important than their words when determining how serious they really are about what they say. Words and deeds must be consistent. Exemplary leaders go first. They go first by *setting the example* through daily actions that demonstrate their commitment to their beliefs. As Prabha Seshan, principal engineer for SSA Global, told us, "One of the best ways to prove something is important is by doing it yourself and setting an example." She discovered that her actions spoke volumes about how the team needed to "take ownership of things they believed in and valued." There wasn't anything she asked others to do that she wasn't willing to do herself, and, as a result, "while I always trusted my team, my team in turn trusted me." For instance, she wasn't required to design or code features, but by doing some of this work, she demonstrated to others not only what she stood for but also how much she valued the work they were doing and what their end user expected from the product.

The personal-best projects we heard about in our research were all distinguished by relentless effort, steadfastness, competence, and attention to detail. We were also struck by how the actions leaders took to set an example were often simple things. Sure, leaders had operational and strategic plans. But the examples they gave were not about elaborate designs. They were about the power of spending time with someone, of working side by side with colleagues, of telling stories that made values come alive, of being highly visible during times of uncertainty, and of asking questions to get people to think about values and priorities.

Modeling the way is about earning the right and the respect to lead through direct involvement and action. People first follow the person, then the plan.

Inspire a Shared Vision

When people described to us their personal-best leadership experiences, they told of times when they imagined an exciting, highly attractive future for their organization. They had visions and dreams of what *could* be. They had absolute and total personal belief in those dreams, and they were confident in their abilities to make extraordinary things happen. Every organization, every social movement, begins with a dream. The dream or vision is the force that invents the future. *Leaders inspire a shared vision.* As Mark D'Arcangelo, system memory product marketing manager at Hitachi Semiconductor, told us about his personal-best leadership experience, "What made the difference was the vision of how things could be and clearly painting this picture for all to see and comprehend."

Leaders gaze across the horizon of time, imagining the attractive opportunities that are in store when they and their constituents arrive at a distant destination. They *envision exciting and ennobling possibilities.* Leaders desire to make something happen, to change the way things are, to create something that no one else has ever created before. In some ways, leaders live their lives backward. They see pictures in their mind's eye of what the results will look like even before they've started their project, much as an architect draws a blueprint or an engineer builds a model. Their clear image of the future pulls them forward. Yet visions seen only by leaders are insufficient to create an organized movement or a significant change in a company. A person with no constituents is not a leader, and people will not follow until they accept a vision as their own. Leaders cannot command commitment, only inspire it.

Leaders have to *enlist others in a common vision.* To enlist people in a vision, leaders must know their constituents and speak their language. People must believe that their leaders understand their needs and have their interests at heart. Leadership is a dialogue, not a monologue. To enlist support, leaders must have intimate knowledge of people's dreams, hopes, aspirations, visions, and values. Evelia Davis, merchandise manager for Mervyns, told us that while she was good at telling people where they were going together, she also needed to do a good job of explaining why they should follow her, how they could help reach the destination, and what this meant for them. As Evelia put it, "If you don't believe enough to share it, talk about it, and get others excited about it then it's not much of a vision!"

Leaders breathe life into the hopes and dreams of others and enable them to see the exciting possibilities that the future holds. Leaders forge unity of purpose by showing constituents how the dream is for the common good. Leaders stir the fire of passion in others by expressing enthusiasm for the compelling vision of their group. Leaders communicate their passion through vivid language and an expressive style.

Whatever the venue, and without exception, the people in our study reported that they were incredibly enthusiastic about their personal-best projects. Their own enthusiasm was catching; it spread from leader to constituents. Their belief in and enthusiasm for the vision were the sparks that ignited the flame of inspiration.

Challenge the Process

Every single personal-best leadership case we collected involved some kind of challenge. The challenge might have been an innovative new product, a cutting-edge service, a groundbreaking piece of legislation, an invigorating campaign to get adolescents to join an environmental program, a revolutionary turnaround of a bureaucratic military project, or the start-up of a new plant or business. Whatever the challenge, all the cases involved a change from the status quo. Not one person claimed to have achieved a personal best by keeping things the same. All leaders *challenge the process.*

Leaders venture out. None of the individuals in our study sat idly by waiting for fate to smile upon them. "Luck" or "being in the right place at the right time" may play a role in the specific opportunities leaders embrace, but those who lead others to greatness seek and accept challenge. Jennifer Cun, in her role as a budget analyst with Intel, noted how critical it is for leaders "to always be looking for ways to improve their team, taking interests outside of their job or organization, finding ways to stay current of what the competition is doing, networking, and taking initiative to try new things."

Leaders are pioneers. They are willing to step out into the unknown. They *search for opportunities to innovate, grow, and improve.* But leaders aren't the only creators or originators of new products, services, or processes. In fact, it's more likely that they're not; innovation comes more from listening than from telling. Product and service innovations tend to come from customers, clients, vendors, people in the labs, and people on the front lines; process innovations come from people doing the work. Sometimes a dramatic external event thrusts an organization into a radically new condition. Leaders must constantly look outside themselves and their organizations for new and innovative products, processes, and services. "Mediocrity and the status quo will never lead a company to success in the marketplace," is what Mike Pepe, product marketing manager at O3 Entertainment, told us. "Taking risks and believing that taking them is worthwhile," he went on to say, "are the only way companies can 'jump' rather than simply climb the improvement ladder."

When it comes to innovation, the leader's major contributions are in the creation of a climate for experimentation; the recognition of good ideas; the support of those ideas; and the willingness to challenge the system to get new products, processes, services, and systems adopted. It might be more accurate, then, to say that leaders aren't inventors so much as early patrons and adopters of innovation.

Leaders know well that innovation and change involve *experimenting and taking risks.* Despite the inevitability of mistakes and failures, leaders proceed anyway. One way of dealing with the potential risks and failures of experimentation is to approach change through incremental steps and small wins. Little victories, when piled on top of each other, build confidence that even the biggest challenges can be met. In so doing, they strengthen commitment to the long-term future. Not everyone is equally comfortable with risk and uncertainty. Leaders must pay attention to the capacity of their constituents to take control of challenging situations and become fully committed to change. You can't exhort people to take risks if they don't also feel safe.

It would be ridiculous to assert that those who fail over and over again eventually succeed as leaders. Success in any endeavor isn't a process of simply buying enough lottery tickets. The key that unlocks the door to opportunity is learning. Claude Meyer, who is with the Red Cross in Kenya, put it to us this way: "Leadership is learning by doing, adapting to actual conditions. Leaders are constantly learning from their errors and failures." Life is the leader's laboratory, and exemplary leaders use it to conduct as many experiments as possible. Try, fail, learn. Try, fail, learn. Try, fail, learn. That's the leader's mantra. Leaders are learners. They learn from their failures as well as their successes, and they make it possible for others to do the same.

Enable Others to Act

A grand dream doesn't become a significant reality through the actions of a single person. It requires a team effort. It requires solid trust and strong relationships. It requires deep competence and cool confidence. It requires group collaboration and individual accountability. To get extraordinary things done in organizations, leaders need to *enable others to act*.

After reviewing thousands of personal-best cases, we developed a simple test to detect whether someone is on the road to becoming a leader. This test is the frequency of the use of the word *we*. In our interviews, we found that people used *we* nearly three times more often than *I* in explaining their personal-best leadership experiences. For instance, Hewlett-Packard's Angie Yim was the technical information technology team leader on a project involving core team members from the United States, Singapore, Australia, and Hong Kong. In the past, Angie told us, she "had a bad habit of using the pronoun *I* instead of *we*," but she learned that people responded more eagerly and her team became more cohesive when people felt part of the *we*. "This is a magic word," she realized. "I would recommend others use it more often."

Leaders *foster collaboration and build trust*. This sense of teamwork goes far beyond a few direct reports or close confidants. They engage all those who must make the project work—and in some way, all who must live with the results. In today's virtual organizations, cooperation can't be restricted to a small group of loyalists; it must include peers, managers, customers and clients, suppliers, citizens—all those who have a stake in the vision.

Leaders make it possible for others to do good work. They know that those who are expected to produce the results must feel a sense of personal power and ownership. Leaders understand that the command-and-control techniques of traditional management no longer apply. Instead, leaders work to make people feel strong, capable, and committed. Leaders enable others to act not by hoarding the power they have but by giving it away. Exemplary leaders *strengthen everyone's capacity* to deliver on the promises they make. As Kathryn Winters learned working with the communications department at NVIDIA Corporation, "You have to make sure that no one is outside the loop or uninvolved in all the changes that occur." She continually ensures that each person has a sense of ownership for his or her projects. She seeks out the opinions of others and uses the ensuing discussion not only to build up their capabilities but also to educate and update her own information and perspective. "Inclusion (not exclusion)," she finds, "ensures that everyone feels and thinks that they are owners and leaders—this makes work much easier." She has realized that when people are trusted and have more discretion, more authority, and more information, they're much more likely to use their energies to produce extraordinary results.

In the cases we analyzed, leaders proudly discussed teamwork, trust, and empowerment as essential elements of their efforts. A leader's ability to enable others to act is essential. Constituents neither perform at their best nor stick around for long if their leader makes them feel weak, dependent, or alienated. But when a leader makes people feel strong and capable—as if they can do more than they ever thought possible—they'll give their all and exceed their own expectations. Authentic leadership is founded on trust, and the more people trust their leader and each other, the more they take risks, make changes, and keep their organization and movement alive. Through this relationship, leaders turn their constituents into leaders themselves.

Encourage the Heart

The climb to the top is arduous and long. People become exhausted, frustrated, and disenchanted. They're often tempted to give up. Leaders *encourage the hearts* of their constituents to carry on. Genuine acts of caring uplift the spirits and draw people forward. In her personal-best leadership experience Ankush Joshi, the service line manager with Informix USA, learned that "writing a personal thank-you note, rather than sending an email, can do wonders." Janel Aherns, marketing communications manager with National Semiconductor, echoed Ankush's observation. Janel would make notes about important events in other people's lives and then follow up with them directly afterward or simply wish them luck before an important event. Every person was "genuinely touched that I cared enough to ask them about how things are going." She told us that in her organization, "work relationships have been stronger since this undertaking." Janel's and Ankush's experiences are testimony to the power of a "thank you."

Recognizing contributions can be one to one or with many people. It can come from dramatic gestures or simple actions. One of the first actions that Abraham Kuruvilla took upon becoming CEO of the Dredging Corporation of India (a government-owned private-sector company providing services to all 10 major Indian ports) was to send every employee a monthly newsletter (*DCI News*) that was full of success stories. In addition, he started a public recognition program that gives awards and simple appreciation notices to individuals and teams for doing great work. Abraham made sure that people were recognized for their contributions, because he wanted to provide a climate in which "people felt cared about and genuinely appreciated by their leaders."

It's part of the leader's job to show appreciation for people's contributions and to create a culture of *celebrating values and victories.* In the cases we collected, we saw thousands of examples of individual recognition and group celebration. We've heard and seen everything from handwritten thank-yous to marching bands and *This Is Your Life*–type ceremonies.

Recognition and celebration aren't about fun and games, though there is a lot of fun and there are a lot of games when people encourage the hearts of their constituents. Neither are they about pretentious ceremonies designed to create some phony sense of camaraderie. When people see a charlatan exhibiting noisy affectations, they turn away in disgust. Encouragement is, curiously, a serious business. It's how leaders visibly and behaviorally link rewards with performance. When striving to raise quality, recover from disaster, start up a new service, or make a dramatic change of any kind, leaders make sure that people see the benefit of behavior that's aligned with cherished values. Leaders also know that celebrations and rituals, when done with authenticity and from the heart, build a strong sense of collective identity and community spirit that can carry a group through extraordinarily tough times.

Leadership Is a Relationship

Our findings from the analysis of personal-best leadership experiences challenge the myth that leadership is something that you find only at the highest levels of organizations and society. We found it everywhere. These findings also challenge the belief that leadership is reserved for a few charismatic men and women. Leadership is not a gene, and it's not an inheritance. Leadership is an identifiable set of skills and abilities that are available to all of us. The "great person"—woman or man—theory of leadership is just plain wrong. Or, we should say, the theory that only a few great men and women can lead others to greatness is just plain wrong. Likewise, it is plain wrong that leaders can only come from large, or great, or small, or new organizations, or from established economies, or from start-up companies. We consider the women and men we've met in doing our research great people, and so do those with whom they've worked. They are the everyday heroes of our world. It's because there are so many—not so few—leaders that extraordinary things get done on a regular basis, especially in extraordinary times.

To us, this is inspiring—and it should give everyone hope, because it means that no one needs to wait around to be saved by someone riding into town on a white horse, because a generation of leaders is searching for opportunities to make a difference, and because right down the block or hall are people who will seize the opportunity to lead you to greatness. They're your neighbors, friends, and colleagues. And you're one of them too.

There's still another crucial truth about leadership. It's something that we've known for a long time, but we've come to prize even more today. In talking with leaders and studying their cases, a very clear message wove itself throughout every situation and every action: *Leadership is a relationship*—a relationship between those who aspire to lead and those who choose to follow. The quality of this relationship matters most when we're engaged in getting extraordinary things done. A leader-constituent relationship that's characterized by fear and distrust will never, ever produce anything of lasting value. But a relationship characterized by mutual respect and confidence will overcome the greatest adversities and leave a legacy of significance.

Evidence abounds for this point of view. For instance, in examining the critical variables for executive success in the top three jobs in large organizations, Jodi Taylor and Valerie Sessa at the Center for Creative Leadership found the number one success factor to be "relationships with subordinates" (Sessa and Taylor 2000; Taylor 1998). We were intrigued to find that even in this nanosecond world of e-everything, opinion is consistent with the facts. In an online survey, respondents were asked to indicate, among other things, which would be more essential to business success in five years—social skills or skills in using the Internet. Seventy-two percent selected social skills, and 28 percent selected Internet skills (*Fast Company* 1999). Internet literati completing a poll online realize that it's not the web of technology that matters the most, it's the web of people.

Similar results were found in a study by Public Allies, an AmeriCorps organization dedicated to creating young leaders who can strengthen their communities. Public Allies sought the opinions of 18- to 30-year-olds on the subject of leadership. Among the items was a question about the qualities that were important in a good leader. Topping the respondents' list is "being able to see a situation from someone else's point of view." In second place is "getting along well with other people" (Public Allies 1998).

Success in leadership, success in business, and success in life have been, are now, and will continue to be a function of how well people work and play together. Success in leading will be wholly dependent upon the capacity to build and sustain human relationships that enable people to get extraordinary things done on a regular basis.

Leadership is in the moment, and each day provides countless moments to make a difference. The chance might come in a private conversation with someone who reports directly to you or in a meeting with colleagues. It might come over the family dinner table. It might come when you're speaking at a conference on the future of your business, or it might come when you're listening to a friend talk about a current conflict with a peer. There are many moments each day when you can choose to lead and many moments each day when you can choose to make a difference. Each of these moments offers the prospect of contributing to a lasting legacy.

The 10 Commitments of Leadership

Embedded in the Five Practices of Exemplary Leadership are behaviors that can serve as the basis for learning to lead. We call these the 10 Commitments of Leadership (table 2-1). These commitments can serve as a guide as your further explore how leaders get extraordinary things done in organizations.

Table 2-1. The Five Practices and 10 Commitments of Leadership

Practice	Commitment
Model the way	1. Clarify values by finding your voice and affirming shared ideals.
	2. Set the example by aligning actions with shared values.
Inspire a shared vision	3. Envision the future by imagining exciting and ennobling possibilities.
	4. Enlist others in a common vision by appealing to shared aspirations.
Challenge the process	5. Search for opportunities by seizing the initiative and by looking outward for innovative ways to improve.
	6. Experiment and take risks by constantly generating small wins and learning from experience.
Enable others to act	7. Foster collaboration by building trust and facilitating relationships.
	8. Strengthen others by increasing self-determination and developing competence.
Encourage the heart	9. Recognize contributions by showing appreciation for individual excellence.
	10. Celebrate the values and victories by creating a spirit of community.

Source: Kouzes and Posner (2007). Used with permission from John Wiley & Sons.

Further Reading

Bill George with Peter Sims, *True North: Discover Your Authentic Leadership.* San Francisco: Jossey-Bass, 2007.

Daniel Goleman, *Working with Emotional Intelligence.* New York: Bantam, 2000.

Tom Kelley with Jonathan Littman, *The Ten Faces of Innovation: IDEO's Strategies for Beating the Devil's Advocate and Driving Creativity Throughout Your Organization.* New York: Currency Doubleday, 2001.

James M. Kouzes and Barry Z. Posner, *The Truth About Leadership: The No-Fads, Heart-of-the-Matter Facts You Should Know.* San Francisco: Jossey-Bass, 2010.

John Naisbitt, *Mindset: Eleven Ways to Change the Way You See and Create the Future.* New York: HarperCollins, 2006.

Tom Rath and Donald O. Clifton, *How Full Is Your Bucket? Positive Strategies for Work and Life.* New York: Gallup Press, 2004.

References

Fast Company. 1999. FC Roper Starch Survey: The Web. October, 302.

Kouzes, J. M., and B. Z. Posner. 2007. *The Leadership Challenge,* 4th ed. San Francisco: Jossey-Bass.

Public Allies. 1998. *New Leadership for a New Century.* Washington, DC: Public Allies.

Sessa, V. I., and J. J. Taylor. 2000. *Executive Selection: Strategies for Success.* San Francisco: Jossey-Bass.

Taylor, J. J. 1998. Telephone interview with Jodi Taylor, Center for Creative Leadership, April.

About the Authors

James M. Kouzes has been thinking about leadership ever since he was one of only a dozen Eagle Scouts to be selected to serve in John F. Kennedy's honor guard at Kennedy's inauguration. Kennedy's inaugural call to action inspired him to join the Peace Corps, and he taught school in Turkey. That experience made him realize that he wanted a career that offered two things: the opportunities to teach and serve. Upon his return to the United States, he began training community action agency managers, and he found his calling. He has devoted his life to leadership development ever since. He is a best-selling author; an award-winning speaker; and, according to the *Wall Street Journal,* one of the 12 best executive educators in the United States.

Barry Z. Posner makes each day matter. He is a professor of leadership at the Leavey School of Business, Santa Clara University (located in the heart of Silicon Valley), where he served for 12 years as dean of the school. At Santa Clara, he received the President's Distinguished Faculty Award, the School's Extraordinary Faculty Award, and several other outstanding teaching and leadership honors. Described as a warm, engaging, and pragmatic conference speaker and dynamic workshop facilitator, he has made presentations and conducted workshops across the United States and around the globe, from Canada, Mexico, and Europe, to the Far East, Australia, New Zealand, and South Africa.

Chapter 3

Leading to Build the Team

Patrick M. Lencioni

Practically all the executives I've ever come across believe in teamwork. At least they say they do. Sadly, a scarce few of them make teamwork a reality in their organizations; in fact, they often end up creating environments where political infighting and departmental silos are the norm. And yet they continue to tout their belief in teamwork, as if that alone will somehow make it magically appear. I have found that only a small minority of companies truly understand and embrace teamwork, even though, according to their websites, more than one in three of the *Fortune* 500 publicly declare it to be a core value.

How can this be? How can intelligent, well-meaning executives who supposedly set out to foster cooperation and collaboration among their peers be left with organizational dynamics that are anything but team oriented? And why do they go on promoting a concept they are so often unable to deliver?

© 2010 Patrick M. Lencioni. Used with permission.

Well, it's not because they're secretly plotting to undermine teamwork among their peers. That would actually be easier to address. The problem is more straightforward—and more difficult to overcome. Most groups of executives fail to become cohesive teams because they drastically underestimate both the power teamwork ultimately unleashes and the painful steps required to make teamwork a reality. But before exploring those steps, it is important to understand how the compulsory, politically correct nature of teamwork makes all of this more difficult.

Contrary to conventional wisdom, teamwork is not a virtue in itself. It is merely a strategic choice, not unlike adopting a specific sales model or a financial strategy. And certainly, when properly understood and implemented, it is a powerful and beneficial tool. Unfortunately, management theorists and human resources professionals have made teamwork unconditionally desirable, something akin to being a good corporate citizen.

As a result, many of today's leaders champion teamwork reflexively without really understanding what it entails. Pump them full of truth serum and ask them why, and they'll tell you they feel as if they *must* promote teamwork, that anything less would be politically, socially, and organizationally incorrect. "What choice do I have? Imagine me standing up in front of a group of employees and saying that teamwork isn't really all that important here." Ironically, that would be better than what many—if not most—leaders do. By preaching teamwork and not demanding that their people live it, they are creating two big problems.

First, they are inducing a collective sense of hypocrisy among their staff members, who feel that teamwork has devolved into nothing more than an empty slogan. Second, and more dangerous still, they are confusing those staff members about how to act in the best interest of the company, so they wind up trying at once to be pragmatically self-interested and ideologically selfless. The combination of these factors evokes inevitable and sometimes paralyzing feelings of dissonance and guilt.

Executives must understand that an alternative to teamwork exists, which is actually more effective than being a faux team. Jeffrey Katzenbach (2003), author of *The Wisdom of Teams*, calls it a "working group," a group of executives who agree to work independently with few expectations for collaboration. The advantage of a working group is clarity; members know exactly what they can and, more important, *cannot* expect of one another, and so they focus on how to accomplish goals without the distractions and costs that teamwork inevitably presents. (For guidance on deciding whether teamwork is right for your organization, see the sidebar.)

Of course, none of this is to say that teamwork is not a worthy goal. There is no disputing that it is uniquely powerful, enabling groups of people to achieve more collectively than they could have imagined doing apart. However, the requirements of real teamwork cannot be underestimated.

To Be or Not to Be a Team

So how do well-intentioned leaders go about deciding if teamwork is right for their staff? They can start by recognizing that organizational structure is not nearly as important as behavioral willingness. Most theorists will call for teamwork in organizations that are structured functionally, but may not do so for those that are organized divisionally or geographically.

In other words, if the work can be organized in departments that operate largely independently (with regional territories, distinct product divisions, or separate subsidiaries), then the executives at the top can follow suit and function as what Jeffrey Katzenbach (2003) describes as "working units." These are groups made up of individuals who, though friendly and cooperative at times, are not expected to make willing sacrifices to one another to achieve common goals that lead to joint rewards.

However, when executives run an organization made up of departments with structural interdependencies, teamwork is usually presented as the only possible approach for the leadership group. But although this is a sound and reasonable theory when all other factors are considered equal, it is not necessarily advisable in the messy and fallible world of real human beings. Before deciding that teamwork is the answer, ask these questions of yourself and your fellow team members:

- Can we keep our egos in check?
- Are we capable of admitting to mistakes, weaknesses, and insufficient knowledge?
- Can we speak up openly when we disagree?
- Will we confront behavioral problems directly?
- Can we put the success of the team or organization above our individual success?

If the answer to one or more of these questions is "probably not," then a group of executives should think twice about declaring themselves a team. Why? Because more than structure, the willingness of executives to change behavior—starting with the leader of the organization—should determine whether teamwork is the right answer.

The fact is, building a leadership team is hard. It demands substantial behavioral changes from people who are strong willed and often set in their ways, having already accomplished great things in their careers. What follows is a realistic description of what a group of executives must be ready to do if they undertake the nontrivial task of becoming a team, something that is not necessarily right for every group of leaders. (See figure 3-1 for an illustration of the role of a leader in building a team.)

Establishing Vulnerability-Based Trust

The first and most important step in building a cohesive and functional team is establishing trust—but not just any kind of trust. Teamwork must be built upon a solid foundation of vulnerability-based trust. This means that the members of a cohesive, functional team

Figure 3-1. The Role of the Leader in Building a Team

The leader must...

Inattention to results	Focus on collective outcomes
Avoidance of accountability	Confront difficult issues
Lack of commitment	Force clarity and closure
Fear of conflict	Demand debate
Absence of trust	Be vulnerable

must learn to comfortably and quickly acknowledge, without provocation, their mistakes, weaknesses, failures, and needs for help. They must also readily recognize the strengths of others, even when those strengths exceed their own.

In theory—or in kindergarten—this does not seem terribly difficult. But when a leader is faced with a roomful of accomplished, proud, and talented staff members, getting them to let their guard down and risk losing positional power is an extremely difficult challenge. And the only way to initiate it is for the leader to go first.

Showing vulnerability is unnatural for many leaders, who were raised to project strength and confidence in the face of difficulty. And though that is certainly a noble behavior in many circumstances, it must be tempered when it comes to demonstrating vulnerability-based trust to hesitant team members who need their leader to strip naked and dive into the cold water first. Of course, this requires that a leader be confident enough, ironically, to admit to frailties and make it easy for others to follow suit. One particular CEO with whom I worked failed to build trust among his team members and watched the company falter as a result. As it turns out, a big contributing factor was his inability to model vulnerability-based trust. As one of the executives who reported to him later explained to me, "No one on the team was ever allowed to be smarter than him in any area because he was the CEO." As a result, team members would not open up to one another and admit their own weaknesses or mistakes.

What exactly does vulnerability-based trust look like in practice? It is evident among team members who say things to one another like "I screwed up," "I was wrong," "I need help," "I'm sorry," and "You're better than I am at this." Most important, they only make these statements when they mean it—and especially when they really don't want to.

If all this sounds like motherhood and apple pie, understand that there is a very practical reason why vulnerability-based trust is indispensable. Without it, a team will not, and probably should not, engage in unfiltered productive conflict.

Inciting Healthy Conflict

One of the greatest inhibitors of teamwork among executive teams is the fear of conflict, which stems from two separate concerns. On one hand, many executives go to great lengths to avoid conflict among their teams because they worry that they will lose control of the group and that someone will have their pride damaged in the process. On the other hand, others avoid conflict because they see it as a waste of time. They prefer to cut meetings and discussions short by jumping to the decision that they believe will ultimately be adopted anyway, leaving more time for implementation and what they think of as "real work."

Whatever the case, CEOs who go to great lengths to avoid conflict often do so believing that they are strengthening their teams by avoiding destructive disagreement. However, what they are really doing is stifling productive conflict and pushing important issues that need to be resolved under the carpet where they will fester. Eventually, those unresolved issues will grow into uglier and more personal discord when executives grow frustrated at what they perceive to be repeated problems.

What CEOs and their teams must do is learn to identify artificial harmony when they see it and incite productive conflict in its place. This is a messy process, and it takes time to master. But there is no avoiding it, because to do so makes it next to impossible for a team to make a real commitment.

Making an Unwavering Commitment

To become a cohesive team, a group of leaders must learn to commit to decisions when there is less than perfect information available and when no natural consensus develops. And because perfect information and a natural consensus rarely exist, the ability to commit becomes one of the most critical behaviors of a team.

But teams cannot learn to do this if they are not in the practice of engaging in productive and unguarded conflict. Only after team members passionately and unguardedly debate with one another and speak their minds can the leader feel confident of making a decision with the full benefit of the group's collective wisdom. A simple example might help illustrate the costs of failing to truly commit.

The CEO of a struggling pharmaceutical company decided to eliminate business and first-class airplane travel to cut costs. Everyone around the table nodded their heads in agreement, but within weeks, it became apparent that only half the room had really committed to the decision. The others merely decided not to challenge the decision but rather to ignore it. This created its own set of destructive conflicts when angry employees from different departments traveled together and found themselves heading to different parts of the airplane. Needless to say, the travel policy was on the agenda again at the next meeting, wasting important time that should have been spent righting the company's financial situation.

Teams that fail to disagree and exchange unfiltered opinions find themselves revisiting the same issues again and again. All this is ironic, because the teams that appear to an outside observer to be the most dysfunctional (the arguers) are usually the ones that can arrive at and stick with a difficult decision.

It's worth repeating here that commitment and conflict are not possible without trust. If team members are concerned about protecting themselves from their peers, they will not be able to disagree and commit. And this presents its own set of problems, not the least of which is the unwillingness to hold one another accountable.

Ensuring Unapologetic Accountability

Great teams do not wait for the leader to remind members when they are not pulling their weight. Because there is no lack of clarity about what they have committed to do, they are comfortable calling one another on actions and behaviors that don't contribute to the likelihood of success. Less effective teams typically resort to reporting unacceptable behavior to the leader of the group, or worse yet, to back-channel gossip. These behaviors are not only destructive to the morale of the team; they are inefficient and allow easily addressable issues to live longer than should be allowed.

Don't let the simplicity of accountability hide the difficulty of making it a reality. Teaching strong leaders on a team to confront their peers about behavioral issues that hurt the team is not easy. But when the goals of the team have been clearly delineated, the behaviors that jeopardize them become easier to call out.

Focusing on a Collective Orientation Toward Results

The ultimate goal of the team, and the only real scorecard for measuring its success, is the achievement of tangible collective outcomes. And though most executive teams are certainly populated with leaders who are driven to succeed, all too often the results they focus on are individual or departmental. Once the inevitable moment of truth comes, when executives must choose between the success of the entire team and their own, many are unable to resist the instinct to look out for themselves. This is understandable—but deadly to a team.

Leaders committed to building a team must have zero tolerance for individually focused behavior. This is easier said than done when considering the sizes of the egos assembled on a given leadership team. And this is perhaps why a leader trying to assemble a truly cohesive team would do well to select team members with small egos.

If all this sounds obvious, that's because it is. The problem with teamwork is not that it is difficult to understand, but rather that it is extremely difficult to achieve when the people involved are strong-willed, independently successful leaders. The point here is not that teamwork is not worth the trouble, but rather that its rewards are both rare and costly. And as for those leaders who don't have the courage to force team members to step up to the requirements of teamwork, they would be wiser to avoid the concept altogether. Of course, that would require a different kind of courage—the courage not to be a team.

Further Reading

Patrick M. Lencioni, *The Five Dysfunctions of a Team: A Leadership Fable.* San Francisco: Jossey-Bass, 2002.

Reference

Katzenbach, J. R. 2003. *The Wisdom of Teams: Creating the High-Performance Organization.* New York: HarperCollins.

About the Author

Patrick M. Lencioni is the author of *The Five Dysfunctions of a Team,* which has been a fixture on *The Wall Street Journal* bestseller list since it was published in 2002. He is the author of seven additional business books with nearly three million copies sold and is also the founder and president of The Table Group, a firm dedicated to providing organizations with ideas, products, and services that improve teamwork, clarity, and employee engagement. Lencioni's passion for organizations and teams is reflected in his writing, speaking, and consulting. His work has appeared in *The Wall Street Journal, BusinessWeek, Inc.* magazine, *USA Today,* and the *Harvard Business Review.* Lencioni consults and speaks to thousands of leaders each year in world-class organizations and at national conferences.

Chapter 4

Strategic Planning: A Leadership Imperative

Leonard D. Goodstein

In This Chapter

- Why strategic planning is an imperative leadership competence.

- A facilitated approach to strategic planning.

- The leadership competencies required for strategic planning.

Long ago, Peter Drucker (1974) insisted that the two most important tasks leaders needed to perform were to establish a strategic plan and to select managers to execute that plan. (I would amend Drucker's prescription to include a third requirement: that leaders need to accept personal responsibility for implementing the plan, for leading the charge to the organization's desired future.)

I regard strategic planning as the most important function of any leader. The strategic planning process should involve establishing an organization's goals and the pathways to reaching them, identifying the potential obstacles that may be encountered en route to these goals and how they can be avoided or minimized, and setting the milestones to measure

---

This chapter is adapted from *Applied Strategic Planning: An Introduction,* 2nd edition, by Timothy M. Nolan, Leonard D. Goodstein, and Jeanette Goodstein. Copyright © 2008 by John Wiley & Sons. Used with permission.

progress along the way. I believe that it should be difficult, if not impossible, for any leader to argue that these are not the highest-priority tasks on the leadership agenda.

Strategic planning involves more than drafting some airy mission statement and posting it on the wall of every cubicle. A strategic plan should be a clear statement of the organization's desired future and the path to reach this future. The planning process should result in a living document that guides the organization's decision making for both the present and the near-term future. An organization's functional strategic plan should help both its managers and rank-and-file members make choices that advance it toward its desired future state. The future is never attainable, however, but always remains in the distance. This elusiveness of the future means that strategic planning must be an ongoing process, done on a regular basis, typically annually. Such annual planning requires the organization and its leaders to take stock of how much progress has been made in reaching last year's milestones, celebrate the successes, account for any failures, and readjust the goals for the coming year.

When strategic planning is woven into an organization's cultural fabric, it becomes the basis for day-to-day decision making, even though planning sessions occur only annually. Between these sessions, the organization's leaders use the plan to assess progress and to evaluate both their methods and the outcomes they produce or fail to produce. The plan also focuses the leaders' activities and prods them to remind rank-and-file employees of their importance, in both group and one-to-one encounters.

The Importance of Strategic Planning

The metaphor of the racing shell that is propelled by a team of rowers illustrates the importance of strategic planning. Despite the rowers' best efforts to move the shell, the crew's success depends on the coxswain to steer the boat to the finish line and to coordinate their efforts. Without the leadership of the coxswain, greater effort by the crew could simply result in the shell going round and round, but ever faster. The steering and coordinating of team efforts is the task of the organizational leader, a process that is best done through strategic planning. Without such leadership exercised through the strategic planning process, the organization most likely will be directionless.

Although considerable value lies in having a well-developed strategic plan, the process of strategic planning is more important than its product. As Dwight D. Eisenhower, commander in chief of the Supreme Headquarters Allied Expeditionary Force in World War II and later president of the United States, observed, "In preparing for battle, I have always found the plans are useless, but the planning is indispensable." The planning process enables us to clarify our objectives, to determine where we now stand with respect to those objectives, to assess our present resources and how they need to be augmented to accomplish our objectives, and to prepare for the unexpected. The planning process causes the leadership and the organization as a whole to temporarily put aside their usual preoccupation with solving immediate operational problems and to think strategically about the future and the organization's role and function in that future.

The long-term focus of the organization's leaders that emerges from the strategic planning process is a far more important outcome than the plan itself. As Louis Pasteur, the great French chemist and bacteriologist, observed, "Chance favors only the prepared mind." Strategic planning is the best way that we know to prepare the minds of leaders—to move leadership to think and behave strategically.

Values Clarification and Strategic Planning

A proper strategic planning process should involve clarifying the values on which the organization is based; these values most often reflect the values held by the organization's leaders. All important organizational decisions are values based, and a well-functioning organization has a set of clearly articulated values that is widely shared throughout the organization and forms the basis for most of its decisions. Though many businesses pretend that the only value that matters is represented by the financial bottom line, a brief discussion invariably amends that view. For example, if there are profits, the question arises of how they are to be used. Are the profits to be used for executive bonuses, to increase shareholder dividends, to support expansion or acquisitions, to pay down debt, for research and development, or what? And are there limits to the businesses practices that will lead to profitability? Clearly, the answers to these questions are based on deep-seated values, and they typically should be clarified and articulated through the strategic planning process.

I am not suggesting that strategic planning is a process of eliminating or even reducing risk. Risk is an inevitable element of organizational functioning. But the values clarification piece of strategic planning is useful in identifying the *right* risks that leaders should take and in assessing risks rationally rather than emotionally. Risks that advance the organization to its desired future state and are congruent with its espoused values are legitimate; those that do not meet those twin criteria are not.

In most strategic planning processes, the values clarification stage is one of the most conflictual elements. The exploration of the values that underlie an organization's decision making often reveal that its leadership has not behaved in laudatory ways, creating a gap between its espoused values and actual behavior. Though painful, this process of values clarification can go a long way toward producing a set of values that the organization's leaders can endorse and live with—connecting the video with the audio.

The Process of Strategic Planning

I strongly support a strategic planning process that directly involves an organization's leadership. In my experience, the alternative of engaging a consulting group to do the planning is distinctly less useful. My reasons for this strong preference are twofold: One, we own things that we create, including strategic planning; and two, all too often the strategic plans developed by consultants are simply filed away and not implemented.

The approach I advocate is contained in the definition of *applied strategic planning* developed by my colleagues and me (Goodstein, Nolan, and Pfeiffer 1992; Nolan, Goodstein, and Goodstein 2008b). Applied strategic planning is *the process by which the guiding members of an organization envision its future and develop the necessary procedures and operations to achieve that future.* This is an internal organizational process driven by an organization's leadership and facilitated by an experienced and skilled external consultant or facilitator. This process should be judged by the degree to which the resulting plan is successfully implemented—hence the use of the word *applied* in the term.

But before we briefly review the steps in the process of applied strategic planning, we must answer the question of how an organization can proceed if, for whatever reason(s), it is unwilling or unable to implement this applied strategic planning approach to planning. Does this conclusion mean that an organization must forgo strategic planning altogether? No! It is possible to engage a consulting team to gather the necessary data, analyze it, and present the plan that the consultants have developed. Following this course of action, however, requires recognizing that even this approach involves considerable time and effort by the organization, especially by its leadership, if the process and its outcomes are to have any relevance to the organization.

Experience with the latter approach to planning has led me to conclude that, without strong input and guidance from the leadership of the organization, the ownership of the plan resides with the consultants, which is highly unlikely to lead to its implementation—a massive waste of time and resources. In any event, as noted above, the critical test of any planning process is whether it culminates in its implementation, and the implementation of a plan cannot be delegated to outside parties. A plan created by an external consulting team requires a relatively seamless handoff to the leaders of the organization, each of whom needs to be committed to its successful implementation. Though implementation in such circumstances is not an impossibility, it has rarely happened in my experience. Creation, rather than delegation, is far more likely to lead to ownership.

The Applied Strategic Planning Model

How, then, does the leadership of an organization go about the process of applied strategic planning? This process, spelled out in great detail elsewhere (Goodstein, Nolan, and Pfeiffer 1992; Nolan, Goodstein, and Goodstein 2008a, 2008b), involves nine sequential steps and two continuous ones. The applied strategic planning model is depicted in figure 4-1. The two continuous elements—environmental monitoring (inputs) and application considerations (outputs)—are shown on the sides of the figure, and the nine sequential steps are shown in its center, in order from top to bottom. The following description of the model is intended to provide only the briefest overview and, it is hoped, to whet the reader's appetite to learn more from the original sources.

Environmental Monitoring and Application Considerations

These two continuous steps—the monitoring of the environment and promptly responding to whatever new information such monitoring reveals—is a competence rarely exhibited by the leadership of most organizations. Our planning process forces an in-depth review and analysis of how well the leadership of any organization goes about scanning the several environments in which it operates and how its information access can be improved. The process requires that any gaps in environmental monitoring be addressed immediately and that a proper process be put in place for the organization's leadership to deal promptly and decisively with any threats or opportunities that such monitoring reveals—the application considerations.

Planning to Plan

The first of the continuous steps is planning to plan, where the organization's leadership determines the readiness of the organization to engage in strategic planning, who should be involved in the process, the time frames for the process, how nonparticipants in the process will be informed about its progress, and other details that need to be resolved. The leadership role here involves a high level of planning and organizing, along with a well-above-average level of communication skills.

Organizational Values and Culture

The importance of clarifying organizational values and culture for an organization's success prompted the introduction of this topic earlier in the chapter. It is critical that an organization's leaders confront the differences in values that exist, differences that have been submerged in the past but have led to miscommunications and poor decision making. This is where the leaders must surface and make public their values, the values that underlie the implicit code of conduct that drives—and should drive—the organization.

Figure 4-1. The Applied Strategic Planning Model

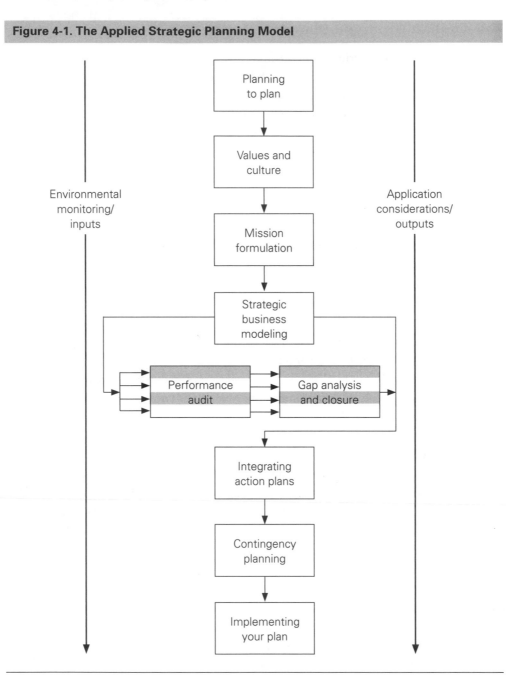

Source: Nolan, Goodstein, and Goodstein (2008b). Used with permission from John Wiley & Sons.

Such a clarification of differences is often the most contentious segment of the planning process and requires more than a bit of courage on the part of leadership to face and resolve the issues that surface.

Mission Formulation

Mission formulation involves identifying the desired future state of the organization—what leadership really wants to achieve in specific, measurable terms. Formulating the mission involves answering four basic but thought-provoking questions:

- What business are we now in, and what business do we want to be in for the future?
- Who are our current customers, and who should they be in the future?
- How do we go about meeting our customers' wants and needs?
- Why do we exist? What fundamental societal needs do we meet?

The answers to these questions should result in a brief mission statement that provides clarity about the organization's future direction, both internally and externally, and should identify the organization's distinctive competence. Here leadership needs to exercise a high degree of creativity, an ability to think outside of the box.

Strategic Business Modeling

The strategic business modeling process involves moving the organization from the abstractions involved earlier to developing specific, detailed plans that will move the organization along the path toward its desired future state. This stage defines the desired future in tangible, measurable terms. It specifies what businesses the organization will be in, what the critical success indicators will be in each of those businesses, and what needs to be done to create movement along the path toward the desired future, as well as establishing mileposts to track the movement forward. This stage of the planning process entails developing a detailed plan for how and when the organization will move toward the achievement of its desired future—how it will fulfill its mission. Managing this process requires both toughness and creativity on the part of leadership to squarely face the way forward.

Performance Audits

Conducting a performance audit involves squarely facing the current state of the organization and identifying how well it is performing and the implications of its current performance for implementing the strategic business model. Here is another test for the organization's leadership, because this stage requires an objective, realistic examination of the state of the organization, warts and all.

Gap Analysis and Closure

The gap analysis and closure segment involves a realistic evaluation of the gap between the present state of the organization and its desired future state and the development of a plan to bridge this gap. The gap between the resources currently available and those needed to move toward the desired future state can be resolved in two ways: by increasing resources, or by reducing the quality of the desired future state. Most frequently, some combination of these two tactics is necessary, but brutal honesty is required of the organization's leadership if closure of the gap between the present and future is to be achieved. Leadership requires the ability to recognize the difference between a stretch goal and mission impossible.

Integrating Action Plans

During the integration of action plans, the organization's leadership must work to develop both a plan and a process for monitoring the plan to knit together the various operational plans that are required to move the organization toward its desired future state. The typical elements of such an integration include plans for additional financial capital, human capital, equipment, and space. Such integration requires setting priorities, planning the timing, paying careful attention to detail, and resolving to do whatever is necessary to move the plan from the conceptual to the operational.

Contingency Planning

Whereas strategic planning identifies the ideal future state of the organization, alternatives typically also need to be identified, both of the desired end state and of the various paths to achieve that end state. The critical leadership requirements are creativity and flexibility—the ability to look into the future, to see alternatives, to assess risks, and to promptly take action when necessary.

Implementing Your Plan

The critical issue of applied strategic planning is implementation. The world's most innovative and creative plan is worthless without implementation. The central task of leadership is to implement the strategic plan—a point that I cannot stress sufficiently. The strategic plan should become the template that guides all important future organizational decisions. The task of leadership is to model how the plan is to be used, to hold the managers and other decision makers in the organization responsible for implementing their portions of the plan, and to serve as cheerleaders for its utilization.

Leadership Competencies for Strategic Planning

Although some of the critical leadership competencies required for leading a successful strategic planning process and its implementation have been mentioned in passing, these are sufficiently critical that I conclude this chapter with a review of these competencies and how they affect both the development and implementation of the strategic plan.

What is striking about most discussions of leadership competencies is their failure to include developing and implementing a strategic plan for the organization as a critical leadership competency. A cursory review of the literature on leadership competencies fails to reveal a single instance even of strategic thinking as a critical leadership competency, with of course the exception of Peter Drucker.

Two recent literature reviews of leadership competencies (Gibbons and others 2006; Tett and others 2000) have included strategic planning as a necessary leadership competency, but both these reviews have given strategic planning short shrift, simply identifying it as one of a number of leadership competencies. Tett and others (2000, 247) classify strategic planning as one of 13 traditional leadership competencies, defining it as developing "long-term plans to keep the organization aligned with future demands," while Rupp and others (2009, 104) never mention strategic planning per se, but include planning and organizing, including making "effective short- and long-term plans" one of the competencies for "approaches to work." Though it may be argued that these reports simply reflect the current status of strategic planning in the world of leadership practices, I expected greater attention to be paid to this critical competence.

Of all the components inherent in leading an organization in developing and implementing a strategic planning process, none is more important than the capacity for strategic thinking and creative thinking. Strategic thinking involves what is termed *downboard thinking* in chess—that is, understanding not only what moves you will make several turns in the future but also what moves your opponent is likely to make in the future and how you will counteract those moves. Without such downboard or strategic thinking, the organization is left with only a thrust-and-parry approach, which is scarcely likely to succeed in these hypercompetitive times. One important outcome of applied strategic planning is to foster, support, and reward strategic thinking, not only in the organization's senior leadership but also throughout the organization. Neither of these literature reviews even touches upon strategic thinking as a necessary leadership competence.

Creative thinking, a critically important complement to strategic thinking, involves thinking outside the box, that is, developing innovative solutions to organizational problems. Developing and implementing effective strategies almost always involves the continued use of the two thinking skills. Tett and others (2000, 248) include creative thinking as a leadership competence but define it as fostering "creative thinking within the organization," rather than as a personal competence of leaders. Gibbons and others (2006) do include *creativity* as an essential leadership competency but do not tie creativity to planning or any of the other competencies on their list.

The recent history of organizational failures throughout the global business world is replete with examples of how the lack of strategic and creative thinking were among the root causes of many of these failures. It is often noted that insanity can be defined as continuing to do the same thing repeatedly and expecting a different result. I suspect that until the leadership literature begins to focus on the criticality of strategy as a function of leaders, such failures will continue to haunt us.

A number of other competencies are also required for effective planning and execution, including an objective mindset—one in which the data rule and where a questioning of assumptions, an openness to hearing bad news, and a lack of defensiveness are paramount characteristics of the leader. There also needs to be a lack of sentimentality, that is, an ability to suppress emotionality and to rely on data rather than emotions. This implies a certain degree of toughness, a willingness to hear and integrate bad news and then to move ahead. François-Henri Pinault—the CEO of PPR, the French luxury retailer that includes Gucci, Chateau Latour, Puma, and many other such firms—makes the point that sentimentality about a line of business owned by the company can lead to failure: "It is a big danger to get too attached to a firm's activities." His strategy is to develop a business, set a strategy, put the people in place to execute the strategy, and then to grow it over 10 to 15 years. "We don't define the exit. It's not based on ratios but on the degree of maturity of the business" (quoted by Gumbel 2009, 80).

This often means making hard decisions. Yet this is not to suggest that compassion and caring about others are not important leadership competencies; rather, these need to be put on hold during the strategic planning process.

In some ways, strategic planning is an extension of the role of leader, but at a higher level of complexity. As I noted above, the strategic planning process involves more than a little planning and organizing, skillful communicating, and assessing risks, both present and future.

However, as I also stated, the most critical competencies required for a successful strategic planning process and its implementation are the leaders' thinking skills—both strategic and creative. Without these, none of the other competencies will be sufficient. Strategy is about moving an organization from where it is now toward an unclear future. As Alan R. Mulally (2009), the CEO of Ford Motor Company, recently stated, his job is "to help connect a talented group of people to a bigger goal, a bigger program and help them move forward to even bigger contributions."

References

Drucker, P. 1974. *Management: Tasks, Responsibilities, Practices.* New York: Harper & Row.

Gibbons, A. M., D. E. Rupp, L. A. Snyder, A. S. Holub, and S. E. Woo. 2006. A Preliminary Investigation of Developable Dimensions. *Psychologist-Manager Journal* 9, no. 2: 99–122.

Goodstein, L. D., T. M. Nolan, and J. W. Pfeiffer. 1992. *Applied Strategic Planning: How to Develop Plans that Really Work.* New York: McGraw-Hill.

Gumbel, P. 2009. The New King of Luxury. *Fortune,* September 14, 76–92.

Mulally, A. R. 2009. Corner Office: Planes, Cars and Cathedrals. *New York Times,* September 6.

Nolan, T. M., L. D. Goodstein, and J. Goodstein. 2008a. *Applied Strategic Planning: Consultant's Toolkit,* 2nd ed. San Francisco: Pfeiffer/Wiley.

———. 2008b. *Applied Strategic Planning: An Introduction,* 2nd ed. San Francisco: Pfeiffer/Wiley.

Tett, R. P., H. A. Guterman, A. Bleier, and P. J. Murphy. 2000. Development and Content Validation of a "Hyperdimensional" Taxonomy of Managerial Competence. *Human Performance* 13: 205–251.

About the Author

Leonard D. Goodstein, PhD, is a consulting psychologist based in Washington who specializes in strategic planning, executive assessment, selection, development, and coaching. He is one of the coauthors of *Applied Strategic Planning: A Consultant's Toolkit,* 2nd edition, with Timothy M. Nolan and Jeanette Goodstein (2008). His other books include *Using Individual Assessment in the Workplace: A Practical Guide* (2006) and *A Practical Guide to Job Analysis* (2009), both with Eric P. Prien. He is a frequent speaker to professional and lay audiences and contributor to the professional literature.

Five Critical Communication Skills for Leaders of the Future

Dianna Booher

··· **In This Chapter** ·······························

▓ How communication via social networking media can be useful for decision making.

▓ The importance of listening to a diverse constituency.

▓ How to focus on and shape simple, crystal-clear messages.

▓ Characteristics of persuasive communication.

Communication is the soul of leadership: analysis and solid decisions translated into clear messages that influence people to act and feel good about their performance" (Booher 1994). This is truer today than it was 15 years ago when I first published this statement. And it will be truer 15 years from now than it is today. Why? Governments cannot lead. Technology cannot lead. Strategy cannot lead. Only people put all these things in motion through their communication. Leaders drive action with their lives and their lips: clear, focused, persuasive, relevant, and memorable messages.

Tracking Communication Technology

Emphasizing the importance of the human dimension of communication does not mean that technology will grow less important. On the contrary. Not many years ago—before

---

© 2010 Dianna Booher. Used with permission.

Blackberrys, Palm Treos, and iPhones—a CEO friend of mine said smugly, "I don't do email. My assistant handles all that." Today, some executives exhibit the same attitude about social networking media: "I don't Tweet. Our marketing people do that." But leaders of the future really must understand the new communication technology and how useful it can be for their decision making, not just sit and watch the tweets go by.

For example, take Twitter. Let's say an organization wants to find out what consumers think about its new product, service, or policy. A search function on Twitter lets users track tweets mentioning their products or services, then analyze them to spot trends and changes in consumer opinions. This information can help executives make more accurate decisions about whether to increase inventories, put particular items on sale to dump product, abandon an unpopular policy, or even raise pricing on a service that customers currently consider a bargain.

Huaxia Rui, Andrew Whinston, and Elizabeth Winkler (2009), all at the Center for Research in Electronic Commerce at the University of Texas at Austin, have built a model to conduct such research using Twitter. To test their model, they conducted a study to predict box office receipts on given dates for three movies that premiered on the same day. Because Twitter returns only the most recent 1,500 tweets for each keyword-search query, they knew they could miss a sudden surge. To prevent that from happening, they gathered the data on 20 servers running at different times of the day to collect the tweets and then deposit them in one central database.

With the advanced-search function, they analyzed tweets for positive or negative comments (emoticons to represent sad or smiley faces and other positive, negative, or neutral words). The results? Two days before the movies opened, they gathered data. The tweet chatter was low about two of the movies, corresponding to ticket sales on opening day of $1.28 million and $7.13 million, respectively. For the third movie, the tweet chatter was 10 times as heavy as for the other two, and the box office receipts more than doubled, totaling $16.7 million.

The research held true for staying power. For the first two movies, sales peaked on the opening weekend and sharply declined at a rate of 50 percent each week after their release. For one of these first two movies, an analysis of the tweets showed that the comments were mostly neutral. And overall sales proved to be mediocre. The second movie performed slightly better; most tweets after its release also proved to be neutral, but there were decidedly more positive and negative tweets than with the first movie.

But the third movie again had more staying power. Word-of-mouth tweet buzz kept moviegoers interested for a longer time than with the other two movies opening on the same day.

So what does all this have to do with leaders who don't go to the movies? It's about the medium: You need to understand the capabilities of the communication media at your disposal so you can make them work for you. Here's a quick, three-step strategy until you have time to develop your own:

- Listen to customers on social networking media websites.
- Spot the shifts.
- Tee off the trends.

Let's look briefly at each step.

Listen to Customers on Social Networking Media Websites

Users post frequently on social networking media websites like Twitter, Facebook, LinkedIn, and blogs. They express their likes and dislikes about products, services, and policies and what they want to see as improvements for next-generation products. They offer their complaints about the competition—your inroad to new opportunities!—and their concerns about the industry.

Spot the Shifts

As a leader, your goal in tuning in to the social networking media chatter is not necessarily to change all negative opinions but to watch for trends, hot buttons, and shifts in opinion. If you've changed what you thought was an unpopular policy and customers are still complaining, consider that issue a red-herring concern—not the real problem. If you're working on improving customer service and you notice fewer and fewer negative comments, then that chatter confirms your success. If you launch a new service and notice a flood of negative posts, then you know you need to fix a problem quickly before it wreaks havoc with your stock prices or sends your customers to the competition.

Tee Off the Trends

On its home page, Twitter has a "trending topics" feature to show the 10 most discussed issues. Granted, these could be the latest pop star's paternity suit or a new peanut allergy. But the list is worth monitoring for topics that may be relevant to your industry or organization. Whether there's an opportunity or a crisis, you as a leader can react immediately.

Those who understand today's communication technology earn the right to lead others in analysis and decision making for the future.

Listening to All Constituencies, Not Just the Louder Voice

In the next 20 years, you can expect the organization you lead to grow more, not less, diverse. And the higher you climb in your organization, the harder it will be for you to hear the truth. The reasons for this situation will be understandable:

- Leaders typically think they've already heard it all.
- They *have* already heard much of it.
- Some of what they've heard has changed—but nobody thought to tell them and they didn't think to ask.
- People fear reprisal for giving bad news.
- People fear giving negative information that may imply the leader shares responsibility for a bad situation.
- People withhold bad news about their own mistakes, bad judgment, and poor performance until they have time to "correct the situation" before reporting.
- Listening takes time, and leaders are busy people.

Whatever the reasons, the result can be deadly. The challenge of the future will be to continue to listen to all constituencies for their information, insights, and contributions—the engaged worker, the disengaged worker, all four generations in the workforce, and the global community. The second, closely related challenge will be to listen to what they're *not* saying as well as what they're saying.

Not listening before acting can be as disastrous as pulling out into traffic on a major freeway without checking the rearview mirror. Not only is listening important to leaders as decision makers, but it's also important for personal credibility. Voltaire said, "The shortest route to a person's heart is the ear." Leaders earn followers one by one, as they earn trust and gain buy-in.

Ask citizens why they plan to vote for a particular political candidate, and overwhelmingly they'll say, "I feel that he is listening to the American people" or "I believe that she reflects my values and opinions." Nothing gets someone's attention like listening to them.

As technology tends to isolate people from personal contact with each other, the leader who can still connect warmly one on one has an edge. The best leaders listen as though they care.

Acknowledge that you hear what others communicate to you—both verbally and nonverbally. Rather than interrupting or telling your own story, communicate concern through your words and body language: good eye contact, appropriate facial expression, focused posture. Listening also involves acknowledging what someone says:

- "I certainly understand where you're coming from on that issue."
- "That's a big step you're taking."
- "That's a risky move—you must have second thoughts at times."
- "You must have felt proud of that accomplishment."

And it involves probing, clarifying, or confirming with care:

- "So tell me your next step."
- "When do you think that you'll . . . ?"
- "What do you think caused her to do X?"
- "Why do you think he set that policy?"
- "So you feel that you really made the best decision under the circumstances?"
- "So what would you like to see happen in the next few years here?"
- "In what ways do you think a mentor would help prepare you for promotion?"
- "What kind of outcomes do you think would be in your best interest in a situation like that?"

However, these are *not* empathic comments—no matter how many times you've heard them around the water cooler:

- "It could be worse. We could be announcing a layoff."
- "Looks like you'll just have to tough it out."
- "You think you've got it bad—you should hear what we went through last year in my area."
- "This may be a blessing in disguise."

Listening means focusing on others with sincere, compassionate interest—not just politely waiting your turn to talk.

Focusing On and Shaping a Single, Simple Message

Every year more noise—more information, more advertising, more videos, more statistics, more opinions, more surveys, more blogs, more ezines—pollutes the airwaves and competes for the attention of your employees, your customers, and your strategic partners. And the more noise, the more likely people will be to tune out. Thus, your challenge for the future: Cut the clutter clamoring for their attention and keep them tuned in.

My most frequently retweeted message ever posted is this: "If you can't write your message in a sentence, you can't say it in an hour." Unfortunately, this must resonate with many meeting attendees sitting in conference rooms, befuddled and bemused by ramblers.

Executives often call our office to give a quick briefing about a senior manager they're sending for coaching: "He's very technically competent—in fact, brilliant. But when speaking to clients or presenting information in a board meeting, he gets far too detailed. And with questions, he can easily get sidetracked. He just has so much information, and it's difficult for him to stay focused on the key points that we need to drive home to the audience." So I listen to the executive vice president's briefing as if it's the first time I've heard such a comment.

Then the senior manager arrives for coaching. He delivers the presentation to me, and I discover his boss's assessment to be true. So we start to work to reshape the message.

"What is it that you really want to say to these people?" I ask.

The manager begins to stumble, sputter, and stutter. Looking guilty, he flips through the slides. "Way too many, huh?"

I nod.

"My XYZ supervisor sent these six slides to me from his deck. And my team lead pulled these three slides from her presentation last week. Then John added these four slides from the presentation he gave in his standard briefing." He begins to see the problem. "So I guess I have too much information here, right?"

I nod. "So what's your real purpose and point? Today. For this audience? What's their interest in all the information you just told me? What do you want them to know, believe, buy, consider, approve, buy into, do about all this?"

He finally gives me an awkward sentence or two. We reshape it to make it a simple, single, complete message. He nods.

It's at about this point that a big grin spreads across his face, and I hear some version of this comment: "You know, I demand this from my own people all the time. When they burst into my office and ramble all over the place, I cut them off. I demand that they cut to the chase. But for some reason, I don't seem to be able to do it myself."

Hmmm.

In any communication—whether a speech, email, report, meeting, cafeteria poster, or trade show hospitality suite—identify your purpose: to inform, persuade, inspire, coach, commend, warn, entertain, introduce, address concerns, or answer questions.

The ability to cut through the extraneous details to the core message, problem, solution, situation, or issue is a critical leadership skill. Say it in a sentence so it's crystal clear to all. Focus and prioritize. Make that summary your road map for the remainder of your message.

Make Your Facts Tell a Story

Have you ever researched a "fact" on the Internet and then found contradictory data? The fact is that "facts" can be false, wrong, misleading, or misinterpreted—purposefully or accidentally. According to Mark Twain, writing in his autobiography, "There are three kinds of lies: lies, damned lies, and statistics." Even if a statement or "fact" happens to be correct, it doesn't always double as a reason. Facts are just facts, until you interpret them as reasons "for" or "against" something. Track facts, keep score, call a winner.

The only thing worse than stacking your speech, slides, emails, or reports with fact after fact after fact is not shaping them to tell your story. What story do your facts tell? What trail do the facts leave?

Tell how your division exploded with the introduction of the new widget, and your head count climbed from three to 68 engineers in the first two years in business. Then tell how you grew lax in your quality control. Tell about your reject rates. Show how the customer satisfaction numbers plummeted. Show how orders started dropping off as fast as they were logged onto the computer screen. Then circle back to the layoff of 58 engineers three years later. Then out of the ashes came. . . . Well, you get the picture. . . . Drama. Dialogue. Climax. Denouement.

Set the scene at the trade show. How many competitors were there? How many attendees? Of those, how many did your booth attract? Why? What was the attraction—or nonattraction? What did the competitor do to drive customers your way? What kind of lead follow-up or closing ratio do you have to do after the trade show to make your competitors eat dust?

Music, lights, camera, action. Facts alone will never feed the mind—at least for long.

Take a Point of View

Having been hired to help an investment company develop and shape its message, I listened to four executive vice presidents as they presented their segments of the "official" company overview. The general counsel presented his overview of real estate investing and the new laws and regulations related to them. When he finished, I asked him, "Do you think real estate is a good investment for high-net-worth individuals today?"

"Absolutely," he said. "The best. For several reasons." And he listed them for me.

"Why didn't you include those reasons in your presentation?" I asked.

"I did."

"I missed them."

> *"Numbers are the language of business. Unfortunately, it is a boring language when spoken by most leaders."*
>
> —Boyd Clarke and Ron Crossland, *The Leader's Voice*

"Maybe they didn't come across as reasons. But the facts were there. The investor could have drawn that conclusion."

"But why would you leave it to the listener to draw that conclusion?"

"Well, I'm a lawyer. I didn't want to come across as a used car salesman."

For the next hour, we discussed the difference between hype and a persuasive presentation. After all, his organization spent several million dollars annually flying in estate planners, financial advisers, brokers, and potential clients to persuade them to invest in real estate. Why would he not want to lead them to a conclusion?

Be clear about your purpose. If you're asked just to dump information, do it. But far more often than not, you're expected to take a point of view about the information you provide. That point of view involves what I call the four Ss of persuasion to make sure your listeners arrive at the same destination: solid facts, sound logic, straightforward language, and strong structure.

Make Your Bottom Line Your Opening Line

If you're telling a joke, directing a screenplay, or writing a TV sitcom, your audience will give you a few minutes to interest them before they walk away, walk out, or flip the channel. Business colleagues aren't always that patient.

Audiences for your email, your briefing, or your proposal want your bottom line up front, for several reasons:

- It's difficult to understand the details if you don't have a summary of the big-picture message first.
- Attention wanes quickly. You'll need to grab listeners fast before they exit, sleep, or text-message their spouse.
- People expect applicable messages. With more than 500 TV channels to select from; thousands of newspapers, magazines, and ezines; hundreds of headlines; and blogs and tweets popping online faster than popcorn, people expect choices.

Whether the news is good or bad, competent communicators understand the value of getting to the point. Get attention by summarizing and shaping your message succinctly. Then follow up with the details that shape your story.

Be Direct with Bad News

And what if you're message is negative? Decide to be direct. Whatever the difficult conversation, announcement, issue, or situation—defensiveness, emotional immaturity, poor performance, fear of losing star performers, fear of admitting personal mistakes, disgruntled customers—honest communication can lead to change.

Kind people sometimes confuse circuitous communication with courtesy. But direct language doesn't necessarily mean being blunt, brash, or harsh. You can be clear but still courteous and respectful. Direct communication embraces rather than evades the truth, involves clear words, and focuses on the facts. Consider these principles for communicating reality in a reassuring way:

- *Break the silence:* Start talking. Just because you're not talking about the situation doesn't mean others aren't talking about it. It just means that you, your information, your viewpoint, and your positive influence are not part of the conversation.
- *Acknowledge mistakes*—your own or those of your organization—and how those have contributed to the bad situation.
- *Stop the sugarcoating:* This doesn't mean you must agree with the doom and gloom around you. It just means that others will reject glib comments. Instead, say it like it is and invite others to do the same. Invite them to express fears openly and honestly in front of the group. Otherwise, others will be doing it in the parking lot, in the cafeteria, and on Twitter.
- *State the reality of the unknown future*—that things may or may not work out for the better. Nobody knows what the future holds, and you will lose credibility if you pretend that you do. Acknowledging chances that things can go either way sends the message that you know you're talking with reasoning adults, not children.
- *Outline positive choices for dealing with the future:* State your faith in your colleagues or staff as competent and committed people. Acknowledge the fear, the risk, and the difficulty—and then the rewards of overcoming the situation with the positive choices they can make to improve it.

What's the good news in delivering bad news? It's that straight talk in tough times can build bridges in ways that motivational hype in good times never can. Communicating clear, direct messages creates a climate of trust. And this trust pays big dividends in a competitive environment.

Remember: Your most important job as a leader is to help others cut the clutter clamoring for attention and communicate the crystal-clear, priority message of the moment.

Articulating a Vision Understandable to a Less-Educated Workforce

A few weeks ago, coupons landed in my mailbox for "$10 off a purchase of $30 or more" at a national department store chain. Because I was going to that store anyway, I took the coupons along. At the checkout counter, I presented the coupons with my seven items. I said to the cashier, "This adds up to more than $60, so would you use both coupons please."

"Oh, sure, no problem," she said. "But we have to ring it up on two separate tickets of at least $30 each."

My turn to say, "No problem." I waited.

She pulled three items into one pile and the other four into another pile, and then she rang the first group up. "This won't work. This group comes to a total of only $29.28 without the tax. You can't use the coupon."

"Okay," I said. "Then switch one of the items, so that both groups add up to $30."

"Oh," she said. "I didn't think of that."

She started over on the ticket. On the second go-round, she started with the second pile and then said, "Oh, this doesn't work either; this pile is less now. "This adds up to only $28.92."

"Okay, then." I tried to be helpful. "You switched the wrong item. You have a bath towel that cost the same in each group. Leave it. You have a washcloth that cost the same in each group. Leave it. That means a $12 item and a $4 item and an $8 are dissimilar. Switch those to different piles so that the more expensive item is in one pile and the two cheaper items are in the other pile. The seventh item can go in either pile."

"Oh," she said, "I get it now."

She didn't get it. I reached across the counter and stacked up the piles for her. She finally managed to check me out on the fourth try.

This is not an isolated incident. Today's workforce is less educated than ever before, and the situation is likely to grow worse in the near future. You walk into fast food places where pictures have replaced numbers on the cash registers. The correct change is made automatically. Operating instructions for equipment are written in the simplest form. The average newspaper in the United States is written at the fifth-grade reading level.

Consider what this means for you as a leader, communicating with a diverse group of employees at all educational levels. Take this situation to heart as you speak with your employees, your customers, and the media. Remember the same issues when you blast out emails of policy, commendation, or change.

And it's not just the lower-ranking employees you address who'll want, need, and demand more clarity.

Translate concepts like "vision," "strategy," and "initiatives" into specifics. If you're writing to or speaking with an audience larger than one and using these vague terms, people are going to have different tasks in mind for their next week's to-do list. "Vision" in Asian corporations often refers to plans to be executed 20 to 50 years into the future, whereas vision in American companies may refer to next quarter.

Political candidates receive as much criticism for vagueness on implementing their campaign promises as they do for their positions on controversial issues. People demand the particulars. Give them what they need to get the job done for you.

Here's a reminder from Friedrich Nietzsche on this subject: "They who know that they are profound strive for clarity; those who are not strive for obscurity."

Make Your Message Memorable

Consider the slogans from some of the most memorable advertising and political campaigns in recent history:

- "Where's the beef?"
- "It's the real thing."
- "We'll leave the light on for you."
- "Are we there yet?"
- "Just do it!"
- "Real men don't . . . X."
- "Show me the money!"
- "Smile. Be happy."
- "I love New York."
- "Don't mess with Texas."
- "What happens here—stays here."
- "Man Law."

How important are structure and word choice for these slogans? What if we changed these slogans slightly? Consider these changes:

- From "Where's the beef?" to "Where's the hamburger patty?"
- From "It's the real thing!" to "It's the old product we love."
- From "We'll leave the light on for you" to "Our hotels and hospitality make you feel like you're at home."
- From "Are we there yet?" to "I'm tired of traveling—have we arrived?"
- From "Just do it!" to "Act now—stop delaying."
- From "Real men don't . . . X" to "Prove you're a man by . . ."
- From "Show me the money!" to "I don't do anything until I get paid."
- From "Smile. Be happy" to "Life is easy. Relax."

- From "I love New York" to "New York is a great place to live."
- From "Don't mess with Texas" to "Don't litter across Texas."
- From "What happens here—stays here" to "You'll have a great time in Las Vegas."
- From "Man Law" to "This is an axiom generally accepted by men in all situations."

Take the time to make your point memorable.

Create Impact with Stories

Captain Charlie Plumb—a jet fighter pilot who was shot down, parachuted into enemy hands, and was held as a prisoner for nearly six years during the Vietnam War—tells a fascinating story. Several years after he was released from the prisoner of war camp, he accidentally ran into the man who had packed his parachute! His story makes the point that none of us ever knows the impact we are having on the lives of others. And the point is so powerful that audiences remember it for years—even recapping it to their friends on the Internet and calling him years later to tell their own tales.

Whatever your message, stories will make it stronger—communicating courage, determination, commitment, persistence, customer service, vision, caution, and change. Consider all the stories that have created the rich cultures and legendary CEOs. There's the story about the employee who made a costly mistake at IBM that cost the company $10,000, and walked into CEO Tom Watson's office to offer his resignation. Watson's famous line: "Why would I want your resignation? I just paid $10,000 for your education."

Then there's the Disney story of Walt himself walking the theme park, picking up trash. There's the story of Sam Walton driving to work every day with his lunch in a brown bag. There's the story of the Marriott bell captain giving his hotel guest his own shoes to wear for his early morning job interview.

As a teenager, in my first job at the Six Flags Over Texas theme parks, I heard stories about hosts and hostesses being sent home from work if they got a drip of chocolate ice cream on their white tennis shoes. You can be sure we didn't show up with dirty shoes or disheveled hair if we wanted to be issued a uniform for the day and keep our summer jobs.

Such culture-creating stories still surface during my consulting projects. Perry, a financial adviser and now regional manager of a large brokerage house, encourages his trainees to use more stories in their sales presentations with clients by telling his own story of an earlier lost account. He was competing with another brokerage house for the 401(k) funds at a large hospital system in the Northeast. The hospital invited both him and a competitor to make presentations to the group of employees, after which the employees could choose where to invest their 401(k) funds.

Perry walked in with all the facts on his side—better yields, better customer service ratings, wider fund choices, more flexibility in the plans. His competitor walked in with a better presentation. She focused on a few stories of how her company got involved in the lives of its clients, helping them to achieve their personal goals, particularly in times of crisis.

She walked away with 92 percent of the employee accounts; Perry, with 8 percent. He attributed the loss solely to his competitor's use of stories to make her points memorable.

A few years ago, I heard Colin Powell address an audience in Chicago, where he captivated the crowd—not with platitudes, statistics, and studies about leadership but with stories of leadership and what makes America great. He ended with a story about a Chicago restaurant owner and a group of foreign exchange students who couldn't pay their dinner bill for the evening. Powell's point was that the generosity of America would be demonstrated to the world individual by individual rather than through acts of government.

Drive your point home with a well-chosen story. On the other hand, never use a $100 story in a three-minute time slot to make a nickel point. Make sure the point deserves a story. If so, create, shape, and deliver it accordingly.

Use Analogies and Metaphors to Evoke Emotion and Deepen Understanding

Analogies lead to a conclusion based on a specific comparison. Jeff Bezos, CEO of Amazon, used this analogy in a report to shareholders:

> Long-term thinking is both a requirement and an outcome of true ownership. Owners are different from tenants. I know of a couple who rented out their house, and the family who moved in nailed their Christmas tree to the hardwood floors instead of using a tree stand. Expedient, I supposed, and admittedly these were particularly bad tenants, but no owner would be so shortsighted. Similarly, many investors are effectively short-term tenants, turning their portfolios so quickly they are really just renting the stocks that they temporarily "own" (quoted in Booher 2007).

We talk about "prime real estate" in referring to the home page of a website or placement above the fold in a newspaper or product catalog. Many human resources managers talk about "cafeteria" benefits with their employees. With just one word, this analogy implies that employees have a "menu" of benefits from which to select, that a "parent" has agreed to cover the "total" invoice up to a certain amount, and that employees can select according to "taste or preferences" from that menu.

Such comparisons as these don't exactly solicit an emotional response; they simply clarify a complex concept.

Metaphors, however, imply a comparison and typically evoke an emotion and a mindset. Both comparisons can be succinct yet powerful ways to manage how people think about an idea or situation.

If you wanted to make the point that someone was not fully engaged with his or her colleagues in a mission, you might use a war metaphor: "John ducks into his cubicle as if it were a foxhole. He needs to stick his head out occasionally and help the rest of us fight the war. Otherwise, the parent company is going to take over the entire department."

If you wanted to talk about how indifference to quality customer service could destroy your business, you might put it in these terms: "Our poor customer service has become a cancer eating away at our business. I see customers walk in here and wait 10 minutes before being greeted. Then once we do help them locate what they need in the store, they have to wait again at checkout. Then they wait again at the loading dock. The longer a customer stays in our store, it's like our cancer metastasizes rather than goes into remission."

If you were making a point to your colleagues about the importance of living a balanced life, you might use a sports metaphor: "Most of us would agree life has many dimensions or tracks, all important to our overall well-being: mental, physical, spiritual. But some of us are spending all our time on one track and ignoring the rest, thinking we're going to find satisfaction and fulfillment along the way. It's not going to happen. That's like entering a triathlon and practicing only the bicycling for the three months before the race."

Metaphors and analogies, by their very selection, create a powerful way of thinking about an issue and often evoke a strong accompanying emotion that makes ideas memorable.

Planning a Persuasive Case for Skeptical Employees, Customers, and Shareholders

Winston Churchill once remarked, "A lie gets halfway around the world before the truth has a chance to get its pants on." Today, people call it spin. And with current technology, I'd revise Churchill's quip this way: "Spin gets around the world before the speaker leaves the stage."

As we move further into the future, our audiences will have become even more skeptical, cynical, and thus expert at fact-checking, double-checking, and slicing and dicing as people speak. Their skepticism and cynicism will be the "new normal," considered a good attitude and high employee morale.

As a leader, get used to it. Prepare by understanding what it takes to meet this challenge.

Consider those people you know personally today. Do you always believe and trust what they say? Recall conversations with your financial adviser, for example, a person with whom you have an ongoing trust relationship. After all, you tell him or her your salary, net worth, lifelong goals and dreams, matters of wills and estates.

Imagine saying to your adviser, "I'm getting a sizable bonus at the end of the year. Where do you recommend that I invest it?"

Without batting an eye, your adviser responds, "Life settlements. Most people don't know much about them, but they're a great alternative to the stock market. Basically, you buy life insurance policies from elderly people who need the cash. This kind of investment helps you manage your risk and protects you from the volatility of the stock market. You can pretty much count on a return of about 15 to 18 percent—year in, year out, and often much, much better. They're based on actuary tables of life spans just like life insurance companies use—good hard statistical data. The only downside is that they're not very liquid unless you're in a pool with other investors."

Would you buy? The adviser's making a strong, logical case. Or, in a similar situation, would you be thinking, I wonder what her commission is on this product she's trying to sell me? What's lacking in such a conversation about the life settlements? What would increase your confidence in the adviser's recommendation on life settlements as a good investment? Knowing the adviser has your best interest above her best interest? What if you knew she got no commission at all on this investment?

Consider the credibility Bernie Madoff and Allen Stanford created with their multitudes of investors whom they persuaded to give them millions year after year. Bernie Madoff, the manager of a hedge fund, Ascot Partners, pulled off a $50 billion Ponzi scheme, the largest fraud in history. The Texas financier Allen Stanford, operating both within the United States and in the Caribbean, persuaded more than 30,000 investors to give him $7 billion before the Securities and Exchange Commission rang his doorbell.

Clearly, these two financial wizards mastered the secrets of influence. So obviously, these attributes and skills can be learned. But influence doesn't just boil down to skills, suits, status symbols, and stature. Mother Teresa was as welcome and comfortable in the world's boardrooms as Bernie Madoff. At just five feet tall, dressed in her traditional habit, with few earthly possessions to call her own, Mother Teresa had one secret that Bernie Madoff and Allen Stanford lacked. And unfortunately, this one—or its absence—takes awhile to surface: character.

For 45 years, armed with little but her integrity, her tongue, and her ability to make CEOs feel the plight of the poor, Mother Teresa persuaded them to finance orphanages, hospices, leper houses, hospitals, and soup kitchens. By the time of her death in 1997, 610 missions in 123 countries on six continents had felt her presence.

I'm convinced that Mother Teresa studied Aristotle because back in the fourth century, he identified these same three essentials of persuasion:

- logical argument (the ability to articulate your points clearly)
- emotion (the ability to create or control emotion in your listeners)
- demonstration of character (the ability to convey integrity and goodwill).

And that turned out to be a big deal.

In the Greek world of Aristotle's day, the ability to persuade with such arguments carried high social status. Winning a war of words paralleled the warrior's victory on the battlefield. Recall, from college assignments, the great debates between the main characters in the *Iliad* and the *Odyssey*, interspersed between the war scenes. The battle of wits became as fierce as the battle of brawn.

Times haven't changed all that much. Being a persuasive communicator still grants social status and power. Think how often pundits and voters alike extol a candidate's speaking ability—or lack thereof. Not only do we expect our presidents and celebrities to speak well; that has become the expected norm in the boardroom, the conference room, and the community. Persuasive communication is the key to leadership in politics and in the corporate world, both now and in the future.

To lead change, to sell an idea, to raise funds, to win a contract, to strike a partnership, to shore up investor confidence during a stalled economy, to improve employee morale—all such endeavors create the need to build a persuasive case for a skeptical audience. Your success as a leader demands it.

Last Thoughts

Communication makes the "top three" in many lists today—the most vital skill in job-interviewing success, the most frequent complaint employees cite as their reason for leaving an organization, the most frequent reason top talent joins a new team, the biggest challenge leaders experience in times of change and upheaval. Communication makes leadership possible.

Further Reading

Dianna Booher, *E-Writing: 21st Century Tools for Effective Communication.* New York: Simon & Schuster / Pocket Books, 2001.

———, *Speak with Confidence: Powerful Presentations to Inform, Inspire, and Persuade.* New York: McGraw-Hill, 2003.

———, *The Voice of Authority: 10 Communication Strategies Every Leader Needs to Know.* New York: McGraw-Hill, 2007.

Paul Chaney, *The Digital Handshake: Seven Proven Strategies to Grow Your Business Using Social Media.* New York: John A. Wiley & Sons, 2009.

Rober Cialdini, *The Psychology of Influence and Persuasion.* New York: HarperCollins, 2006.

Danny Cox, *Leadership When the Heat Is On: 24 Lessons in High-Performance Management.* New York: McGraw-Hill, 2007.

John C. Maxwell, *The 21 Irrefutable Laws of Leadership: Follow Them and People Will Follow You.* Nashville: Thomas Nelson, 2007.

Reference

Booher, D. 1994. *Communicate with Confidence: How to Say It Right the First Time and Every Time.* New York: McGraw-Hill.

———. 2007. *The Voice of Authority: 10 Communication Strategies Every Leader Needs to Know.* New York: McGraw-Hill.

Rui, Huaxia, Andrew Whinston, and Elizabeth Winkler. 2009. Follow the Tweets: By Monitoring Comments on Twitter, Companies Can Predict Where Next Week's Sales Are Heading. *Wall Street Journal,* November 30. http://online.wsj.com/article/SB10001424052970204731804574391102221959582.html#articleTabs%3Darticle.

About the Author

Dianna Booher works with organizations to increase their effectiveness through better communication—oral, written, interpersonal, and organizational. The CEO of Dallas–Fort Worth communication training firm Booher Consultants, she is also the author of 44 books, published in 23 countries and in 16 languages. Her most popular books include *Speak with Confidence, E-Writing, Communicate with Confidence, The Voice of Authority,* and *Booher's Rules of Business Grammar.* Several have been selected by major book clubs. She has been interviewed on critical workplace issues by Good Morning America, *The Wall Street Journal, Forbes, The New York Times, USA Today,* Bloomberg, and NPR, and *Successful Meetings* magazine named her to its list of "21 Top Speakers for the 21st Century."

Chapter 6

Influence Tactics
for Leaders

Gary Yukl

In This Chapter

- Types of influence tactics available for leaders.
- How to use the influence tactics with subordinates, peers, and bosses.
- How leaders can increase influence skills and effectiveness.

Interpersonal influence is an essential skill for leaders. To be effective, leaders need to influence many people in the organization, including those who report directly to them, peers, bosses, and those outside the organization, such as suppliers and clients. A leader must influence people to carry out requests, provide resources and assistance, support proposals, and implement decisions. Some of the necessary influence is provided by the formal authority and the power associated with a leadership position, and this authority can be exercised by making a simple request or command. However, formal authority and power are not sufficient to gain the cooperation and commitment needed for effective leadership. For some influence attempts, it is also necessary to use proactive tactics.

This chapter describes what has been learned about the effective use of influence tactics by leaders and ways to improve influence skills. The chapter begins with a brief

---

© 2010 Gary Yukl. Used with permission.

description of the different outcomes that can result from an influence attempt. Next, it describes the different types of influence tactics that have been identified in empirical research on managers. Then the conditions that determine tactic effectiveness are discussed, including how different tactics are combined and sequenced, the amount of authority and power possessed by the leader, and the type of interpersonal relationship that exists between a leader and the target persons to be influenced. The chapter's final section describes three ways for leaders to improve their influence skills and effectiveness, including how to plan for an influence attempt, how to increase learning from experience after using influence tactics, and how to use multisource feedback to improve self-awareness about influence behavior.

Influence Outcomes

The success of an influence attempt depends on the target person's response, and the outcome can take three different forms (Falbe and Yukl 1992):

- Commitment occurs when the person agrees internally with a request and makes a strong effort to carry it out effectively.
- Compliance occurs when the person is willing to carry out a request but is apathetic rather than enthusiastic and will make only a minimal effort. This outcome is likely if the person is not convinced that the requested action is necessary or is the best way to accomplish the objective but recognizes that the request is consistent with the leader's authority.
- Resistance occurs when the person is strongly opposed to a request. The person may refuse to carry out the request, try to persuade the leader to withdraw or change the request, delay acting in the hope that the leader will forget about the request, ask higher authorities to overrule the request, or pretend to comply but try to sabotage the task.

Commitment is the most successful outcome for a complex, difficult task that requires enthusiasm and initiative from the individual being influenced. Commitment has several advantages, including more effort, persistence initiative, and creativity by the person in carrying out a requested task. However, commitment is not always necessary. For a simple, routine task, compliance may be all that is necessary to accomplish the influence objective. Resistance is usually an unsuccessful outcome, but it can be beneficial if it helps the leader avoid making a serious mistake. For example, you have developed a detailed plan for a new project, but subordinates are reluctant to implement it until several serious flaws are corrected.

Influence Tactics

Several scholars have conducted research to identify specific types of proactive influence tactics that are commonly used by leaders (for example, Falbe and Yukl 1992; Kipnis, Schmidt, and Wilkinson 1980; Yukl, Lepsinger, and Lucia 1992). Building on the earlier research, I developed a more comprehensive taxonomy of 11 proactive influence tactics (Yukl, Seifert, and Chavez 2008). These 11 tactics are listed and defined in table 6-1. The four tactics most likely to elicit commitment are called core tactics and include rational persuasion, inspirational appeals, consultation, and collaboration. The remaining seven tactics are exchange, legitimating, personal appeals, pressure, and coalitions. These tactics are much less likely to elicit commitment, but they can be useful for eliciting compliance. Moreover, some of these other tactics can be combined with core tactics to increase the success of an influence attempt. In the following subsections, each of the 11 proactive tactics is described in more detail, and the situations where a tactic is most useful are briefly identified.

Rational Persuasion

The tactic of rational persuasion involves the use of explanations, logical arguments, and factual evidence to show that a request or proposal is feasible and relevant for attaining task objectives. Rational persuasion can take many forms, including

- explaining in detail why a request or proposal is important
- using facts and logic to make a clear case in support of a request or proposal
- explaining why a proposal is much better than the alternatives
- providing evidence from a pilot project or experiment that a proposed change or project is feasible.

Rational persuasion is most appropriate for influencing someone who shares the leader's task objectives but does not recognize that the leader's request or proposal is the best way to attain them. This tactic is unlikely to be effective if the leader and the target person have incompatible objectives, or if the person does not perceive the leader to be a credible and trustworthy source of information, evidence, and predictions about the future.

Apprising

The tactic of apprising involves an explanation of how a request or proposal is likely to benefit the individual. The benefits may involve the individual's career advancement, job satisfaction, compensation, or achievement of personal objectives. When used to influence an outsider, apprising may include information about the likely benefits for the person's organization. Apprising is most useful when a leader has information about potential benefits that are

Table 6-1. Proactive Influence Tactics

Rational persuasion: Use logical arguments and factual evidence to show that a request or proposal is feasible and relevant for attaining important task objectives.

Apprising: Explain how carrying out a request or supporting a proposal will benefit the person or help to advance his or her career.

Inspirational appeals: Appeal to the person's values and ideals or seek to arouse the person's emotions to gain commitment for a request or proposal.

Consultation: Ask the person to suggest improvements or help plan a proposed activity or change for which the person's support is desired.

Collaboration: Offer to provide assistance or necessary resources if the person will carry out a request or approve a proposed change.

Exchange: Offer something the person wants, or offer to reciprocate at a later time, if the person will do what you ask.

Ingratiation: Use praise and flattery before or during an attempt to influence the person to carry out a request or support a proposal.

Personal appeals: Ask the person to carry out a request or support a proposal as a personal favor based on friendship or the person's kindness.

Legitimating: Seek to establish the legitimacy of a request or to verify that you have the authority to make it.

Pressure: Use demands, threats, frequent checking, or persistent reminders to influence the person to do something.

Coalition building: Enlist the support of others to help you in influencing the person, or use an endorsement of your request or proposal by others in your influence attempt.

Source: © 2001 by Gary Yukl. Used with permission.

not already obvious to the person. Unlike with exchange tactics, the benefits described in this tactic are a by-product of carrying out the leader's request, not something the leader will directly provide. For example, when asking a subordinate to carry out a task that is different from previous responsibilities, the leader explains how it will help increase skills that the subordinate needs for promotion to a higher-level position.

Inspirational Appeals

The tactic of inspirational appeals involves an emotional or value-based entreaty, in contrast to the logical arguments used in rational persuasion. An inspirational appeal is an attempt to develop enthusiasm and commitment by arousing strong emotions and linking a request or proposal to a person's needs, values, hopes, and ideals. Some bases for appealing to most people include the desire to be important, to feel useful, to accomplish something worthwhile, to perform an exceptional feat, to be a member of the best team, or to participate in an exciting effort to make things better. To formulate an effective appeal, one must have insight into the values, hopes, and fears of the person or group to be influenced. This tactic is not very useful when the requested task or change does not involve ideals, values, or emotions. Its effectiveness also depends on communication skills, such as the leader's ability to use vivid imagery and metaphors and employ voice and gestures to generate enthusiasm and excitement.

Consultation

The tactic of consultation involves asking an individual (or the members of a team) to suggest ways to attain a task objective or implement a proposed change. Consultation can take a variety of forms. One example is to present a general objective and ask people to suggest specific action steps for implementing it. Another is to present a detailed proposal or plan and ask people if they have any doubts, concerns, or suggestions for improving it; after hearing these concerns, the leader can explain why they are unwarranted or modify the proposal to reflect the person's concerns. Active involvement in planning can result in commitment if people begin to take ownership of the strategy or plans they helped to develop. The successful use of consultation requires at least moderate agreement that the objective is worthwhile; otherwise, there will be no interest in developing an effective strategy or plan for attaining the objective.

Collaboration

The tactic of collaboration involves an offer to provide the necessary resources or assistance if the person will carry out a request or approve a proposal. Examples include offering to show how to complete the requested task, offering to provide the equipment or technical assistance needed to perform a requested task, and offering to help the person deal with a problem that would be caused by carrying out the request. This influence tactic is very useful when an individual or team initially believes that a proposed activity or change is too risky or difficult to justify their enthusiastic support. Like exchange, collaboration involves an offer to do something for the person; however, exchange usually involves an impersonal trade-off of unrelated benefits, whereas collaboration usually involves a joint effort to accomplish the same task or objective.

Exchange

The tactic of exchange involves the explicit or implicit offer to reward someone for carrying out a request. This tactic is especially appropriate when the person is indifferent or reluctant about complying with a request because it offers no important benefits and would involve considerable effort and inconvenience. An exchange makes compliance with a request more acceptable, because the person will receive something desirable such as tangible rewards, scarce resources needed for another task, or help in attaining another objective that is important to the person. Sometimes the promise involved in an exchange may be implicit rather than explicit, such as suggesting that in return for doing what is asked, you will owe the person an unspecified favor in the future. A limitation of this tactic is the cost of providing a reward to the person, which may be more than is feasible or justifiable.

Ingratiation

The tactic of ingratiation is an attempt to make the person feel better about the leader. Ingratiation can take many forms, such as giving compliments, doing unsolicited favors, acting deferential and respectful, and acting especially friendly. For example, when asking a subordinate to do a new task, the leader says that the subordinate is the most qualified person to do it. When ingratiation is perceived to be sincere, it tends to strengthen positive regard and make a person more willing to consider a request. However, if it is perceived as an attempt to manipulate the person, it can have negative effects. Ingratiation is more likely to be viewed as insincere when used just before making a request, especially if it is not directly relevant to the request. Therefore, ingratiation is less useful for an immediate influence attempt than as a part of longer-term strategy to improve relationships with people.

Personal Appeals

The tactic of personal appeals involves a request based on friendship or an appeal to the target person's kindness and generosity. Examples include asking for a personal favor as a friend, asking if the person will do a favor before saying what it is, and explaining that you are in a difficult situation and would really appreciate the person's help. This tactic is not feasible when the person dislikes you or is indifferent about what happens to you. The stronger the friendship or loyalty, the more you can ask the person to do. A personal appeal is most likely to be used for requesting assistance in dealing with a difficult problem, or for obtaining a personal favor unrelated to the work.

Legitimating

The tactic of legitimating involves an attempt to establish the authority or right to make a particular type of request. A legitimating tactic may be needed when a request is unusual, it clearly exceeds your authority, or the person does not know who you are or what authority you have. There are several types of legitimating tactics; examples include explaining that a request or proposal is consistent with organizational policies and rules, with legal statutes or precedents, with professional role expectations, or with the terms of a contract or prior agreement. Sometimes it is helpful to use a document to verify that a request is legitimate (for example, a work order, policy manual, contract, and a charter or bylaws for the organization).

Pressure

Pressure tactics include threats, warnings, and assertive behavior such as repeated demands or frequent checking to see whether the person has complied with a request. These tactics are sometimes successful in inducing compliance with a request, but they are unlikely to result in commitment and may have serious side effects. The harder forms of pressure (for example, threats, warnings, and demands) are likely to cause resentment and undermine working relationships. Sometimes hard pressure tactics are necessary to obtain compliance with a rule or policy that is important to the organization, such as safety rules and ethical practices. However, in most cases, the softer forms of pressure (for example, persistent requests and reminders that the target person promised to do something) are more likely to gain compliance without undermining the relationship.

Coalition Building

Coalition-building tactics involve getting other people to help influence someone. The coalition partners may be peers, subordinates, superiors, or outsiders. Coalition tactics can take many forms, including

- mentioning the names of others who endorse a proposal when asking the target person to support it
- getting others to explain to the target person why they support a proposed activity or change
- bringing someone along for support when meeting with the target person to make a request or proposal.

If you use an endorsement, it should be provided by someone the target person likes or respects. A coalition partner may use any of the other 10 tactics to influence the target person, and sometimes different tactics are used by different coalition partners. For example, in a version of the "good cop, bad cop" strategy, you use soft tactics such as consultation and collaboration, and the coalition partner uses a harder tactic such as pressure.

Determinants of Influence Outcomes

Some proactive influence tactics are generally more effective than others, but there is no guarantee that any tactic will result in the desired outcome. Any tactic can result in resistance if used in an unskillful way, in an inappropriate situation, or for an unethical objective. Even though some tactics are generally more useful than others, success is not guaranteed for any individual tactic or combination of tactics. The outcome of an influence attempt depends in part on what tactics are used, how they are combined and sequenced, and the skill of the influencer. The outcome also depends on other relevant aspects of the influence situation, including the type of authority and power relationship and the quality of the interpersonal relationship (that is, the depth of mutual trust and friendship). In the following subsections, each type of outcome determinant is briefly explained.

Combining Influence Tactics

An influence attempt is more likely to be successful if two or more compatible tactics are combined. Rational persuasion is a very flexible tactic, and it is usually compatible with any of the other proactive tactics. Rational persuasion is often combined with another core tactic. For example, one way to combine rational persuasion with consultation is to clarify why a proposed change is important and then invite the person to help find a good way to implement the change. One way to combine rational persuasion with inspirational appeals is to show how a proposed new product will save lives as well as increase profits. And one way to combine rational persuasion with collaboration is to explain why a new task is necessary and offer to show the person how to do it.

The other three core tactics can also be used together. For example, when consultation reveals concerns about obstacles, the leader can offer to help the person deal with these obstacles (a form of collaboration). Inspirational appeals can create enthusiasm for a proposed initiative, and consultation can be used to involve people in planning it.

Apprising is another tactic that can be combined with rational persuasion for many influence attempts. For example, you can explain why a proposed change will improve sales, then explain how much the person's annual bonus is likely to increase as a result of higher sales.

Some tactics are less compatible. A hard form of pressure is usually incompatible with personal appeals or ingratiation because it undermines the feelings of friendship and loyalty that are the basis for these tactics. Pressure can also undermine the trust necessary for the effectiveness of a tactic such as consultation. Nevertheless, when assistance is needed from a person who does not agree with the leader's task objectives, substantial pressure may be necessary before consultation will be feasible. Threats or warnings may help to convince the person that cooperation is more beneficial than noncooperation. However, the benefits of using pressure in this way must be weighed against potentially adverse side effects, such as lingering resentment and hostility.

Sequencing Influence Tactics

An influence attempt often involves a series of separate influence episodes that span a period of days or weeks. Some tactics are more appropriate for an initial influence attempt, and other tactics are more appropriate for follow-up influence attempts. It is prudent to initially select tactics that are likely to gain the desired outcome (compliance or commitment) with the least effort and cost. Initial influence attempts with subordinates or peers often involve either a simple request or a relatively weak form of rational persuasion, because these tactics are easy to use and entail little in the way of costs. If some resistance is anticipated, then it may be necessary to use a stronger form of rational persuasion, along with other soft tactics such as consultation, collaboration, apprising, and inspirational appeals. In the face of continued resistance, the leader will either escalate to "harder" tactics such as pressure, legitimating, or appeals to higher authority (a form of coalition-building tactic) or abandon the effort if the request does not justify the risks of escalation.

The sequencing of tactics can affect how people perceive your motives. Ingratiation (for example, praising the person's ability) is more credible when used early as part of the rationale for a request. Consultation may be viewed as more sincere if used initially rather than saving it until an influence attempt has already faltered.

Legitimating may be used either early or late in the process of attempting to influence someone, but it should be used early if the person is likely to have doubts about the legitimacy of a request. Exchange can be costly when used to gain compliance with a request that would otherwise be resisted, because it usually requires expending a valuable resource. Thus, exchange should not be used early in an influence attempt unless it is clearly necessary. Pressure involves the risk of undesirable side effects such as resentment and hard forms of pressure should be used only as a last resort after other tactics have failed.

Coalitions are most often used as a follow-up tactic in Western cultures after an initial influence attempt has encountered resistance. When used in this way, a coalition tactic may be viewed as a form of pressure and can elicit resentment. To gain support for a change that is likely to be costly and risky, it is useful to plan how to use coalition tactics earlier in the influence process. For someone who is likely to be doubtful about a proposed change or new initiative, showing that it has strong support from others can help to avoid initial resistance.

Authority and Power

Success in influencing others depends in part on authority and power. Authority involves the types of requests and commands that are viewed as proper for a leader, and many organizations have written policies, rules, and procedures to guide the actions of middle- and lower-level leaders. When a request or command is clearly legitimate, it is much more likely to elicit compliance. The likely success of an influence attempt is also increased when it is made by someone who has substantial "position power" derived from control over the allocation of rewards, resources, and punishments and access to information and important people. Leaders usually have more reward and coercive power over subordinates than over peers. Except in rare cases where they participate in the appraisal of a manager's performance, or in democratic organizations where they elect managers, subordinates have little power over managers.

Several tactics require at least a moderate amount of leader power to be feasible and effective. Exchange is not very useful unless a leader has control over some resources desired by the target person. Collaboration is also limited when a leader has few resources that would help the target person to carry out a request. Rational persuasion is limited when a leader has limited access to essential information. Apprising is limited when a leader has little knowledge about reward contingencies in the organization or career opportunities, as would be the case for a newly hired manager relative to subordinates and peers with years of experience in the organization. A leader's authority may deny a leader the use of some types of influence tactics. For example, forms of pressure such as threats to fire, demote, or reduce the pay of a subordinate are allowed in some organizations but not others. Likewise, forms of exchange such as the promise of a promotion, pay increase, or better assignment are permitted in some organizations but not others.

In light of these determinants and constraints on the use of influence tactics and the types of requests or commands that can be made, it is not surprising that managers use different tactics in dfferent situations. A tactic is more likely to be used if one has an appropriate power base for it and it is socially acceptable in the culture of the organization. Thus, exchange, pressure, ingratiation, and legitimating tactics are used more in a downward and lateral direction than in an upward one. Coalitions are more often used in influence attempts with peers and managers than with subordinates. Consultation is used more often with subordinates than with managers. Apprising is used more often with subordinates than with peers or managers.

Interpersonal Relationships

The proactive tactics are usually more effective when the leader is trusted and perceived to be ethical and competent. Moreover, in a cooperative, trusting relationship, there is less need to use the proactive tactics. Thus, it is beneficial for the leader to develop a good relationship with the target person, and to preserve a reputation for integrity and competence. The credibility and integrity of leaders is very much affected by how they use their power and influence. Any tactic can be used in a way that is unethical. For example, rational persuasion and apprising may involve lies and distortion. Inspirational appeals based on emotions such as fear or envy may be used to influence people in destructive ways. Collaboration and exchange may be based on empty promises. Ingratiation may be insincere. Unless a leader is trusted, these tactics may be viewed as an attempt to manipulate the target person. The proactive tactics should be used in ethical ways to accomplish shared objectives, not to exploit others for the leader's personal gain. Leaders should be careful to avoid using tactics in a way that is deceptive or manipulative.

Improving Influence Skills

Many leaders assume that the same type of influence strategy is applicable in every situation, or that they can get sufficient commitment by relying on formal authority and power. Both assumptions are incorrect. Research on interpersonal influence during the past quarter century provides a more comprehensive and accurate picture of the factors that determine influence success (Yukl 2010).

Leaders can improve their skill in identifying and using an effective influence strategy. The first requirement is a good understanding of the different types of influence tactics that are available and the conditions where each type of tactic is relevant. Understanding the determinants of influence outcomes is another important requirement. This chapter provides a foundation for both types of knowledge.

Several things can be done to improve the effectiveness of influence attempts and build skills in the use of influence tactics. Here are three practical suggestions:

- Invest more time in planning an influence strategy for requests that are unusual, controversial, difficult, or risky.
- Reflect on influence attempts afterward to learn from experience.
- Develop a better understanding of one's influence behavior and skills by participating in multisource feedback workshops and training programs involving the use of influence tactics.

Each of these approaches is briefly described in the following subsections.

Planning an Influence Strategy

An influence attempt is more likely to be successful if you carefully analyze the influence situation. It is important to determine the influence objectives, the people whom you need to influence, what you want them to do, the likely motivation and attitudes of each person with regard to your request, and the tactics most likely to be relevant for the situation. These questions can be used to guide the situational analysis:

- Whom do you need to influence, and what is the formal relationship with each person?
- What kind of working relationship do you have with each person?
- Why do you need to influence these people, and what do you want them to do?
- What is the desired level of commitment or compliance?
- What potential benefits and costs are there for the organization or team?
- What potential benefits and costs are there for the individuals you want to influence?
- Do these people share your task objectives, and what are their values and priorities?
- What obstacles or constraints are there, and how can they be surmounted?
- Are there reasons for likely resistance to your request or proposal?
- Are concerns or doubts likely regarding the importance and feasibility of the request?
- Are these persons able to suggest ways to improve your proposed plan of action?

Given what you know about the person you want to influence and the situation, you can develop an influence strategy. Identify the influence tactics that appear to be relevant for the situation. Taking into account your own skill in using each type of tactic, develop an influence strategy. Select the tactics that are most likely to be useful and determine an optimal timing and sequencing for them. Then determine how a conversation with that person might go.

Learning from Experience

To increase your influence skills, reviewing an influence attempt afterward to consider what happened and why is a valuable exercise. After the influence attempt is completed and the outcome can be determined, these questions are useful for reviewing what happened and what can be learned from the experience:

- What tactics were used, and how were they sequenced?
- What was the outcome, and was it the desired one?
- What went well during the influence attempt?
- Were there any surprises or things that did not go as expected?
- What things could have been done better?
- What did you learn about yourself and your influence skills?

When an influence attempt is unsuccessful, it may be difficult to discover the true reasons for the failure or what if anything could have been done better. One way to facilitate learning from experience is to get assistance from an executive coach who has relevant knowledge about interpersonal influence. The coach may be able to obtain relevant information about the reasons for the failure and can also provide advice about plans for future influence attempts. If the failure is related to a continuing conflict that needs to be resolved, the coach may be able to serve as a mediator to help resolve the conflict.

Feedback and Training Programs

Feedback from others about a leader's use of the proactive influence tactics can be used to improve the leader's influence skills. Three field experiments (for example, Seifert, Yukl, and McDonald 2003) found that feedback workshops can increase the use of the core tactics in influence attempts with those who report directly to a manager and peers. Because influence tactics are not used in the same way to influence subordinates, peers, and bosses, it is desirable to learn how often a manager uses each proactive influence tactic in influence attempts made with each type of target person. For each tactic, the mean score from each type of target person is compared with the mean score on the focal manager's self-rating of how much the tactic is used to influence that type of target person. Sometimes the ratings are also compared with norms for similar managers or other managers in the same organization. The focal managers and the workshop facilitator analyze the results to identify strengths and weaknesses for the managers. As in most leadership feedback programs, the workshop includes some skill-building activities, such as role plays and action planning for influence scenarios relevant to the real job situations of the managers. At least two feedback cycles are recommended, and follow-up coaching also increases the benefits of the feedback.

Summary

Success in influencing people requires skill in diagnosing the situation and determining which influence strategy is relevant. These general principles are relevant for improving success in your influence attempts:

- Understand the attitudes, values, and emotions of the individuals you need to influence.
- Maintain a good relationship with the people whose cooperation and support are needed.
- Plan in advance what proactive influence tactics are appropriate for a difficult influence attempt.
- Identify any core tactics that are relevant for an influence attempt.

- Combine tactics that are mutually compatible for a difficult influence attempt.
- Sequence tactics in a way that will maximize the positive effects.
- Learn from experience in making successful and unsuccessful influence attempts.
- Acquire the skills needed to use proactive influence tactics effectively.
- Use power and influence in ways that are ethical and appropriate.

Further Reading

Robert Cialdini, *Influence: Science and Practice,* 5th ed. Needham Heights, MA: Allyn & Bacon, 2008.

Allan Cohen and David Bradford, *Influence without Authority,* 2nd ed. New York: John Wiley & Sons, 2005.

John C. Maxwell, *The 360 Degree Leader: Developing Your Influence from Anywhere in the Organization.* Nashville: Thomas Nelson, 2005.

Gary Yukl, *Leadership in Organizations,* 7th ed. Upper Saddle River, NJ: Prentice Hall, 2010.

References

Falbe, C. M., and G. Yukl. 1992. Consequences for Managers of Using Single Influence Tactics and Combinations of Tactics. *Academy of Management Journal* 35: 638–653.

Kipnis, D., S. M. Schmidt, and I. Wilkinson. 1980. Intra-organizational Influence Tactics: Explorations in Getting One's Way. *Journal of Applied Psychology* 65: 440–452.

Seifert, C., G. Yukl, and R. McDonald. 2003. Effects of Multisource Feedback and a Feedback Facilitator on the Influence Behavior of Managers Towards Subordinates. *Journal of Applied Psychology* 88: 561–569.

Yukl, G. 2010. *Leadership in Organizations,* 7th ed. Upper Saddle River, NJ: Prentice Hall.

Yukl, G., R. Lepsinger, and A. Lucia. 1992. Preliminary Report on Development and Validation of the Influence Behavior Questionnaire. In *Impact of Leadership,* ed. K. Clark, M. B. Clark, and D. P. Campbell. Greensboro, NC: Center for Creative Leadership.

Yukl, G., C. Seifert, and C. Chavez. 2008. Validation of the Extended Influence Behavior Questionnaire. *Leadership Quarterly* 19, no. 5: 609–621.

About the Author

Gary Yukl received a PhD in industrial-organizational psychology from the University of California, Berkeley. He is currently a professor of management at the State University of New York at Albany, and his research interests include leadership, power and influence, and management development. He has published many articles in professional journals and has received several awards for his research. He is also the author or coauthor of several books, including *Leadership in Organizations,* 7th edition (Prentice Hall, 2010) and *Flexible Leadership* (Jossey-Bass, 2004). He is a fellow of the American Psychological Association, the American Psychological Society, the Society for Industrial-Organizational Psychology, and the Academy of Management. His leadership development programs have been used in many organizations.

Chapter 7

Leading Change: A Conversation with John P. Kotter

Interviewed by Elaine Biech

In This Chapter

- A discussion about leadership and change.
- John Kotter's views on change in a changing world.

Elaine Biech (EB): You are regarded as the "world's foremost authority on leadership and change." How do you feel about that? How do you feel about being renowned the world over as the guru of change?

John Kotter (JK): Well, it is hard for me to believe that statement. What I truly enjoy is finding places where people have managed to successfully take something that I've discovered or developed and used it in their organizations or lives and have achieved better results. I receive emails daily, and most are very gracious and sweet. I think I'm blessed. My work appears to be helping people, and that is very gratifying. I must admit that I have mixed feelings about being publicly recognized. I appreciate it very much, and it encourages me to go out and do even more.

EB: What competency is most important for a leader to be successful at implementing change?

JK: It's probably having a "sense of urgency." Our research during the 1980s led to a great deal of analysis during the 1990s, and this led to a basic set of conclusions that have been tested over and over again. The rate of change is increasing everywhere for everyone, no matter who you are or what you do. The increasing rate of change is very volatile today. We all feel the effects.

If an organization wants to prosper, it must be better at dealing with change, not small changes, not Kaizen—but bigger leaps. To reinvent themselves, organizations must think ahead to the change required as big leaps: Change to version 2.0 of an enterprise, 3.0, or maybe 4.0. So how do leaders gain mastery over the change process? How do they learn? Most people do a terrible job. In fact, 70 percent either shy away or don't do it well at all. Or they may achieve half the desired change at twice the cost and twice the time. However, the good news is that there are examples of people doing it well. We have seen a successful pattern in industry as well as government when organizations follow an eight-stage pattern [table 7-1]. In those cases, when we determine which of the eight steps is the most challenging or the most crucial for leaders to get right, the answer, without a doubt in my mind, is the first step, "Establishing a sense of urgency." This step must rise to a high enough level in the organization so that it provides the foundation for a difficult and complex change process.

EB: Creating that sense of urgency is certainly critical. What about the other end of your eight steps: "Anchor new approaches in the culture?" I've seen the sense of urgency being created, but then nothing happens. The planned change doesn't become reality.

JK: Of course the implementation steps are important. Why that doesn't occur could be due to a number of reasons. People can talk about something, even plan for it, but then it doesn't become reality. It usually fails somewhere in steps 5, 6, or 7. But step 8 can be a

Table 7-1. John Kotter's Eight Stage Process

1. Establish a sense of urgency.
2. Create the guiding coalition.
3. Develop a vision and strategy.
4. Communicate the vision.
5. Empower employees.
6. Generate short-term wins.
7. Consolidate gains and produce more change.
8. Anchor new approaches in the culture.

Source: From *Leading Change* © 1996 John P. Kotter. Used with permission.

problem too. The last step is all about getting the change grounded. It means ultimately that the culture changes. This is the making-it-stick step. The reason I didn't state that the last step is that the most critical is because most people do not get that far—sad to say.

EB: You mentioned your earlier research and analysis regarding step 1. You have a new book, *A Sense of Urgency,* that addresses this one step alone. What convinced you to put emphasis on this step?

JK: After putting *A Sense of Urgency* to bed, I'm even more convinced of its importance. I am certain that if you establish a sense of urgency and you get it right, it makes the following steps move easier and faster. If you establish a sense of urgency, it's easier to find a large enough group at the leadership level who have the required strengths and competencies— that's step 2. You won't have to force them onto a committee to drive the change. Most will volunteer. You can find volunteers who have credibility in the organization. There will be little problem scheduling meetings because people want to show up. During meetings, team members will come to the point and get it right. They will get to work.

Instead of focusing on the first step to ensure a solid foundation, leaders often run past it. They don't notice complacency. Or they see lots of frenetic activity occurring and think it is urgency; but I call this false urgency. It is not driven by a positive sense that we are going to grab a big opportunity. Instead, people are meeting, meeting, meeting and there is talk, talk, talk. But it is not aimed at some kind of big opportunity; nor is it productive. Urgency is as much a feeling as it is action. Real urgency is wanting to get up every day to accomplish something. Leaders who understand the role that urgency plays can figure out the biggest opportunity, and make sure everyone is on the same page. Leaders who have a true sense of urgency re-architect their calendars. As they consider meetings or activities, they realize that some of the events may be a waste of time. These leaders will either have someone else do it or just cancel the event.

EB: If you do not start out with the first best step, you are probably not going to get the best results. There are many analogies we could use for change. For example, when preparing a new recipe, if you don't have the best ingredients, it's not going to turn out right and no amount of spice added along the way will fix it.

JK: If you get the first step wrong, nothing afterward will work well. Someone recently counted the pages in my book *Our Iceberg Is Melting* and assigned them to each of the eight steps. The fable is about 100 pages long, so if each step was equal, there should be about 12 pages for each step. However, one step has by far the most pages, and that is the first, "Create a sense of urgency." I did not plan it that way, but it naturally matches reality. This is another example of how much time it takes to get the first step right—even in a fable.

One other point is that in the fable, the one who gets it all going is not on the top of the pyramid. It is someone without a title, Fred. Fred started down the road to success when he saw that his iceberg wouldn't last forever. People tell me all the time that they are in the middle of the organization and feel that nobody will listen to them. I say go read the fable; that's where Fred started. The one who launches the process is not always the person at the top of the pyramid.

EB: How do leaders gain mastery? How do they learn?

JK: The most common way is from experience. In terms of change skills, that means leaders have been lucky enough to have seen successful transformations and learn from them. Best of all, they were able to participate in the big changes, to make decisions. The ideal is to go through three or four big, successful changes. You always learn more from experience, like learning to drive a car. In addition, it helps enormously if their leadership instincts are good. It doesn't mean leaders know everything. It does mean that they learn easily from experience. We need to improve upon how to help these people. This has been a big focus of mine in the last year. How do you get people to raise their hand and say, "We need to transform this place and I don't know how to do it! I need help." How do you go about helping them to reach this point?

Some people can't be helped, because they do not listen. Or they don't know what they don't know. When they don't listen, what are you going to do? But you can help those who are willing to ask for help, who have some leadership capacity, and who are not condescending jerks. You seem to need more than one person to help them grow into a leadership role. You can do it over time. Doing it in traditional classroom, like at Harvard, can be helpful, but actually walking alongside leaders as they go through change, and being able to help in real time, is critically important.

It is coaching in the moment, but I resist the term "coaching" because the responsibility really is on the person providing the leadership, not the coach. Coaching is, of course, a sports analogy where the coaches are more the boss. Thinking about our famous New England Patriots, for example, everyone writes about Belichick and his coaching skills. From what we've seen in a corporate environment, great coaches don't help the "quarterback" by telling him what to do. Their role is more like a guide. I have been searching for words that help describe this important aspect of learning. People we coach often just need to follow their instincts to do what should be done. They often don't follow their instincts because they don't receive enough confirmation. So a great coach helps provide that confirmation. He or she also guides, informs, inspires, and engages much more then tells.

EB: What do you predict will be different regarding leading change in the future—say 20 years from now?

JK: First of all, with the curve we are on, the rate of change is going up and up, and there is increasing volatility. This trend will probably continue for another 10 years, at least. There are too many macro forces driving change, so the trend is not going to level off soon. This means that organizational capacity to deal with shocks or leaps caused by new technology has to go up or you don't succeed. Bureaucratic organizations that move slowly, even with a capacity for incremental change, will suffer more and more.

Second, the kind of leadership required will be a leadership that can implement the right change process, such as my Eight Steps. That's clear. But the most basic response to the question "What type of leadership we will need in 10 years" is "more." Simply more. We need more people to serve as leaders. We need more leaders from all stations in society. We do not have anything close to the number of leaders we need. We need leaders at the middle and lower levels; on and off the job. We need leaders for local political parties, community organizations, churches, education, and so on. We need a lot more people stepping forward and trying to show some leadership. How do you create more of this leadership? Beat the drum. Get out there to draw attention to the issue. The more drama, the better. The more you help people understand why we need leaders, the better. Many people have been raised to believe that leadership has nothing to do with them and that leadership only involves the person at the top. But that's not true, and in an increasingly changing world that outlook is not good for anyone. We need to help people recognize the need for much more leadership and that they too have a role.

Third, we need to encourage people to take the potential they have and develop it into skills, and then actually use those skills. We need to find a way to show that when people use their potential to be leaders, it is a worthwhile and rewarding endeavor. Certainly there are some risks in leadership. Potential leaders need to stick their necks out. They'll find some pushback. Unfortunately, people often see the risks as bigger than they really are. It's easier to find cases of failure than success and that shapes our outlook. This is where the inspirational part of guiding people to leadership positions can be helpful. People need to get the message that "You can do it! You may take a couple arrows, but it is really worthwhile." The reality is that people who step out and provide leadership receive enormous personal benefits, not just career benefits.

I wrote a biography of Konosuke Matsushita, the founder of Panasonic. He had seven brothers and sisters who all died before he was 30, but he made it to 94. His father lost all the family wealth in bad business deals, and his formal education ended at the age of nine. Despite this, Matsushita's persistent efforts and determination led to his success. People who knew him believed that his success had to do with his relentless attempts to provide leadership in a number of ways, including building a company and helping to rebuild Japan after World War II. After he retired, he initiated national dialogues, authored books, created a school of leadership, and created the Japan Prize. Providing all this leadership created a powerful form of something that flowed back to him. When you give, it always comes back. Once you feel it, you know it. We need to spread this message.

EB: If you could give leadership development professionals one piece of advice, what would it be?

JK: Give trainers advice? Training is tough because you never have enough time. Even in the university, we only have a few hours, a few days a week. A typical trainer may get only two days in a year. When you add that time up, it's really only a drop in the ocean. Therefore, a logical conclusion might be that the more we can turn students on to leadership, in an honest sense, the better. So if trainers can spread the message that leadership is for everyone, not just for bosses, that can be powerful; that no matter what a person is doing right now, the odds are high that he or she can probably do a better job. We need to get the message out that taking on leadership responsibilities will not only help you, your career, and your company, but it will also do good things for society and for your personal well-being. No one will figure out how to be a leader in a three-day class, so we need to encourage them to go forth with the knowledge that they do learn and then gain more experience with that knowledge at their jobs. This will make a difference. Simply because of the reality of the little time trainers have, it's logical that trainers must focus on helping others take the right action after the training to grow. That can be very powerful. I am not dismissing great teaching techniques that develop people's skills during a program. That's not the point. But to answer your question, the one piece of advice I would give trainers is to find ways to encourage future leaders to develop themselves on the job.

EB: I've heard you discuss "bold change." Can you define "bold change" and tell us what unique leadership competencies are required for bold change?

JK: Bold change is associated with significant changes that you try to make happen even while facing significant obstacles or when you have a seemingly impossible time frame. For example, you don't have 20 years to make the change; you have two. You don't face one or two obstacles; there are 15.

EB: Well it sounds like a leader making bold change must have a very focused sense of urgency. Are there other skills or attributes that will help a leader be successful in making bold change?

JK: Sure, there are many. But a leader must have a strong sense of urgency. If a leader doesn't have a really, really, really strong, gut-level sense of urgency, it's tough for him or her to be successful these days [table 7-2]. The leader must have more than just a general sense of urgency, more than just, "oh yeah, it's important." You need a fiery sense of urgency.

And the leader must use all the tactics available to help others start to gain that degree of urgency too.

EB: Are we as people getting better with ensuring that change happens? Is there a difference worldwide?

JK: There's good news and bad news from what I've seen. The good news is that we are improving. We are learning from our own mistakes. The bad news is that the rate of change is going up so fast, you worry that the gap between what we know and what is needed—between the leadership that's provided and the leadership that's needed—may not be shrinking but growing. So, it's a good news–bad news situation. We are getting better, but the need may be growing faster.

EB: Who do you admire as the greatest leaders (current or historical) and why?

JK: My answer isn't going to be a particularly surprising list. I'd put Nelson Mandela first. It's not just that he achieved a great deal of change with a minimum of disruption. He really handled a mammoth challenge. People predicted his country would blow up! Other leaders, on the political side, would include Winston Churchill. It is amazing what he did

Table 7-2. Tactics to Increase a Sense of Urgency

1. Bring the outside in:
   - Reconnect internal reality with external opportunities and hazards.
   - Bring in emotionally compelling data, people, videos, sights, and sounds.
2. Behave with urgency every day:
   - Never act content, anxious, or angry.
   - Demonstrate your own sense of urgency always in meetings, one-on-one interactions, memos, and emails and do so as visibly as possible to as many people as possible.
3. Find opportunity in crises:
   - Always be alert to see if crises can be a friend, not just a dreadful enemy, in order to destroy complacency.
   - Proceed with caution, and never be naïve, because crises can be deadly.
4. Deal with the no-nos: Remove or neutralize all the relentless urgency killers, people who are not skeptics but are determined to keep a group complacent or, if needed, to create destructive urgency.

Source: From *A Sense of Urgency* © 2008 John P. Kotter. Used with permission.

in World War II. The British suffered hugely, yet they did not give up. Part of it was much more than British culture, but the leader who led them to destroy the enemy of humankind. In the business sphere, I would pick Konosuke Matsushita as one of the greatest leaders, because what he did is also astonishing. In addition, more well-known to Americans would be Sam Walton. During his lifetime, he had thousands and thousands of senior managers, middle managers, and employees who were dedicated to building Walmart by following a few key principles: customer, customer, customer, treat them right. Finally, at his peak, which may have been in the 1930s, I think Thomas Watson Sr. was quite amazing. If you hear some of the stories about what he did at IBM to create this very unusual organization, they are impressive. Among other things, he helped our country through the Depression. Pretty incredible.

EB: What's your favorite change story—success or failure?

JK: I've heard lots. Do I have a personal favorite? One I love is both a change and leadership story. Between 1860 and 1863, the United States was going in a direction that was by any standard not good. Historical events were leading us toward two nations—two very different nations, probably with ongoing confrontations. One nation living by some values most of us today would find horrible. The United States may have never emerged as a world leader of democracy if the country had been split up, if there were two parts quarreling with each other. We may not have had the strength to engage in World War I or World War II to at least, in a little way, help save the whole world. Yet the country curved around in a direction that almost all historians say was not just a little bit better but a lot better. I like the story because it is so dramatic. I also love the story because Lincoln was a man who didn't have much formal schooling, certainly from no elite educational organization, who didn't have money to launch his career, and who—talk about obstacles—came up against horrible circumstances in 1860. He started changing the attitude of the Army to prepare for what was to come. He created a vision of what the United States should be and rallied enough people behind it. And he convinced people to make sacrifices and work to achieve that vision. And they did change a trajectory in the way events were heading. It's a very dramatic story.

EB: You mentioned that change is coming at us at a faster rate, creating urgency of its own. Does this make it more difficult for a leader to create a sense of urgency?

JK: Yes, the task is more difficult in the sense that you need a greater sense of urgency to deal with greater change. And yes, in the sense that it often becomes even more difficult for an executive to see if the urgency he or she has created is high enough to deal with the increased speed of change. But the biggest challenge of all is that after some point, the entire process needed to create successful change doesn't simply become more difficult, it becomes different.

I have drafts of various parts of six or seven books in my computer. I am finishing the next one, on buy-in, right now. But the book after that one was slated to be called *Winning Hearts and Minds.* I now think that will have to wait. My wife, who is a Harvard MBA class of 1984, and I founded a company called Kotter International, which is dedicated to building change leadership competencies around the world. One of the insights I have already had from working with Kotter International clients is that people often don't know what they don't know about what is required to deal with a changing world. I sit in front of many executives who say "We need to change." And then they say "Yeah, but we've changed before. It's tough, but we know how to do it." If you pursue this, what you discover is that the changes they have faced before required going 30 miles per hour, yet now they need to go 70 miles per hour. And you can't take your methods of going 30 and incrementally improve them until you are able to go 70.

A metaphor that I like relates to riding bicycles. The company knows that walking is not the answer; bikes are. They see the distances they must go and the speed they must go is increasing. So they put healthier and stronger people on the bikes. They may even send their technical people out to find tires that have less friction resistance so you can speed up. So they say, we know how to change. We have been doing just that for some time now. But they don't see that the speed and distances will continue to increase and that at some point bikes will become irrelevant. They will need a car, car mechanics, car drivers, and so on. And yet they don't even know what a car is. And they don't know to even ask the .question "Will we need to abandon bikes and do something very different?" So they are still honing the current process, as opposed to looking for a new process. They are still reacting with comments such as, "There may be more bumps in the road, but we can find a way to make our bikes handle them." They don't know that at some point their methodology is no longer applicable. It's not a quantitative difference they face. It's a qualitative difference.

EB: So how do you help people who don't know what they don't know, and how do you get that point across to them?

JK: That is really a tough one. I suspect one of the most critical characteristics of the best leaders is that they will admit there are things they don't know. They will ask for help. They are not afraid to be vulnerable.

EB: Where are you with the concept of charismatic leaders?

JK: As I mentioned, a working title for one of my future books is *Winning Hearts and Minds.* It presents a basic thesis that great leaders throughout history do win the hearts and minds of people and, in the process, mobilize individuals to make great things happen. These leaders are often characterized as "charismatic." That is to say, there is a causal logic that goes like this: A charismatic personality draws people in and mobilizes them to achieve these great things. I am wondering more and more if that is true. Is charisma more an effect than a cause? People take certain actions, and we aren't talking about supermen. These actions win over hearts and minds and move people to achieve astonishing outcomes. Then in retrospect, people look back at the person who started it all and say, wow, what a charismatic leader. This is very important, because if it's true, then it means you can have very powerful, very effective leaders who do not need to have compelling personalities. There is even a problem for those few people who do have magnetic personalities. It's too easy for them to win people over. You don't have to have a sensible vision. These charismatic leaders may then take people off cliffs. Therefore charisma is both positive and dangerous. And it's not a force that is necessary to ensure that great outcomes happen. That is what, in part, that book will be about.

EB: Your *Harvard Business Review* articles have sold more than two million copies [more reprints than any of the hundreds of other distinguished professors who wrote during the period Kotter published those articles] and your 17 books have sold more than 2.5 million copies worldwide [well within the top 1 percent of sales on Amazon]. Why do you think they are so popular?

JK: And it is only six articles, not 10 or 15. It is amazing, but there's nothing magical about it. I work very hard to understand what is happening in the world. I am always focused on outcomes, on performance, on what makes things better. I seem to have a talent for what you might call pattern analysis. I can look at a number of situations and see a pattern that is sometimes very subtle, that relates to outcomes that are better or worse. And I communicate what I know simply and clearly. Some people question my work because I don't use four-syllable words and hundreds of footnotes. However, if you wish to help people, I've learned, the more clearly and simply—not simplistically—you communicate the patterns, the more people can pick it up and do something with it.

EB: Which book is your favorite?

JK: That's like asking which child is my favorite! I like the first book, but I don't like the first one as much as the second. And I like the third more than the second, and so on. I like each subsequent book more because each tries to focus on more important topics, each is written a little better, and each is a little more useful. All the books have been great learning experiences for me. The day that I stop learning, I'll just hang it up.

EB: Chapter 12 in *Leading Change* is "Leadership and Lifelong Learning." What do you do to ensure that you are a lifelong learner?

JK: I think the more you have ridiculously high aspirations for what you want to do with your life, that helps because it pushes you to continue to learn. I think the more you keep your ego under control and listen, the more you will listen, and that helps learning. One of the lessons I drew from studying Matsushita is that listening kept him growing. He kept listening, even when he was extremely wealthy, because he honestly believed he could learn from other people. The problem that occurs when you become successful is that you can see other people as not as smart and not as successful so you don't listen as much. Therefore, you grow less. I work very hard to remind myself that we are all human beings and we are all in the same family and you can learn from anybody anytime. So if you believe that, listen, look around all the time, and you have the energy to do that because you have big aspirations, you can keep growing.

EB: What exciting project are you working on today? What is your big aspiration?

JK: The vision for Kotter International, a vision coming from me, is "millions leading, billions benefiting." The group that started the firm sat down with a facilitator who helped us work through a mission, vision, and values statement. The number of people who have used my books and taught other people the concepts is already in the millions. I wanted our vision to be even bigger and to have many more people benefit from that knowledge. There are one billion people today on Earth living in conditions that are so dreadful that they are beyond our comprehension. There are possibilities with our weapons of mass destruction that we could all be wiped out tomorrow. There are negative effects of industrialization, which could destroy the planet. We have developing countries walking tightropes right now, China being the big one, and if they fall it will hurt us all because it's an interdependent world. On the other side of this most distressing scenario, there are incredibly promising technologies being developed to keep us healthier and fitter. I am convinced that if you can help more people to provide leadership in their space, we will all benefit a great deal.

I mentor an Indian student in Bangalore who is creating a movement called "The Million Leader Mandate." I've been encouraging him to think big like that because India is at an interesting point in its history with China sitting above it, growing fast, and with huge political challenges within India, a caste system that's not going away—Muslims and Hindis living together, 1.1 billion people. Their problems are our problems in a globalized economy. Their problems flow everywhere and affect our children. We need more leadership from more places, and it will benefit billions of people.

EB: You mentioned book projects. What's the name of your next book?

JK: The working title is *Buy-In*. The focus is about how people shoot down good ideas and how you can save the good ideas. The reality is that good ideas are shot down constantly. Not just ideas, but *good* ideas. The book presents insights on how to deal with people who are skilled at putting something down or wounding a proposal so badly that it can never get off the ground. The book talks about what you can do and how you can deal with the problem better, so that not only is an idea saved, but in the process, people also come to understand and support it more. There is a method. The first half of the book is a fiction story. I think the story is fun. This fictional story is followed with an analysis. You've just read something fun and interesting; now let's analyze what happened and the method being employed. The book will be very practical—not just for senior executives, but for everyone because the skills we are talking about are very basic life skills. The book will be published in October 2010.

EB: The world probably can't imagine you as anything but the guru of leadership and change. If you had not become a professor focused on leadership and change, what would you have done with your career?

JK: I'd love to be an architect and create beautiful functional structures that help us all do our work better and make our cities or houses more pleasant. I admire great buildings. Centuries ago, the Europeans gave us the astonishing, gigantic catholic churches. Today, outside the United States, the Petronas Twin Towers in Kuala Lumpur are amazing. The Walt Disney Concert Hall in Los Angeles is fascinating. I could list about 50 buildings that I admire, and all of them for different reasons. But in all cases, they have a combination of both aesthetic and functional appeal. Beyond that, I don't know. I so much enjoy what I'm doing, it's hard to imagine doing anything else. I am sure the 10-year-old boy in me would love to play professional football, but the 18-year-old boy is smart enough to know it's not a good idea, even if I had the skills, because you end up at age 50 with a body that is so messed up that football is not really worth it.

EB: What legacy do you want to leave the world?

JK: Two healthy great children, doing what they want, who contribute to the world, and are happy about it. Ideas, books, and techniques that are communicated to others, though it doesn't matter through what vehicle, as long as it has some endurance. Hopefully, I will leave ideas that capture something that has staying power. That is why leadership and change are such fundamental topics for me, instead of inflation accounting or reengineering. I'd like people to look back and view me as a person who tried very hard. I'd like to be seen as someone who helped build a greater community. And I'd like to be thought of as a pretty good guy.

Further Reading

John Kotter, *The Heart of Change.* Boston: Harvard Business Press, 2002.
———, *Leading Change.* Boston: Harvard Business Press, 1996.

————, *Matsushita Leadership*. Boston: Harvard Business Press, 1997.

————, *Our Iceberg Is Melting*. New York: St. Martins Press, 2006.

————, *A Sense of Urgency*. Boston: Harvard Business Press, 2008.

————, *What Leaders Really Do*. Boston: Harvard Business Press, 1999.

About the Author

John P. Kotter is an award-winning business and management thought leader, *New York Times* best-selling author, inspirational speaker, and the Konosuke Matsushita Professor Emeritus of Leadership at Harvard Business School. He is the founder and chief innovation officer at Kotter International. His ideas, books, and speeches have helped mobilize people around the world to better lead organizations, and their own lives, in an era of increasingly rapid change. In October 2001, *BusinessWeek* rated him the number one leadership guru in America based on a survey of 504 enterprises. He is the author of 17 books, with more on the way. His books have been printed in more than 120 foreign-language editions, and total sales exceed two million copies. His articles in the *Harvard Business Review* over the past 20 years have sold more reprints than those of any of the hundreds of distinguished authors who have written for that publication during the same period. His books are in the top 1 percent of sales from Amazon.

Chapter 8

Managing Talent

Kevin Oakes, Holly Tompson, and Lorrie Lykins

In This Chapter

- The importance of defining talent management.

- The most common elements of talent management integration.

- The state of succession planning in corporations.

- Ownership and responsibility for talent management success.

- Best practices in human capital measurement.

- The role of technology in effective talent management.

Despite its high-priority status on the agendas of organizational leaders, talent management remains an elusive concept. Even its definition is debatable; is talent management the sum of its components—recruitment, development, succession planning, performance management, and the like—or something more?

Research shows that a key to effective talent management is integration: successfully intermingling components across organizational silos to share meaningful data, coordinate resources, and reap positive outcomes. Ultimate responsibility for managing talent varies from one firm to the next, but human resources (HR) typically plays a key role, and sources agree that effective talent management requires senior leaders' support. More important, research suggests that companies that manage talent well tend to fare better in financial and performance measures than their less-people-capable competitors. Execution of strategy, talent acquisition and retention, provision of customer service, and the pressures of competition drive talent management initiatives and fuel the development of strategies to address this concern.

Definitions and methodologies aside, talent management appears to be growing increasingly integrated and valuable as a strong component of organizations' responses to uncertain economic times. As the field matures, talent management's effectiveness as a constituent of overall business strategy is likely to be borne out.

Today, leadership is recognized as a challenge best met with a cadre of talent—no heroes needed. And those at the top clearly understand that one of their major roles is to identify, assemble, and prepare the talent needed to lead their organizations into the future. Most senior executives know intuitively that effectively developing and managing this talent is the key to long-term organizational success.

But when it comes to *talent management,* there couldn't be a more polarizing phrase in today's human capital profession. Some managers scoff at the term, regarding it as little more than a vaguely defined, overhyped business buzzword or as a shiny new bottle for age-old concepts such as leadership development, succession planning, or HR management. But others see it as much more than that, identifying it as a term that represents an important paradigm shift in the way organizations think about and manage skilled personnel. They argue that managing talent well gives companies major advantages in the marketplace.

Where does the truth lie? Research conducted by the Institute for Corporate Productivity (i4cp) suggests that both groups have a point. Talent management really is a poorly defined concept in many companies, and there's no consensus in the business community about who owns or executes it. On the other hand, better talent management does seem to be linked to better market performance, and companies that define and frequently use the term also tend to think they're better at managing talent.

Defining Talent Management

What does the term "talent management" really mean? A universally recognized definition is elusive. It can mean everything from performance management or succession planning to high potential development, depending on whom you ask. Talent management means different things to different individuals, and its meaning can even differ widely by function, location, or business unit within an organization. Clearly, talent management is not a one-size-fits-all proposition, and though some organizations define it in terms of their entire workforce, others view it as being exclusive to executives, essential core talent, and those with particularly high potential.

From a historic perspective, there are several reasons why a universally accepted definition of talent management does not exist. Talent management is still an unexplored frontier for many organizations, partly because an emphasis on it is still relatively new. Although it was first mentioned in McKinsey & Company's 1997 publication of its War for Talent research, the majority of companies are just beginning to explore talent management. As a testament to the lack of experience with this, fewer than 5 percent of the respondents to i4cp's 2008 global survey reported that their organizations have had talent management in place 10 years or longer (figure 8-1; i4cp 2008; i4cp 2009a).

When the term "talent management" first emerged, the concept encompassed three primary activities:

- the development of an employee value proposition
- the identification of sources of talent
- the systematic removal of underperformers.

Today, however, talent management means so much more. In an earlier study conducted by i4cp and ASTD, the term was defined as "a holistic approach to optimizing human capital, which enables an organization to drive short- and long-term results by building culture, engagement, capability and capacity through integrated talent acquisition, development, and deployment processes that are aligned to business goals." Though too long, this definition captures many of the elements that companies are attempting to affect. In fact, 83 percent of 518 human capital professionals surveyed agreed with the definition; only 2 percent of respondents said they didn't (i4cp 2007a, b).

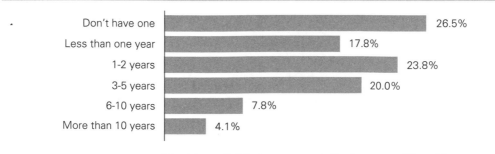

Figure 8-1. How Long Has Your Organization Had an Integrated Talent Management Approach?

Correlation with talent management effectiveness r = .33; p<.01

Although the definition of talent management often varies from one organization to another, most companies admit that it varies significantly even within their own organization. In fact, more than 75 percent of respondents surveyed by i4cp and ASTD said their organizations do not have a standard definition (table 8-1).

Deborah Wheelock, head of global talent management for Mercer, contrasts her firm's definition—"getting the right people in the right place at the right time for the right cost"—with concepts added by client companies, which include finding, developing, engaging, and retaining talent, and may extend to strategic objectives, alignment of workforces and organizational design, and workforce planning. Wheelock adds that "depending on the maturity of the company and its situation, talent management can range from isolated practices to a holistic approach" (i4cp/ASTD 2008).

So does it matter that a formal, universally recognized definition of talent management doesn't exist? Not necessarily, but what is required is a common understanding across an entire organization of the scope and purpose of talent management, and arriving at this understanding should start with determining the business outcomes the organization wants to achieve.

Whether an organization chooses to articulate a formal definition or not, there are three basic requirements for talent management success:

1. An organization's understanding of talent management needs to match its strategic goals.
2. An organization's understanding of talent management must be supported by its senior leaders and reinforced by its culture.
3. There needs to be a common understanding of talent management among stakeholders.

A fourth important concept to understand about talent management is that it must integrate several key areas within an organization.

Table 8-1. Does Your Organization Have an Agreed-on Definition of Talent Management?

	All Respondents	Best Market Performers	Best Talent Management Performers
Yes	24.7%	32.8%	43.8%
No	75.3	67.2	56.2

The Importance of Integration

In 2009, ASTD's Talent Management Committee defined integrated talent management as follows:

> Integrated talent management is a practice which strategically unites all human capital functions to maximize organizational effectiveness.

Thought leaders in talent management agree that integration is the key to realizing the full potential and benefits of talent management. But most companies do not have an integrated talent management approach. Only 5 percent of the i4cp/ASTD study respondents reported that their organization integrates the various components of talent management to a high extent (table 8-2). A full third of the respondents reported that their organization integrates talent management below a moderate extent, or very little.

But what are the components that need to be integrated? The i4cp/ASTD survey on talent management identified 20 different talent management activities that covered the employee life cycle (table 8-3; i4cp/ASTD 2008).

Software vendors often define integrated talent management at its most basic as a database that gathers and evaluates information or multiple integrated databases. Organizations might be considered to have integrated talent management if they have two or more talent management applications from the same vendor. But it should be noted that integration is not only (or even primarily) achieved through technology. The integration of processes, goals, and data should be well thought out before a new technology system is adopted and implemented. Technology can facilitate integration but is not a substitute for it.

Table 8-2. Opinions About the Organizational Integration of Talent Management

To what extent would you describe talent management as integrated with other human capital processes and strategies in your organization?

Opinion	All Respondents	Best Market Performers	Best Talent Management Performers
Very little	13.7%	9.3%	2.6%
Below moderate extent	21.2	14.2	3.9
Moderate extent	39.2	42.0	30.1
Above moderate extent	20.9	28.4	49.7
High extent	5.0	6.2	13 7

Table 8-3. Components of Talent Management

Which of these components do you think are included in talent management?
(select all that apply)

Component	All Respondents	Best Market Performers	Best Talent Management Performers
Leadership development	89.1%	88.5%	91.6%
Career planning	88.1	91.2	89.5
High-potential employee development	87.6	87.2	89.5
Performance management	84.6	86.5	88.8
Succession planning	86.7	89.2	88.8
Learning and training	83.8	85.8	85.3
Competency management	81.9	79.7	82.5
Retention	79.6	77.7	82.5
Professional development	79.3	77.0	81.8
Critical job identification	70.8	70.3	71.3
Recruitment	66.0	64.9	71.3
Compensation and rewards	68.9	70.9	69.2
Employee feedback	62.0	66.2	68.5
Workforce planning	62.7	59.5	67.1
Culture and values	59.1	60.8	64.3
Diversity management	52.7	48.6	56.6
Integrated HR management systems	55.6	56.8	55.9
International assignments	38.0	39.2	49.7
Benefits	34.2	39.9	38.5
Labor relations	17.8	14.9	20.3
Other (please specify)	5.7	5.4	7.0

A key issue about integrated talent management is that many organizations view integration as more process driven, and this speaks to the nature of the traditional silo structure of HR, which has inherent challenges in terms of integration. A company's compensation group, for example, might have a certain set of guidelines and processes that are well integrated vertically but are not well linked horizontally to the performance, succession planning, or recruitment cycles, which doesn't support the overall business outcome perspective.

Ironically, organizations that are just beginning the journey of developing talent management processes are often able to integrate them more quickly than organizations with more established processes. This is true for two key reasons: First, there are no silos that need to be confronted or egos that need to be considered. Second, it is often easier to build in a place where nothing existed before that might need to be torn down.

As one i4cp member observed: "We have established great performance management processes—development curriculum and work/life programs—but I don't think we would have designed them the same way if [we] started fresh today with the overall goal of talent management" (i4cp 2009a).

All 20 components of the 2008 i4cp/ASTD study are positively correlated with talent management effectiveness to some degree. Based on regression analysis, seven components taken as a group explained 49 percent of the variance in talent management effectiveness. To put it another way, an organization starting talent management today could begin with these seven in mind and be assured of building on a solid foundation.

Succession Planning

Of the many human capital components that need to be integrated, most organizations cite succession planning as a critical talent management consideration in the development of long-range future planning. And findings from i4cp's research in this area consistently indicate that most leaders believe the importance of succession planning will increase in the future. Succession planning was identified as the number one challenge organizations faced in 2008, according to a Society for Human Resource Management (SHRM) survey of more than 500 executives—half from the United States—who were asked to rank their top five challenges. Moreover, the top four challenges cited—succession planning, recruitment and selection, engagement and retention of talent, and success-skills building for leaders—pertain to succession planning strategies (SHRM Foundation 2007).

But given the importance of succession planning, how effective is it within organizations? Shockingly, a brand new i4cp/ASTD Succession Planning Survey finds that a mere 14 percent of respondents describe their succession planning efforts as effective to a high or very high extent (i4cp/ASTD 2010). Most admitted their level of success is moderate, or less (table 8-4). Also, though many organizations acknowledge the importance of planning for successors for leadership and other vital positions, fewer than half of those surveyed (44.5 percent) say their organizations have a formal planning process in place (table 8-5).

Table 8-4. Opinions About Succession Planning (percent)

To what extent do you agree with the following statements?

Response	Don't Know	Not at All	Small Extent	Moderate Extent	High Extent	Very High Extent
Overall, our succession planning efforts are effective.	11.8	5.1	29.2	40.0	12.1	1.8
Our succession planning efforts are not just "something we have to do"—we really depend on this process and use it when leadership vacancies occur.	8.0	15.2	28.6	28.4	16.9	2.9
Our succession planning efforts effectively identify and develop candidates for leadership positions.	6.3	10.3	30.5	31.6	17.6	2.6
Our succession plans are fluid and flexible enough to change when different types of leaders or skill sets are needed.	8.6	14.1	25.3	26.8	20.9	4.2
Our succession planning efforts extend far enough throughout the organization that key positions beyond senior management have pipelines in place.	7.2	25.9	28.5	21.7	14.0	2.6

Table 8-5. Status of the Succession Planning Process (percent)

Does your organization have a formal succession planning process?

Response	Percent
Yes	44.5
No	55.5

Among those in firms that do not have a formal plan, just over half noted that their firms do have informal plans. However, a good deal of ambivalence seems to exist, as shown by the significant number of respondents who said they either didn't anticipate that their firms would formalize a plan or that they simply didn't know whether their firms might do so.

Most often, companies vest ultimate responsibility for succession planning with their entire executive teams. However, many respondents say their organizations are extending their succession planning well beyond top management levels, choosing to include managerial, technical, and professional positions in their planning efforts as well. The greatest proportion—72 percent—of respondents said their succession planning addressed positions at the vice president level. In addition, many confirmed their use of technology to enhance speed, efficiency, and accuracy in handling information pertaining to various aspects of succession planning.

Clearly, recent data reinforces the significance of succession planning now and in the future. The next step for businesses is to follow up their own words with action by implementing and managing an effective strategy, and by incorporating it into a broader talent management strategy.

Who Owns Talent Management?

There is no consensus about who is or should be responsible for owning and executing talent management. Results of an i4cp survey found that the "HR function generally" was most often seen as the group responsible for talent management ownership (37 percent) and execution (38 percent) of talent management among respondents overall (table 8-6; i4cp 2007 a, b).

However, respondents from the best market performers as well as the best talent management performers saw things a little differently. Although similar percentages saw HR as having ownership of talent management, they were more likely to select "all managers"

111

Table 8-6. Organizational Responsibility for Talent Management (percent)

Who is responsible for the execution and ownership of talent management in your organization?

Aspect	Human Resources Generally	Training Function	CEO	Executive Team	All Managers	All Employees	Other
All Respondents							
Execution of talent management	38	7	4	20	25	5	2
Ownership of talent management	37	4	9	23	19	5	3
Best Market Performers							
Execution of talent management	31	6	2	20	33	7	1
Ownership of talent management	36	4	6	20	23	7	3
Best Talent Management Performers							
Execution of talent management	31	3	3	21	31	10	2
Ownership of talent management	31	1	10	24	22	9	3

as being responsible for the execution of talent. No one group claimed a clear majority in either ownership or execution in any group of respondents, indicating that responsibility for talent management is divided (and perhaps in flux).

"More and more, I see end-to-end organizational structures emerging, where a single leader owns talent acquisition, talent development, performance management, and succession," asserts Susan Burnett, chief learning officer at Yahoo! Yet even though this approach to managing talent management may be becoming more popular, it may not create the most effective results, for two reasons. First, if HR solely "owns" talent management and is responsible for the success of the process, managers who "live" with the talent have little incentive to comply with, let alone embrace, the processes (i4cp/ASTD 2008).

Second, in addition to the obvious reasons why HR cannot be the sole owner of talent management, there is a deeper issue: Talent management is about the organization's long-term survival and success. This goal may present dynamics that are diametrically opposed to a manager's short-term goals and objectives; therefore, senior managers need to build the right incentives into the rewards philosophy and execution.

Although it is critical for senior leadership to steer the ship when it comes to talent management, HR cannot abdicate its responsibilities to the business. The most successful models have shared responsibility:

- HR is responsible for developing and maintaining the tools and processes to enable successful talent management.
- Individual managers are responsible for carrying out and executing the intent of the processes.
- The executive team is responsible for creating the organizational incentives, monitoring the progress, and rewarding (or withholding rewards for) behaviors in line with the talent management objectives.

If a manager meets his or her business objectives but is not engaged in the talent mindset, should this affect his or her performance bonus? Many organizations struggle with this issue, especially those trying to implement or integrate talent management processes. What guidelines have some organizations established? The Institute for Corporate Productivity has uncovered several best practices:

- Employee movement/promotion is measured at the individual manager level.
- Managers of high-potential employees have specific objectives to meet regarding developing the high-potential employee.
- Managing high-potential employees is a reward for the manager.
- Low termination rates, low absenteeism rates, and high engagement scores are measured and rewarded at the team level.

- Managers who select/onboard high performers are rewarded.
- Managers who demonstrate success in recruiting and selection are included in selection teams for other areas, as in small and medium-sized enterprises.
- HR leaders are rewarded for having an impact on business outcomes.
- HR is measured as to the quality, ease, and effectiveness of talent management processes.

Along with rewards, the importance of training, performance reviews, and development is vital to the effective execution of talent management. Line managers, and especially new managers, must receive training that addresses managerial and supervisory skills such as time management and communication and team performance. Companies need to proactively do several things in training and development for talent management to be effective:

- Train managers to clarify/standardize expected behaviors.
- Educate managers in overall talent management concepts, especially how talent management adds value.
- Make talent management part of daily managerial duties.
- Include consideration of talent implications in decision-making criteria.
- Emphasize through the culture that managing talent is an essential management function.
- Leaders/managers' performance ratings should include talent components.

Ultimately, however, without senior-level support, talent management is doomed to fail no matter how good the training and rewards.

The Importance of Support

Even in a prosperous environment, organizations need to understand the investment proposition for talent management programs and processes, and senior leadership must champion talent management. By starting with the business drivers for talent management processes, HR professionals are in a better position to articulate the value these processes bring to the organization. For organizations that acknowledge they are not effective in managing talent or would like to become more effective, this is the cornerstone of the value proposal.

As stated above, in many organizations HR is solely responsible for the success of talent management processes. But when talent management is HR's exclusive responsibility, the success is limited. HR alone is not empowered to make the day-to-day decisions of selecting, onboarding, training, developing, and rewarding employees. This is a process between managers and employees, but often managers are not fully equipped to manage talent management strategies.

In most cases, management already values talent management, so there doesn't need to be a lot of selling. Research findings demonstrate that well-executed talent management provides organizations with solid financial data, improved customer service and satisfaction, and a competitive edge derived from forward planning and the projection of future conditions, ensuring stakeholder benefits and the long-term health of the organization. But what does need to be communicated effectively is how the data gathered strengthens the organization—how it benefits managers and their profit centers by improving engagement, performance, and retention; and how it lowers the costs of turnover and recruitment, which in turn saves time and money and makes each profit center more productive.

The most succinct message regarding the business case for talent management is that research shows that high-performing organizations view talent management as a strategic imperative for sustainable organizational success. High performers rely on talent management to assess and address issues that include tying training to employee development as well as overall organizational goals, measuring productivity and performance of business units, and identifying key talent. So why isn't everyone doing it?

The scenario described in the quotation below is not unique. For most organizations, the biggest line item in the budget is salary and other people-related expenses, yet only 2 percent of chief financial officers report that they understand to a great extent the return on their aggregate investment in human capital.

Perhaps because the importance of good talent management processes seems so obvious to HR professionals, they often seem unprepared to answer the questions that invariably come up each year: "What would happen if we cut the dollars for these programs?" or "What is the business case for talent management?" Without effective measurement, the answers to these questions will remain elusive.

Measurement Is Critical

Talent management professionals cannot tell a story that will resonate with the C-suite unless they are able to link talent management to business outcomes. The reasons why an organization is investing in talent management—beyond processes, systems, optimizing

> "We spend four months per year on the budget process, but we hardly spend any time talking about our talent."
>
> —Jim Robbins, Cox Communications
> (quoted by Michaels, Handfield-Jones, and Axelrod 2001)

operational efficiency, and compliance—need to be very clearly articulated. These questions must be answered:

- Why are we doing this?
- What is the business outcome?
- How do we really know that talent management will maximize shareholder value?
- Will this give our organization a clear view of current and future needs?
- Will this give our organization a healthy succession pipeline?
- Will talent management help manage the risk for key roles?
- Will the success of talent management, as we define it, actually move us to our strategic outcomes?

Metrics help create accountability—what gets measured gets done. But if the process of gathering data becomes the primary focus, organizations run the risk of coming up short in making the connections necessary to address gaps and making certain that they have the talent in place for current needs and future growth. Metrics need to be linked to very clear business outcomes. Most organizations require different kinds of metrics, including accountability metrics, awareness or business case metrics, and metrics on return-on-investment (ROI) or impact.

The Human Capital Institute argues that exact ROI calculations are not needed because there is no proven methodology "to put a number on 'the value of human capital'" (Anonymous 2004). Though probably true, this may not be a successful argument come budget time. There are three common challenges to calculating the ROI of talent management:

- Clear outcomes for talent management have not been identified.
- Many of the benefits, such as "soft cost avoidance," make calculating a positive ROI difficult.
- Organizations either have not agreed on assumptions and/or have not captured the metrics needed to calculate an ROI.

When building an ROI or presenting a budget for talent management practices, organizations should start with the stated goals of the processes and determine how they align with business objectives or issues. This is the answer to the question "What would happen if these processes were not funded?" For this reason, it is important to have executive support for the processes and to have management appreciation of the intent and value of the processes. But during the budget cycle, it is probably too late to build this support and appreciation. Ideally, human capital professionals will be in the position of only needing to remind stakeholders rather than having to try to convince them of the merits of talent management.

Although it is true that the majority of the value of talent management is "soft"—including cost avoidance, opportunity costs, and other subjective measures—a positive ROI is possible. Before the budgeting process begins, HR should work with the units responsible for finance, marketing, and/or process improvement (for example, Six Sigma or total quality management) to learn what assumptions these units are using for their calculations. Each of these areas uses sophisticated models that require assumptions about the value of market share, a customer, or an individual unit. They often use assumptions for an hour of labor, benefits, and overtime. It isn't necessary to try to reinvent the wheel. If these assumptions exist, HR needs to use them in its ROI calculations. If they do not exist, the task shifts to working with finance to build annual assumptions that can be used for this purpose.

When looking at what is often measured, half of the companies surveyed by i4cp in 2009 distinguished between turnover rates (leaving a position due to termination, transfer, promotion, or other movement within the organization) and termination rates. The poll of 556 firms found that turnover rates were the most popular measure, followed closely by both voluntary and involuntary termination rates. The sidebar lists various categories of HR measures, noting the ones that are most often measured with regular frequency (i4cp 2009b).

Many organizations believe they already have the proper metrics in place; after all, they pay millions for HR information systems (HRISs) that are supposed to store, report, and analyze employee and talent data. However, the majority of HRISs are used as payroll systems and are not true information systems. This means that data on such things as promotions, movement, termination reasons, and even job codes may be suspect.

Although many HRISs purport to have the ability to hold talent management, development, and performance management data, the reality is that few organizations use HRISs as designed. More often, each HR function has adopted technologies that meet its specific needs but may not integrate well with those of others. This is another reason that breaking down HR silos can be so difficult.

Technology as a Panacea

Technology software and platforms can streamline and make data tracking more efficient, allowing HR to focus on strategy while building a record of performance that can be compared from year to year. Automation is critical for many reasons, but a common pitfall is the expectation that purchasing software will resolve the talent management question. Organizations should not rely on talent management vendors to drive decisions. Strategic planning must come before investment and deployment; it is critical that organizations first determine what they want to accomplish strategically and how effective talent management can help them achieve their strategy.

Checklist of Common HR Measurements

- Termination/attrition—turnover rates (81.3 percent), voluntary termination rate (81.0 percent), involuntary termination rate (78.5 percent).
- Revenue/income—planned operating profit growth (76.2 percent), planned revenue growth (77.5 percent), sales/revenue (73.4 percent).
- HR—payroll or labor expense as a share of total operating cost (72.6 percent), ratio of HR to total staff or ratio of employees to HR staff (66.9 percent), HR expense, as a share of the company's operating costs (59.1 percent).
- Training/development—dollars dedicated to employee training and development (73.0 percent), reactions of participants to training programs (70.8 percent), average training hours per employee (55.0 percent).
- Compensation—total compensation as a share of revenue (71.7 percent), pay for performance or variable compensation (incentive awards, profit sharing) as a share of total compensation (61.9 percent), total cash compensation of high performers versus market (43.3 percent).
- Diversity—people metrics such as hiring, promoting, and terminating (64.1 percent); employee opinions/culture metrics (61.6 percent); compliance or completion rate of business diversity action plans (33.4 percent).
- Hiring/acceptance—hiring cycle time (average days of open position) / time-to-fill positions (59.9 percent), planned head-count growth (59.6 percent), cost to fill (51.2 percent).
- Effectiveness—satisfaction surveys (68.5 percent), employee engagement index/surveys (65.9 percent), audits (63.4 percent).
- Age—average age of full-time employees (75.1 percent), share of employees eligible for retirement (65.1 percent), average age of part-time employees (51.0 percent).
- Output/cost measures—total labor to cost revenue percent (55.1 percent), ratio of employee to productivity output (27.7 percent).
- Promotions—promotions from level to level (38.3 percent), promotions by demographics variables (27.7 percent), cycle time to full productivity (18.1 percent).
- Employee movement (lateral, upward, and downward)—employee movement from job level, classification or rank (34.2 percent); measure by types of employee moves, including lateral, upward, downward, short-term, and the like (28.7 percent); employee movement by demographic variables (23.1 percent).

Source: i4cp/ASTD (2008); i4cp (2009a).

Some organizations may have a process that works reasonably well for a certain smaller subset of the staff—such as salaried employees or the top 25 percent—and based on this they decide to expand this process to the rest of the organization. But the expectation that automating and providing everyone with access means that the organization now has a performance management process that works well is not entirely realistic. Invariably,

> "I believe that technology is fundamental because that is the way that organizations can operationalize processes and strategies. It's the cleanest and fastest way to push the message out and do what needs to be done and for the organization to mine the data, study it, and figure out what to do next. But it could be as easy as an Excel spreadsheet; it doesn't necessarily have to be a complex software package. The process needs to be as easy as email, and that's something that some software vendors have managed to create."
>
> —Ranjani Iyengar, head of learning and development, Kraft Foods
>
> (Quoted in i4cp 2009a)

some employers find that once they automate, whatever weakness existed in the system will be magnified, and, as a consequence, the focus will become ironing out problems with the technology.

Moreover, once a system is in place, it can continue to dominate the process, and attention is thus too often diverted from the mission to the system. This distraction can remove the focus from the conversations that need to take place between managers and employees or between leaders and managers.

Organizations that are considering making an investment in talent management software should keep in mind that the field of talent management is relatively young and, though vendors may claim to be talent management experts, they are almost all very new to the field, and their products are often missing critical components. Some questions to ask:

- How long has the vendor been in business?
- How financially healthy is the vendor?
- What major clients does the vendor serve?
- Is the vendor's solution configurable for global markets?
- What applications in the talent management continuum is the vendor missing?
- How easy is the software to implement and integrate with other systems?
- What will happen if the vendor is acquired?

These are only a few of the questions that need to be asked when selecting the right technology supplier.

Most would agree that the amount of hyperbole from vendors claiming to have the "fully integrated talent management suite" can be mind-boggling. And typically, it just plain isn't true; most vendors sell products that are lacking major core components that are needed to be considered fully integrated. Corporations need to look at talent management software with a very critical eye for the next few years—there will clearly be several mergers and acquisitions as vendors all try to add the necessary components to vie for the brass ring of a fully integrated suite.

Conclusion

The implementation of integrated talent management benefits organizations when a clear-cut definition of talent management is established across the organization, a business outcome strategy is developed, and data is properly linked. It's not enough that a system is in place and the data flows; it needs to flow in a correct format that will help organizations make the right decisions. Integration should take place both at the strategy and process levels, and data must be linked to specific business outcomes. Like other initiatives, training and leadership are critical to the success of talent management.

Organizations can become more adroit at managing talent if they adopt certain strategies, including the following:

- Integrate talent management components more effectively, especially as they relate to the areas of selection, development, leadership, succession planning, retention, and engagement.
- Focus talent management neither too narrowly nor too broadly. Identify "talent," and then create programs to support it.
- Make an executive team rather than just a single HR leader responsible for talent management.
- Ensure that leaders see talent management as vital and that the culture supports it.
- Hold managers accountable, and give them the right skills to manage talent.
- Continuously improve talent management programs.
- Use technology to help the organization manage talent, but don't expect it to be a silver bullet.
- Measure talent management, especially in terms of training and development effectiveness.
- Align talent management with business goals, and make sure that your processes and policies support it.

In the end, there's reason for optimism. Integrated talent management remains a relatively new phenomenon, and organizations generally seem to get better at it over time. New research, techniques, and technologies are emerging to improve the management of talent. Nonetheless, effective and integrated talent management isn't easy to achieve. It is, in essence, a system with many different parts. The sooner organizations learn to create and nurture these systems, the sooner they'll be able to turn their talent base into a genuine competitive advantage.

Further Reading

Aberdeen Group, Talent Acquisition Strategies: Employer Branding and Quality of Hire Take Center Stage, July 2008.

Eddie Blass, *Talent Management Cases and Commentary.* Chippenham, U.K.: CPI Antony Rowe, 2009.

Ed Michaels, Helen Handfield-Jones, and Beth Axelrod, *The War for Talent.* Boston: Harvard Business School Publishing, 2001.

Pat Galagan, "Talent Management: What Is It, Who Owns It, and Why Should You Care?" *T&D,* May 2008, 40–44.

Matt Guthridge, Emily Lawson, and Asmus Komm, The Strategic Priority of Talent: Part 2. *Office World News,* May–June 2008, 12–14.

i4cp (Institute for Corporate Productivity), *Taking the Pulse: Succession Planning.* Seattle: Institute for Corporate Productivity, 2008.

———, *Taking the Pulse: Talent Branding.* Seattle: Institute for Corporate Productivity, 2008.

Kevin Oakes, "The Emergence of Talent Management," *T+D,* April 2006, 22.

"Talent Management: Now It's the Top Priority for CEOs and Their Organizations," *HRfocus,* February 2008, 8–9.

Andy Teng, "Making the Business Case for HR: Talent Management Aids Earnings," *HRO Today,* May 2007.

Lesley Uren, "From Talent Compliance to Talent Commitment," *Strategic HR Review,* March–April 2007, 32–35.

References

Anonymous. 2004. A Simpler Way to Determine the ROI of Talent Management. *HRfocus,* 3–4.

i4cp (Institute for Corporate Productivity). 2007a. *Talent Management Survey 2007.* Seattle: Institute for Corporate Productivity.

———. 2007b. *Survey Results: High-Potential Assessment.* Seattle: Institute for Corporate Productivity.

———. 2008. *Major Issues Survey 2008.* Seattle: Institute for Corporate Productivity.

———. 2009a. *Talent Management Playbook.* Seattle: Institute for Corporate Productivity.

———. 2009b. *Taking the Pulse: HR Metrics Survey.* Seattle: Institute for Corporate Productivity.

i4cp (Institute for Corporate Productivity) / ASTD. 2008. *Talent Management Practices and Opportunities.* Seattle and Alexandria, VA: Institute for Corporate Productivity and ASTD.

———. 2010. *Improving Succession Plans: Harnessing the Power of Learning and Development.* Seattle and Alexandria, VA: Institute for Corporate Productivity and ASTD.

Michaels, Ed, Helen Handfield-Jones, and Beth Axelrod. 2001. *The War for Talent.* Boston: Harvard Business School Publishing.

SHRM Foundation. 2007. Strategic Research on Human Capital Challenges. *Human Capital Challenges Report,* 10–21, 24.

About the Authors

Kevin Oakes is the CEO and founder of the Institute for Corporate Productivity (i4cp), the world's largest private network of corporations focused on improving workforce productivity. He has been a leader in the human capital field for the last two decades, and was most recently the president of SumTotal Systems, the largest provider of talent and learning solutions in the world, which he founded in 2003 by merging Click2learn, where he was CEO and chairman, with Docent. Completing a five-year board term, he was the 2006 chairman of ASTD, and he was the 2008 chair of the ASTD Board Selection Committee.

Holly Tompson, PhD, is a senior research analyst at i4cp. Previously, she taught human resource management at the University of Tampa to undergraduates and MBA students, and today she serves as an executive coach, working with the University of Tampa's Focused Leadership Program. She has a BS in business and psychology from Trinity University in San Antonio and a PhD in organizational behavior and human resources management from the University of South Carolina. Her work has been published in the *Journal of Management, Employee Rights and Employment Policy Journal, Journal of International Business Studies,* and *Small Business Journal.*

Lorrie Lykins is i4cp's managing editor and has been involved in human capital research for 10 years. She has an MFA from Queens University and has authored numerous reports and white papers on subjects ranging from corporate volunteerism to health care and wellness to disaster preparedness and women's issues. She is an adjunct professor at Eckerd College in St. Petersburg, Florida, and is a longtime correspondent for the *St. Petersburg Times.* She is a member of the Society of Professional Journalists and the National Book Critics Circle. Her work has been published by *Talent Management* magazine, the American Management Association, and HR World.

 Chapter 9

Getting Results: Our Journey to Turn Leadership Competencies into Outcomes

Dave Ulrich and Norm Smallwood

······················· **In This Chapter** ·······················

◼ How to turn leadership competencies into results by considering the "so that" aspect.

◼ How leaders define and accomplish four specific results—related to employee competence, commitment, contribution; to organization capabilities that help deliver strategy; to customer share through leadership brand; and to investor confidence through intangibles.

◼ What leaders can and should know and do to make results happen—the leadership code.

In the thicket of works on leadership, we too often overlook an obvious fact: Leaders must deliver results. All the emotional intelligence, judgment, empathy, vision, or ability to learn does not matter much if leaders cannot deliver results. For the last 12 years, we have been working to define more clearly the results leaders should deliver to employees, organizations, customers, and investors. When these results are clearly defined, then we can identify the knowledge and skills leaders must demonstrate to make results happen. This chapter reviews our journey to turn leadership competencies into meaningful outcomes.

© 2010 Dave Ulrich and Norm Smallwood. Used with permission.

If you Google the words "leader" and "leadership," there are more than 420 million hits. That's an awful lot of information. Clearly, much has been written about leaders and leadership. In the last decade, we have addressed the issue of how leaders make an impact by contributing to this huge volume of work with four books and many articles. In this chapter, we review this work and synthesize how we believe we've contributed a unique perspective with respect to four ideas:

1. Leadership is about more than individual, psychological competencies; it's also about delivering results. An effective leadership formula is leadership = attributes $\times$ results (Ulrich, Zenger, and Smallwood 1999).

2. Leaders must focus outside the firm on investors and customers as well as inside because results are tied to multiple stakeholders both inside and outside the organization. When this is done well, greater market value occurs (Ulrich and Smallwood 2003).

3. Individual leaders matter, but leadership matters more. It's critical to pay attention to leadership as an organization capability, not just to leaders as individuals. When this capability ensures the desired customer experience, both customers and investors are served (Ulrich and Smallwood 2004, 2007).

4. There are two kinds of individual leader competencies; one is a set of fundamental competencies, the leadership code; and the other is a set of unique competencies that relate to how leaders connect employees with customers, the differentiators (Ulrich and Smallwood 2008).

Let's review the evolution of these ideas.

Results-Based Leadership: The Kickoff

In the late 1990s, we had a simple insight: Much of the practice of leadership was focused on individual, psychological competencies. Practically every book we could find then, and to a great extent now, was aimed at individual, leader competency development (what we called the attributes of leaders). Popular examples include

- seven habits of highly effective people
- authenticity
- leadership secrets of . . . Attila the Hun, Thomas Jefferson, Buddha, Santa Claus, and so on
- emotional intelligence
- the extraordinary leader
- and so on.

In seminars, we frequently ask "What makes an effective leader?" The response is often the same: setting a vision, having integrity, communicating, being bold, making things happen, and other personal attributes. Frequently, leadership development experiences are organized with a day on each attribute.

We proposed that this approach was half right. Leaders do need to have effective attributes, but leadership is also about getting results. So in our book *Results-Based Leadership* (Ulrich, Zenger, and Smallwood 1999), we explored four results that leaders need to deliver:

- Investor-leaders must build investor confidence in the future as seen in intangible value.
- Organization-leaders must build sustainable capabilities that shape an organization's identity.
- Customer-leaders must ensure customer delight as seen in share of customers.
- Employee-leaders must increase employee competence and commitment as evidenced in productivity and retention.

It was at this time we realized the importance of the relationship between attributes and results. Neither alone is enough; it's the virtuous cycle between them that makes all the difference. We connect attributes and results with *so that* and *because of* (figure 9-1). One simple application is that when a leader receives 360-degree feedback about his or her individual competencies, the leader must ponder the "so that" query: I must improve this competency "so that" I can deliver a particular result to one of my stakeholders. Alternatively, another leader delivers results and should consider the "because of" rationale: I delivered this result "because of" this competency I have (or lack).

Figure 9-1. The Virtuous Cycle of Attributes and Results

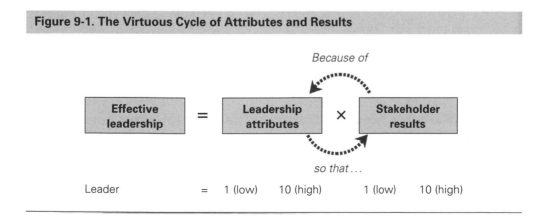

Figure 9-1 has guided the last 10 years of our writing and applications for leadership. To turn this simple idea into a tool, have participants think of several leaders. For convenience, we'll pick a few Democratic presidents—Jimmy Carter, Bill Clinton, and Barack Obama. On a scale of 1 to 10 (1 is low and 10 is high), rate each leader on attributes and results. Most will score Clinton and Carter exactly the opposite—Clinton high on results and Carter high on attributes, giving them both a similar score. Obama tends to score high on both.

Let's quickly overview each of four results, and then show how we have explored each of them in the last decade:

- *Investor results:* What happens inside the organization also affects investor confidence for the future. Investors invest based on industry favorableness, firm performance, and the quality of leadership and organization. We believe that the leadership and organization dimension is often the most difficult to specify, but also one that may hold a key to a firm's overall market value.
- *Organization results:* Organization theory has shifted the focus from structure, shape, and morphology to capabilities. Capabilities are the DNA of companies and determine how things are accomplished. Sample capabilities include speed of change, learning, collaboration, innovation, service, efficiency, and culture or shared mindset. These capabilities become the key to sustained strategy execution, the deliverables of human resources (HR), and the core identity of the organization.
- *Customer results:* Ultimately, what happens inside an organization needs to deliver value to customers outside the organization. The tag line being "the employer of choice" makes more sense if we are the employer of choice of employees our customers would choose. Using customer criteria as the filter for internal management actions validates those actions.
- *Employee results:* We have articulated a simple formula for employee results: competence × commitment × contribution. Leaders must enable employee results in all three areas. Employee competence means that the individual has the skills to do the job. Commitment or engagement is about investing discretionary energy to do what it takes to get things done. Contribution is about finding meaning in work.

Investor Results: Why the Bottom Line Isn't (or How Leaders Add Value)

We began with a very simple question: "Which of the four result areas are senior executives most interested in?" With a few notable exceptions, senior executives tend to be interested in what investors want because it aligns with the executives' personal interests and because it sustains the longevity of the firm. So we began to read and ask questions about how market value was derived. Pretty soon we were reading the work of Baruch Lev, an economist at New York University who was the world's expert on intangibles. At about this time, we felt as though our approach to leadership was going in a very different direction than what we knew our colleagues were studying, and we were excited about what we were learning.

Since 1990, financial results have played a decreasing role in market value, so that across industries, by 2008, market value was half earnings and the other half intangibles (figure 9-2). Intangibles are the factors that give investors confidence in the future of your company versus other competitors in the same industry. These intangibles determine why two companies in the same industry with similar earnings might have vastly different market values. We synthesized a number of studies on intangibles into an architecture for intangibles that explains how leaders increase confidence in future earnings (figure 9-3).

These intangibles define what leaders must do to build capabilities that investors value. We found that intangibles exist in both up and down markets:

- Keep our promises: The organization has a track record of delivering earnings in a consistent manner.
- Create a clear, compelling strategy: There is a shared direction with which we will win in our industry.
- Align core competencies: We have developed targeted core competencies that are consistent with our strategic direction.
- Enable organization capabilities: We have distinct social capabilities that allow us to win through our people and organization.

Figure 9-2. Financial Results and a Company's Market Value

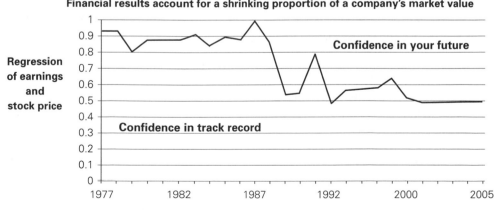

127

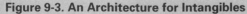

Figure 9-3. An Architecture for Intangibles

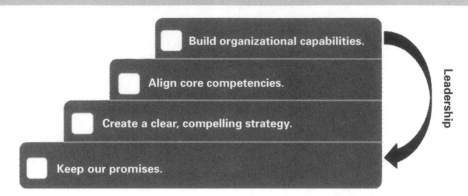

Organization Results: Capitalizing on Capabilities

About a year after the publication of *How Leaders Build Value,* we published an article, "Capitalizing on Capabilities" (Ulrich and Smallwood 2004), that defined, identified, and operationalized organization capabilities. Organization capabilities are the fourth level of the architecture for intangibles. We had a fondness for these issues because we realized that organization capabilities are the deliverables of strategic HR and because they have a direct line of sight to improving market value. Leaders at companies like GE, Singapore Airlines, P&G, and many others discovered how to increase investor confidence by building capabilities of leadership, talent, culture, and customer connection. In this work, we suggested that once leaders have defined strategy, they should create organization capabilities that enable and sustain that strategy. These capabilities outlast any individual leader, management event, or HR practice.

In particular, we wanted to examine internal organization capabilities from the outside/in. For example, HR at Intercontinental Hotels sponsored an "Organization (or intangibles) Audit," in which they solicited feedback from not only employees and leaders but also franchisers, key customers, analysts, and institutional investors. The process of obtaining this organization-level feedback and determining how to act on it was new ground. The results spoke for themselves—Intercontinental fought off a hostile takeover and was able to convince analysts that it should not continue cost cutting but invest in customer service.

We continue to reflect on the capabilities organizations have required to achieve sustainable success. In our recent writing, we have added to our original list the capabilities of simplification, social responsibility, and managing risk. When capabilities integrate diverse HR practices and when they are linked to customer expectations, they build long-term sustainability.

Customer Results: The Leadership Brand

As we turned to the customer results, we focused on the importance of a brand that distinguishes a firm by making and acting on promises to customers. We liked the metaphor of brand because it is so clearly tied to business results. As a marketing concept, brand starts with the customers. Traditionally individual competencies for leadership are defined exclusively inside the company by interviewing high- versus low-performing leaders and then linking the identified competencies to strategy execution.

The more we started with firm brand and the identity of the firm in the mind of the customer then worked to identify leadership behaviors consistent with that external brand, the more we were sure that we had struck gold. We captured our thinking with two conceptual shifts:

1. individual (focus on the leader as a person) versus organizational (focus on leadership as a capability)
2. inside the firm (focus on what happens inside the person or the firm) versus outside the firm (focus on customer and investor expectations.)

These two shifts are shown in figure 9-4.

- Competent leaders: As we've pointed out before, this is where most companies spend their time and it's an important quadrant, trying to determine the knowledge and skills of the individual leader:
- Leadership systems: Aligning selection, development, compensation, and retention systems so integrated and helpful to leaders.
- Celebrity leaders: Famous leaders who are known to customers and investors help by drawing attention to the firm—think Steve Jobs or Bill Gates.

Figure 9-4. Conceptual Shifts

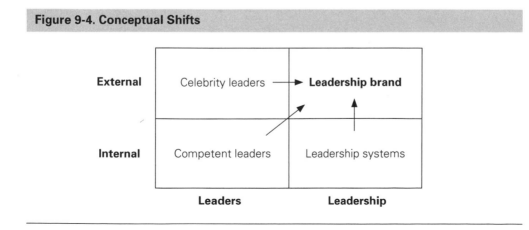

- The leadership brand: Leaders at every level who are recognized both by employees as well as customers and investors for their ability to deliver results in a manner consistent with the firm's brand identity. Confidence in the future drives the price; earnings multiply and a higher market value results.

The leadership brand is created when external customer expectations are translated into internal leadership behaviors so that leaders ensure that employees deliver the desired customer experience whenever they touch the customer. To do this, the firm must not only build good individual leaders but must also develop leadership as an organization capability, recognized inside the firm and also by the market (figure 9-5).

An early adopter of these ideas was a global financial company, which identified three elements describing its desired firm brand:

- effective collaboration
- prudent innovation
- disciplined execution.

This perspective guides HR practices and leadership development initiatives. HR practices such as selection, development, performance management, and retention must all be integrated with effective collaboration, prudent innovation, and disciplined execution. As action learning projects are identified for emerging leaders, they are also structured to deliver the firm brand elements:

- Effective collaboration: Each project will be sponsored by a member of the administration committee and staffed by two to three participants in the cohort. In

Figure 9-5. The Relationship Among Customer Experience, Firm Brand, and Employee Actions

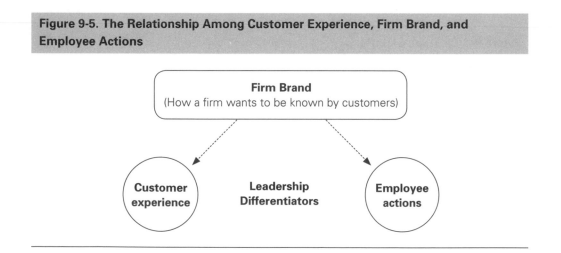

this way, collaboration occurs among the people on the project and between the project team and senior executives. In addition, projects are identified that cross departments to ensure collaboration across organization boundaries.

- Prudent innovation: This cultural capability can be developed by scoping the project so that it delivers a level of impact on the numerator or the denominator, for example, a $150,000 impact.
- Disciplined execution: Tight time frames ensure disciplined execution. Therefore, each project must be completed in eight, 10, or 12 weeks. Each project must also be measured for impact and a short white paper written that describes what the project intended to accomplish and key learning by the team. This information is made available to future cohorts.

In our consulting practice and in our research with Hewitt on Top Companies for Leaders (published by *Fortune* every two years), we discovered that the leadership brand may be created through the six integrated steps shown in figure 9-6. We attempted to link customer expectations to leadership actions so that employees can see a line of sight from what they did to what customers expect.

Figure 9-6. Architecture to Build the Leadership Brand

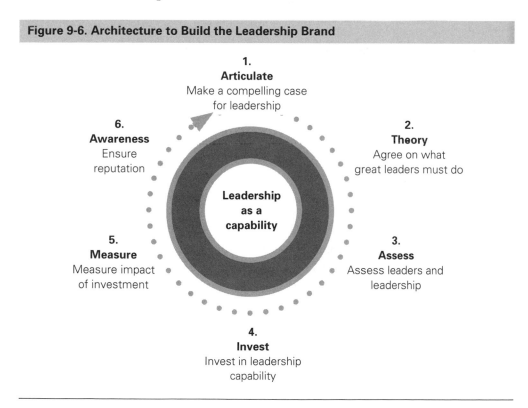

1. Articulate
Make a compelling case for leadership

2. Theory
Agree on what great leaders must do

3. Assess
Assess leaders and leadership

4. Invest
Invest in leadership capability

5. Measure
Measure impact of investment

6. Awareness
Ensure reputation

Leadership as a capability

Employee Results: Managing Talent and Abundance

We have written indirectly about employee results by helping frame the ways in which the HR function can deliver value (Ulrich and Smallwood 2005). When HR departments, practices, and professionals align their work with the goals of the company and with the preferences of customers, HR builds employee commitment.

We are currently working to further understand employee results in two ways. First, we have synthesized the key insights that general managers should know about talent. To do this, we have created a "talent menu" of 10 things that a general manager needs to understand to build better talent. These include defining, assessing, and investing in talent, as well as managing diversity, matching people and position, and measuring talent. Second, we are working to further clarify how people create meaning at work. Though employees may be competent (able to do their job) and committed (willing to work hard), when they also feel a sense of making a contribution or creating meaning, they are more productive. We call this "creating the abundant organization" and draw insights into this phenomenon from multiple disciplines like positive psychology, demographics, high-performing teams, commitment, and social responsibility; see *The Why of Work* (Ulrich and Ulrich 2010).

We clearly believe employee results matter and deserve attention, but we have focused on leadership for achieving investor, organization, and customer results.

The Leadership Code: Back to the Basics

During 2008, we realized that we really had not affected how the majority of firms pursued leadership development. Rather than fight this tide, we decided to do integrative and synthesizing research on attributes that would allow leadership practitioners to move on and join us in our quest to integrate attributes with results.

Faced with the incredible volume of information about leadership, we asked our colleague Kate Sweetman to join us and then turned to recognized experts in the field who had already spent years sifting through the evidence and developing their own theories. These thought leaders had each published a theory of leadership based on a long history of leadership research and empirical assessments of what makes effective leadership. Collectively, they have written more than 50 books on leadership and performed well over two million leadership 360-degree assessments. They are the "thought leaders" of this field. In our discussions with them, we focused on two simple questions whose answers had always been elusive:

- What percentage of effective leadership is basically the same?
- If there are common rules that all leaders must master, what are they?

We wanted to understand if an effective leader at, say, Wal-Mart in any ways resembles an effective leader at Virgin Airlines. Does an effective leader in a bootstrapping nongovernmental organization in any way resemble an effective leader at the famously bureaucratic United Nations? Does an effective leader in an emerging market resemble an effective leader in a mature market? Does an effective leader in organized crime in any way resemble an effective leader in organized religion? Does an effective leader in a Swiss pharmaceutical company share any underlying characteristics with an effective leader at Google?

To the first question, the experts' answers varied as they estimated that somewhere in the range of 50 to 85 percent of leadership characteristics were shared across all effective leaders. The range is fairly broad, to be sure, but consistent. From the body of interviews we conducted, we concluded that 60 to 70 percent of leadership effectiveness would be contained in a leadership code—if we could crack it. Synthesizing the data, the interviews, and our own research and experience, a framework emerged that we simply call the Leadership Code.

In an effort to create a useful visual, we have mapped out two dimensions (time and focus) and placed what we are calling personal proficiency (self-management) at the center as an underlying support for the other two. Figure 9-7 synthesizes the Leadership Code and states the five rules of leadership that capture leadership DNA. These five rules can be readily applied to any group of leaders. Let's briefly look at each.

Rule 1: Shape the future. This rule is embodied in the strategist dimension of the leader. Strategists answer the question "Where are we going?" and make sure that those around

Figure 9-7. The Leadership Code

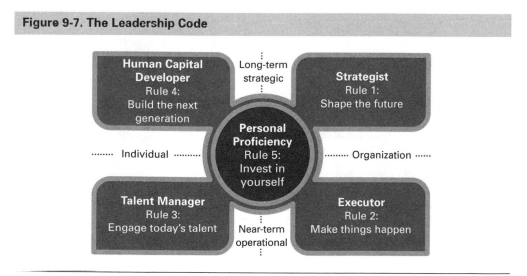

them understand the direction as well. They not only envision but also can create a future. They figure out where the organization needs to go to succeed, they test these ideas pragmatically against current resources (money, people, organizational capabilities), and they work with others to figure out how to get from the present to the desired future. Strategists have a point of view about the future and are able to position their organization to create and respond to that future. The rules for strategists are about creating, defining, and delivering principles of what can be.

Rule 2: Make things happen. Turn what you know into what you do. The executor dimension of the leader focuses on the question "How will we make sure we get to where we are going?" Executors translate strategy into action. Executors understand how to make change happy, to assign accountability, to know which key decisions to make and which to delegate, and to make sure that teams work well together. They keep promises to multiple stakeholders. Executors make things happen, and they put the systems in place for others to do the same. The rules for executors center on the disciplines for getting things done and the technical expertise to get the right things done right.

Rule 3: Engage today's talent. Leaders who optimize talent today answer the question "Who goes with us on our business journey?" Talent managers know how to identify, build, and engage talent to get results now. Talent managers identify what skills are required, draw talent to their organizations, engage them, communicate extensively, and ensure that employees turn in their best efforts. Talent managers generate intense personal, professional, and organizational loyalty. The rules for talent managers center on resolutions that help people develop themselves for the good of the organization.

Rule 4: Build the next generation. Leaders who are human capital developers answer the question "Who stays and sustains the organization for the next generation?" Talent managers ensure shorter-term results through people, while human capital developers ensure that the organization has the longer-term competencies required for future strategic success. Just as good parents invest in helping their children succeed, human capital developers help future leaders become successful. These developers, throughout the organization, build a workforce plan focused on future talent, understand how to develop the future talent, and help employees see their future careers within the company. These developers ensure that the organization will outlive any single individual. And these developers instill rules that demonstrate a pledge to build the next generation of talent.

Rule 5: Invest in yourself. At the heart of the Leadership Code—literally and figuratively— is personal proficiency. Effective leaders cannot be reduced to what they know and do. Who they are as human beings has everything to do with how much they can accomplish with and through other people. Leaders are learners—from success, failure, assignments, books, classes, people, and life itself. They are passionate about their beliefs and interests, and they expend enormous personal energy and attention on whatever matters to them. Effective leaders inspire loyalty and goodwill in others because they themselves act with integrity and trust. Decisive and impassioned, they are capable of bold and courageous moves. Confident in their ability to deal with situations as they arise, they can tolerate ambiguity.

As we have worked with these five rules of leadership, we have learned enough to make some summary observations:

- All leaders must excel at personal proficiency. Without the foundation of trust and credibility, you cannot ask others to follow you. Though individuals may have different styles (introvert versus extrovert, intuitive versus sensing, and so on), any individual leader must be seen as having personal proficiency to engage followers. This is probably the toughest of the five domains to train, and some individuals are naturally more capable than others.
- Effective leaders have one towering strength. Most successful leaders have at least one of the other four roles in which they excel. Most are personally predisposed to one of the four areas. These are the signature strengths of leaders.
- All leaders must be at least average in their "weaker" leadership domains. It is possible to train someone to learn how to be strategic, execute, manage talent, and develop future talent. There are behaviors and skills that can be identified, developed, and mastered.
- The higher up the organization that the leader rises, the more he or she needs to develop excellence in more than one of the four domains.

It is very bold to say that these five domains synthesize and summarize leadership, but we continue to believe that we have captured the essence of the attributes that effective leaders need.

What's Next?

After a decade, we are more confident than ever about our balanced formula for leadership: attributes × results. This simple formula allows us to organize the theory, research, and practice of leadership. A summary of our publications on leadership is given in figure 9-8.

We know there is more to do. As we look ahead, there are more stakeholders that have results for which leaders can build value. For example, we are interested in communities and how leaders can ensure social responsibility. We're also interested in how investors, venture capitalists, private equity funds, sovereign wealth funds, and others determine quality of leadership during due diligence processes. Our initial research in this area and on global

Figure 9-8. The Formula for Effective Leadership

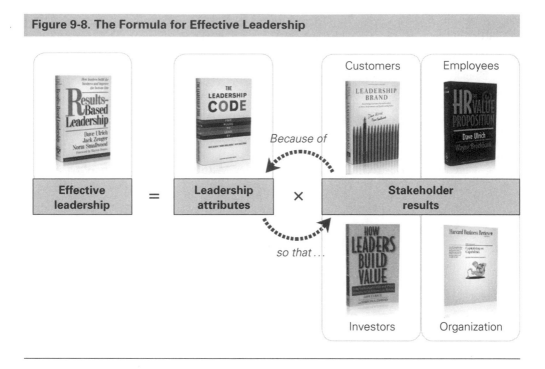

economic conditions suggests that current approaches are relatively primitive. This future work will continue to flesh out the mix of attributes and results that characterizes effective individual leaders and organization leadership capabilities.

As we have done this body of work, we have better defined the importance of both leaders as individuals and leadership as systems, of both attributes of effective leaders and results of effective leadership, and of leaders serving stakeholders both outside and inside their organizations. We have many ideas for continuing to build on this logic over the next decade and hope to use fewer words to have more impact.

Further Reading

Dave Ulrich and Norm Smallwood, "Building Your Leadership Brand," *Harvard Business Review,* July 2007.

————, "Capitalizing Your Capabilities," *Harvard Business Review,* June 2004.

————, *Leadership Brand: Developing Customer-Focused Leaders to Drive Performance and Build Lasting Value.* Boston: Harvard Business Press, 2007.

————, *The Leadership Code: Five Rules to Lead By.* Boston: Harvard Business Press, 2008.

————, *Why the Bottom Line Isn't.* New York: John Wiley & Sons, 2003.

Dave Ulrich and Wendy Ulrich, *The Why of Work: How Great Leaders Build Abundant Organizations That Win.* New York: McGraw-Hill, 2010.

Dave Ulrich, Jack Zenger, and Norm Smallwood, *Results-Based Leadership.* Boston: Harvard Business Press, 1999.

References

Ulrich, Dave, and Norm Smallwood. 2003. *Why the Bottom Line Isn't: How to Build Value Through People and Organization.* New York: John Wiley & Sons.

————. 2004. Capitalizing On Capabilities. *Harvard Business Review,* June.

————. 2005. *The HR Value Proposition.* Boston: Harvard Business Press.

————. 2007. *Leadership Brand: Developing Customer-Focused Leaders to Drive Performance and Build Lasting Value.* Boston: Harvard Business Press.

————. 2008. *The Leadership Code: Five Rules to Lead By.* Boston: Harvard Business Press.

Ulrich, Dave, and Wendy Ulrich. 2010. *The Why of Work: How Great Leaders Build Abundant Organizations That Win.* New York: McGraw-Hill.

Ulrich, Dave Jack Zenger, and Norm Smallwood. 1999. *Results-Based Leadership.* Boston: Harvard Business Press.

About the Authors

Dave Ulrich is as a professor of business at the University of Michigan and a partner in the RBL Group, a consulting firm focused on helping organizations and leaders deliver value. He studies how organizations build capabilities of speed, learning, collaboration, accountability, talent, and leadership by leveraging human resources. He has helped generate award-winning databases that assess alignment between strategies, human resource practices, and human resources competencies. He has published more than 100 articles and book chapters and 22 books. He has won numerous lifetime achievement awards and has consulted with more than half the *Fortune* 200 companies.

Norm Smallwood is a recognized authority on developing businesses and how their leaders can deliver results and increase value. His current research centers on increasing business value by building organization, strategic human resources, and leadership capabilities that have a measurable impact on market value. He is cofounder, with Dave Ulrich, of the RBL Group. He has coauthored six books and hundreds of articles, book chapters, and newspaper columns. For several years, *Leadership Excellence* has ranked him one of the Top 100 Global Voices in Leadership.

Chapter 10

Engaging and Retaining Talented People in Any Economy

Beverly Kaye and Sharon Jordan-Evans

In This Chapter

- Why engaging and retaining talented people should be a perennial effort, no matter what the economy.

- How leaders can best initiate an engagement and retention process.

- Tried-and-true strategies for engaging and retaining talent.

Whether the economy is good or bad, a leader's most talented people always have choices about where they work. Will they choose to stay with your organization? Effective efforts to engage and retain talent shouldn't be turned on and off, syncing to the latest economic blip and the corresponding concern about keeping talent. They work best when they are authentic and perennial, when you clearly believe in them and demonstrate it daily in your actions toward the people you want on your team.

As a leader at any level, you have phenomenal clout and responsibility in the ongoing race for engaged, productive talent. To help you win this race, we've identified 26 strategies for

---

This chapter is adapted from *Love 'Em or Lose 'Em: Getting Good People to Stay*, 4th edition, by Beverly Kaye and Sharon Jordan-Evans. Copyright © Beverly Kaye and Sharon Jordan-Evans. All rights reserved. Used with permission.

creating and maintaining an effective talent engagement and retention process (please note that because this chapter is an excerpt, not all strategies will appear here). In this chapter, we give an overview of all these strategies and then provide the details for just a few to further illustrate how this process really works. And best yet, we provide hands-on tips that you can start using immediately.

Hot Economy or Not

"It's a recession. My employees aren't going *anywhere.*" Have you ever heard complacent leaders say something like this? Have you said it? Don't be so sure it's true. And when the economy's lights come back on (as they always do), many talented, overworked, demoralized employees seek—and find—greener pastures. Dr. Phil, television's popular psychologist, would say to those complacent leaders, "So how did that work for you?" Not so well.

Talent is everything. You've heard it before. Do you believe it? Is it true in your field? Your workplace? One executive said this about a recent acquisition: "We all have access to technology. We all have access to money. The only differentiator is the people. We paid $7 billion for the people [in the firm we acquired] and what we hope they'll be able to create for and with us in the future."

Talent loss also costs a lot. Experts agree that the cost of replacing a talented employee can easily run one to two times his or her annual salary. And the cost is even greater (four to five times an annual salary) to replace platinum workers, those with specialized, hard-to-find skills.

What's your experience? Have you ever lost a key employee—a solid contributor, someone you really could not afford to lose, but who left anyway? How many times have you said:

- "If I'd only known."
- "Why didn't I see that coming?"
- "The answer was easy. I could have fixed that."
- "Why didn't I ask?"

And what about employees' engagement? Some talented employees could do worse than leave you. They might mentally and emotionally "quit" while they physically stay. Thus, they might withdraw their discretionary effort—the effort beyond the call of duty that you need for your team to succeed. Gallup, Towers Perrin, and other pollsters concur that more than 50 percent of employees are not engaged and that 20 percent are so disengaged that they poison the workplace (Gallup 2010; Towers Watson 2010). With a disengaged employee, you're better off when he or she calls in sick. The cost of disengagement to organizations in the United States alone has been estimated at $350 billion a year. What is it costing you?

The Buck Stops with Leaders

The good news is that employee engagement and retention are strongly correlated. The work that engages talented employees likewise encourages them to stay—at least a little while longer. And many of these "stay factors" can be strongly influenced by leaders. Successful leaders—those who engage and retain good people—thus have a talent-focused mindset. And they maintain this mindset through economic highs and lows.

Have you ever wondered what will actually keep the most talented people on your team and keep them engaged while they're on it? We've wondered, and we've asked. In fact, we've asked more than 17,000 people why they stayed with their organizations for a while. In descending order of frequency of response, here is what they said (note: 91 percent of respondents listed at least one of the first two items among their top reasons for staying):

1. exciting work and challenge
2. career growth, learning, and development
3. working with great people
4. fair pay
5. supportive management/good boss
6. being recognized, valued, and respected
7. benefits
8. meaningful work and making a difference
9. pride in the organization, its mission, and its product
10. great work environment and culture
11. autonomy, creativity, and sense of control
12. flexibility: work hours, dress, and so on
13. location
14. job security and stability
15. diverse, changing work assignments
16. fun on the job
17. being part of a team
18. responsibility
19. loyalty, commitment to the organization or co-workers
20. inspiring leadership.

How many of these "stay factors" can you, as a leader, influence? Probably quite a few.

Where Should You Start?

Although we do see commonality of response regarding the stay factors listed above, we also see great diversity of responses. Thus, while one person wants career growth, another will not be engaged if the mission or product of the organization isn't in sync with his or her values. Yet another person insists on fun and flexibility at work. You won't know what your treasured employees really want unless you ask. Conduct a "stay interview" with every employee you hope to keep.

Imagine this. Your boss calls you in and says:

> I probably haven't told you this often enough, but you are important to this team and to me. I can't imagine losing you. I know we've been through a rough time lately, and I want you to know how much I appreciate all you've done and how you've done it. I'd like you to know that I want you to hang in here. I'd like to know what you want next. What do you want to learn? What career goals are you thinking about? What can I do to help you reach those goals? I'd like to know what will keep you here. And I'd like to know what could entice you away.

Has a manager ever held this kind of interview with you? In the seminars we conduct, when we ask this question, very few hands go up. When we ask those few people how it felt, we hear, "Good, Great, I felt important and valued." One person said, "It felt a little late—it was in the exit interview." Everyone laughed at the irony—leaders often find out what their most treasured talented people really wanted as they exit the organization.

Why don't leaders (including you) conduct stay interviews? Usually they don't ask because of *fear*.

What If You Can't Give Talented Employees What They Want?

Some leaders don't hold stay interviews because they fear they won't be able to deliver on the request. That is particularly true during economic downturns and associated belt-tightening. If you think you can't deliver on employees' requests, follow these four steps:

1. Tell them (again) how much you value them—for example, "You're worth that to me and more."
2. Tell the truth about the obstacles you face—for example, pay freeze, project closing down.
3. Show you care enough about them to look into it—for example, "I hear your request. Let me look into it, and let's meet again next Friday to talk about possibilities." (If not now, then when? If not this, then what?)

4. Ask "What else?" Research shows clearly that people want more from work than just a paycheck. When you ask the question "What else?" we guarantee you'll be told about at least one thing your talented employees want that you can supply.

When you're bold enough to hold stay interviews with the talented employees you hope will remain on your team and produce for you, two things will happen. First, these employees will feel great that you cared enough to ask. And second, you'll collect the information you need to take action—to customize your employee engagement and retention efforts for each unique individual.

And remember: You don't have to have all the answers. Ask your employee to think about how they could make their request work—for you, teammates, the organization, and for him or her. Brainstorm possibilities and create a plan together. Try it out, then fine-tune it until it works.

A manager said to us, "If I tried this 'stay interview' thing, my employees would fall over in a dead faint. I don't even say 'hi' in the hallway." We said, "You might want to ease into this then. Start with 'hi' in the hallway." So if you need to ease into it, that's OK, but don't wait too long.

Engagement and Retention: As Easy as A-B-C—and A to Z

After the stay interview, you'll know more about what will keep your talented people engaged and on your team. Then it's time to act and to customize your efforts for each employee, based on his or her unique wants and needs. Our stay factor research led to 26 strategies—coded to the alphabet (in the following figures, note the large letters to the left of each item; because this is an excerpt, not all 26 strategies appear)—that will help you. These strategies are clustered in three areas: development and growth, management style, and work environment. The figures and summaries that follow will give you a good idea of the strategies that fall in a particular cluster. Then, for each cluster, we provide sidebars giving an example of one strategy and the engagement actions you could take, starting tomorrow.

The Development and Growth Cluster

Successful leaders start off by doing a great job of selecting people who fit well into the organization (figure 10-1). Then they continuously look for ways to enrich and enliven their employees' work and to support their growth. They uncover possibilities to do more of what people love to do. They link their talent to other people—to mentors, feedback providers, leaders up the ladder, and colleagues in other departments. They help their employees see

Figure 10-1. Encouraging Development and Growth

multiple options for career growth, and they serve as mentors in the strongest sense of the word. Employees who are learning and growing are less likely to search for greener grass. For an example, see the sidebar, "Enriching and Energizing the Job."

If you help employees enrich their jobs, you can benefit them, their teams, and the entire organization. Stay alert to enrichment opportunities for all your employees. Encourage them to suggest ways to enrich their own jobs. And watch their "job EKGs" spike.

The Management Style Cluster

Talent-focused leaders have a management style that breeds loyalty (figure 10-2). They are truth tellers and feedback providers. Preserving the dignity of others greatly matters to them. They respect differences and value diversity. These leaders also tend to be great listeners. They think outside the box and question the rules in support of talented people and their needs. They give power and the spotlight to others without a second thought, and they look for creative ways to reward and recognize talent. These leaders watch their own behaviors when under stress. They don't take out their bad moods on their team. Employees have been known to leave money on the table to stay with a leader they admire. For an example, see the sidebar, "Jerk—Don't Be One."

If you believe (or find out) that you often exhibit the jerk-like behaviors described in the sidebar, decide to change. Get feedback, some coaching, and then more feedback to ensure

Enriching and Energizing the Job

What if you learned in the stay interview with a key employee that he's feeling a bit bored? That his "job EKG" has gone flat? Did you know that your most valued employees are the most likely to suffer this sense of job discontent? By definition, they are savvy, creative, self-propelled, and energetic. They need stimulating work, opportunities for personal challenge and growth, and a contributing stake in the organizational action.

Plenty of job enrichment possibilities are in your control. And most will cost you little or nothing to implement. This means you can use them to engage and retain your talent during both good times and bad. Here are some techniques that work if you're careful to match them with individual wants and needs:

- *Form teams:* Self-directed work groups can make a lot of their own decisions. They can redistribute work, so that team members learn more, have more variety, and follow more projects through to completion.
- *Touch the client:* For example, a computer systems troubleshooter might be more effective knowing the needs of real people and units rather than responding only to problems as they occur. Assign one troubleshooter to one department, and make him or her accountable for the computer system. Give him or her a client, which can be inside or outside the organization. It's amazing how many employees never see their clients.
- *Rotate assignments:* New responsibilities can help an employee feel challenged and valued. Employees can acquire important new skills that add depth to the workforce. Do rotational assignments sound like chaos? Suggest the idea, and let your employees propose the "who" and "how" part; you'll be surprised at their expertise in making it happen smoothly.
- *Increase feedback:* Do more than annual reviews. Find ways to develop peer review and client review opportunities. Employees want to know about their performance, and continual feedback allows them to be their own quality control agents.
- *Establish participation opportunities:* Employees are empowered and motivated when they take part in decisions that have an impact on their work, such as budget and hiring decisions, or ways to organize work and schedules. Involvement allows employees to see the big picture and make a contribution they find meaningful.
- *Nurture creativity:* Untapped creativity dwindles. If employees rarely think for themselves, they simply go through the paces, undermotivated and disengaged. You can help by asking employees for creative ideas and rewarding them, by giving them the freedom and resources to create, and by challenging them with new assignments, tasks, and learning.
- *Teach someone:* Teaching another person is motivational for many. If an employee has a particular niche or specialty and enjoys passing this knowledge on, you have a perfect win–win.

Figure 10-2. The Management Style of Talent-Focused Leaders

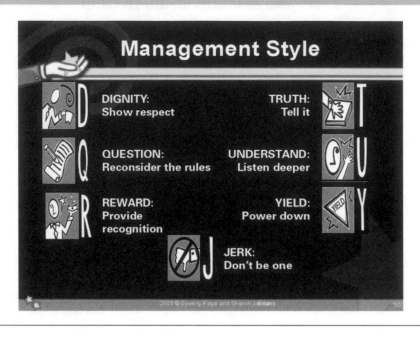

you're heading in the right direction. Talented employees today simply will not work for a jerk—at least not for long. They'll disengage or depart. Changing jerk-like behaviors may be the most important action you can take to keep talented people on your team.

The Work Environment Cluster

Great leaders create a work environment that people love (figure 10-4). They support fun in the workplace, encourage wellness, and create a guilt-free departure at the end of the day or for a well-deserved vacation. They assign work according to employees' passions, and they show they care about their employees' private lives (without prying). These leaders communicate often and honestly with their people, and they strive to align their values with

> *"We spend a lot of time teaching leaders what to do. We don't spend enough time teaching leaders what to stop. Half the leaders I have met don't need to learn what to do. They need to learn what to stop."*
>
> —Management expert Peter Drucker, quoted by Marshall Goldsmith in *What Got You Here Won't Get You There,* 2007

Jerk—Don't Be One

Do you know anyone who should be wearing the shirt shown in figure 10-3? You know, the person who occasionally exhibits jerk-like behaviors? People cautioned us not to write about this topic, or at least not to use this title. But to avoid this topic is to avoid discussing a primary reason why people leave their jobs. If employees don't like their bosses, they will leave even when they are well paid, receive recognition, and have a chance to learn and grow. In fact, disliking the boss is one of the top causes of talent loss.

Figure 10-3. The Shirt of a Jerk

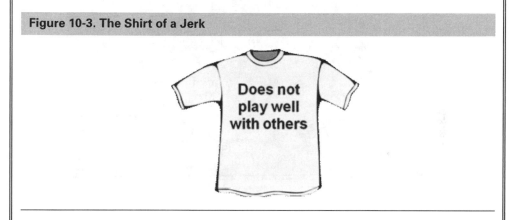

We asked dozens of people, "What do jerks act like or look like?" (The book and movie *The Devil Wears Prada* certainly portrayed some of the worst of these behaviors, but our research found many more.) Here is a subset of the 50 jerk-like behaviors we've uncovered:

- Being intimidating.
- Slamming doors, yelling.
- Withholding praise.
- Belittling.
- Acting superior, smarter.
- Withholding information.
- Acting arrogant.
- Stealing credit for the spotlight.
- Not listening.
- Demanding perfection.
- Acting sexist or racist.
- Acting above the rules.
- Humiliating or embarrassing.
- Blaming.
- Betraying trust.
- Having "sloppy" moods.
- Motivating by fear.
- Setting impossible deadlines.
- Not caring.
- Breaking promises.
- Distrusting.
- Micromanaging.

Do you know anyone who exhibited any of those behaviors? And what about you? Do you ever accidentally exhibit any? How would you know if you were the jerk at work?

Show the jerk checklist to a good friend at work. Ask if you ever exhibit any of these behaviors. (If you don't have any friends at work, there's a clue for your clue bag.) Ask family members to give you insight as well. If others agree that you often exhibit more than one or two of those behaviors, you are at high risk for losing talent. Jerk-like behaviors are so damaging that even one or two can negate all your other strengths as a boss.

Figure 10-4. The Work Environment of Great Leaders

their work. They give employees the freedom to work in their own creative ways, the space to be self-directed, and the support to think in new ways. Employees find it difficult to leave a work environment they love. For an example, see the sidebar, "How to Give Space."

Last Thoughts

Allowing job sharing, flextime, telecommuting, or someone to work on the lawn on a laptop is not pampering. As the example described in the last sidebar shows, there are ways to meet your business goals. This means listening to what people want, going to bat for their

---

How to Give Space

Anyone who has raised a teenager (or remembers being one) knows the phrase "give me some space." Someone who feels fenced in, overcontrolled, or frustrated by his or her lack of power over his or her own situation usually says it.

Think about the last boss you had who dictated your every move, held stringently to the policy manual, or was never open to new ways of doing anything. How long did you stay in that job? (We hope you are not there now.) That boss didn't understand that he or she needed to give you some space.

How space friendly are you as a leader? Imagine that your talented people come to you with this array of strange requests:

- I want to come in and leave a half hour earlier three days a week.
- I want to complete this task in a brand new way.
- I want to wear casual clothes to work.
- I want to put a team together to complete this task.
- I want to take six weeks off (without pay) to build my home.
- I want to put my vacation pictures on my wall.
- I want to bring my baby to work for a while.
- I want to bring my dog when I work Saturdays.
- I want to complete the first five steps of this project before you review it with me.
- I want to learn that skill from a mentor instead of the class you recommended.

To which of these would you say, "Sure, no problem?" To which would you say, "Hmmm, let me look into that and see what we can do?" And to which might you say, "No way. We've never done that—or—the policy manual forbids that, or if I give it to you I'll have to give it to everyone?"

There's a story behind every one of these requests—a story about the managers who collaborated with the requesters, got creative, and found a way to make it work (sometimes against all odds). And there's a happy ending to the stories. The managers' openness and support for employees' needs created work environments that people loved. Employees worked harder and stayed longer in those workplaces. Today's workers expect space—flexibility, balance, autonomy, and so on—in fact, many Generation X and Generation Y workers will select or leave a workplace based on this factor alone.

Some leaders worry about fairness. We hear, "How do I give one employee time off on Friday afternoon and not give it to everyone?" But being fair does not mean treating everyone identically. (Do you have more than one child? If so, do you give them all identical holiday gifts? Probably not.)

The answer is "mass customization"—sounds like an oxymoron, doesn't it?—which offers a new kind of institutional fairness. The workforce is more differentiated, and one policy simply does not fit all. (Who said management was easy?) Listen to your talented employees' requests, and brainstorm with them to create innovative solutions that are fair, both to them and to their hard-working, talented teammates—whom you also want to keep.

Other leaders worry that being flexible means they'll lose control or employees will goof off, take advantage, not deliver. If you manage by objectives, you'll have much more room to give your talent some space.

One leader said, "I feel like you're suggesting I give, give, give. What do I get, get, get?" We said, "You'll get engaged, productive employees who'll stick around and do their best work for you." That's the quid pro quo.

> *"Of course, there's a catch. Sure, you can take Friday off to train for the Ironman Triathlon or to attend your kid's soccer match. Just make sure you do your job—and figure out how to do it better than anyone else. With freedom and flexibility come responsibility and accountability—lots of it."*
>
> —Paula Lawlor, MediHealth Outsourcing

needs, and ultimately giving them options and opportunities to do things differently. And these same kinds of considerations for your employees apply to all the other strategies we've suggested in this chapter.

In exploring the example of giving space, you can learn about doing several things: to truly listen to the unique requests your employees bring you, to ask them to provide ideas for how a particular change might work—for you, the team, and the organization—and to make an honest attempt to win flexibility and improved working conditions for your people. And again, these same kinds of approaches apply to the other strategies discussed above.

Space to play, have a good time, take breaks, celebrate successes, creatively attack problems—all these make for a retention culture in today's organizations. Likewise, for the other strategies, if you pay attention to your most talented employees' development and growth, style of being managed, and work environment by following the strategies outlined here, your reward will be loyalty and commitment from your best people.

Further Reading

Beverly Kaye and Sharon Jordan-Evans, *Love It, Don't Leave It: 26 Ways to Get What You Want at Work.* San Francisco: Berrett-Koehler, 2003.

J. M. Bardwick, *One Foot Out the Door: How to Combat the Psychological Recession That's Alienating Employees and Hurting American Business.* New York: AMACOM, 2008.

C. Benko and A. Weisberg, *Mass Career Customization: Aligning the Workplace with Today's Nontraditional Workforce.* Boston: Harvard Business School Press, 2007

P. Cappelli, *Talent on Demand: Managing Talent in an Age of Uncertainty.* Boston: Harvard Business Press, 2008.

F. K. Klein, *Giving Notice: Why the Best and Brightest Leave the Workplace and How You Can Help Them Stay.* San Francisco. Jossey-Bass, 2008.

E. E. Lawler, III, *Talent: Making People Your Competitive Advantage.* San Francisco. Jossey-Bass, 2008.

J. Phillips and L. Edwards, *Managing Talent Retention: An ROI Approach.* San Francisco. Pfeiffer, 2009.

References

Gallup. 2010. Employee Engagement: A Leading Indicator of Financial Performance. http://www .gallup.com/consulting/52/Employee-Engagement.aspx.

Kaye, B., and S. Jordan-Evans. 2008. *Love 'Em or Lose 'Em: Getting Good People to Stay.* San Francisco: Berrett-Koehler.

Towers Watson. 2010. The New Employment Deal: How Far, How Fast, and How Enduring. Insights from Towers Watson's 2010 Global Workforce Study. http://www.towerswatson.com/ global-workforce-study.

About the Authors

Beverly Kaye is an internationally recognized authority on career issues and retention and engagement in the workplace. She was named a "Legend" by ASTD. She has also been named by *Leadership Excellence* as one of North America 's 100 top thought leaders. As founder and CEO of Career Systems International and a best-selling author on workplace performance, she has worked with a host of organizations to establish cutting-edge, award-winning talent development solutions. Her first book, *Up Is Not the Only Way* (Davies Black) became a classic, and although it was published in the early 1980s it is still very relevant today. In it, she foresaw the effects that leaner, flatter organizations would have on individual careers and the subsequent need for workers to take charge of their own careers. She also developed systems for leaders and employees to work together to help employees achieve their developmental goals.

Sharon Jordan-Evans, president of the Jordan Evans Group, is a pioneer in the field of employee retention and engagement. She has a master's degree in organization development and is a professionally certified coach. She serves as a speaker for numerous conferences and works with *Fortune* 500 companies such as American Express, Boeing, Disney, Lockheed, Cheesecake Factory, Monster, MTV, PBS, Sony, and Universal Studios. She also serves as a resource for a number of national media, including *Business 2.0, Chief Executive, CIO, Harvard Management Update, Working Woman, Investor's Business Daily, BusinessWeek*, and the *Los Angeles Times*.

Kaye and Jordan-Evans have coauthored two *Wall Street Journal* bestsellers. The first, *Love 'Em or Lose 'Em: Getting Good People to Stay,* is the world's best-selling employee retention book and has been translated into 20 languages. The second, *Love It, Don't Leave It: 26 Ways to Get What You Want at Work,* offers easy-to-implement strategies for increasing job satisfaction and has been translated into 15 languages.

✎ Section II

Leadership Development

What keeps your organization's leaders up at night? Most leaders will tell you that it is a lack of talent, and most specifically the talent—the skills and capabilities—it will take to lead the organization. Does the organization have the talent in the next generation of leaders, the bench strength, to carry out its strategy and meet its goals?

The most critical investment any organization can make is in choosing and developing its future leaders. Some organizations rely on a generic model with the same leadership competencies as every other organization: setting direction, managing change, delivering results, building teams, and inspiring employees. Indeed, these are critical leadership skills—a place to start. But they are just the beginning of a solid leadership development program.

The specific competencies are no secret. Most organizations groom their leaders in these skills. However, successful organizations need more than a list of competencies. Because each organization faces its own challenges, has its own goals, and maintains its own reputation, it seems logical that it also needs to ensure that its leaders have the specific skills and capabilities required to carry out the strategy. The upcoming leaders must deliver a competitive advantage.

The most successful organizations link their leadership development plan to the organization's strategy, its culture, and its vision for the future. The six chapters in this section address the "how" of developing leaders:

- How do you define an effective leadership development strategy?
- How do you identify the right competencies?
- How do you avoid making mistakes with 360-degree feedback?
- How can you use mentoring by other leaders?
- How can you enhance the potential for learning on the job?
- How can you use coaching to change behavior?

In chapter 11, "Leadership Development Strategy," the daughter-father team of Tacy Byham and William Byham present five strategies for individual leadership development and delineate the roles of both the developing leaders and their supervisors.

In chapter 12, "Identifying Real-World Leadership Competencies," Mark David Jones presents his findings from interviews with leaders of successful corporations to show why leadership competencies are important and how to identify competencies connected to corporate culture and the organizational brand.

For chapter 13, "Worst Practices in 360-Degree Assessments: Why Feedback Fails," we are fortunate to have an author with Craig Chappelow's immense experience with 360-degree assessments. Here he takes a how-*not*-to approach, which we hope will help you learn from others' mistakes.

In chapter 14, "Leaders as Mentors and Teachers: Time-Tested Leadership Development Strategies," Edward Betof explains the benefits of using leaders as mentors and teachers of other leaders. You will find that the learning benefits both mentors and learners.

Don't let the simple title of chapter 15, "Learning on the Job," fool you; this chapter by Ellen Van Velsor is filled to overflowing with information about what people learn and how they learn on the job. The chapter tackles the conundrum of why learning from experience can be difficult and what can be done to enhance the potential for learning on the job.

In chapter 16, "Coaching Leaders to Lead," Marshall Goldsmith—who is considered one of the top leadership coaches in America and is certainly one of the most recognized—presents his simple but effective coaching process to assist in encouraging leadership growth.

The topic of this section could easily take up several handbooks—or an encyclopedia's worth! If you want more depth, a great companion to this section is the Center for Creative Leadership's *Handbook of Leadership Development*, edited by Cynthia McCauley and Ellen Van Velsor, who are both authors of chapters in the present handbook.

Chapter 11

Leadership Development Strategy

Tacy M. Byham and William C. Byham

In This Chapter

- Why only a small fraction of leaders take action on their assessment feedback.

- Five practices that define an effective leadership development strategy.

- The roles of the individual leader and his or her supervisor in planning and successfully completing development activities.

- The development activities most appropriate for leaders at different organizational levels.

Successful leadership development is driven by actionable information and individual accountability, but there is often a disconnect between these two requirements. In many organizations, individual leaders are assessed and receive feedback on the basis of their strengths and development areas. Yet surprisingly few leaders act on the feedback they receive by actually pursuing their further development.

This chapter examines the reasons why leaders fail to act on the basis of assessment feedback. In addition, five practices are identified that constitute an effective leadership development strategy whereby individual leaders receive the support they need and are held accountable for their own development.

A talent crisis is looming around the world. Global companies are aware that they need to grow leadership capability—and they need to do it soon—or face being hamstrung in executing their business strategy. Yet awareness of the problem is not translating into progress toward resolving it. Consider these facts:

- 55 percent of CEOs and senior leaders (globally) expect business performance to suffer in the near future due to a lack of leadership capability (DDI and Economist Intelligence Unit 2008).
- 46 percent of leaders around the world did not get the support they needed to be successful in their most recent promotion (transition) (DDI 2008a).
- Leaders report that their most difficult challenge is the need to understand the hurdles at the next level and how to prepare for them (DDI 2008b).

Clearly, organizations need to develop global leadership capability, and they are doing too little. But what should they be doing to be successful? We believe that their actions should be marked by two indispensable requirements: better information and greater accountability. From our work with leading organizations around the world, we have seen firsthand how the use of accurate, predictive information helps drive decision making about who has the talent to succeed in key leadership positions, how to develop leaders faster, and where to deploy these leaders when they are ready to step up. Better information also helps organizations reduce risk and ensure success throughout their entire global leadership pipelines.

But high-quality information is of little value if the use of this information for development is not accompanied by accountability. Strategically, we view the accountability for development on two levels: (1) the organization's leadership development strategy and (2) the individual leader's personal commitment to leadership development activities. The successful development of leaders demands processes on both levels that are well planned and properly executed.

Most high-performing organizations today purport to have a sound process for *organizational leadership development* in place. However, with respect to *individual leadership development,* we believe that while millions of leaders at all organizational levels may make plans to improve their leadership and management skills, relatively few (probably less than 10 percent) actually act to change their behavior, develop skills, overcome personality derailers, or acquire new knowledge and experience to optimize their current performance and prepare for higher-level positions. We believe this poor record is attributable to

- inaccurate determination of development needs—individuals either don't know or don't fully accept their leadership strengths and weaknesses relative to their current or future jobs
- inappropriate prioritization of development needs—leaders don't consider the organizational importance of their development targets
- poor selection of development activities—the most effective development tools are not applied
- poorly conceived and implemented development plans—individuals don't have opportunities to practice their newly developed skills in a timely manner
- lack of emphasis on measuring progress toward, and the achievement of, development goals.

In this chapter, we propose an individual leadership development strategy, defined by five strategic practices, that is, in some regards, radically different from the common strategy used by most organizations. In proposing this strategy, we assume that two common human resources (HR) practices or tools are in place.

The first practice or tool is *success profiles*—well-defined job profiles that describe what is needed to be a successful leader at each organizational level. Organizational leadership development strategists should begin by identifying the three to five business drivers that are most relevant to the organization's strategy and future success. Creating alignment and accountability and forging strategic alliances are examples of business drivers that may resonate with senior leaders. The choice of business drivers will determine the success profiles upon which subsequent assessment measures and development activities will be based. The success profiles, in turn, include job challenges (preparatory experiences) and organization knowledge needed, along with behaviorally defined competencies and important personal attributes (personality factors) that can enable leaders to succeed or cause them to derail.

A success profile represents a complete picture of what's required for an individual to succeed in the target job or role. Unfortunately, most organizations don't take such a holistic view of development targets. In their leadership development programs, they focus only on assessing and developing competencies and a few personal attributes, although they may informally consider the experience and organizational knowledge required for promotions or development.

The second practice or tool is *performance management*—a system that includes evaluations of the competencies important at each organizational level and that accurately measures job performance. As a requirement for the effective use of a performance management system, managers should have been trained to communicate strengths and weaknesses, give explicit examples illustrating both positive and negative behavior, and do so in a timely manner throughout the year.

Strategic Practice 1: Help Individuals Understand and Buy into the Strengths and Weaknesses Revealed in 360-Degree or Assessment Center Feedback

An organization can have sound organizational development approaches and programs, but if individual leaders don't recognize and accept their development needs, then these approaches and programs are wasted. This is why the first thing most organizations do to effectively demonstrate strengths and weaknesses in relation to the full success profile is supplement feedback from the individual leader's immediate manager with feedback from other sources. Assessment measures most used to illuminate elements of the success profile are multi-rater (360-degree) surveys and assessment centers (simulation-based assessments), which often include personality tests.

Multi-Rater (360-Degree) Surveys

Many organizations rely heavily on 360-degree feedback to provide insights into positive and negative areas of current job performance and to convince people of their need to develop. Feedback from a 360-degree survey is a wonderful way for an individual leader to learn how others see him or her on the job, as the individual's manager, peers, and subordinates complete a rating of competencies. As part of this process, the individual also provides a self-rating.

However, less than 10 percent of the people receiving 360-degree feedback actively change their behavior in a positive way and sustain that change for several years (Byham and Weaver 2005). Why? We believe that some are confused by the definitions of the competencies being rated, and they may wonder if the competencies are truly related to important measures of organizational success. Others see their feedback as a report card rather than as a road map for development. Most important, many have difficulty accepting the need for taking action on their 360-degree feedback. Those who hold this view frequently make comments such as

- "All my ratings are in the favorable range. I am just dealing with different degrees of goodness."
- "All my ratings are above average or above the norms presented with the feedback."
- "My average rating is favorable, even if some competencies are low."
- "I've made it to where I am without being proficient in all these competencies, so I don't need to change now."

Or they dismiss the results due to what they perceive as shortcomings in the 360-degree process:

- "I had the wrong raters."
- "The raters don't understand why I do things."

- "I've changed since they rated me."
- "These ratings were influenced by poor morale or other factors outside of my control."

Whether or not 360-degree feedback is accepted depends upon how the output of the survey is communicated. Even the most comprehensive assessment is meaningless unless the person being assessed acknowledges the accuracy and value of the data and willingly recognizes the diagnosed development needs. To work toward making this happen, after the 360-degree evaluation is complete, the subjects (that is, the individual leaders who have been rated) should meet with a skilled person who can explain why the competencies were chosen and why the results are important. (What shouldn't happen is that the subject receives the results, with little or no explanation. Yet even though this can have an adverse impact on the individual's acceptance of the feedback, it's common practice in most organizations today.)

In a well-conducted feedback discussion, the individual leaders are asked to draw connections between the insights from peers and their supervisor and additional feedback they have received on or off the job. These discussions often elicit comments such as "I've heard this before from others" or "My spouse tells me that all the time." These comments amount to the individual's confirmation and acceptance of the 360-degree feedback.

When 360-degree feedback is communicated properly and supported with meaningful discussion, the result is a significant increase in the process's return on investment.

Assessment Center Experience and Personality Inventories

Although a 360-dgree assessment allows leaders to hold a mirror of self-insight up to their performance in their *current* jobs or roles, an assessment center experience foreshadows capabilities for *future* jobs. A typical assessment center for leaders involves component parts such as role-play interactions, email-based judgment items, the development of a strategic plan, an oral presentation, and a personality test. The experience is job-relevant, realistic, and covers a broad range of leadership challenges so that leaders can be observed using their entire repertoire of skills.

Today's assessment centers employ state-of-the-art technology and world-class facilities, ensuring that participants encounter an engaging process that is challenging and developmental from the outset. This degree of process realism contributes to assessment centers producing significantly richer information on candidate strengths and development needs than do 360-degree assessments. Another benefit of this realism is that subjects are more likely to accept feedback from an assessment center than from other assessment methods.

A personality assessment is typically included in a full assessment center experience. Personality characteristics play an important role in enabling those concerned to understand why leaders succeed and why they sometimes fail, despite having strong skills. Traditionally, personality assessments have been seen as a window into the bright side of personality, the dark side of personality, and the values and other factors that motivate individuals. Together, these assessments provide a rich picture of the personal attributes that underlie leadership performance. For example, they can reveal early indicators of whether confidence may veer toward arrogance, whether passion may slide into volatility, or whether highly sociable individuals may become self-promoting. These personality derailers can have significant consequences.

Assessment center feedback must be delivered to the individual leader by a highly skilled internal or external consultant trained in the holistic integration of assessment data. This is because assessment centers are usually designed to evaluate individuals relative to higher-level, future-focused jobs, and also because of the large quantity of information gathered during assessment. The vast majority of the leaders who participate in assessment centers agree that the assessment experience provides personal insights into knowledge, skills, and abilities (95 percent), and serves as a catalyst for change (81 percent; DDI 2003).

A Combination of Data Points Produces the Most Accurate Diagnosis

Generally, the more sources of job-related data (360-degree feedback, assessment center feedback, and so on), the better the accuracy and the higher the likelihood that the individual leader will accept the feedback. Consistent findings across various methodologies lead to increased believability and acceptance. Table 11-1 shows the quantity and quality of information that can be gleaned from common options.

Once the assessment data is effectively communicated and the individual has acknowledged that the feedback is both valid and actionable, he or she should be encouraged to focus development efforts on one strength area to build on and one weakness to shed. After those are completed, two more can be selected.

Table 11-1. Quantity and Quality of Assessment Information Provided by Assessment Methodologies

Assessment Tool	Competencies	Experiences	Knowledge	Personal Attributes
Simulations	XXX			X
Multi-rater (360°) surveys	XX			X
Personality inventories	X			X
Behavior-based interviews	XX	XX	XX	

Note: The Xs denote the quantity and quality of information; the more Xs, the greater the quantity and quality.

Strategic Practice 2: Ensure that Development Goals Have an Impact on Current Job Performance

Research and experience show that strong manager support is the key driver of sustainable leadership development at all levels. This support is critical because most leaders, especially those with high potential, have more on their plates than they can easily handle. As a result, time pressures often make development difficult. If the support of their managers is lacking, the majority of leaders will put off their development activities to the following year—a delay that greatly lessens the likelihood that the development will be completed at all. Considering organizational and group needs when prioritizing development needs is the key to an individual obtaining the support of his or her manager.

When left to their own devices, individual leaders can choose inappropriate development priorities. For example, they may select development targets that are

- too easily achievable, convenient to correct (they know there is a training program available), or socially acceptable (for example, looking to be placed on a project team that includes several peers)
- of particular interest to them but that are not the development targets that would have the greatest impact on their own, their team's, or the organization's performance
- undoable because of competing job demands (they likely will later claim that "work got in the way of my development") or because resources or cooperation from other parts of the organization probably will not be forthcoming.

Managers can remedy these challenges by helping leaders properly view their strengths and weaknesses with respect to the needs of their unit or of the organization (figure 11-1). Such a view leads to more accurate insights into the relative payoffs possible from achieving alternative development goals. Having goals directly related to areas of positive unit or organizational impact will increase the likelihood that more people will have a vested interest in the individual's success. For example, a manager will be less likely to pull a person from a training program or cut off a development opportunity. Hence, rather than work getting in the way of development, good development priorities ensure that work *is* the way to development.

An example would be an individual who has been put in charge of an important company-wide task force, the success of which is an objective on the individual's manager's performance plan (group goal/need). For instance, originally, the individual had chosen to learn French (personal goal/need) as a development priority because the company is French owned. He rightfully thought that knowing how to speak French would be important for his advancement in the company (organizational goal/need). But his manager, knowing

Figure 11-1. Identifying High-Payoff Development Priorities

the importance of the task force and having a vested interest in it succeeding, instead suggested that the individual focus on meeting leadership, a competency identified as a deficiency when the individual went through an assessment center. Because improving meeting leadership skills is critical to the success of the task force, and this success means that the manager will meet his own performance goals, the manager will clear the deck for the individual to get trained in meeting leadership and will point out individuals who are particularly good in this area and assure that the individual will have the time to observe them.

The time available for development will always be limited, so the individual leader's efforts must support those goals that represent the highest payoff for him or her, the group, and the larger organization, and that can ideally be integrated into normal job responsibilities.

Now let's shift the level of our conversation up from the individual's commitment to development to the organization's leadership development strategy. From up here, we see that too often individuals who receive assessment center or 360-degree feedback use the person delivering the feedback (usually an HR professional or someone from outside the organization) as a sounding board for determining development priorities. Though the person communicating the feedback may be extremely competent and willing to help, we believe the best sounding board is the individual leader's manager and that the individual and his or her manager should make development priority decisions together.

The manager's involvement in setting development priorities is critical because the manager is able to

- assist the individual in targeting the competencies, knowledge, experience, and personal attributes that will have the greatest immediate and long-term impact on the individual's career, and the success of his or her group and the organization
- provide growth opportunities (for example, job assignments, membership on a team)
- arrange access to organizational experts, training, or other support
- help the individual execute on his or her development plan
- deliver ongoing feedback on the individual's development and provide coaching as needed
- provide ideas on possible measurements for tracking progress.

Having an HR or training specialist discuss priorities and development plans is certainly better than the individual leader not discussing them with anybody, but it is not an optimal solution.

Strategic Practice 3: Help Leaders Select the Most Efficient and Highest-Impact Development Solutions

Leaders can develop competencies in many different ways, with a combination of methods often proving the most effective approach. Surveys of successful leaders from all organizational levels have shown the value in a combination of development options—a 70/20/10 development mix—for achieving development goals (see figure 11-2; the specific competency or other area of the success profile being developed will dictate a method's appropriateness):

- Seventy percent of development should entail learning from experience—new job assignments, in-place developmental assignments, off-the-job experiences, cross-functional assignments, stretch assignments, and job rotations. Leaders learn most from experience when they have a chance to understand a skill or knowledge area in depth, when it is critical to demonstrate a skill, and when they can practice the skill in a real-world setting.
- Twenty percent of development should include opportunities to learn from others—feedback from mentors, leaders, peers; 360-degree feedback; ongoing, real-time observation and coaching; shared experiences; job shadowing; and networking. Leaders get the most from learning from others when the skill is new or unique and risk of failure is moderate to high. This approach is also beneficial when a person has low confidence and needs encouragement from a more skilled person.

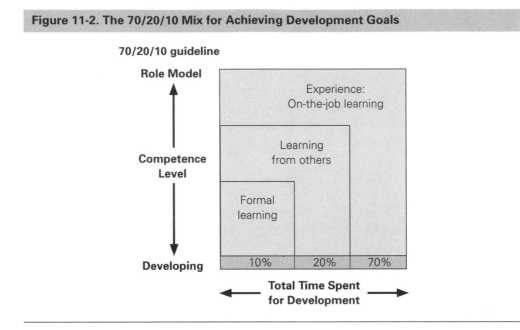

Figure 11-2. The 70/20/10 Mix for Achieving Development Goals

- Ten percent of development should be devoted to attending training sessions—online, web-based, instructor-led, self-study, reading, seminar, or industry-related conferences. Leaders get the most from training sessions when creating or enhancing basic skills or knowledge, or when they are trying to gain cognitive knowledge or a framework from which learning and skill building will occur.

It's also important to consider two other factors when planning high-impact development activities. First, consider the individual leader's preferred learning styles (learning by experiencing, reflecting, thinking, or doing) and his or her motivation to make positive change in a competency or some other target. Second, consider the individual's level within the organization (table 11-2). Formal training is most important for first- to middle-level leaders when they are trying to gain cognitive knowledge or a framework from which learning and skill building will occur on the job. Coaching and key stretch assignments or experiences will need to play a predominant role at senior levels in the organization.

After development goals are prioritized, the logical next step for a leader is to seek help in determining how development will be accomplished. As in prioritizing development goals, usually the best guidance comes from the individual's manager, because the manager is familiar with the individual's job and therefore understands the opportunities to acquire and practice skills. In addition, when the manager is involved, he or she will have even

Table 11-2. Decreasing Rank Orders of Learning Activities by Leader Level

Overall	First/ Middle	Higher/ Senior	Source of Learning
1	4	1	Supervisors at my company
2	1	3	Trial and error
3	2	4	Special work assignments
4	6	2	Co-workers (not including your supervisor) at my company
5	3	5	Observing others
6	7	7	Formal educational experiences
7	8	6	Reading
8	5	9	Formal on-the-job training
9	9	8	Formal training experiences
10	10	10	Professional colleagues at other organizations
11	11	11	Family and friends
12	12	12	Internet or online resources

Note: A rating of 1 = most-valuable experience.

Source: DDI (2007).

more ownership of the individual's development plan. Thus, for instance, when the individual needs to miss some work to accomplish a development objective, the manager will likely understand the situation (maybe the manager even suggested the learning experience) and agree that the development action must take priority.

If an educational effort is involved, such as selecting an appropriate training program, then representatives from HR should also be involved in the discussions. This is because HR, as the entity that designs and implements most leadership development programs, will have specific insights and information about the knowledge or skills that will be imparted by a training program.

In many cases, the prioritization of development objectives and the planning for accomplishing the objectives are handled in the same meeting between the individual leader and his or her manager. But sometimes a second meeting is required. Development planning forms are an invaluable tool for facilitating these meetings and for helping to decide how development will be accomplished.

Strategic Practice 4: Have Individuals Complete a Development Planning Form After Discussion with Their Managers

A story that we've heard told at professional development conferences goes something like this: In the mid-1950s, researchers surveyed graduating students at Yale University and found that only 3 percent had written down clearly defined goals. Twenty years later, the members of that particular class were polled again, and researchers found that the 3 percent who'd had the written goals had accumulated wealth worth more than the other 97 percent combined. As it so happens, this story is untrue (Tabak 2007), but it has become the stuff of urban legend.

Within the realm of what is true, we have actual data suggesting that leaders who craft well-thought-out written development plans are more likely to accomplish their development goals. In 2002 and 2003, Tacy Byham interviewed 79 midlevel leaders from a manufacturing organization a year after they had received development feedback based on several assessment instruments, including an assessment center, personality tests, and a 360-degree survey. Though, anecdotally, most of these leaders reported that the assessment and feedback had been the "most rewarding development experience of their careers," few had made ongoing efforts to correct deficiencies and build on strengths.

Tacy was curious as to whether these individuals completed the recommended individual development plan (IDP) for each goal that was provided as part of their assessment feedback and if that plan made any difference in their development. The results were not encouraging: Only 11 percent of the leaders actually created a written development plan, although the organization expected that they would do so. Most of the others (42 percent) favored a "mental plan" with no actions put in writing. The rest (47 percent) did not follow up on their development at all. Those who completed an IDP were significantly more likely to take development actions and view their development efforts as a success (Byham 2005). This data is amazingly close to a survey by Bersin & Associates (2009), which indicated that 52 percent of managers have development plans but only 8 percent have high-quality plans.

What constitutes a high-quality development plan? Effective plans deal with three issues:

1. *How the skills, knowledge, and competencies will be acquired (if necessary).* What training or coaching will be needed before the individuals can practice or apply the target skills, competencies, and the like? Also, it is important to anticipate and articulate barriers or challenges to success that may arise (for example, not being able to attend a training program, getting pulled out of training due to job demands, not having the time or travel funds to pursue a task force opportunity). Anticipating barriers

or challenges prepares the individual leader to discuss with his or her manager what support or resources will be needed to avoid them.

2. *How the skills or knowledge will be practiced (or applied).* Leaders should enlist the help of their managers in coming up with creative application opportunities. For example, if a leader needs exposure to the organization's international operations but is unable to take a long-term assignment abroad, the individual's manager may provide support by organizing a short-term role in a global initiative, such as the international rollout of a new product.

3. *How learning will be measured.* Progress and outcome measures capture the degree to which leaders are developing new skills. We discuss these below.

An IDP should be completed for each development goal. The best practice is for the manager and the individual to talk through each section of the form during the development planning meeting. The role of the HR person is to facilitate the process with actions such as suggesting how two needs can be grouped under one goal or recommending measurement options. HR's role is not to create or dictate the plan. Instead, the IDP should be a mutually agreed-to plan between the individual and the manager.

Strategic Step 5: Insist That Leaders Set Measurable Development Goals and Review Progress

The last part of an IDP is an agreement on how the plan's progress will be monitored and how it will be determined if the development objectives have been met. This agreement is especially critical if the plan will take months (or even years) to complete. Tentative decisions on how progress will be tracked should be made when the development plan is discussed and agreed to. Often, identifying measurable objectives will serve to firm up the plan and improve its focus on key objectives.

Measurement should occur on both the individual and organizational levels. For the individual, three forms of measurement are important:

1. *Measurement associated with competency or knowledge acquisition (progress measures).* Progress measures capture the degree to which development targets are achieved. They provide quick feedback that aids the individual leader in honing skills or changing behavior. They can cover a wide range of measurement options that fall across two categories: measures of perceptions (for example, feedback from the people who can observe behavior or decisions made by the leader) and short-term operating data (for example, weekly or monthly statistics on business performance that are tied to the individual leader's performance).

2. *Measurements associated with the application of what is developed (outcome measures).* The best outcome measure of the use of a competency or knowledge is the successful completion of a relevant project or assignment. For instance, to develop skills in project management, one might have been given a task demanding the coordination of the work of several groups. Success in carrying out this task would offer clear evidence of the individual's successful application of project management skills.

3. *Measurements associated with continued application of what is developed.* The function of these measurements, which capture the impact on the organization of the individual's ongoing use of a competency or knowledge, is to help maintain focus and motivation to continue applying the new skills or knowledge. These measures will reveal if the individual is slipping back to old, less-effective ways.

For example, some areas to measure that would indicate continued application could include

- the number of leaders promoted internally (measured against status quo)
- the retention of key leaders and/or those with high potential
- time to mastery for defined leadership capabilities at each level.

Key metrics should be defined up front to truly drive the leader and the manager to be accountable for development. Defining key metrics in advance provides assurance that individual leaders will maintain their focus on their development and that their managers will remain committed to helping them.

As illustrated in figure 11-3, research shows that a measurement focus significantly affects the quality of a leadership development strategy.

Conclusion

Today's global organizations need more leadership capabilities, and the key to satisfying this need is doing a better job of developing leaders. Toward this end, both organizations and individual leaders must quit fooling themselves that quick fixes or easy cures will produce results.

Developing leadership and management skills takes time and effort. Too often, people choose training programs that promise a change in attitude or increased personal awareness. But these programs don't build new leadership skills and don't provide opportunities to practice or apply new skills or knowledge. It's like watching a yoga video but never practicing the movements—there is little chance of successfully acquiring the needed development.

Figure 11-3. The Relationship Between Measurement and Leadership Development Quality (percent)

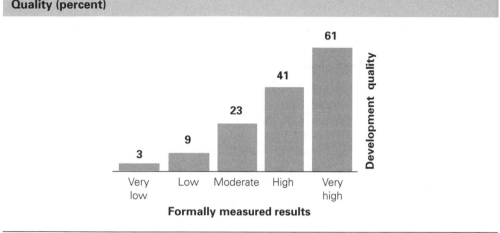

Source: DDI (2009).

To improve, leaders need an accurate diagnosis of their development needs, the opportunity to acquire needed skills or knowledge through training or other means, and on-the-job experiences that offer opportunities to not only apply new skills and knowledge to ensure success, but to also continue to build on them. They need to work with their managers to attain buy-in and ensure they get the support they need to make development happen.

Organizations also need to realize that development is not the job of the HR or training department. Those responsible for these functions can only act as catalysts and coaches. The responsibility for development must rest with the learner and his or her manager to build the knowledge, competencies, and personal attributes needed for success—for the leader, the manager, and the organization.

Further Reading

Ann Barrett and John Beeson, *Developing Business Leaders for 2010.* New York: Conference Board, 2002.

William Byham, *What Now? The Little Guide to Using Your Assessment Center Results to Make Big Things Happen.* Pittsburgh: DDI Press, 2005.

William Byham, Audrey Smith, and Matthew Paese, *Grow Your Own Leaders.* Upper Saddle River, NJ: Financial Times / Prentice Hall, 2002.

Richard Lepsinger and Antoinette D. Lucia, *The Art and Science of 360-Degree Feedback.* Hoboken, NJ: John Wiley & Sons, 2009.

References

Bersin & Associates. 2009. *2009 Talent Management Fact Book: Best Practices and Benchmarks in Talent Management.* Oakland: Bersin & Associates.

Byham, W., and P. Weaver. 2005. *Multisource (360) Feedback That Effects Changes in Leaders' Behavior.* Pittsburgh: Development Dimensions International.

DDI (Development Dimensions International). 2003. *The Impact of DDI Assessment Centers.* Pittsburgh: DDI. (Revised 2007.)

———. 2008a. *Leadership Forecast 2007–2008.* Pittsburgh: DDI.

———. 2008b. *Leaders in Transition: Stepping Up, Not Off.* Pittsburgh: DDI.

———. 2009. *Global Leadership Forecast 2008–2009.* Pittsburgh: DDI. http://www.ddiworld.com/pdf/globalleadershipforecast2008-2009_globalreport_ddi.pdf.

DDI (Development Dimensions International) and Economist Intelligence Unit. 2008. *Growing Global Executive Talent: High Priority, Limited Progress.* Pittsburgh: DDI and Economist Intelligence Unit.

Tabak, Lawrence. 2007. If Your Goal Is a Success, Don't Consult These Gurus. http://www.fastcompany.com/magazine/06/cdu.html.

About the Authors

Tacy Byham, PhD, is a manager in Development Dimensions International's Executive Solutions Group. She provides consulting across organizational strategic talent needs, including talent strategy, talent management, talent assessment, development planning, and executive development. She is currently managing the launch of Business Impact Leadership, a new development system for midlevel leaders that ensures the action-oriented alignment of leaders relative to organizational business imperatives. Her research received the national ASTD Dissertation Award at the International Conference and Expo in 2007.

William C. Byham, PhD, is chairman and CEO of Development Dimensions International. He founded the company 40 years ago to help organizations make better hiring, promotion, and management decisions, and the firm continues to be internationally renowned in human resources consulting. He has forged important innovations in HR that have had an impact on organizations worldwide. As a best-selling author, he continues to write books and articles and deliver speeches on important management advancements and how they are affecting businesses.

Chapter 12

Identifying Real-World Leadership Competencies

Mark David Jones

··· **In This Chapter** ···

▧ Why leadership competencies are important.

▧ How identifying competencies with the right fit is critical for long-term success.

▧ The connection between identifying effective leadership competencies, corporate culture, organizational brand, and financial results.

▧ Implementation tips from renowned, consistently successful organizations.

To effectively implement leadership competencies, it is crucial to have an understanding of what particular leadership abilities are needed by an organization. Once this foundation has been established, the organization can better align, communicate, and implement its guidelines for all operational efforts to achieve excellent results. And the best sources for identifying how highly competent leadership can lead to proven results are those organizations that are consistently producing them. The different industries showcased in this chapter reflect a wide variety of philosophies and tactics for best developing leadership throughout an organization—whether large or small, private or public sector.

Introducing Leadership Competencies

Are you considering identifying leadership competencies as a tool to improve your organizational results? You're not alone. The importance of leadership for the success of any operation cannot be overstated. Most organizations eventually explore this tool to clarify and focus the selection, development, and assessment of their leaders. Unfortunately, most professionals view identifying competencies as some mysterious process—especially when considering tactically implementing them into their business.

There are several challenges when attempting to actually implement leadership competencies. The first is that there are so many definitions of what specifically makes up a competency.

Established leadership talent management firms such as Lominger, Development Dimensions International, and Personal Decisions International have built their corporations on providing large-scale, statistically sound systems for leadership competencies, yet they each have differing approaches: "Organizations sometimes get hung up on the words, and then miss what they really mean" (Crosby 2009).

For the purposes of this chapter, I generically define a competency as the ability to use either knowledge or a skill in the performance of a role. In other words, what must a leader know and be able to do to become successful?

In addition to this definition, there are two types of competencies most commonly accepted in this field of study: conceptual competencies (what you know, such as past experiences, qualifications, and the like) and behavioral competencies (how you use what you know). The conceptual type is the first (internal) step toward mastery. However, to be deemed fully competent, an organization's leaders must progress to the more measurable (external) behavioral competencies. In the metrics-minded business world, success means achieving measurable results.

Finally, competencies generally pertain to three different dimensions: position level (formal span of responsibility within the organization—individual, manager, or executive level?), skill level (is the person skilled or unskilled?), and specific type of competency (skill or knowledge?).

> *"Of course leadership competencies are important. What's the alternative? Leadership incompetencies?"*
>
> —Lee Cockerell, former executive vice president of operations,
> Walt Disney World Resort

Another common challenge regarding leadership competencies is the tendency for businesses to address competencies in a conceptual manner that has little relevance for their day-to-day functional operations. Organizations often get so bogged down in theoretical concepts that the competencies they identify lack relevance and fail in the implementation phase. According to Claudio Diaz (2009), chief human capital officer of the renowned accounting firm Wipfli, "Competency models are at the core of every [human resource] process that will make you successful and ultimately get you exceptional leadership in your organization. If you put your competency model together correctly, you will be engaging your highest performers first. From there, they will influence the next level to follow—similar to a shock wave."

This chapter illuminates why organizations select particular competencies to guide their leaders. Successful implementation requires understanding why, so you can know what leadership competencies to implement and how to best implement them. The goal is to provide insights and tools that overcome the obstacles to making the most of leadership competencies.

Proven Real-World Results

When searching for business solutions, most professionals make the mistake of grasping at the trendy business management fad of the day. But rather than chasing such unproven theories, the most successful professionals benchmark organizations that have a proven record of consistent, long-term success. The key is not to simply analyze what they do tactically but also to understand how they think. Implementing the process of achieving success allows adapting to ongoing changes in any work environment—regardless of the industry.

The first step in creating sustainable business results is to understand how outstanding organizations all around the world earn their rank as best-in-industry leaders. According to J. Jeff Kober, chief executive officer of World Class Benchmarking, LLC, a consulting firm that actively showcases proven world-class business excellence, "there is an amazing consistency in the formula that nearly every industry-leading organization follows to achieve exemplary results. They have done the essential work of connecting the dots between business results and the root causes of those results" (Kober 2009). World Class Benchmarking's Chain Reaction of Excellence Model reflects this formula, as shown in figure 12-1.

Figure 12-1. The Chain Reaction of Excellence Model

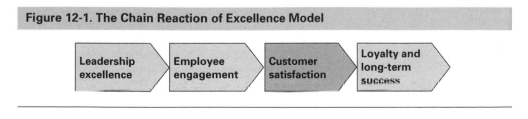

Looking at the model portrayed in figure 12-1 from right to left, customer loyalty and long-term business success are the natural consequences of customer satisfaction, which is created by employee engagement and excellent service. And the catalyst for the entire process is leadership excellence. Leaders throughout an organization influence the environment within which the resulting steps in the formula take place. The potential of any organization, therefore, is directly linked to the abilities of its leaders—thus spotlighting the crucial importance of leadership competencies.

Kober (2009) continues, "Ironically, focusing solely on the financial results at the end of the formula severely undermines the outcome. Like any formula, the secret to achieving the desired outcome is to focus on what precedes the end result. That is the aspect we can control. Improving the quality of the early parts of the formula will naturally result in improvements to the results at the end."

A key part of the never-ending effort to achieve corporate growth is identifying the most beneficial opportunities for improvement along the entire chain of operational touch points. Let's review the Chain Reaction of Excellence Model from a competencies (knowledge/ behaviors) perspective; we'll call this the Competency-Success Chain Model, as shown in figure 12-2. The leader's competencies (knowledge and behaviors) create an employee experience that influences those employees' competencies. This, in turn, affects the quality of customers' experience, which influences their knowledge and behaviors (that is, they become more loyal), which results in the long-term success of the organization.

On the basis of these consistent dynamics, the most successful organizations have discovered a key competitive insight: Any organizational improvement effort is, at its core, a leadership improvement initiative—and not simply for leaders with formal titles at the top of the organizational chart but also influential leaders throughout the organization. To achieve the best possible corporate culture, external service, and financial results, organizations must select the leader with the right fit for their unique situation: "If you don't design what matters into your leaders, then the rest of your operational efforts are a waste of time" (Crosby 2009). Simply put, improved leadership begins a chain reaction of improvements that, when implemented correctly, have a positive impact on every aspect of the organizational experience.

Figure 12-2. The Competency-Success Chain Model

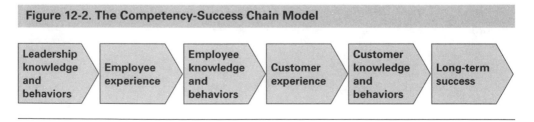

Given that an organization's leaders have such a profound influence on its health, it makes sense to optimize every leader's knowledge and behaviors to improve the results for all aspects of the organization. Most companies typically start the process by asking "What are the best leadership competencies?" However, considering the dynamics of the Chain Reaction of Excellence Model, the most renowned organizations instead ask "What do we ultimately want to accomplish and how will we know when we've succeeded?" These two questions create a more comprehensive frame of reference for addressing the systemic nature of their business—and the answers to these questions provide a better context for identifying the right competencies for their unique circumstances.

Been There, Doing That

Contrary to the popular opinion that the ultimate role of the leader is merely to drive financial results, proven world-class organizations are convinced that the leader's role is to affect every part of the organization so that the natural consequence is long-term success. Once a person is promoted to a position of leadership, his or her professional tools are no longer things; they are people and ideas, communication and processes—summed up in their leadership competencies. Leaders must orchestrate their front line's knowledge and behaviors while influencing the people who actively implement these competencies. To be truly successful, leaders throughout the organization must consider the corporate ramifications of their decisions, but execute in cooperation with their local teams to make it happen (Meath 2009).

To better understand the pragmatic implementation aspects of the tool of identifying leadership competencies, executives from renowned organizations in vastly different industries were interviewed to provide insights about selecting, implementing, and best leveraging this tool; see table 12-1. Despite the differences in their history, industry, and organizational dynamics, these organizations have one thing in common: They have become extraordinarily successful. They are all known for exemplary internal cultures that have generated legendary service and raving advocates—resulting in consistent industry-leading growth and profits. The next section of this chapter explores how each of them has addressed competency-related issues, bridging the gap between theory and tactical application to achieve proven results.

Success by Design: Steps Toward Competency Engagement

For every organization, there comes a crossroads regarding whether or not it is satisfied with the status quo. Benchmarking how the most successful organizations navigate this process becomes a portal to discovering what creates leadership competencies that really work in the real world.

Table 12-1. Contributing Interview Subjects

Name/Position	Company	Background
Lee Cockerell, former executive vice president of operations and author of the best-selling book *Creating Magic*	Walt Disney World Resort	In the 1990s, Disney World initiated Performance Excellence, a company-wide organizational improvement initiative that included a transformation of leadership with Great Leader's Strategies. The results have become known as the "Disney Decade" of record-breaking growth and profits.
Michelle Crosby, former senior vice president of human resources	Starwood Hotels and Resorts	In 2004, Starwood Hotels, home of brands such as Westin, Sheraton, St. Regis, and W, began a systematic transformation effort to align its cultures and brands into a unifying whole—resulting in dramatically improved metrics across all divisions, brands, and job levels.
Jack Roddy, director, partner resources	Starbucks Coffee Company	Earning multiple-year awards for the most prestigious accomplishments—*Fortune*'s best companies to work for, top 10 most admired companies, best corporate citizen, top brands list, and so on—Starbucks attributes its global success to their strategically established competencies.
Pat Jannausch, vice president of culture and organization development	Con-way, Inc.	This $5 billion freight transportation and logistics services company changed its industry by focusing on leadership competencies that support innovation and employee engagement.
Gerard Q. Pierce, senior vice president of human resources; and Anne Meath, director of organization development	Wegmans	This multiple-award-winning major supermarket chain is one of the largest private companies in the United States. Considered the benchmark experience of supermarket chains worldwide, it is attributed to consistent competency implementation.
Claudio Diaz, chief human capital officer	Wipfli LLC	Voted as one of the best accounting firms to work for in the nation (*Accounting Today*), Wipfli ranks among the top 25 accounting firms in the United States. The competency-driven Wipfli Way creates a unique experience for both clients and associates.
J. Jeff Kober, chief executive officer and co-author of *Lead with Your Customer*	World Class Benchmarking, LLC	International benchmarking firm that partners with best-in-class organizations to implement innovative world-class leadership, culture, service/brand, and operational solutions.

Walt Disney World came to that awareness in the early 1990s. The economy was struggling and its competition was heating up. As the executive in charge of all operations, Lee Cockerell knew that Disney needed to reach its potential to thrive in such a difficult environment. The solution? Transform the culture. "It's about creating a great inclusive environment for the cast members [employees] so they want to do a great job. I made myself the chief environmentalist at Walt Disney World, so my job was to focus on the things that would help our business environment. Number one was to make sure I was involved when we selected new leaders. Great leaders create a great environment for people to do great things, . . . and everyone wants to be part of something great—both cast members and customers" (Cockerell 2009b).

Once an organization truly understands the Chain Reaction of Excellence Model strategy, it becomes obvious that any effort to transform its operations must begin with the root cause of leadership—and weave in all aspects of both its internal culture and external brand. Those who are passionate about realizing their potential get serious and commit to taking an active, strategic role in creating their results by design rather than by default.

In 2006, Starwood Hotels and Resorts realized that its impressive holdings of hotel brands (that include Westin, Sheraton, St. Regis, and W) were not operating as effectively as they could, and it launched a company-wide initiative across 900 hotels in more than 90 countries operated by more than 150,000 associates around the world. Michelle Crosby, the vice president of organizational capability, led the effort to create a branded service culture: "We had numerous different brands that we had purchased, each with their own culture and ways of doing business. Internally, different functions across brands weren't connected with each other, which limited effectiveness. We realized that we needed to find a way to align everyone that tiered up, not just within a single hotel, but among all hotels in that brand. We then expanded that thinking to include aligning all the Starwood brands so they would complement each other with strong hotel brand but also unify under the Starwood corporate banner—realizing efficiencies throughout the entire corporation" (Crosby 2009).

For Con-way Inc., a $5 billion freight transportation and logistics services company, the interest in leadership competencies was sparked by an epiphany during an executive meeting. Pat Jannausch, the vice president of culture and organization development, was collecting some data about retirement trends when the CEO raised the issue of succession planning. "Years ago, the leadership competencies tended to focus on personality and making your numbers," jokes Jannausch. "We soon realized that our leadership hiring and promoting process was based too much on gut instinct and not enough on a more formal approach that included seeking out and testing for specific leadership competencies. We have since developed leadership criteria for succession planning and are continually expanding this effort to include every facet of the Con-way culture—from hiring to retiring. What we've done is definitely not something that is typical for a company in the transportation and shipping industry" (Jannausch 2009).

Accomplishing extraordinary long-term results demands a sustainable, comprehensive, and fully integrated plan. Many organizations use a rollout plan similar to the Competency Engagement Plan Checklist, which consists of seven steps:

1. Assemble the team and clarify the core.
2. Document all relevant processes.
3. Create an initial competency list and categorize.
4. Secure team validation and buy-in.
5. Connect to the operation.
6. Create an accountability infrastructure.
7. Revisit, learn, celebrate, and improve.

Each of these steps is directly connected to the Chain Reaction of Excellence Model—strategically reinforcing the links of the process to optimize the results at the end of the formula.

Step 1: Creating the Core

Step 1 of the implementation plan is to gather a focus group of influential role models from all parts of the organization to serve as a task force. It is critical that all functions of the organization are represented. "This isn't (human resources) work, though they facilitate it. It's really the operations that must own it. That's where the results are measured" (Crosby 2009). One of the key insights from the most successful world-class organizations is that any competencies must be aligned with the core components of the organizational culture. The degree of organizational integrity is completely dependent on the degree of alignment every part of the organization has with the core. The core consists of the components of the culture, such as the values, vision, mission, operational guidelines, and so forth. The significance of this first step is critical to the success of the entire organization transformation effort.

One reason that so many change initiatives fail is because they become just another complicated responsibility added to the leaders "plate." Consider this brief analogy from the book *Lead with Your Customer* (Jones and Kober 2010): If someone has a plate piled full of cooked noodles and you were to add yet another serving of cooked noodles on top of the mound, what would be the natural consequences? Unless you were to hold the noodles on, they would slide off the plate. The same dynamic occurs when people have additional responsibilities forced onto their already-full workload as part of a new initiative (as a matter of fact, we often hear people say that their "plate is already full"). The new program may last for some months, but eventually, when the effort of "holding the noodles on the plate" cannot continue, the noodles fall off the plate.

What world-class businesses do differently and better is that they take the organization's nonnegotiable aspects—the things that should never change, like its vision and values—and make them "the plate." The key is to design the core of your company so that it is dependably reliable and valid. There will always be things in the environment that are changing—like the economy, your competition, social issues, technology changes, and new competition—that will require attention, but when the core is set, all that additional time and effort can be reinvested into handling the issues on the plate (Jones and Kober 2010). Gerard Pierce, the senior vice president of Wegmans Supermarkets, ranked one of the best places to work by *Fortune* magazine, states that their core (known as the "Four Ws": What we believe, Who we are, What we do, and What we measure) is "the road map for our business plan. Having a common goal that is clearly understood by everyone makes sure we are all moving toward the same goals—even though we may start from different places" (Pierce 2009). "Follow the customer from two steps ahead" is a Wegmans saying that illustrates its ongoing commitment to staying focused on the customer at all times while anticipating his or her wants and exceeding his or her expectations (Meath 2009).

Once you have established the core, you can move to step 2, which is to begin documenting and understanding what people in your organization do on a day-to-day basis.

Step 2: That Voodoo That You Do So Well

Whereas step 1 addresses the purpose of why particular competencies should be embraced, step 2 begins to identify the deliverables required of your business. This helps set the stage for exploring what knowledge and skills are specifically needed in your unique operation to successfully complete the processes of step 2.

This process and deliverable review is most effective when considered not only from the company's perspective but also from that of the customer. Not only does this activity create insights about the integrity between the company's core and the organizational culture, but it also identifies alignment with your brand. Ultimately, the goal is to exceed expectations while making it easy to do business with you—inside and out.

Step 3: Getting Competent About Competencies

Step 3 is when you will begin to create the initial list of competencies most relevant to your unique organization. One way to think about this is that the most successful companies review their internal best practices and identify which competencies fit them best, rather than force-fitting generic leader characteristics onto their culture. To illustrate this, table 12-2 gives many of the competencies commonly found in organizations all around the world.

The remarkable fact about this concept list is that it actually reflects an elementary school student profile. Isn't it interesting how expectations of human nature apply to people of all ages? Leaders, as role models, "are expected to perform the same kinds of competencies as younger people"—just on a different level (Cockerell 2009b).

The goal of this step is not so much what competencies other organizations use but more why you want to be competent in a particular area. This step is also about how implementing the right competency for you will improve how you consistently achieve results by exceeding the expectations of your employees and your customers.

Numerous methods are used to brainstorm concepts—most involve decks of cards that are discussed and sorted through a series of forced-choice selections. The goal here is to begin the discussion about the concepts and their importance as part of how you produce your most important deliverables.

One vital criterion at this phase is to keep it very simple. Just the most critical competencies should make the cut. "It's easy to be complicated. It's much harder to distill down to what really matters" (Crosby 2009). An effective rule of thumb is to "consider current role models of excellence as a template for the competence level for everyone in that role, and then articulate that clearly for every member of that organization" (Diaz 2009).

Imagine that everyone on your team had the knowledge and abilities of your star leader. That is the value of developing competencies with the right fit for your unique operation. The final aspect of step 3 is to place the draft competencies into collections of likeminded categories, for maximum simplification of competencies critical for success. This is typically the final act of the original one- or two-day task force meeting. What you want to avoid at all costs is having the executive group create the competencies and hand them off to be implemented. According to Jack Roddy, director of partner resources at Starbucks, getting only the executive team to approve the competencies is "a false 'promised land.'

Table 12-2. Sample Competencies

Principled	Inquiring	Caring	Tolerance	Open-minded
Integrity	Thinking	Enthusiastic	Respect	Risk-taking
Committed	Creative	Communicating	Empathetic	Confident
Well balanced	Reflective	Independent	Cooperative	Curious

The intent of the competencies is to be used as a tool by the people out in the operation running the company. If those out in the field don't buy in, you don't have anything" (Roddy 2009).

Step 4: Getting Engaged

Step 4 is the initial effort to share the decisions made by the task force and get the rest of the company (at the lowest appropriate level) involved in generating feedback. This also is an informal validation step to test the work of the task force for both the operational aspects and the planned accountability methods. The bottom line: "If you don't connect correctly, you haven't done your job" (Roddy 2009).

One reason to use influential team members who are well-respected in the task force is how they interact with the rest of their teams during this step. Having these informal leaders accessible to explain their decisions and show genuine support for the competency tool generates confidence and a sense of control by the rest of the team.

Another valuable benefit of involving people throughout the organization early is that they get the chance to be involved in the process. Not only does the company gain their feedback for a more valid tool, but their involvement also creates ownership and buy-in to the process—making it more likely that they will support the implementation phase.

Step 5: Execution, in a Good Way

Step 5 consists of taking the refined and final product of step 4 and using the new competencies as an aligning filter for every aspect of the organization. Once you have the road map (the core), every role and function in the operation must align to optimize integrity. The consequence of this step is consolidation of your support resources—you are consistently reinforcing the same types of efforts for the same reasons.

One way to design and develop this step is to do a process map of your employees as well as your customers. Every experience requires some kind of knowledge or behavior to execute. Compile these touch points and the corresponding competencies to determine expectations—and what will exceed expectations—in each instance.

Remember to do the difficult work of distilling down everything to its essence and make it as simple as possible. If the process is too unwieldy to be realistically and consistently implemented in day-to-day operations, the plan will soon give way to the previous, less effective approach. This is the time to be audacious, disciplined, and committed. The reason for initiating the improvement effort is because the ordinary approach is no longer acceptable.

Step 6: Accountability

Step 6 occurs in tandem with step 5. As the new processes and procedures are rolling out, the accountability systems should be implemented as well. "Management must be measured on the values of the organization. A lot of companies have their values posted on the wall, but if employees can't see the values in their manager or their fellow workers, then those values really don't exist" (Pierce 2009). Anne Meath (2009), Wegmans' director of organization development, adds that "the real differentiator is the demonstration of values."

Clarifying the specific goals and how your entire team will work together to achieve them must be measured to serve as an objective road map for everyone's guidance. This feedback infrastructure is the lifeblood of any sustainable system.

The benchmark accounting firm Wipfli has an interesting approach to providing information as part of its performance management system. "One tool that has been helpful is using a positive rubric at all levels when assessing performance. We use a traditional Likert scale to rate associates, but instead of describing negative behaviors with the lowest two numbers, we decided to have all five numbers reflect varying degrees of positive outcomes for that competency. It's a practical application of the now famous transition from 'good to great'" (Diaz 2009).

Just as with any transition, more care must be taken to ensure a nurturing environment supports the learning curve of the competency or improvement initiative. The changes will assuredly create some level of confusion, anxiety, and intense emotions as people adjust. Fortunately, the need to provide justification for decisions and behavior parameters consistently leads back to the newly established core. Because there are now direct links between results, knowledge, and behaviors for service and culture and the new leadership competencies, there is natural motivation for anyone who cares about the core (values, vision, and mission). Accountability support systems reinforce the methods and results that everyone aligned with the newly stated direction desires.

Step 7: Making Common Sense Common Practice

Step 7 is the flywheel that keeps the process moving forward, building momentum with each cycle and nurturing the effort each and every day: "It takes time. Changing an organizational culture is like cleaning up a polluted lake. At first, it starts off muddy and murky, but with discipline and commitment, it eventually gets clearer and drinkable again. With people, they earn more trust, become more engaged, and eventually get happy from providing extraordinary service to their guests" (Cockerell 2009b). Make the effort to revisit the purpose, process, and payoff of the "new normal." Reminders that are part of the typical day-to-day operation—daily team huddles, weekly department meetings, monthly newsletters, and so on—maintain the urgency and motivation to continue the improvement process. These opportunities allow for two-way communication so everyone can continuously learn from the process and celebrate—both the successes and the failures along the way. "One of the activities we've done consistently over the years with the highest return-on-investment is to have extended leadership sessions and simply talk about how we can better live the values" (Pierce 2009).

In his book *Creating Magic*, Lee Cockerell (2009a, 263) comments on his experiences during this part of the process: "As a leader, you have to make many tough choices, and that process starts now. And when making those tough decisions, always consider their impact on each leg of what Disney calls the three-legged stool: guests (customers), cast members (employees), and business results. By clearly thinking through the effect your choices will have on these three legs, you are taking everyone's concerns into account. Once you do, go ahead and make your decision and act on it."

Finally, in addition to gathering insights, sharing those insights throughout the organization leverages the benefits exponentially. If a leader's responsibility is to grow the business, then by definition, growing employees' competence is a nonnegotiable requirement. Building competence is the intent of leadership competencies, but many lose sight of this when it comes to the rest of the organization.

Ending at the Beginning

Identifying leadership competencies is too often used as a superficial tool to select, develop, and hold leaders accountable for compensation purposes. But the most successful world-class organizations realize the opportunity to expand well beyond that limiting perspective, and they apply the effort to building competence throughout the company—for a transformational shift toward future achievements.

The act of identifying relevant competencies that are the right fit for the leaders of an organization should be the start of a fresh, new beginning for all its operations. An organization's leader is a role model who ultimately influences its internal culture, external brand, and financial results. Approached strategically, identifying and implementing the right leadership competencies that work for your organization will help you achieve the same kinds of proven results achieved by the world's most renowned organizations.

Further Reading

Ram Charan, Stephen Drotter, and James Noel, *The Leadership Pipeline: How to Build the Leadership-Powered Company*. San Francisco: Jossey-Bass, 2000.
Lee Cockerell, *Creating Magic: 10 Common Sense Leadership Strategies from a Life at Disney*. New York: Doubleday, 2008.

Mark David Jones and J. Jeff Kober, *Lead with Your Customer: Transform Your Culture and Brand into World-Class Excellence.* Alexandria, VA: ASTD Press, 2010.

Michael M. Lombardo and Robert W. Eichinger, *FYI: For Your Improvement.* Minneapolis: Lominger International, 2009.

Dave Ulrich and Norm Smallwood, *Leadership Brand: Developing Customer-Focused Leaders to Drive Performance and Build Lasting Value.* Boston: Harvard Business School Press, 2007.

References

Cockerell, L. 2009a. *Creating Magic: 10 Common Sense Leadership Strategies from a Life at Disney.* New York: Doubleday.

———. 2009b. Interview by the author, October 16.

Crosby, Michelle. 2009. Interview by the author, October 15.

Diaz, Claudio. 2009. Interview by the author, October 30.

Jannausch, Pat. 2009. Interview by the author, October 15.

Jones, M., and J. Kober. 2010. *Lead With Your Customer: Transform Culture and Brand into World-Class Excellence.* Alexandria, VA: ASTD Press.

Kober, J. Jeff. 2009. Interview by the author, October 20.

Meath, Anne. 2009. Interview by the author, October 30.

Pierce, Gerard Q. 2009. Interview by the author, October 27.

Roddy, Jack. 2009. Interview by the author, October 29.

About the Author

Mark David Jones is currently the president of Small World Alliance, leading a team of former Disney leaders to help corporations achieve business excellence. Before this venture, his 26-year career with the Walt Disney Company involved numerous leadership roles, including being responsible for customer service, creativity and innovation, and leadership initiatives. In recognition of his contributions, he was nominated for Disney's highest corporate accolade, the Partners in Excellence Award. Jones' business transformation work with dozens of *Fortune* 500 companies is showcased in his book *Lead with Your Customer: Transform Your Culture and Brand into World-Class Excellence,* published by ASTD Press.

 **Chapter 13**

Worst Practices in 360-Degree Assessments: Why Feedback Fails

Craig Chappelow

In This Chapter

■ The most common mistakes organizations make when launching a 360-degree feedback initiative.

■ What your organization can do to avoid these mistakes.

This chapter is *not* a how-to guide for conducting a 360-degree feedback initiative in your organization. Those resources already exist, and four good ones are listed at the end of this chapter. Nor is the information contained here particularly scientific. If you are looking for empirical evidence, hundreds of journal articles slice and dice nearly every aspect of the way 360-degree assessments behave—some of it in subatomic detail. Rather, this chapter is a how-*not*-to guide, which reflects my opinions about why 360-degree feedback initiatives fail in organizations, based on my experience during the past 15 years managing the Center for Creative Leadership's (CCL's) 360-degree assessment business and working with organizations to implement 360 initiatives. All too frequently, our work starts with the heavy lifting of undoing the damage from a previous 360 initiative these companies conducted that somehow went wrong. In most cases, we can help the organization right the 360 ship and return with a stronger position than before—but not always.

Why a chapter about failed 360 efforts? Because, as the philosopher John Dewey said, "Failure is instructive." We can learn a lot from the mistakes of others that can help us avoid similar traps. The other reason is because I got tired of attending session after session at human resources conferences listening to people talk about the great successes they have had with 360-degree assessments while hearing nothing about the perils involved. There is no doubt that, when done well, 360-degree feedback has many upsides for developing leaders in organizations. The problem is when a 360 goes wrong, it can have a lasting negative impact on the people involved and taint future initiatives. As the Yiddish proverb says, "From success to failure is one step; from failure to success is a long road."

On the basis of my experience working with organizations, when 360-degree feedback initiatives fail, it is usually a result of botched implementation, and almost never because the survey failed to contain the exact right content or because the questions weren't phrased precisely the right way. Yet the relative proportion of time I see clients spending on these issues seems to be reversed. In this chapter, I summarize eight of the most common worst practices I have observed in companies with which I have worked that caused their 360 initiative to fail. Some became CCL clients and some did not, but I learned something important from each one.

I have already mentioned two caveats about this chapter: long on opinion, short on science. Let me add two more. First, all my examples showcase organizations that implemented or were considering implementing 360-degree feedback initiatives for groups of leaders, because initiatives that involve multiple participants tend to be trickier to conduct. Second, CCL's experience with 360s is in the arena of assessment for development. Its assessments have been designed and validated for the purpose of helping an individual increase his or her self-awareness and provide the basis for creating a development plan. Its 360s have not been designed for assessment for administrative uses like hiring, promotion decisions, salary determinations, or any other use that would involve issuing the feedback report to the organization. There are vendors that do offer responsibly developed, high-quality assessments for these purposes—it just doesn't happen to be the space CCL occupies in the market, and therefore not where its experience lies. Now let's look at eight common worst practices:

- unclear purpose
- dumbing it down
- project bloat
- no support from senior executives
- misreading the organization's readiness
- growing your own
- poor communication
- confusing assessment with development.

Worst Practice: Unclear Purpose

Several years ago, CCL was approached by a United States–based multinational chemical company to bid on a large 360-degree initiative it was planning to start, and the turnover time for submitting the proposal was unusually short. At CCL, we had less than three days to formulate our response. Even after reading the lengthy request for proposals several times, I could not determine why this firm wanted to do a 360 to begin with. The request was, to put it mildly, fuzzy. When I contacted the human resources (HR) vice president to collect more information, he told me that they were under a mandate from their CEO to roll out and complete the entire process over the next five months. They were prepared to make a considerable investment in this effort, and I got the strong impression that they were eager to hit the ground running. When I again asked the prospective client why they wanted to introduce 360 assessments into their organization, this beleaguered (but honest) HR vice president, after talking in general terms for several minutes, admitted that he wasn't sure. He then revealed that their CEO had just returned from a trip and had read an article on 360s in an in-flight magazine. The article just happened to mention one of their competitors, and the CEO didn't want to get left out by comparison.

The use of 360s in organizations has become so pervasive that if your company is not currently using one (or several), it might feel as if you are somehow missing out. But by merely keeping up with the Joneses instead of making a strategic decision about how they planned to use a 360 and what they wanted to accomplish from it, this company's leaders would be hard pressed to determine if their investment, when concluded, actually made any difference. Before proceeding, any organization that hopes to use 360s successfully must be clear about the answers to these three key questions:

- *Why?* What is the specific business problem you are trying to solve by implementing a 360, and how will the 360 help you with this problem? Without clarity on the answer to this first question, it will be difficult to identify the best assessment, process, and target participants, or to determine whether or not the work was successful.
- *Why now?* What is it about today's situation that makes this a priority? Has there been a change in your organization or the economy that is prompting this initiative?
- *Why you?* How will you determine who to include to best solve the business problem you have identified? Depending on the business problem, different companies use different approaches. Some might target young staff with high potential, managers facing a critical transition, or everyone who reaches the general manager level as a part of their managerial ramp up—just to cite a few examples.

Finding clarity about the answers to these three essential questions establishes a basis from which to operate, and informs the way the message is communicated to the organization. If a potential client is not clear about these answers, then the value CCL can bring is to help it gain clarity before it engages a vendor and invests in an assessment process.

Worst Practice: Dumbing It Down

The process of 360-degree feedback is not for everyone in an organization, and should not be force-fit. As companies with which CCL works become increasingly careful about how they spend their development dollars, I have noticed a dramatic shift in the way they deploy 360s. Years ago it was not unusual for clients to deploy 360s to an entire level in their company. Nowadays these efforts are more targeted. Companies are being more selective and are focusing on high-potential leaders, new managers, and other people facing critical transitions. Perhaps as a result, when I sit down with assessment participants to discuss their feedback reports, I am seeing them taking their data more seriously. If I had to describe the ideal target for a 360, it would be someone who is motivated and sees the 360 as an opportunity, not a threat. In my experience, these individuals who are facing critical transitions in their careers are the most engaged of all. So, money is tight, and targeting the right participants is critical, yet I still see some organizations dumbing down their 360 process to accommodate (and protect against) the opposite kind of participant: the lowest common denominator.

One large organization designed a 360-degree feedback process and approached us at CCL to use one of our assessments. By the time their staff members engaged with us, they had already done a good job of addressing the three key questions (Why? Why now? Why you?). They decided to use our customizable 360, and they had invested a considerable amount of time fleshing out their competency model and vetting it within their company. They targeted 60 senior managers across the organization as the target participants, and did a fine job of setting up a reasonable timeline with key milestones and a solid communication plan. They arranged for each participant to have a confidential one-to-one session with a trained facilitator to review their reports.

So far so good. The unusual thing was that they wanted to insert several strict rules (they called them "safeguards") in their process that the participants would be required to follow. The first was that the organization, not the individual participant, would determine who each participant would select as his or her raters. The participants were not allowed to add to or delete from the rater list. The other rule came in to play at the end of the process. After each participant met with his or her facilitator in a one-to-one session, the participant's manager would be waiting to go directly into a meeting with the participant to discuss his or her development plan. We probably could have worked through those issues with the client, but the third rule they put in place ultimately became the deal breaker. They planned to issue each manager a copy of the participants' feedback reports. We consulted at length with this client to suggest other, less restrictive options for their process. We suggested that the participants pick their own raters (to increase their degree of buy-in), and if the organization still wanted to have input, they could suggest additional raters they would like the participant to include.

We also worked with this client to give the participants more space after their one-to-one session for reflection, and then for meeting with their managers the following week. We particularly tried to help them understand the downsides of issuing the managers the feedback reports. It was in these discussions that the client revealed that the controls they originally requested to put in place were all directed toward one individual, whom I will call Steve. They were certain that Steve would not take the process seriously and would do everything he could to take the easy way out. They were convinced he would only include raters who would give him positive-only feedback, would never follow up and meet with his manager if left to his own devices, and certainly could not be trusted to work on the right things.

Ultimately, this client used another vendor and proceeded with the "Steve rules" in place. Several months later, I received a call from my contact at the organization, who asked, "Can we just get to the part where you say 'I told you so'?" She told me that there was a predictable backlash against the rules by the participants, who felt, in their own words, as if they were being treated "like children." The firm started the initiative, but it stalled after fewer than 20 participants finished the process. She recounted that because the participants did not have a say in who they used as raters, some used that as an excuse to ignore their results. She also suggested that other, more serious problems were created by issuing copies of the feedback reports to the participants' managers.

If a "Steve" slips through the cracks and doesn't do everything he is supposed to do, so be it. Invest your development dollars in the way that makes the biggest difference. Carefully design your 360-degree initiative. Gear it to the people who deserve the extra attention and will appreciate it and use it. You never know; Steve might just rise to the occasion.

Worst Practice: Project Bloat

In 2009, a schoolteacher from Ohio set a world record when she brought a pumpkin weighing 1,725 pounds to the scales. That, my friends, is one big gourd. The thing is, it wasn't even the biggest one grown that year. Other gardeners have grown bigger pumpkins, but they didn't make it out of the garden to be weighed. We seem to have reached a tipping point in the maximum amount of weight that a pumpkin's architecture can support. They lay in the garden soaking up the sunlight and thousands of gallons of water all summer long, and when the farmer rigs them to be lifted—splat! The giant pumpkins collapse under their own weight.

There seems to be a similar maximum-size principle for organizational 360-degree initiatives. I have yet to see a huge 360-degree feedback initiative work as planned. CCL was once approached to provide a feedback initiative for 1,500 managers over the course of one year—an ambitious number. In practical terms, that would mean that the client would have started almost 30 new participants per week, every week, for a year. Its staff members' first question to us was whether or not CCL could handle that type of volume (except they used the current buzzwords, "Will your system scale?"). My answer was yes, and that we process hundreds of surveys every day. That part of the work is easy for CCL to administer because the data collection, scoring, and feedback report production is managed on an efficient technology platform.

What this client wasn't willing to do in support of its large initiative was to put in place the administrative capacity to coordinate the human element of the project—identifying the participants, communicating with them, ensuring the confidential management of the finished feedback reports, scheduling people for workshops and one-to-one interpretive sessions, rescheduling missed sessions, and responding to problems or questions. Typically, either the client manages this aspect of the project, CCL manages it, or the client and CCL team up and each takes a part of it. This particular client was unwilling to choose any of these options, because it was convinced that it could set up a completely "participant-driven" process from the beginning.

Ultimately, we at CCL had to walk away from what would have been a lucrative piece of business, but it was so full of open issues that it seemed too big *not* to fail. All the warning signs told us that this project, as described, could never be conducted and still meet our quality expectations and accomplish the client's goals, and that in the end it would set the participants up for disappointment. This potential client did find another vendor to take on the work as originally described, and plop—pumpkin pie. It later rebid the work in a series of smaller segments.

The key to avoiding project bloat is to keep the project to a scale that ensures that the first person and the last person going through the process will have the same high-quality experience. The mistake this organization made was that its leaders had already decided that they were going to "process," as they described it, an entire division in one calendar year, no matter what. In doing so, they underestimated the amount of support 1,500 human beings (and their 10,000-plus raters) would need.

With very few exceptions, we at CCL have seen smaller initiatives work better than massive initiatives. Conducting a successful 360-degree feedback process involves a multitude of moving parts, all dependent on people doing what they are supposed to do within a certain time frame. For these larger initiatives, we recommend that the client start with a small pilot group. Ideally, the pilot group would be made up of a small number of senior executives, and this would have several benefits. It would help expose the executives to the content and process of the 360-degree initiative. It would engage their peers and those reporting directly to them as they filled out their surveys, and would probably cause them to ask themselves, "I wonder what people would say about me on all these questions?"

Worst Practice: No Support from Senior Executives

The other benefit of starting a larger initiative with a pilot group made up of senior executives is that it demonstrates to the organization that these executives are taking this seriously and are willing to set an example and go first rather than creating a perception in the organization that this is something we are going to do to other people. When I started working with one new client, I could tell that their 360-degree initiative was on thin ice as soon as we engaged with them. The project details were a constant moving target as the client kept changing the scope and deployment of the work in what seemed to be daily shifts.

First, the numbers of participants started at 200, then decreased gradually until we were only working with 30 people at the end. Second, the implementation date continued to be pushed back. And, most telling of all, the contract deadlines came and passed with no word from the client. When I contacted them, they would say, "We're definitely going to do this, we're just making sure we have everything nailed down first." Third, more than a month beyond the original kickoff date requested by the client, they asked us to produce return-on-investment (ROI) proof that our 360s actually work. We put a substantial amount of work into gathering the latest on ROI studies and defending the efficacy of 360s in general.

Eventually, our client contact admitted to us that their CEO was resistant, had not been on board at all from the start, and he was just throwing up roadblocks—one of which was the ROI request. The client did ultimately deploy one of our 360s to a group of 30 middle managers without the support of the executive team, and the participants saw the initiative as, in their words, "another HR thing."

Another organization that contracted with CCL to build a customized 360 started with its executive team. Even though the 360 was designed to support this client's newly created leadership competency model, while completing its own self-surveys, its executives did not agree that this content was the right thing to be measuring. They stopped the process in midstream to decide what to do. As it turns out, none of the executives had had input on the survey content, and only one of them had even been consulted to provide input into the new organizational competency model. We at CCL did what we could to help them salvage the investment of time and money that they had already made, but they ended up changing a substantial amount of their survey content after the fact—an expensive but critical decision.

Still another organization carefully designed its 360-degree feedback initiative but rolled out the initiative from the bottom up. The first to receive their feedback as participants were the lower-level managers, then upper managers, and, finally, nearly a year after the start of the process, the senior executives (and at that, fewer than half elected to participate). As you can guess, the program got off on the wrong foot and was perceived by the managers not as a development opportunity but as something "being done to them" by senior management and HR.

It has become clear to me in considering the experiences of the organizations with which I have worked that senior management support is critical, and the more visible and earlier the better. Even though it was years ago, I am still impressed by my memory of watching a CEO who flew back early from business in China to stand in front of a group of high-potential leaders to kick off their 360 process by addressing the three key questions: Why? Why now? Why you? He told them that this was one of the most important things they would do for their own development. He also told a story about when he had used the same assessment a few years earlier and what he had learned about himself.

Worst Practice: Misreading the Organization's Readiness

Sometimes it's just not the right time for a 360-degree assessment. A midsized telecommunications company selected one of CCL's 360s to use, but as we worked with them to plan the rollout, we started hearing warning bells. Several of the people with whom we talked revealed that during the prior year, the company (under different leadership) had rolled out a 360 with disastrous results. The participants were told that the results would be confidential—that no one would see the results except them. In reality, the HR department kept a copy of the feedback reports in the employee file.

This all came to the surface when one underperforming employee was called into a performance counseling session and the HR representative pulled out the individual's 360 and used the results to justify putting him on probation. That story circulated like wildfire, and, as a result, potential participants were suspicious. The damage went so deep that it even affected the annual employee opinion survey, which was returned by only about half as many respondents as the previous year. The reality in some organizations may be that it is just too soon to try again, and there are other development activities that for the moment would work better until trust can be restored.

Another readiness issue relates to the work the company has done (or not done) to create an underlying management/leadership model. A new client approached CCL with three separate competency models: one for hiring, another for performance appraisal, and a third applied to 360-degree assessment. Each of these overarching models had three separate sets of competencies, depending on the individual's organizational level. Nine models and counting. Employees got to the point where they weren't sure which model they were supposed to pay attention to. One participant told me that he had model fatigue.

A low-technology, family-owned manufacturing business had a strong culture of feedback avoidance. In particular, it was very unusual for a subordinate to give feedback upward. This firm put a 360 in place for its senior managers and received a very low return rate from those reporting directly to these managers (and, I suspect, inflated ratings from those who did respond).

All three of these cases, while different, point out the need to pay attention to an organization's culture, recent experience with 360s, and clarity of purpose as they affect readiness for a 360.

Worst Practice: Growing Your Own

Years ago, one of CCL's clients, determined to save money by using untapped time within its internal information technology (IT) group, started out by creating their own survey content, survey system, and technology platform to manage scoring and report production. The IT department, a group of people capable of maintaining the organization's finance systems, had little or no experience creating survey software or understanding the process flow of a 360 system. The project practically consumed the small IT group for almost a year. After a considerable amount of time and money, the IT department finally got a system off the ground.

The resulting system was balky, to say the least. The web-based user interface was awkward, and I was overwhelmed by the number of navigation options on every single page. Efficient web surveys typically contain three navigation options: "Go back," "Next," and "Save/complete later." This homegrown interface had up to 12 navigation options on some pages. One button simply said "OK." After several months of use and hundreds of participants later, the client discovered that the algorithms its staff members had constructed were faulty and the data that every participant report had so far produced contained errors. Even if the technology issues can be resolved, often participants and their raters are not convinced that a homegrown system will provide the same confidentiality as a third-person provider.

There are so many 360 vendors available now that it doesn't make sense for most organizations to reinvent the wheel. It does require due diligence on the part of the purchasing organization, and it is critical to select a vendor that can manage the scale of the project you are considering and shares a similar philosophy regarding the collection and managing of feedback data—particularly as it affects the confidentiality and anonymity of the results.

Some vendors of 360s use their assessment business principally to leverage their consulting business. Make sure that the vendor you select will be there to support your implementation of the process after the sale closes. Before contracting with a 360 vendor, call their user support number and see how long it takes to reach a real person who can answer your 360 implementation questions.

One clear advantage to using an established vendor is to have access to its survey content. It is expensive and time consuming to develop research-based competencies and items, and this is not a task that organizations usually want to take on. Another organization discovered this the hard way. Its staff members made a noble attempt to create their own survey content, but the participants and raters complained that they found it impossible to answer the questions. Some questions asked about things that were not observable, like participants' attitudes and thought processes. Some questions were double-barreled, and the raters would answer the question differently depending on which part of the question they were answering.

Worst Practice: Poor Communication

One of CCL's research partners told of a 360 initiative it had conducted two years earlier that was a disaster. No one involved knew what they were supposed to do, what the purpose of the 360 was, what the timeline was, or who would see the feedback report. This seems to be a common theme in assessment activities. There is a lot of heavy lifting involved before anyone starts completing surveys. A thorough communication plan is critical, particularly for those directly involved with the 360 assessment process—including the participants, the managers, and all other raters.

Your vendor should help you understand the various roles involved with a 360, particularly the administrative roles within your organization. Someone will need to be identified to be responsible for coordinating logistics. This includes monitoring rater return status, workshop scheduling and feedback event coordination, and ongoing communication with the vendor.

Figure 13-1. Sample Checklist for Avoiding Common Problems with Using 360-Degree Feedback

1. Is the purpose clear? Can everyone involved describe
   - ☐ Why?
   - ☐ Why now?
   - ☐ Why you?

2. Is the initiative designed *up*?
   - ☐ Processes give people credit for taking responsibility for outcomes.
   - ☐ Participants have input on rater selection.
   - ☐ Rules provide structure but allow for participant choice.

3. Is the project size manageable?
   - ☐ Administrative duties have been clearly defined and assigned.
   - ☐ Pilot group(s) have been identified and a feedback debrief scheduled.
   - ☐ Feedback facilitators are identified and scheduled.

4. Do senior executives support the initiative?
   - ☐ Human resources and training and development staff are clear on how the 360 supports business drivers.
   - ☐ Executives have been involved on competency development.
   - ☐ Communication plan involving senior executives is in place.

5. Is the organization ready for a 360-degree assessment process?
   - ☐ Confidentiality rules are in place and understood by all involved.
   - ☐ Any previous issues with 360s have been addressed and resolved.
   - ☐ Measurement objectives, like competency models, are concise and clear.

6. Has thorough consideration been given as to whether to build your own assessment or contract with a vendor?
   - ☐ Internal review of information technology capability and availability has been thoroughly reviewed.
   - ☐ If external, vendor has similar assessment philosophy.
   - ☐ Vendor has research-based content and robust assessment tools.

7. Has a communication plan been developed?
   - ☐ A realistic timeline with clear milestones has been created.
   - ☐ The purpose of the initiative has been made clear, particularly about confidentiality of data and anonymity of rater responses.
   - ☐ All potential raters have been involved and exposed to an opportunity for rater training/ orientation to the assessment.

8. Are post-assessment plans in place?
   - ☐ Expectations of what participants are expected to do with their data are clear.
   - ☐ Participants have an opportunity to meet with a feedback coach in a private, confidential one-to-one session.
   - ☐ Expectations for creating a developmental plan are clear, as are the support mechanisms being provided by the organization.

Worst Practice: Confusing Assessment with Development

Once a participant has received a completed 360-degree feedback report and has met with a facilitator to discuss the results, the only thing that has happened so far is assessment—not development. The assessment process must be tied to a development planning step and then to an implementation and feedback loop by the participant.

Development is what happens *after* the individual has seen his or her data, come to terms with it, and decided what he or she is motivated to change. It usually involves conversations with the staff member's manager about whether he or she is targeting the right things to work on and what kind of support he or she can expect to get for working on the development plan. If there's no accountability or way to measure behavioral change, an organization will never be sure if it got its money's worth for the initiative. I don't have just one client example for this worst practice because it is so prevalent—easily the one I see the most often. I would estimate that nearly half the organizations that engage CCL for a 360 initiative do no formal follow-through. It is typical for organizations to focus intensely on the assessment aspect of the 360 initiative and then leave the participants on their own to create and deploy a development plan with no challenge or support from the organization.

Summing Up

In summary, this chapter has not given an exhaustive list of every reason 360-degree assessments can go wrong. It has simply given an overview of some of the most common ways organizations have botched 360-degree feedback initiatives. By keeping some of these pitfalls in mind, you can avoid making some of these same mistakes in your organization, and thereby tap into the benefits that 360-degree assessment has to offer. Use the checklist given in figure 13-1 to help your organization avoid these mistakes.

Further Reading

David Bracken, Carol W. Timmereck, and Allan H. Church, eds., *The Handbook of Multisource Feedback: The Comprehensive Resource for Designing and Implementing MSF Processes.* San Francisco: Jossey-Bass, 2001.

John W. Fleenor, Sylvester Taylor, and Craig Chappelow, *Leveraging the Impact of 360-Degree Feedback.* San Francisco: Pfeiffer, 2008.

Richard Lepsinger and Antoinette D. Lucia, *The Art and Science of 360-Degree Feedback.* San Francisco: Pfeiffer, 1997.

Walter W. Tornow and Manuel London, eds., *Maximizing the Value of 360-Degree Feedback: A Process for Successful Individual and Organizational Development.* San Francisco: Jossey-Bass, 1995.

About the Author

Craig Chappelow is the global assessment portfolio manager at the Center for Creative Leadership and has written extensively on the subjects of leadership and 360-degree assessment. Most recently, he coauthored a chapter on executive derailment in the book *The Perils of Accentuating the Positive* (Hogan Press, 2009) and coauthored the book *Leveraging the Impact of 360-Degree Feedback* (Pfeiffer, 2008). As a freelance writer, he has published articles in a wide variety of periodicals, from the *Harvard Business Review* to *Southern Living.* He was originally trained as a biologist, and he worked at Glidden Corporation and National Starch and Chemical Company. He holds a bachelor's degree from MacMurray College and a master's degree from the University of Vermont.

 **Chapter 14**

Leaders as Mentors and Teachers: Time-Tested Leadership Development Strategies

Edward Betof

In This Chapter

- Mentoring and teaching by leaders is a time-tested leadership development strategy dating back centuries before the birth of Christ.

- The six primary benefits of leaders serving as mentors and teachers.

- Organizations gain competitive advantages when their experienced leaders serve as mentors and teachers for both nascent leaders and their overall workforce.

- Five mentoring formats for leaders serving as teachers and mentors.

> *Mentoring: . . . a brain to pick, an ear to listen, and a push in the right direction.*
>
> —Source unknown

What do the following individuals, groups, and professionals have in common?

- great philosophers such as Plato, Aristotle, and Socrates from the Golden Age of Greece
- elders, shamans, or medicine men from early native civilizations
- leaders of the great religions over the centuries
- artisans or skilled craftsmen beginning in the Middle Ages
- Girl Scouts, Boy Scouts, and 4H leaders in the 20th and 21st centuries
- experienced physicians and nurses through the history of medical education
- labor union craft masters and foremen
- senior military and law enforcement personnel for many hundreds of years
- contemporary business leaders in selected high-performance companies
- great elementary school and university educators
- athletic and performance arts coaches
- sage friends and trusted advisers
- parents and grandparents.

The common element for all these is that they are examples of leaders who have served as mentors and teachers. Simply defined, mentoring is the helping and guiding of an individual's development.

Leaders have served as mentors and teachers since centuries before the birth of Christ in ancient civilizations around the globe. Basic means of survival, customs, and traditions were taught by elders to the young. The great religions passed their teachings from one generation to another. From these teachers, leaders emerged and continued the cycle of teaching–learning–surviving–thriving.

Mentoring and teaching are centuries-old strategies for the development of leaders that have withstood the test of time. As a documented developmental strategy, mentoring dates back to the Greek poet Homer's epic, the *Odyssey*. In fact, the word "mentor" comes from the Greek word meaning *enduring* and is derived from the name of a person who appears in this classic epic. As Odysseus (Ulysses, in the Latin translation) readied himself to leave and fight in what was to become the 10-year-long Trojan War, he is faced with leaving his young son and only heir, Telemachus, behind. Telemachus is unprepared to assume the crown, so Odysseus enlists the help of a trusted and experienced family friend named Mentor to be his son's teacher and guide. Mentor became the key developmental resource and, in effect, his guidance and teaching became the key developmental strategy that was employed to help Telemachus learn to be a leader and, eventually, the king.

This brief history lesson is a window into the importance, dynamics, and the staying power of successful mentoring and teaching experiences. It provides insight into several key characteristics of excellent leader-mentors and teachers. Effective mentors, and to a large degree teachers, share knowledge, experience, perspective, and counsel. They are also sensitive to others' needs and personalities, which enables them to establish, build, and sustain supportive, trusting, and confidential relationships. In short, they are trusted advisers who create opportunities for learning, growth, development, and positive change in others. The examples of individuals, groups, and professionals listed above are models of these characteristics.

Now dial forward from the ancient civilizations to today's complex organizations with their need and inherent competition for talented leaders. Leaders who serve as mentors, teachers, and coaches are vital organizational resources who support the development of current and emerging managers and executives. The use of mentors and leader-teachers can be a highly effective leadership development strategy. This is particularly the case when these approaches are used to complement a sound job challenge and assignment-based approach for the growth and development of leaders.

Leader-mentors and teachers are highly valued in many contemporary businesses, government, educational, and human services organizations. However, despite the demonstrated and time-tested value of leaders serving as mentors and teachers, many organizations place themselves at a competitive or talent disadvantage by failing to utilize these developmental resource people, who are typically experienced, motivated, and highly engaged. These can be lost developmental opportunities for many organizations—but usually not for those that have established themselves as best in class for the development of leaders.

The Six Major Benefits of Leader-Mentors and Teachers

Many organizations now use some form of a leader-mentor or leader-teacher approach as part of their leadership development and learning initiatives. These approaches can take many forms and are described later in this chapter. But when their leaders serve as mentors and teachers, on a small or large scale, organizations gain these six primary benefits:

- Helps drive business results.
- Stimulates the learning and development of leaders and associates.
- Improves the leadership perspective and skills of those who teach.
- Strengthens the organizational culture and communications.
- Promotes positive business and organizational change.
- Reduces costs by leveraging top talent.

This chapter focuses on two of these business and organizational benefits when leaders serve as mentors and leaders:

- Stimulates the learning and development of leaders and associates.
- Improves the leadership perspective and skills of those who teach.

Stimulating the Learning and Development of Leaders and Associates

A key reason to implement a leaders-as-mentors-and-teachers approach is that it is a catalyst for the learning and development of the leaders and associates who participate as mentees, protégés, or learners in mentoring, development, or learning programs. This dynamic occurs in three ways: role modeling, creating a safe environment for feedback, and building networks (Betof 2009).

Role Modeling

One of the most meaningful ways learners experience what is really important in an organization is through role modeling by their leaders. Imagine the impact of your CEO, presidents of global or national businesses, school superintendents, and functional leaders when they are perceived as dedicated mentors, teachers, and role models by leaders in their respective organizations. In a more formal teaching mode, imagine further the effect of these same leaders teaching principles of leadership and strategy and candidly addressing other topics that are vital to the success of their organizations.

The impressions made and lessons learned by leaders and professionals in mentoring and teaching-learning scenarios like these are vital to the success of any business, educational, governmental, or human service organization. Call it matching word and deed or walking the talk. The impressions are bold, and they can have a long-lasting, positive impact. When executives and administrators are also mentors and teachers, leaders who work under their influence, guidance, and direction benefit in many important ways. They will deeply understand business and organizational strategy as well as key priorities and how to address them. They often also receive invaluable input that can affect their career hopes and aspirations. And crucially, they also learn what is important about an organization's culture. This helps to accelerate the learning and development of leaders as well as helping to provide insulation from both common and organizationally specific career derailment factors. The impact that positive role models such as mentors and leader-teachers have tends to stay with mentees, protégés, and learners for many years.

Ask any leader this question: Who are the top five people who have most influenced your career, and possibly even your lives? Also ask: What did they do to influence you, and how did they do it?

As leaders answer these questions, you are very likely to hear enthusiastic stories about caring people who took a great interest in others and who served as mentors, teachers, guides, and coaches. The lessons learned are very durable. Additionally, these lessons have a ripple effect on others. Leaders who are valued as mentors and teachers by others are some of the most important role models in leaders' lives.

Creating a Safe Environment for Input and Feedback

Leaders have opportunities to gain perspective and learn from the experience of mentors and leader-teachers who take an authentic interest in them as unique and valued individuals. They are able to test their ideas and assumptions about their business and organizational strategies, their ideas for innovation, and how to handle particularly difficult or sensitive people situations.

Perhaps most important, they can also find a safe haven for testing their ideas about their own career development. They are also able to learn from and react to ideas concerning their development posed by their mentors. In some mentoring situations, these can be ideas that the mentee might not have even considered. This is the effect of mentors when they provide a trusting yet challenging and confidential environment that a mentee may not find elsewhere.

By its very nature, leadership development is the land of the uncomfortable, a term coined by the leadership expert Bob Eichinger. This is especially true in big, stretching, tough, and unfamiliar across-the-grain leadership roles. As a development strategy, in most situations, high-challenge, assignment-based development has been demonstrated to have the greatest potential for the growth of leaders. As a complement to this kind of challenging assignment-based development, mentors can have some of their greatest impact, in at least two ways. The first is by providing a longer-term career perspective of how such an assignment fits into one's overall development, no matter how tenuous or even scary the challenge may feel in the short term. The second way is when mentors provide input and feedback in a manner that shapes a leader's understanding of himself or herself. This desired effect happens because of the respect that the leader has for the mentor's courage, candor, and actions.

When executives teach courses as part of an organization's leadership development curriculum, leaders are able to consider ideas and practice skills and behaviors in other types of challenging yet safe environments conducive to development and learning. Leaders in these situations are able to obtain candid feedback from leader-teachers as well as peers before trying to implement them in their real work settings.

Also, in these types of learning environments, participants have opportunities to hear from, have ideas sparked by, and interact with leaders other than those with whom they regularly work. There are many advantages when leaders teach institutional knowledge, cultural expectations, and skills expected of managers and associates. When these are considered and practiced in the classroom, learners are able to try out what is uncomfortable and hear perspectives and receive feedback in a place other than their normal work settings. Ideas can be tested to determine if they are practical. Skills can be practiced.

When leaders teach in these kinds of situations, they are able to provide points of view and observations that have an inherent value often greater than what professional trainers can add by themselves. The combination of leader-teachers who co-train with learning and development professionals may provide the best of both worlds for leaders in a learning mode. In these types of facilitated teaching and learning environments, learners have an opportunity to assess their ideas and creatively explore possible solutions to the problems and challenges they face every day with leader-teachers and learning professionals, both of whom can serve as short-term mentors, coaches, facilitators, and advisers in and outside the classroom.

Building Networks

In both mentoring and teaching settings, mentees and learners have opportunities to build important networks with leader-mentors and teachers who can be resources for helping them with current and future leadership challenges. These relationships can be helpful in other ways as well. One common area is in the exploration of career growth possibilities and in making difficult career and career-related life decisions. These could include decisions about leadership experiences to be gained and roles to pursue, accept, or turn down.

These kinds of decisions might also involve possible relocations, expatriations, or taking on any other types of expanded responsibilities that could affect the nature of one's family, relationships, health, or available time for other valued aspects of one's life. On a team or organizational level, these types of meaningful networks and interactions with leader-mentors and teachers can foster a robust learning and developmental culture that is so important in building strong leaders and talent pipelines.

As leadership networks expand within organizations as a result of leadership development experiences, mentees and learners also have opportunities to make positive impressions on those leaders who are mentors and who teach. In addition to being identified as mentees and learners, sometimes by nomination for selected programs, these same emerging leaders may have opportunities to co-teach with more experienced leaders. They may, themselves, assume mentoring roles and become part of mentoring networks, which further increases the likelihood of additional interactions and visibility with senior or more experienced leaders. It is not uncommon for relationships to form in these types of situations that can have a profound and lasting impact on an individual's career.

In addition, in many organizations senior leaders are talent scouts looking for leadership capabilities to meet the challenges of their organization through various talent management and succession planning processes. Mentoring and teaching situations can create opportunities to identify talent further along in the pipeline or elsewhere in the organization that simply would not have occurred had the mentoring and teaching not been done. This kind of organizational matchmaking often happens naturally, whether or not it is a stated goal of mentoring or leader-teacher processes.

Conversely, mentees and learners also have opportunities to do reverse talent scouting of more senior leaders in the organization, whom they might later ask to become mentors or, when the timing is right, with whom they might seek opportunities for new roles in their respective teams or organizations. This type of multidirectional talent scouting can be a very healthy dynamic in an age of employee free agency and at a time when employees are increasingly being asked to assume primary responsibility for their career development. Whether or not it is a stated goal of mentoring and leader-teacher programs, organizations with strong mentoring and leader-teacher processes can help create and add to the conditions that foster high employee performance and the retention of top talent, in addition to explicitly helping to build a strong leadership pipeline.

Improving the Leadership Perspective and Skills of Mentors and Those Who Teach

Stimulating the learning and development of leaders and associates has been described above as one of the key business and organizational benefits when leaders serve as mentors and teachers. A second key benefit is that it improves the leadership perspective and skills of the leader-mentors and teachers themselves.

These benefits are realized in at least five ways. First, when leaders are mentors and teachers, they crystallize and then communicate their most strongly held beliefs on a range of important leadership and business topics. Then they must hone and polish the way they articulate these ideas, strategies, and values to be able share their perspectives and the lessons they have learned from their years of successes, disappointments, and even failures.

Consider the value gained by mentors and leader-teachers as they sharpen their leadership perspectives on vital topics such as

- keys to growing a business
- exceeding customer expectations
- how to achieve one's potential
- how teams or organizations can work at very high levels
- the values and ethics essential for success
- the role that mentoring, teaching, and coaching have in bringing out the best in others
- the role of courage and fierce resolve in achieving goals
- the place that humility has in successes and effectiveness in working with others.

Many mentors and leader-teachers report that they are better able to model their desired leadership behaviors in their full-time role as a result of their preparation and actual performance as mentors and teachers. Mentors first need to be clear and honest with themselves about their own points of view, behaviors, and skills to serve in the role of trusted advisers to other leaders. Additionally, when leaders prepare to teach others, they learn the content of the program—either the actual specific content or the leadership, management, and functional or technical concepts that underlie the program—more deeply than they had previously. These, of course, are for the most part the same concepts they are expected by others and expect themselves to model in their actual work.

Second, mentors and leader-teachers frequently move out of their comfort zone. Job challenges of different types, sizes, shapes, and intensities are the "genetic material" that enables leaders to learn, grow, change, and develop. For many leaders, mentoring and teaching is a very significant job challenge—it requires many leaders to step out of their comfort zone and to work across the grain of what they do best and most frequently. Some leaders may be mentors for the first time. They may also be in a mentoring relationship with leaders who have very different backgrounds, work preferences, or value systems than their own. They may be called on to provide advice and counsel on sensitive topics with which they are uncomfortable. Advice on career or even strategic issues may require the mentors to deal with areas where they have less experience. Each of these situations and many others stretch one's comfort zones and are frequently developmental and growth-enhancing experiences for mentors.

There are additional reasons why teaching for leaders can also be a significant growth experience. Sometimes leader-teachers must teach or facilitate the teaching of content areas that are new, different, or even uncomfortable and strange for them. Experiences like this stimulate their learning and development. For experienced leader-teachers, teaching can also be a learning and developmental experience of a different kind. For example, this might occur when they teach others with whom they are not familiar or who work in functions or areas of the company where they have little or no exposure. They may need to handle unanticipated issues that arise in class with which they may not be comfortable and for which they may not have had any time to prepare. To teach effectively, leader-teachers must simultaneously be firm in their convictions and spontaneous and agile in their thinking.

Third, mentors and leader-teachers often come away from their mentoring and teaching assignments with a much more grounded approach to what is really going on in the organization and what others are thinking. These are information and organizational perspectives that they likely would not have gained had they not offered their time and experience as a mentor and as leader-teacher.

Fourth, mentoring and teaching encourages self-improvement by reducing the dissonance between what they say or teach and what they actually do and how they act in their leadership role. Leaders regularly report that they feel a strong responsibility to model in their roles what they teach and share as mentors or in a classroom. Whether it is a sense of responsibility, personal learning, pride, or even guilt, leader-teachers benefit and often grow by reducing or eliminating any gap between what they say and teach and the way they act on a daily basis. I have frequently heard individuals report that they are better leaders as a result of teaching. The same can be said about their mentoring experiences as well. They are clearer about where they stand on issues, and they often improve their ability to speak on issues for which they take positions or feel strongly. Consistently, mentors and leader-teachers report that they do not like the dissonance of saying and teaching one thing and doing something else. So almost all remove the dissonance by continuing to mentor and teach but by also improving how they perform day to day.

Fifth, mentors and leader-teachers can learn by being members of developmental communities of practice. Mentors can share what they learn and, without breaching confidentiality, develop and become better mentors by understanding how others deal with their mentoring and teaching responsibilities. Leader-teachers can co-teach with other leaders. They often share and discuss program content before, certainly during, and frequently after the program has ended. Co-trainers or teachers make self-corrections to improve their own teaching. As trust builds, they make suggestions and exchange teaching feedback with fellow leader-teachers. Also, a remarkable number of learning and developmental opportunities arise when leader-teachers take advantage of the available informal time to interact with fellow leader-teachers as well as students. Frequently, these opportunities occur during trips to and from programs, while leader-teachers are having discussions between themselves as learners and are involved in group discussions, problem-solving activities, or case study work, and during breaks and after-hour sessions.

From Homer's *Odyssey* to Mentoring for the Masses: Examples of Different Forms of Leadership Development Mentoring Formats

From its documented roots in Homer's *Odyssey* in ancient Greece to today's Web 2.0 technology-enabled social learning, the mentoring of leaders for developmental purposes has taken many forms. Though there are more than 50 ways in which leaders can contribute as teachers, the remainder of this chapter focuses on five examples or approaches to mentoring (Betof 2009).

Historically, the most common mentoring method has been a one-to-one relationship between mentor and mentee, sometimes called a protégé. There are also group mentoring processes. Developed more than a decade ago, a third mentoring method is referred to as mentoring circles, which is a type of group mentoring approach that uses a very specific format and protocol. Still another group mentoring approach is called a peer assist. A fifth, and most recent, form of mentoring is technologically enabled and can involve considerably larger numbers of mentors and mentees than more traditional approaches. It can also have an open system of information sharing. All forms of mentoring are designed to be inherently developmental for leaders and professionals. Let's look very briefly at each of these approaches.

One-to-one relationship between mentor and mentee: Dating back to the original documented relationship between Mentor and Telemachus, individualized mentoring relationships have benefited leaders and future leaders for centuries. At their best, this and other forms of mentoring are goal specific and time bound. Although some one-to-one mentoring relationships continue for many years because they are mutually satisfying and productive, typically, they last from several months to one or possibly two years. Individualized mentoring can be combined with or could also be an offshoot of some form of group mentoring.

Group mentoring formats facilitate opportunities for one or several mentors to provide guidance and support for an intact group or team of mentees. Though possibly not as personalized as one-to-one mentoring, it does begin to address the issue of having only a very limited number of people being mentored in individualized settings.

Mentoring circles typically utilize an experienced mentor with an ongoing group of protégés for a defined time such as nine or 12 months. In addition to sage advice from the mentor, mentoring circles have the advantage of using peer mentoring and coaching. There is usually a defined format or topic for each mentoring circle session.

Peer assist is a unique variation of group or peer mentoring. The peer assist methodology applies the power of an intact group or a team's experience to one person's challenge, problem, or opportunity. In a carefully facilitated format, a typical peer assist group mentoring session takes approximately one to two hours.

The most recent form of mentoring uses *current advances in social networking and social learning.* It combines these advances with Web 2.0 technology so that a small or larger number of mentors can reach significantly larger numbers—the "masses"—of mentees who may be in numerous locations and time zones. A broader adaptation of this approach uses social learning technology combined with the best practices of mentoring and knowledge management for just-in-time knowledge and resource sharing for potentially very large numbers of employees.

This chapter has concluded with brief descriptions of five different formats for individual and group mentoring. Each of these is designed to enhance the development of leaders in organizational settings, ranging from businesses to schools to human service and governmental organizations. Thus, mentoring and teaching form a key element of leadership development, whether one is a mentor or a recipient of the mentoring.

Further Reading

Chip R. Bell, *Managers as Mentors: Building Partnerships for Learning.* San Francisco: Berrett-Koehler, 1996.

Laura M. Francis, "Shifting the Shape of Mentoring," *T+D,* September 2009, 36–40; www.3creek .com/resources/research/TD_Sep09.pdf.

Susan H. Gebelein and others, eds., *The Successful Manager's Handbook.* Minneapolis: Personnel Decisions International, 2005.

John C. Maxwell, *Mentoring 101.* Nashville: Thomas Nelson, 2008.

Carson Pue, *Mentoring Leaders: Wisdom for Developing Character, Calling, and Competency.* Grand Rapids: Baker Books, 2005.

Reference

Betof, E. 2009. *Leaders as Teachers: Unlock the Teaching Potential of Your Company's Best and Brightest.* Alexandria, VA: ASTD Press; San Francisco: Berrett-Koehler.

About the Author

Edward Betof is a member of the faculty of the University of Pennsylvania, where he is the senior fellow and an academic director for the first-of-its-kind doctoral program at a major university designed for the preparation of chief learning officers. Previously, he served as vice president for talent management and chief learning officer at BD (Becton, Dickinson and Company). He is a faculty member of the Institute for Management Studies. He is the author of *Leaders as Teachers* (ASTD Press and Berrett-Koehler) and the lead author of *Just Promoted!* (McGraw-Hill). He served a three-year term from 2004 to 2006 as a member of ASTD's Board of Directors. He was also elected as the chair of the Executive Committee of the Conference Board's Council on Learning, Development, and Organizational Performance, and served in that capacity in 2006 and 2007. He serves on Pennsylvania State University's Outreach Advisory Board. He received his doctoral degree from Temple University in 1976.

Chapter 15

Learning on the Job

Ellen Van Velsor

In This Chapter

- What people learn from job experiences.

- How they learn from these work-related events.

- Why learning from experience can be difficult.

- What can be done to enhance the potential for learning on the job.

When people consider how learning and development take place, they tend to think of formal training and to look to these kinds of classroom or e-based opportunities as benefits and as necessities. But when we ask people to describe the *most important* learning experiences of their careers, these kinds of experiences typically do not take center stage. The learning that sticks with people for 10, 20, or even 30 years tends to come from events that happen naturally on the job, experiences such as challenging assignments, business crises, mistakes, and personal failures, and having an exceptional boss or having to deal with a very bad boss.

Some of these events happen almost by chance, others are intentionally designed by a boss or mentor for the manager's development, and some are self-initiated. Yet people not only remember these events as if they happened yesterday, but they can discuss at length what they learned, how or why they believe they learned from those events, and how that learning has affected the leader they have grown to be. However, much of this learning is almost accidental, in that it is often unplanned and unsupported. The assignments and relationships people remember were most often not planned for intentional learning. And few of the experiences recounted by managers were intentionally supported or made part of a systematic development approach so that learning could be maximized.

Of course, many organizations use job rotation to develop skills—for example, moving a new fast-track human resources (HR) recruit through compensation, recruitment, assessment, and training assignments to develop the skills and perspectives needed in an HR generalist or HR manager. But the emphasis of job rotation is often about learning the business of the function, picking up a variety of technical skills (in this example, understanding compensation systems, recruitment processes and skills, onboarding, and training), and gaining a broad view of the function's role in the organization. Though that is certainly important, particularly at an entry level, many organizations do not use and integrate learning from the broad variety of challenging experiences (assignments, relationships, and setbacks) that take place on the job to intentionally enhance the leadership capabilities of people from the start of their careers onward.

This chapter focuses on how to understand and enhance learning from these job experiences. It takes an in-depth look at what people learn from job experiences, how they learn from these work-related events, why learning from experience is hard, and what can be done to enhance the potential for learning on the job. How managers describe various kinds of potent work-based experiences and what they learn from them is the subject to which we now turn.

What People Learn from Job Experiences

Over the course of 30 years, significant research has been done, by the Center for Creative Leadership and by others, to better understand how people learn, grow, and change over the course of their careers. Through a series of studies—beginning in the United States and now including interviews with senior managers in China and India, public- and private-sector leaders in Singapore, and male and female senior executives who attend the Center for Creative Leadership's Leadership at the Peak program from all sectors of the economy—it has become clear that job experiences can both deepen and broaden an individual's overall learning and development. Certain experiences are key to workplace learning. Here, I discuss three types of non-classroom-based learning experiences: work assignments, developmental relationships, and work-related mistakes and setbacks. These are among the most frequently cited events that lead to workplace learning.

Work Assignments

When we think about learning on the job, work assignments probably first come to mind as sources of opportunity, and in fact research bears that out. We often think of assignment-based learning as "development in place," because learning from the challenges encountered in one's day-to-day work often does not require a major job shift or moving to a new organization to learn (McCauley 2006). Instead, one can learn from challenges that arise in the context of a current job, when the context for the work changes in some way or because new elements are added to the job. Among the assignments most frequently described as developmental across many studies (McCall, Lombardo, and Morrison 1988; Morrison, White, and Van Velsor 1992; Douglas 2006; Yip and Wilson 2010) are the following:

- an increase in scope of responsibilities
- an assignment in which the individual is responsible for creating change
- a significant project or cross-functional team
- an international assignment.

Although some of these assignments signify a job change, others are experiences that can come in the context of one's current role. We also know that there is a great similarity across cultures in the kinds of job assignments that people see as developmental, but there are also some differences (Yip and Wilson 2010). For example, one of the most frequently reported learning experiences in a recent study conducted in China was an event called "organizational reform," usually referencing a powerful learning experience Chinese managers had been working in an organization under transformation from a state-run entity to a private-sector firm (Zhang, Chandrasekar, and Wei 2009).

People tend to learn a variety of lessons from events like these. Table 15-1 illustrates some of the many lessons people report learning from the events listed above. Tables 15-2 and 15-3 provide useful tools for (1) assessing the developmental quality of a job or job enlargement and (2) facilitating learning from a developmental assignment.

Developmental Relationships

Learning can also come from engagement in job-based developmental relationships that challenge and support a person. These can be in the form of good relationships with a helpful boss, a mentor, or a formal or informal coaching arrangement. Bosses, mentors, and coaches can play many roles. Though many think of relationships mainly as ways to gain support (and they certainly are), the best developmental relationships also provide challenges in the forms of ongoing feedback, evaluation of strategies for change, standards for self-evaluation, perspectives different from one's own, pressure to fulfill commitments to learning, and serving as an example of competence in one's desired area of development.

Table 15-1. Key Lessons from Four Types of Job Assignments

From an increase in scope:
- To manage and motivate subordinates
- To develop others
- What it means to be an effective manager and leader
- The technical aspects of running a business
- How to build relationships with superiors and peers
- Operational execution
- Team management

From responsibilities for creating change:
- Confidence
- To be innovative and entrepreneurial
- To manage change
- Strategic skills
- Communication skills
- Enhanced self-awareness

From a significant project or cross-organizational team:
- To manage those who report directly to a manager (with project management)
- Technical skills
- Project management skills
- How to influence without authority

From an international assignment:
- Cultural adaptability
- Strategic skills
- Valuing diversity

McCauley and Douglas (2004) describe several strategies for using developmental relationships to enhance job learning, including

- regarding the boss as a partner in development
- seeking out multiple relationships for development
- figuring out which roles are needed to help with current learning goals (for example, feedback provider, sounding board, assignment broker, cheerleader) and finding the right people to meet these needs
- making full use of lateral, subordinate, and external relationships
- not assuming relationships need to be long term or intense to be helpful
- being especially aware of the need for help during times of transition.

Table 15-2. Assessing the Developmental Quality of a Job: Questions to Ask

- Will I be required to accomplish goals, focus on tasks, or take on responsibilities with which I am unfamiliar (for example, in a new function, first supervision, work in new markets)?
- Will I need to create change, reorganize, or start something new?
- Am I likely to inherit problems left over from a former job incumbent, from outdated systems, or old structures?
- Will I be managing employees with known performance problems or histories of grievances or morale issues?
- Are results, decisions, or actions in this job likely to have high visibility with upper management or externally (for example, with the media)?
- Does the job have scope and/or scale that is beyond what I have handled in the past? Are there significantly more people reporting directly to be managed, is it a first supervision opportunity or a first chance to manage managers? Is the budget or business responsibility significantly larger than any I've been responsible for in the past?
- Will I need to influence people over whom I have no direct authority to be effective and successful in achieving group goals? Will there be organizational politics to be managed?
- Will I need to negotiate with external parties (for example, unions, nongovernmental organizations, partners) in this work? Will there be other kinds of external pressure as part of this job?
- Will there be opportunity to interact with people in other cultures or to deal with global aspects of the business?
- Will the group I am part of be more diverse than any I have worked with in the past?

Source: Adapted from McCauley (2006).

Table 15-4 provides a tool, in the form of a set of questions, that can be helpful in assessing a potentially developmental relationship. These questions are probably best used when one can pair a developmental relationship with another new learning opportunity, such as a change in job or new challenges added to one's current role.

Relationships don't have to be positive to provide learning opportunities. Research shows that even experiences with an inept or negative boss can produce learning (McCall, Lombardo, and Morrison 1988; Douglas 2006). From these negative role model experiences, managers learn lessons, such as how not to treat people, integrity, and managing upward.

Table 15-3. Questions to Ask to Facilitate Learning from a Developmental Assignment

---

About yourself:
- What strengths do I bring to this job? What will help me?
- What are my development needs? What might hinder me from being successful?
- What aspects of this job might be particularly challenging for me? For example, is the role clear or ambiguous? Will I have the authority I need? How might I overcome any obstacles?
- What can I learn from this job? What do I want to learn?
- What might make it difficult for me to learn?
- What kind of help or advice am I likely to need?
- What are my career goals? How does this job relate to those?

About the assignment:
- What are the organization's goals for me in this job?
- What are my own goals in this job?
- How does this job fit with the organization's mission, values, and goals?
- What do I know about the tasks, responsibilities, and challenges of this job?
- What are the people reporting directly to me, my boss, and my peers like?
- Am I likely to encounter any resistance? How might I overcome that?
- Who can help me and provide support?
- What other resources do I have available?
- Is there anything I would change about this assignment?

During and after the assignment:
- How can I monitor my learning? For example, will I keep a journal, find a learning partner, seek feedback?
- What am I learning? Anything I did not expect?
- What am I not learning that I had hoped I would? Why?
- How will I know I have learned what I wanted and needed to learn?
- What was the most challenging part of this assignment for me?
- What did I do when I felt particularly challenged? How did I behave? What was the result?
- What will I do differently if faced with a similar situation in the future?
- What mistakes have I made? What have I learned from them?
- What was my greatest success? What contributed to it? What did it teach me?
- What are my next steps? How can I take better advantage of the learning opportunities in my next assignment?

Source: Adapted from Ohlott (2004).

Of course, a constructive boss is most frequently cited as a developmental relationship on the job. From good bosses, people report learning things like how to effectively manage those who report directly to them, strategic skills, and guiding principles for facing the challenges of leadership. The impact of a good boss is evident across cultures as well, and may be particularly strong in countries where superiors garner more respect and authority. In India and Singapore, for example, constructive bosses are seen as playing a significant role in helping subordinates learn from job assignments (Yip and Wilson 2010).

Table 15-4. Questions for Exploring a Developmental Relationship

What will I need?	Who can provide this?
Will I be practicing new behaviors that will benefit from feedback?	Who is in a position to observe me? Who is good at providing feedback? Whom do I trust to be straightforward?
Will I encounter dilemmas I need to think through?	Who is good at thinking out loud and considering alternatives? Who has faced these same dilemmas before? With whom can I share my uncertainties?
Will I need someone to help me gather or make sense of feedback?	Who is good at making sense of data? With whom am I willing to share feedback? Whom do others trust to gather feedback?
Do I need to understand new perspectives?	Who has a perspective different from my own? Who is good at dialogue and examining assumptions? Who is good at the role of devil's advocate?
Will I need help in gaining access to added challenges?	Who can sponsor me when certain jobs become available? Who can help me add challenge to my job?
Do I need someone to hold me accountable for learning?	Can my current boss do that? Is there someone else who wants me to achieve a learning goal?
Do I need to watch someone who is skilled in my learning area?	Who would be a great role model for me? Who can give me good learning strategies?
Am I likely to become frustrated?	With whom can I share my feelings? Who can be both empathetic and objective? Who can see through my excuses and procrastination?
Will I need encouragement to stick with needed learning?	Who is able to make me feel competent? With whom can I share small successes? Who is in a position to reward me?

Source: Adapted from McCauley and Douglas (2004).

Mistakes and Setbacks

Job-related crises, large and small, both organizational and personal, are often crucibles for learning (Moxley and Pulley 2004). These are often unexpected but significant events that usually cause some sense of loss (of confidence, status, credibility, or the like) with which the individual must deal. Mistakes, particularly when visible to others or when causing significant business losses, are one kind of setback remembered as painful and yet rich in learning by many managers. From making mistakes, people learn resilience, technical and management skills, and often something about their own strengths and limitations. Career setbacks, such as being fired, downsized, demoted, or simply plateaued (formally advised as no longer promotable), cause managers to reassess actions, performance, and goals and to develop new understandings of self and work-related strengths and weaknesses. In all these situations, it often takes time and support for people to be able to draw lessons from the experience of a work-related hardship, but it is often rich and introspective learning—and hard won.

How People Learn from Job Experiences

A job is a kind of "holding environment"—a virtual classroom that can work to stimulate and challenge an individual to learn and grow or can deaden the mind with a repetition of tasks and no new demands. People learn from their experiences when they recognize that the experience demands new ways of thinking or new skills; when they have the opportunities needed to apply and practice those; and when they have support from superiors, co-workers, and the organizational culture. If that is not the case (that is, if people are underchallenged or not supported), they can easily lose motivation to learn and to perform, even in their areas of expertise.

My colleagues and I believe that the best development experiences are those that contain three elements—assessment, challenge, and support (McCauley, Van Velsor, and Ruderman 2010). Many assignments that leaders mention contain, almost by definition, heavy doses of challenge. That's part of what causes them to be remembered (degree of difficulty, loss, interpersonal problems). What's often missing are the assessment and support elements—which actually may either be simply missing or not remembered because they were not an intentional part of the development system.

Assessment is important because of the role self-awareness plays in learning and development (Hall 2004). Self-awareness is commonly understood as the ability to recognize various aspects of your identity, to understand your own strengths and weaknesses, and to appreciate the impact of those on others. For most individuals, self-awareness is an area to be developed throughout a career, and many managers have a self-perception that is not entirely in line with how their skills and behaviors are seen by others (Harris and Schaubroeck 1988; Mabe and West 1982). Periodic opportunities to assess or reassess skills and development needs are helpful when starting a new assignment, in particular, because they alert the individual to the changing demands and fit between those demands and his or her current competencies. Assessment can also be helpful in letting someone know when learning has been achieved and skills have improved. Multi-rater feedback is useful in this regard, to help leaders know when the learning they have experienced through a series of developmental experiences has resulted in others being able to see improvement as a result of that learning.

In addition to assessment playing a vital role in learning, we know that the type and degree of challenge an experience holds for an individual are central to the likelihood that one can learn from that experience. In terms of type of challenge, it is clear that opportunities featuring certain kinds of challenges are key to learning on the job (McCauley and others 1994). Unfamiliar responsibilities, such as switching from a line or operations role to a staff role, require individuals to acquire new knowledge, perform in front of new bosses and peers, manage people from different backgrounds, and perhaps use new ways of solving problems. When a job requires focusing on developing new directions, an individual is challenged to create change in an ambiguous environment, reorganize existing structures or systems, or start something new—tasks that require thinking in new ways, encountering resistance, and building systems and structure. In moving into a new job, a manager can also encounter inherited problems, requiring that he or she bring their own skills and perspectives to bear on long-standing issues left behind by the previous incumbent. Jobs that come with inherited problems also help people learn to deal with adversity because solving those problems often requires making tough decisions.

Problems with employees also create developmental challenges for managers, in that they must become motivated to use a variety of approaches to help others improve their performance, learn to be good coaches, acquire the ability and knowledge base about when and how to let someone go, and so on. When an assignment involves high stakes, it provides a challenge because the results are clearly visible and the incumbent has direct accountability for key decisions and often feels intense pressure from higher management. In dealing with high stakes, people often improve their ability to handle stress, become more decisive, and improve their ability to deal with top management.

A job that involves significant responsibility for people, budgets, or large portions of the organization challenges the manager by its scope and scale. When faced with this kind of challenge, managers learn to coordinate and integrate across groups, to create management systems, and to delegate. Influencing without authority can be a challenge in almost any job when the work requires an individual to gain cooperation from peers or higher-ups to be successful. Managers learn to deal with organizational politics more effectively and to work across boundaries. When an individual must engage in handling external pressure, an assignment can require people to hone their negotiation skills, learn to better see things from others' perspectives, and also enhance their ability to collaborate. Working across cultures or in a context of work group diversity gives people the opportunity to become more aware of their own biases, to recognize the need to overcome stereotypes, adapt to different circumstances and individual needs, and persuade people from different backgrounds to work together (Ohlott 2004; McCauley 2006).

Note that many of these job challenges involve some kind of boundary crossing—that is, moving from one function to another, from one level to another, or across boundaries between organizations or even between cultures or countries. Whenever an individual is required to move into a "space" that is new, there is an opportunity, and often a requirement, to acquire new perspectives and knowledge sets, solve problems in different ways, interact with people who see the world differently, and engage in new behaviors to be effective. Boundary-crossing experiences can therefore be rich learning events that provoke significant development (Yip 2007).

In terms of degree of challenge, it is important to remember that while challenge helps people recognize new skills are needed, motivates people to learn, and provides a degree of excitement often unmatched at work, too much challenge can overwhelm a learner. Challenge can get in the way of learning if the level of challenge is too high and without requisite support. Consider the situations depicted in figure 15-1. Situation A is what a developmental experience should feel like when existing skills overlap enough with task demands so as to ensure adequate competency, but there is also sufficient challenge (room for the development of new skills) in the experience. Situation B shows what the same assignment may feel like when an individual has been at it for some time, perhaps having reached what Nicholson and West call the stabilization stage (see the sidebar). At this stage, skills have grown to match job demands, and there is little, if any, room for development in the assignment at this point. Though an individual in this situation would need to add a new challenge to his or her current role, or move into a new role, to learn more, that individual should take care not to move into or create something like situation C, where the task or job demands outstrip his or her current abilities by a wide margin. This third diagram depicts an assignment that is probably too high a risk, both for the individual and for the organization. In the case where someone must be moved into a situation like this, serious attention should be paid to the adequacy and types of support the person will need to both learn and succeed.

Figure 15-1. Developmental Experience

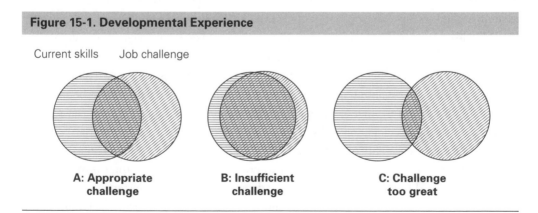

Current skills   Job challenge

A: Appropriate challenge

B: Insufficient challenge

C: Challenge too great

Learning in a Role Transition

Nicholson and West (1988, 1989) identified a process of phases through which a person makes a transition into a role. Each phase involves some form of learning, whether the role is formal (a new job) or more informal (added responsibilities in an existing job). The stages are as follows:

- *Preparation:* The individual develops initial expectations and creates an orientation and attitudes toward the role.
- *Encounter:* The individual explores and makes sense of the role.
- *Adjustment:* The individual changes in response to the role, shapes the role, and develops a network of relationships related to the role.
- *Stabilization:* The individual achieves a level of personal and organizational effectiveness in the role.

This brings us to support, the third aspect important to maximizing learning on the job. In general, support is important in balancing and modulating the challenges people face. Though a low-challenge situation (as in situation B in figure 15-1) probably does not need the same kinds of support needed by a person facing a high-challenge situation (situation A in figure 15-1), if underchallenged, he or she may need support in the form of finding added learning opportunities in the current job or in a new role. Challenges stretch people and put them in a position of disequilibrium, but support helps people know they can handle the struggle of learning and can maintain a positive view of themselves as capable and worthy, even in the face of mistakes and possibly a temporary decline in performance.

Support means different things to different people. Though the largest source of support for many is other people—bosses, co-workers, family, friends, professional coaches, and the like—support can also come from organizational systems (for example, mentoring programs, support groups) or, more generally, from the organizational culture. Support is a key factor in maintaining an individual's motivation to learn. It helps generate a sense of self-efficacy about learning, which in turn helps people exert effort to master challenges. If people do not receive adequate support for their learning, the challenges they are facing, to learn and to perform well, can often overwhelm them.

Maximizing learning on the job also means taking on a variety of experiences over the whole course of one's career (Hall 2004; McCauley 2006; McCauley, Van Velsor, and Ruderman 2010). The more varied one's experience base, the more likely it is that one can develop the broadest array of skills and perspectives, and the more likely it is that good performance can be maintained in the face of changing organizational and market or industry demands. Facing new challenges forces one to use existing strengths in new ways and to develop in areas not yet tested or refined. Challenge can be added to a current job, or one might take on a new job to broaden one's base of experience or develop specific competencies.

Maximizing learning also has to do with understanding readiness. Readiness for learning is a function of how an individual sees himself or herself, personality preferences such as openness, prior experiences, and the other challenges he or she is currently facing (Avolio 2004). As mentioned above, self-awareness (of strengths and weaknesses) is an important facilitator of learning from a challenging assignment and can be facilitated by assessment, using formal means (for example, 360-degree instruments) and/or coaching. Finally, not everyone will be challenged by the same experiences or challenged by the same experience to a similar degree. Challenge is subjective and influenced not only by previously attained skills and perspectives but also by past experience with similar challenges or the degree of preparation for a current challenge. So taking an individualized approach, rather than one size fits all, is imperative.

What Gets in the Way of Learning on the Job

Despite all preparation, learning from one's experiences can be difficult for many reasons. As mentioned above, inadequate readiness, and too few or too many job challenges without adequate support, can get in the way of learning from a potentially developmental job experience. Yet even in a job with appropriate challenges, the press of everyday work can easily get in the way of learning. Time has become a precious commodity, and people focus on devoting precious resources to the most urgent and highest-priority tasks. If learning is not one of those, it will suffer.

When pressed, people often do not give learning the attention or priority necessary to realize development outcomes. This is reinforced in organizations where the achievement of performance goals is more consistently and frequently rewarded than achieving learning goals. In an organizational culture that rewards performance to the exclusion of learning, inertia and past success can be major obstacles to continued learning. People like to use their strengths, to continue to get positive feedback for their behavior, and to continue to be rewarded for what they have been rewarded for in the past. In addition to the comfort this approach can bring, relying on strengths and sticking with tried-and-true behaviors usually seems like it makes the best use of that scarce resource, time.

Learning new skills and developing new approaches takes time and comes with the threat of performance declines, however temporary. Being able to see when new approaches are not working (that is, being focused on learning) requires time to reflect and skill in reflecting. People rarely feel they can take the time to pause and reflect about learning except when they suffer a significant failure. Unfortunately, because learning from failures often focuses only on what went wrong, it has the potential to erode self-esteem and reinforce one's fear of taking risks in new and challenging situations.

For all these reasons, learning from experience feels risky, both to the individual facing added challenges and to the organization faced with providing them. Recognizing the need for new learning is stressful for the individual because it requires the person to admit to himself or herself and possibly to others that what he or she is doing or currently knows is inadequate for future work. No one wants to be perceived as weak or flawed, particularly in an organization where tolerance for weakness or "not knowing" (which often goes hand in hand with tolerance for learning) is low.

So when time is scarce or organizational support is lacking, people are less likely to use the tools that support learning, such as keeping a learning journal. Although one may not have time in the course of a hectic day to sit back and reflect, using a journal to note observations, feelings, thoughts, and critical events can be a useful way of preserving these experiences to reflect on later. Capturing reflections in a journal and reading back through them over time can be a powerful way of learning about work and self—gaining the ability to see oneself grow and change over time (Van Velsor, Moxley, and Bunker 2004).

Personality (or personal preferences) also plays a role in one's comfort with learning. Cognitive capabilities, self-esteem and self-efficacy, and openness to experience can all affect one's ability to learn from work experience. Yet awareness of these can help an individual better deal with the uncomfortable feeling of going against one's grain that a job challenge can impose. These can be taken into account, to the extent that they are known, in making job assignments or adding job challenges. But given a minimum of any of these capabilities, when an individual is ready to learn—given the right opportunities, tools, and organizational support—development is likely to result.

How to Enhance Learning on the Job

There are a variety of tactics available for enhancing learning on the job. Many of these are straightforward and simple in their implementation. Others require taking a more systematic view of learning and development and letting go of the assumptions that classroom training and providing unsupported job challenges are the most effective ways to promote learning or the development of abilities such as leadership. Some ideas for enhancing learning across the organization are presented in table 15-5, organized under the categories of assessment, challenge, and support (although, clearly, some approaches provide more than one of these benefits).

Table 15-5. Enhancing Learning on the Job

Assessment:

- Help individuals become clear about what they want to or need to learn, for their current assignment or their next or future ones.
- Use assessments (360-degree and self-assessments) to provide baseline, enhance awareness of strengths and development needs, and assess readiness for learning.
- Use reflection techniques: journaling, after-action review, end of assignment transition reports. Work to build a culture that supports reflection and values learning.
- Use other kinds of tools periodically—for example, key events question as dialogue tool.

Challenge:

- Encourage managers to play a key role in the career planning processes of the people reporting directly to them and to work with those individuals to match developmental challenges to learning goals.
- Provide and encourage a variety of career experiences and job tasks for every individual.
- Train people to reflect and learn when opportunities present themselves.
- Think about scale in job assignments—for example, startups are valuable at all levels, but start small and build.
- Create practices/climate that help people reflect on their experiences together on a regular basis. Model this and have managers model it.
- Use coaching to challenge leaders to step back and reflect when difficulty is encountered or success is achieved. Reinforce success when behaviors or skills are achieved.

Support:

- Intentionally use developmental relationships in combination with assignments and classroom training.
- Create holding environments for learning—for example, support groups for people who are facing challenges that are new to them, alumni groups from programs.
- Create processes to link classroom training and leadership development programs to job assignments and developmental relationships.
- Provide training to all employees on how to give and receive feedback so individuals feel they can provide good feedback to individuals attempting to learn or change and a climate for development is created.
- Use coaching to help people digest and connect learning from more informal events (good/bad bosses, mistakes) to learning from formal assignments—an external coach necessary for some, such as good/bad boss and perhaps mistakes and career setbacks; consider when a boss might be best coach and when an external coach would be preferable.
- Create forums where people can share their learnings and experts can share rules of thumb for dealing with certain kinds of challenge or situations.
- Create opportunities for effective learners to share strategies for extracting learning from new experiences or situations—find ways to train people in the process of learning and problem solving.
- Tailor type of support to need—supporting assignments is different from supporting mistakes, which is different from supporting a bad-boss experience.

Source: Adapted from McCauley (2006).

Helping individuals become clear about what they bring to a learning experience and what they will have the opportunity to develop is critical to helping them make the most of it. This means assessing both the individual's skills and perspectives, and the challenges inherent in the job. There are various ways to do this assessment, including the use of multi-rater instruments, personality assessments, reflection techniques, and assessments of the jobs used for development in your organization. Formal or informal coaching relationships can also be a source of assessment, either at the beginning of an assignment or as an individual works through it.

Training people to reflect on job experiences is likely to be a challenging task because most managers tend not to have the time or inclination for this. And training in individual reflection techniques such as journaling will not have a positive effect on learning if the culture does not support taking the time to learn and to use tools to facilitate learning. Group reflection on learning can also be used—bringing people together on a regular basis to discuss what is being learned by those in new assignments and allowing more senior managers to model this behavior for others.

Support for learning is probably the most important thing of all to consider, because it is usually the most neglected aspect of creating a culture of learning on the job. Providing training to all employees on how to give and receive feedback can enable them to feel more comfortable providing good feedback to each other as they encounter challenges and opportunities to learn. Creating forums where effective learners can share their strategies or where expert managers can share rules of thumb for dealing with various kinds of challenge are ways to both create a learning culture and help those currently involved in developmental assignments or who will soon be moving into one.

It is particularly important to tailor support to both the level of challenge individuals are facing in their jobs and the kind of challenge they are facing. Supporting a challenging assignment often means supporting the learning curve of new knowledge and skills, and helping to build an employee's confidence if he or she encounters obstacles and frustration. Supporting mistakes and setbacks can mean helping someone draw lessons from loss, rebuild confidence, and either maintain forward movement or find a way to take time away to reestablish some equilibrium. Supporting someone in a bad-boss situation may mean helping him or her deal with stress more effectively, develop effective coping skills, and identify what can be learned about self and leading others in this situation.

Developmental experiences do not have to be expensive, and they do not have to take people away from work. Learning opportunities abound in everyday work experiences. People are encountering challenges daily in their jobs; they are involved in many kinds of naturally occurring, informal or formal relationships at work; and we all make mistakes and encounter failures and setbacks as we learn and progress through our careers. So the raw material for rich learning on the job is readily available, and we all learn as a result. By better supporting and mining these experiences for all the powerful developmental opportunities they could potentially bring, we can easily, and even in these tight economic times, enhance the return on our talent development efforts.

Further Reading

Cynthia D. McCauley, *Developmental Assignments: Creating Learning Experiences without Changing Jobs.* Greensboro, NC: Center for Creative Leadership, 2006.

Marian Ruderman and Patricia Ohlott, *Learning from Life: Turning Life's Lessons into Leadership Experience.* Greensboro, NC: Center for Creative Leadership, 2000.

Ellen Van Velsor, Cynthia McCauley, and Marian Ruderman, eds., *The Center for Creative Leadership Handbook of Leadership Development,* 3rd edition. San Francisco: Jossey-Bass, 2010.

Rola Ruohong Wei and Jeffrey Yip, *Leadership Wisdom: Discovering the Lessons of Experience.* Greensboro, NC: Center for Creative Leadership, 2008.

References

Avolio, B. 2004. Examining the Full Range Model of Leadership: Looking Back to Transform Forward. In *Leader Development for Transforming Organizations,* ed. D. Day, S. Zaccaro, and S. Halpin. Mahwah, NJ: Lawrence Erlbaum Associates.

Douglas, C. 2006. *Lessons of a Diverse Workforce.* Greensboro, NC: Center for Creative Leadership.

Hall, D. 2004. Self-Awareness, Identity, and Leader Development. In *Leader Development for Transforming Organizations,* ed. D. Day, S. Zaccaro, and S. Halpin. Mahwah, NJ: Lawrence Erlbaum Associates.

Harris, M., and J. Schaubroeck. 1988. A Meta-Analysis of Self-Supervisor, Self-Peer, and Peer-Supervisor Ratings. *Personnel Psychology,* 41: 43–61.

Mabe, P., and S. West. 1982. Validity of Self-Evaluation of Ability: A Review and Meta-Analysis. *Journal of Applied Psychology* 67: 280–296.

McCall, M., M. Lombardo, and A. Morrison. 1988. *The Lessons of Experience.* San Francisco: Jossey-Bass.

McCauley, Cynthia D. 2006. *Developmental Assignments: Creating Learning Experiences without Changing Jobs.* Greensboro, NC: Center for Creative Leadership.

McCauley, Cynthia D., and Christina A. Douglas. 2004. Developmental Relationships. In *The Center for Creative Leadership Handbook of Leadership Development,* 2nd edition, ed. C. McCauley and E. Van Velsor. San Francisco: Jossey-Bass.

McCauley, C., M. Ruderman, P. Ohlott, and J. Morrow. 1994. Assessing the Developmental Components of Managerial Jobs. *Journal of Applied Psychology* 79, no. 4: 544–560.

McCauley, C., E. Van Velsor, and M. Ruderman. 2010. Our View of Leadership Development. In *The Center for Creative Leadership Handbook of Leadership Development,* 3rd edition, ed. E. Van Velsor, C. McCauley, and M. Ruderman. San Francisco: Jossey-Bass.

Morrison, A., R. White, and E. Van Velsor. 1992. *Breaking the Glass Ceiling: Can Women Make It to the Top of America's Largest Corporations?* Reading, MA: Addison Wesley.

Moxley, R., and M. Pulley. 2004. Hardships. In *The Center for Creative Leadership Handbook of Leadership Development,* 2nd edition, ed. C. McCauley and E. Van Velsor. San Francisco: Jossey-Bass.

Nicholson, N., and M. West. 1988. *Managerial Job Change.* New York: Cambridge University Press.

———. 1989. Transitions, Work Histories, and Careers. In *Handbook of Career Theory,* ed. M. Arthur, D. Hall, and B. Lawrence. New York: Cambridge University Press.

Ohlott, Patricia. 2004. Job Assignments. In *The Center for Creative Leadership Handbook of Leadership Development,* 2nd edition, ed. C. McCauley and E. Van Velsor. San Francisco: Jossey-Bass.

Van Velsor, E., R. Moxley, and K. Bunker. 2004. The Leader Development Process. In *The Center for Creative Leadership Handbook of Leadership Development,* 2nd edition, ed. C. McCauley and E. Van Velsor. San Francisco: Jossey-Bass.

Yip, J. 2007. Crossing Boundaries. *Leadership in Action* 27, no. 5 (Jossey-Bass).

Yip, J., and M. Wilson. 2010. Learning from Assignments. In *The Center for Creative Leadership Handbook of Leadership Development,* 3rd edition, ed. E. Van Velsor, C. McCauley, and M. Ruderman. San Francisco: Jossey-Bass.

Zhang, Y., A. Chandrasekar, and R. Wei. 2009. *Developing Chinese Leaders in the 21st Century: A White Paper.* Greensboro, NC: Center for Creative Leadership.

About the Author

Ellen Van Velsor is a senior fellow at the Center for Creative Leadership in Greensboro, North Carolina. She is coeditor of the center's *Handbook of Leadership Development,* 3rd edition (2010), and coauthor of *Breaking the Glass Ceiling: Can Women Reach the Top of America's Largest Corporations?* (1987, 1991). She has written numerous book chapters and articles, including "Leadership Development as a Support to Ethical Action in Organizations" (2008), "A Complexity Perspective on Leadership Development" (2007), "Developing Organizational Capacity for Leadership" (2007), and "Constructive-Developmental Coaching" (2006). Her current research focuses on beliefs and practices related to globally responsible leadership. She has a BA in sociology from Stony Brook University, and an MA and PhD in sociology from the University of Florida.

Chapter 16

Coaching Leaders to Lead

Marshall Goldsmith

In This Chapter

- When behavioral coaching won't help.
- Encouraging leadership development.
- Steps in the behavioral change coaching process.
- Does anyone ever really change?

My coaching process is somewhat unusual. My mission is to help successful leaders achieve positive change in behavior—for themselves, their people, and their teams. I work with my clients and their managers to answer two questions: (1) Who are my client's key stakeholders? (2) What are the key behaviors that my client wants to change? The company pays me only after my client has achieved a positive change in key behaviors as determined by key stakeholders.

I've witnessed behavioral coaches receive payment for the wrong reasons. They are paid based on how much their clients like them and how much time they have spent coaching. Neither of these is a good metric for achieving positive, long-term change in behavior.

I have yet to see a study showing that clients' love of their behavioral coach is highly correlated with their behavior change. In fact, when coaches become too concerned with being

---

© 2010 Marshall Goldsmith. Used with permission.

liked by their clients, they may not provide honest feedback when it is needed. In terms of time, my clients are executives whose decisions often affect billions of dollars in expenditures. Their time is valuable. I attempt to take as little of their time as possible to achieve the desired results. The last thing they need from their coach is for me to waste their time.

Knowing When Behavioral Coaching Won't Help

Because I use a "pay only for results" process in behavioral coaching, I have had to learn to *qualify* my coaching clients. This means that I only work with clients that I believe will benefit from the coaching process.

I have found that there are some people who cannot be helped by behavioral coaching. And even the best coach in the world cannot make coaching work with these individuals. The good news is that these "uncoachables" are identifiable. How do you know when someone is uncoachable? How do you detect a lost cause? Let's consider four indicators that you are dealing with one of these people.

First, she doesn't think she has a problem. This successful adult has no interest in changing. Her behavior is working fine for her. If she doesn't care to change, you are wasting your time. Let me give you an example of a nice woman who didn't think she had a problem. My mother, a lovely woman and much-admired first-grade teacher, was so dedicated to her craft that she didn't draw the line between inside and outside the classroom. She talked with all of us, including my father, in the same slow, patient manner, using the same simple vocabulary that she used with her six-year-olds every day. One day, as she graciously and methodically corrected my father's grammar for the millionth time, he looked at her, sighed, and said, "Honey, I'm 70 years old. Let it go." He had absolutely no interest in changing. He didn't perceive a problem. So no matter how much, how hard, or how diligently she coached, he wasn't going to change.

Second, he is pursuing the wrong strategy for the organization. If this guy is already going in the wrong direction, all you're going to do with your coaching is help him get there faster.

Third, they're in the wrong job. Sometimes people feel that they're in the wrong job with the wrong company. They may believe they're meant to be doing something else, or that their skills are being misused. Here's a good way to determine if you're working with one of these people. Ask them, "If we shut down the company today, would you be relieved, surprised, or sad?" If you hear "relieved," you've got yourself a live one. Send them packing. You can't change the behavior of unhappy people so that they become happy: You can only fix behavior that's making people around them unhappy.

Fourth, they think everyone else is the problem. A long time ago, I had a client who, after a few high-profile employee departures, became concerned about employee morale. He had a fun, successful company and people liked the work, but feedback said that the boss played favorites in the way he compensated people. When I reported this feedback to my client, he completely surprised me. He said he agreed with the charge and thought he was right to do so. First off, I'm not a compensation strategist, and so I wasn't equipped to deal with this problem, but then he surprised me again. He hadn't called me to help him change; he wanted me to fix his employees. It's times like these when I find the nearest exit. It's hard to help people who don't think they have a problem. It's impossible to fix people who think someone else is the problem.

My suggestion in cases like these? Save time, skip the heroic measures, and move on. You can't ever win these arguments. My most successful coaching clients are committed to being role models for leadership development and their company's values. My most successful clients encourage leadership development by becoming involved in the process themselves.

Encouraging Leadership Development

While he was chairman and CEO of General Mills, Stephen Sanger openly told 90 of his colleagues: "As you all know, last year my team told me that I needed to do a better job of coaching my direct reports. I just reviewed my 360-degree feedback. I have been working on becoming a better coach for the past year or so. I'm still not doing quite as well as I want, but I'm getting a lot better. My co-workers have been helping me improve. Another thing that I feel good about is the fact that my scores on 'effectively responds to feedback' are so high this year."

Listening to Steve speak so candidly to his co-workers about his own leadership development efforts, I realized how much the world has changed. Twenty-five years ago, few CEOs received feedback from their colleagues. Even fewer candidly discussed that feedback and their personal developmental plans. Today, many of the world's most respected chief executives are setting a positive example by opening up, striving continually to develop themselves as leaders. In fact, the organizations that do the best job of cranking out leaders tend to have CEOs like Steve Sanger who are directly and actively involved in leadership development. That has certainly been my experience. This has also been confirmed by research conducted by Hewitt Associates (2005), one of the largest human resources consulting firms. Hewitt and *Chief Executive Magazine* put General Mills on their list of the top 20 companies for leaders, among such other familiar names as IBM and General Electric.

From its research, Hewitt found that these organizations tend to more actively manage their talent. They put lots of focus on identifying high-potential people, they better differentiate compensation, they serve up the right kinds of development opportunities, and they closely watch turnover. But CEO support and involvement were crucial to all these efforts.

There is no question that one of the best ways top executives can get their leaders to improve is to work on improving themselves. Leading by example can mean a lot more than leading by public relations hype.

Michael Dell, whose company made this same Hewitt list, is a perfect example. As one of the most successful leaders in business history, he could easily have an attitude that says, "I am Michael Dell and you aren't! I don't really need to work on developing myself." But he has the opposite approach. He has done an amazing job of sincerely discussing his personal challenges with leaders across the company. He is a living case study from whom everyone at his firm is learning. His leadership example makes it hard for any leader to act arrogant or to communicate that he or she has nothing to improve upon.

Unfortunately, in the same way that CEO support and involvement can help companies nurture leaders, CEO arrogance can have the opposite effect. When the boss acts like he or she is perfect and tells everyone else they need to improve, that behavior can be copied at every level of management. Those at every level then point out how those at the level below them need to change. The end result: No one gets much better.

The principle of leadership development by personal example doesn't apply just to CEOs. It also applies to all levels of management. All good leaders want their people to grow and develop on the job. Who knows? If we work hard to improve ourselves, we might even encourage the people around us to do the same thing.

Steps in the Behavioral Coaching Process

The following eight steps outline my behavioral coaching process. If the coach follows these basic steps, clients will almost always get better. (These steps are adapted from Goldsmith 2005.)

First, involve the leaders being coached in determining the desired behavior in their leadership roles. Leaders cannot be expected to change behavior if they don't have a clear understanding of what the desired behavior looks like. The people whom we coach (in agreement with their managers) work with us to determine the desired leadership behavior.

Second, involve the leaders being coached in determining key stakeholders. Not only do clients need to be clear on desired behaviors, they also need to be clear (again in agreement with their managers) on key stakeholders. There are two major reasons why people deny the validity of feedback: wrong items and wrong raters. By having our clients and their managers agree on the desired behaviors and key stakeholders in advance, we help ensure their buy-in to the process.

Third, collect feedback. In my coaching practice, I personally interview all key stakeholders. The people I am coaching are all potential CEOs, and the company is making a real investment in their development. However, at lower levels in the organization (that are more price sensitive), traditional 360-degree feedback can work very well. In either case, feedback is critical. It is impossible to be evaluated on changed behavior if there is no agreement on what behavior to change.

Fourth, reach agreement on key behaviors for change. As I have become more experienced, my approach has become simpler and more focused. I generally recommend picking only one or two key areas for behavioral change with each client. This helps ensure maximum attention to the most important behavior. My clients and their managers (unless my client is the CEO) agree on the desired behavior for change. This ensures that I won't spend a year working with my clients and have their managers determine that we have worked on the wrong thing.

Fifth, have the coaching clients respond to key stakeholders. The person being reviewed should talk with each key stakeholder and collect additional "feed *forward*" suggestions on how to improve on the key areas targeted for improvement. In responding, the person being coached should keep the conversation positive, simple, and focused. When mistakes have been made in the past, it is generally a good idea to apologize and ask for help in changing the future. I suggest that my clients listen to stakeholder suggestions and not judge the suggestions.

Sixth, review what has been learned with clients and help them develop an action plan. As was stated above, my clients need to agree to the basic steps in our process. On the other hand, outside the basic steps, all the other ideas that I share with my clients are suggestions. I just ask them to listen to my ideas in the same way they are listening to the ideas from their key stakeholders. I then ask them to come back with a plan of what *they* want to do. These plans need to come from them, not me. After reviewing their plans, I almost always encourage them to live up to their own commitments. I am much more of a facilitator than a judge. I usually just help my clients do what they know is the right thing to do.

Seventh, develop an ongoing follow-up process. This follow-up should be very efficient and focused. Use questions like "Based upon my behavior last month, what ideas do you have for me next month?" to keep a focus on the future. Within six months, conduct a two- to six-item minisurvey with key stakeholders (figure 16-1). They should be asked whether the person has become more or less effective in the areas targeted for improvement.

Figure 16-1. Sample Minisurvey

Do you believe this person has become more (or less) effective *in the past six months* on the following items? (Please circle the number that best matches your estimate of any change in effectiveness.)

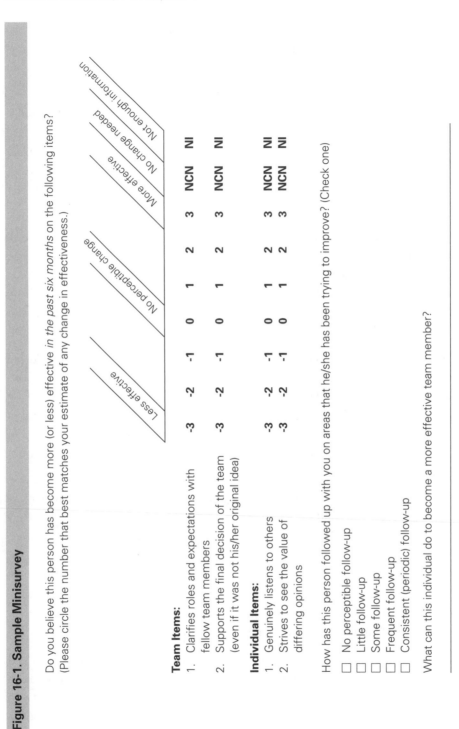

	Less effective			No perceptible change			More effective	No change needed	Not enough information

Team Items:

1. Clarifies roles and expectations with fellow team members

    -3 -2 -1 0 1 2 3 **NCN** **NI**

2. Supports the final decision of the team (even if it was not his/her original idea)

    -3 -2 -1 0 1 2 3 **NCN** **NI**

Individual Items:

1. Genuinely listens to others

    -3 -2 -1 0 1 2 3 **NCN** **NI**

2. Strives to see the value of differing opinions

    -3 -2 -1 0 1 2 3 **NCN** **NI**

How has this person followed up with you on areas that he/she has been trying to improve? (Check one)

☐ No perceptible follow-up
☐ Little follow-up
☐ Some follow-up
☐ Frequent follow-up
☐ Consistent (periodic) follow-up

What can this individual do to become a more effective team member?

_____

_____

_____

Eighth, review the results and start again. If the person being coached has taken the process seriously, stakeholders almost invariably report improvement. Build on that success by repeating the process for the next 12 to 18 months. This type of follow-up will ensure continued progress on the initial goals and uncover additional areas for improvement. Stakeholders will appreciate the follow-up. No one minds filling out a focused, two- to six-item questionnaire if they see positive results. The person being coached will benefit from ongoing, targeted steps to improve performance.

Does Anyone Ever Really Change?

People often ask, "Does anyone ever really change?" The answer is definitely yes. At the top of major organizations, even a small positive change in behavior can have a big impact. From an organizational perspective, the fact that the leader is trying to change anything (and is being a role model for personal development) may be even more important than what the executive is trying to change.

When I was first asked this perfectly reasonable, and for me life-altering, question by a *Fortune* 100 company executive vice president for whose company I was preparing training sessions, I wasn't sure why he had asked me. Perhaps he had an eye on the training budget? It's hard to say. At the time, however, I had trained thousands of people, received fabulous feedback about my coaching, and had dozens of letters from people who believed they had changed. I was a successful coach; I had worked with some of the best companies in the world, and nobody had ever asked me this question. Worse than that, it had never even entered my mind. I never went back to these companies to see if my training sessions had had any effect or if people actually did what they had promised to do in the training sessions. I had just assumed that they understood the benefits of my eminent wisdom and would do what they had been told.

But now, in response to this question, I took immediate action. I became Mr. Follow-Up. I scoured all the research and went back to my client corporations, assembling data that answered the question "Does anyone really change?" The pool of respondents eventually numbered 86,000 participants, involving eight major corporations, each of which had invested millions of dollars a year in leadership programs. (For the complete methodology, statistical results, the companies involved, and conclusions, see Morgan and Goldsmith 2004.) As I studied the data, three conclusions emerged.

First, some people are trainable; some aren't. Not everyone responds to executive development, at least not in the way the organization desires or intends. At the eight companies I surveyed, I asked participants at the end of each session if they intended to go back to their jobs and apply what they had learned. Nearly 100 percent said yes. However, a year later, when I asked those who reported directly to them to confirm that these leaders had applied the lessons on the job, 70 percent said yes, leaving 30 percent who said their bosses did absolutely nothing. Why would 30 percent of executives go through the training, promise to implement the changes, and then do nothing? Quite simply, most of the time they were just too busy and too distracted by the day-to-day demands of their jobs to implement what they had learned. This led me to the second conclusion.

Second, there is an enormous disconnect between understanding and doing. Most leadership development revolves around one huge, and false, assumption: If people understand, then they will do. Don't believe me? Take a look at the adamant smoker. This person knows that smoking cigarettes is bad for his or her health, but refuses to quit. However, this insight didn't tell me if the 70 percent who understand and do actually improved. That's when I realized the missing link was follow-up—not only in my training concepts but also in getting people to change. I rewired my objectives and began measuring people to see not only if they got better but also why. Revisiting five of my eight companies to measure the level of follow-up among the executives, I found that the results were astonishingly consistent. When leaders did little or no follow-up with their subordinates, there was little or no perceived change in the leaders' effectiveness. When leaders consistently followed up, the perception of their effectiveness jumped dramatically. This led to me to the third conclusion.

Third, people don't get better without follow-up. Leaders who don't follow up aren't necessarily bad leaders; they are just not perceived as getting better. Follow-up shows you care about getting better. It shows that you value your co-workers' opinions. Following up consistently, every month or so, shows that you are serious about the process and that you are not ignoring your co-workers' input. Think about it. A leader who seeks input from co-workers but ignores it or doesn't follow up on it quite logically will be perceived as someone who doesn't care much about becoming a better leader.

My experience discovering the value of follow-up taught me a fourth and very valuable lesson: Becoming a better leader (or a better person) is a process, not an event. Executive development is more than an event, training program, motivating speech, or inspiring retreat. It doesn't happen in a day. It doesn't happen because someone understands the training. Leaders develop over time, and the only way to know if someone is getting better by actually doing what he or she learned in a training program is to follow up. Follow-up turns changing for the better into an ongoing process—for leaders, their people, and their teams.

Further Reading

Marc Effron, Robert Gandossy, and Marshall Goldsmith, "Leveraging HR: How to Develop Leaders in "Real Time,'" in *Human Resources in the 21st Century*, ed. M. Effron, R. Gandossy, and M. Goldsmith. San Francisco: John Wiley & Sons, 2003.

Marshall Goldsmith, "Expanding the Value of Coaching: From the Leader to the Team to the Organization," in *The Art and Practice of Leadership Coaching,* ed. H. Morgan, P. Harkins, and M. Goldsmith. San Francisco: John Wiley & Sons, 2005.

———, "Recruiting Supportive Coaches: A Key to Achieving Positive Behavioral Change," in *The Many Facets of Leadership,* ed. M. Goldsmith, Vijay Govindarajan, Beverly Kaye, and Albert Vicere. Upper Saddle River, NJ: Financial Times–Prentice Hall, 2003.

———, "Try Feed *Forward,* Instead of Feedback," *Leader to Leader,* Summer 2002.

Hewitt Associates, *How the Top 20 Companies Grow Great Leaders.* http://www.pecktraining.com/top20.pdf.

Howard Morgan and Marshall Goldsmith, "Leadership Is a Contact Sport," *Strategy+Business,* Fall 2004.

References

Hewitt Associates. 2005. *How the Top 20 Companies Grow Great Leaders.* http://www.pecktraining.com/top20.pdf.

Goldsmith, M. 2005. Coaching for Behavioral Change. In *The Art and Practice of Leadership Coaching,* ed. H. Morgan, P. Harkins, and M. Goldsmith. San Francisco: John Wiley & Sons, 2005.

Morgan, H., and M. Goldsmith. 2004. Leadership Is a Contact Sport. *Strategy+Business,* Fall.

About the Author

Marshall Goldsmith is a world authority in helping successful leaders get even better—by achieving positive change in behavior for themselves, their people, and their teams. In 2007, his book *What Got You Here Won't Get You There* was ranked as America's number one best-selling business book in both the *New York Times* and *Wall Street Journal.* He teaches executive education at Dartmouth College's Tuck School of Business and frequently speaks at leading business schools. His work has been recognized by almost every professional organization in his field. In 2006, Alliant International University honored him by naming their school of business and organizational studies the Marshall Goldsmith School of Management. His 30 books include *The Leader of the Future* (a *BusinessWeek* best seller) and *Coaching for Leadership, and Succession: Are You Ready?* (in Harvard Business Press's Memo to the CEO Series). His newest book, *Mojo* is a *New York Times* bestseller and *Wall Street Journal* number 3 business book in the United States, number 2 in Germany, and number 1 in China. He received his PhD from the University of California, Los Angeles. For more about Goldsmith, go to www.marshallgoldsmithlibrary.com.

⋙ Section III

Attributes of Successful Leaders

Attributes, competencies—what's the difference? While competencies are more about the skills and knowledge leaders need, attributes are about the traits and qualities they must embody to be effective in their organizations. Leadership is not simply about style, a list of skills, how-tos, or achieving high scores in a 360-degree assessment. It is also about the personal qualities, values, habits, and motives that make up a leader's moral fiber. Attributes go beyond skills; they describe the leader's character. Thus attributes are not just what leaders are capable of doing but also what they actually do.

Try Googling "leadership attributes." Go ahead. I dare you. My results included these as the top eight:

- 14 attributes of a leader
- leadership attributes for business success
- connecting leadership attributes (our own Ulrich, Zenger, and Smallwood got a mention)
- 11 leadership attributes
- eight key leadership attributes
- six essential leadership attributes.

Leadership can be difficult to define; it is even more difficult to practice. Leadership is about behavior first, skills second. Leaders are followed because people trust and respect them, rather than the skills they possess. Someone's willingness to follow a leader depends on qualities such as integrity, honesty, humility, sensitivity, empathy, compassion, courage, commitment, sincerity, passion, confidence, and determination. Sometimes this combination may be called "charisma," on which the Zenger-Folkman-Edinger team sheds some light in their chapter in this section.

This section addresses attributes such as inspiration, authenticity, honesty, ethics, and integrity, and its exploration of these attributes is bookended by two important chapters. It opens with Jim Collins discussing what leaders do in "great" organizations. It ends with Bill Gentry sharing his advice for how leaders can avoid derailment—when things go awry.

In chapter 17, "Good to Great: What Leaders Do," Jim Collins explores those practices that do not support change in organizations and what leaders must do to create a great company, on the basis of his best-selling book *Good to Great.*

Ever wonder about that elusive attribute called charisma? In chapter 18, "Unlocking the Mystery of Inspiring Leadership," Jack Zenger, Joe Folkman, and Scott Edinger share their research about how they came to define charisma, the 10 behaviors and qualities that set inspiring and motivating leaders apart from others, and approaches used by leaders to make an emotional connection with others.

In chapter 19, "The Authentic Leader," Bill George uses personal stories and lessons learned from his own experiences to discuss the five qualities of an authentic, principle-driven leader. He also discusses the process by which leaders develop their talents.

A leader's personal character and leadership attributes are truly tested when things go wrong. In chapter 20, "Leading in Turbulent Times," Priscilla Nelson and Ed Cohen present 10 practices to lead employees through turbulent times based on their personal experience at a large high-technology firm in India.

In chapter 21, "Leadership Ethics and Integrity for the 21st Century," Ken Blanchard, long respected for his values and compassion, introduces five ethical practices and clarifies servant leadership for the reader.

In chapter 22, "Trends Shaping Future Leadership Attributes," Karie Willyerd and Jeanne Meister explore the workplace shifts that will affect a leader's ability to be effective and then present the five leadership capabilities that will be required for success.

In chapter 23, "Derailment: How Successful Leaders Avoid It," Bill Gentry presents the history of leadership derailment research to support the five problem areas of derailed leaders, based on extensive research conducted at the Center for Creative Leadership. And he takes this discussion further by offering strategies for avoiding derailment and explaining what to do if a leader has already derailed.

Chapter 17

Good to Great:
What Leaders Do

Jim Collins

In This Chapter

- Explore things that do not support change in organizations.

- Discover what occurs to affect change.

- Identify what leaders must do to create a great company.

Start with 1,435 good companies. Examine their performance over 40 years. Find the 11 companies that became great. Now here's how you can do it too. Lessons on eggs, flywheels, hedgehogs, buses, and other essentials of business that can help you transform your company.

I want to give you a lobotomy about change. I want you to forget everything you've ever learned about what it takes to create great results. I want you to realize that nearly all operating prescriptions for creating large-scale corporate change are nothing but myths:

- *The myth of the change program:* This approach comes with the launch event, the tag line, and the cascading activities.
- *The myth of the burning platform:* This one says that change starts only when there's a crisis that persuades "unmotivated" employees to accept the need for change.

"Good to Great" article first published in *Fast Company*, October 2001. Copyright © 2001 by Jim Collins.

- *The myth of stock options:* Stock options, high salaries, and bonuses are incentives that grease the wheels of change.
- *The myth of fear-driven change:* The fear of being left behind, the fear of watching others win, the fear of presiding over monumental failure—all are drivers of change, we're told.
- *The myth of acquisitions:* You can buy your way to growth, so it figures that you can buy your way to greatness.
- *The myth of technology-driven change:* The breakthrough that you're looking for can be achieved by using technology to leapfrog the competition.
- *The myth of revolution:* Big change has to be wrenching, extreme, painful—one big, discontinuous, shattering break.

Wrong. Wrong. Wrong. Wrong. Wrong. Wrong. Totally wrong.

Here are the facts of life about these and other change myths. Companies that make the change from good to great have no name for their transformation—and absolutely no program. They neither rant nor rave about a crisis—and they don't manufacture one where none exists. They don't "motivate" people—their people are self-motivated. There's no evidence of a connection between money and change mastery. And fear doesn't drive change—but it does perpetuate mediocrity. Nor can acquisitions provide a stimulus for greatness: Two mediocrities never make one great company. Technology is certainly important—but it comes into play only after change has already begun. And as for the final myth, dramatic results do not come from dramatic process—not if you want them to last, anyway. A serious revolution, one that feels like a revolution to those going through it, is highly unlikely to bring about a sustainable leap from being good to being great.

These myths became clear as my research team and I completed a five-year project to determine what it takes to change a good company into a great one. We systematically scoured a list of 1,435 established companies to find every extraordinary case that made a leap from no-better-than-average results to great results. How great? After the leap, a company had to generate cumulative stock returns that exceeded the general stock market by at least three times over 15 years—and it had to be a leap independent of its industry. In fact, the 11 good-to-great companies that we found averaged returns 6.9 times greater than the market's—more than twice the performance rate of General Electric under the legendary Jack Welch.

The surprising good-to-great list included such unheralded companies as Abbott Laboratories (3.98 times the market), Fannie Mae (7.56 times the market), Kimberly-Clark Corp. (3.42 times the market), Nucor Corp. (5.16 times the market), and Wells Fargo

(3.99 times the market). One such surprise, the Kroger Co.—a grocery chain—bumped along as a totally average performer for 80 years and then somehow broke free of its mediocrity to beat the stock market by 4.16 times over the next 15 years. And it didn't stop there. From 1973 to 1998, Kroger outperformed the market by 10 times.

In each of these dramatic, remarkable, good-to-great corporate transformations, we found the same thing: There was no miracle moment. Instead, a down-to-earth, pragmatic, committed-to-excellence process—a framework—kept each company, its leaders, and its people on track for the long haul. In each case, it was the triumph of the Flywheel Effect over the Doom Loop, the victory of steadfast discipline over the quick fix. And the real kicker: The comparison companies in our study—firms with practically identical opportunities during the pivotal years—did buy into the change myths described above—and failed to make the leap from good to great.

How Change Doesn't Happen

Picture an egg. Day after day, it sits there. No one pays attention to it. No one notices it. Certainly no one takes a picture of it or puts it on the cover of a celebrity-focused business magazine. Then one day, the shell cracks and out jumps a chicken.

All of a sudden, the major magazines and newspapers jump on the story: "Stunning Turnaround at Egg!" and "The Chick Who Led the Breakthrough at Egg!" From the outside, the story always reads like an overnight sensation—as if the egg had suddenly and radically altered itself into a chicken.

Now picture the egg from the chicken's point of view.

While the outside world was ignoring this seemingly dormant egg, the chicken within was evolving, growing, developing—changing. From the chicken's point of view, the moment of breakthrough, of cracking the egg, was simply one more step in a long chain of steps that had led to that moment. Granted, it was a big step—but it was hardly the radical transformation that it looked like from the outside.

It's a silly analogy, but then our conventional way of looking at change is no less silly. Everyone looks for the "miracle moment" when "change happens." But ask the good-to-great executives when change happened. They cannot pinpoint a single key event that exemplified their successful transition.

Take Walgreens. For more than 40 years, Walgreens was no more than an average company, tracking the general market. Then in 1975 (out of the blue!) Walgreens began to climb. And climb. And climb. It just kept climbing. From December 31, 1975, to January 1, 2000, $1 invested in Walgreens beat $1 invested in Intel by nearly two times, General Electric by nearly five times, and Coca-Cola by nearly eight times. It beat the general stock market by more than 15 times.

I asked a key Walgreens executive to pinpoint when the good-to-great transformation happened. His answer: "Sometime between 1971 and 1980." (Well, that certainly narrows it down!)

Walgreens' experience is the norm for good-to-great performers. Leaders at Abbott said, "It wasn't a blinding flash or sudden revelation from above." From Kimberly-Clark: "These things don't happen overnight. They grow." From Wells Fargo: "It wasn't a single switch that was thrown at one time."

We keep looking for change in the wrong places, asking the wrong questions, and making the wrong assumptions. There's even a tendency to blame Wall Street for the "instant results" approach to change. But the companies that made the jump from good to great did so using Wall Street's own tough metric of success: a sustained leap in their stock market performance. Wall Street turns out to be just another myth—an excuse for not doing what really works. The data doesn't lie.

How Change Does Happen

Now picture a huge, heavy flywheel. It's a massive, metal disk mounted horizontally on an axle. It's about 100 feet in diameter and 10 feet thick, and it weighs about 25 tons. That flywheel is your company. Your job is to get that flywheel to move as fast as possible, because momentum—mass times velocity—is what will generate superior economic results over time.

Right now, the flywheel is at a standstill. To get it moving, you make a tremendous effort. You push with all your might, and finally you get the flywheel to inch forward. After two or three days of sustained effort, you get the flywheel to complete one entire turn. You keep pushing, and the flywheel begins to move a bit faster. It takes a lot of work, but at last the flywheel makes a second rotation. You keep pushing steadily. It makes three turns, four turns, five, six. With each turn, it moves faster, and then—at some point, you can't say exactly when—you break through. The momentum of the heavy wheel kicks in your favor. It spins faster and faster, with its own weight propelling it. You aren't pushing any harder, but the flywheel is accelerating, its momentum building, its speed increasing.

This is the Flywheel Effect. It's what it feels like when you're inside a company that makes the transition from good to great. Take Kroger, for example. How do you get a company with more than 50,000 people to embrace a new strategy that will eventually change every aspect of every grocery store? You don't. At least not with one big change program.

Instead, you put your shoulder to the flywheel. That's what Jim Herring, the leader who initiated the transformation of Kroger, told us. He stayed away from change programs and motivational stunts. He and his team began turning the flywheel gradually, consistently— building tangible evidence that their plans made sense and would deliver results.

"We presented what we were doing in such a way that people saw our accomplishments," Herring says. "We tried to bring our plans to successful conclusions step by step, so that the mass of people would gain confidence from the successes, not just the words."

Think about it for one minute. Why do most overhyped change programs ultimately fail? Because they lack accountability, they fail to achieve credibility, and they have no authenticity. It's the opposite of the Flywheel Effect; it's the Doom Loop.

Companies that fall into the Doom Loop genuinely want to effect change—but they lack the quiet discipline that produces the Flywheel Effect. Instead, they launch change programs with huge fanfare, hoping to "enlist the troops." They start down one path, only to change direction. After years of lurching back and forth, these companies discover that they've failed to build any sustained momentum. Instead of turning the flywheel, they've fallen into a Doom Loop: Disappointing results lead to reaction without understanding, which leads to a new direction—a new leader, a new program—which leads to no momentum, which leads to disappointing results. It's a steady, downward spiral. Those who have experienced a Doom Loop know how it drains the spirit right out of a company.

Consider the Warner-Lambert Co.—the company that we compared directly with Gillette—in the early 1980s. In 1979, Warner-Lambert told *BusinessWeek* that it aimed to be a leading consumer-products company. One year later, it did an abrupt about-face and turned its sights on health care. In 1981, the company reversed course again and returned to diversification and consumer goods. Then in 1987, Warner-Lambert made another U-turn, away from consumer goods, and announced that it wanted to compete with Merck. Then in the early 1990s, the company responded to government announcements of pending health care reform and reembraced diversification and consumer brands.

Between 1979 and 1998, Warner-Lambert underwent three major restructurings—one per CEO. Each new CEO arrived with his own program; each CEO halted the momentum of his predecessor. With each turn of the Doom Loop, the company spiraled further downward, until it was swallowed by Pfizer in 2000.

In contrast, why does the Flywheel Effect work? Because more than anything else, real people in real companies want to be part of a winning team. They want to contribute to producing real results. They want to feel the excitement and the satisfaction of being part of something that just flat-out works. When people begin to feel the magic of momentum—when they begin to see tangible results and can feel the flywheel start to build speed—that's when they line up, throw their shoulders to the wheel, and push.

And that's how change really happens.

Disciplined People: "Who" Before "What"

You are a bus driver. The bus, your company, is at a standstill, and it's your job to get it going. You have to decide where you're going, how you're going to get there, and who's going with you.

Most people assume that great bus drivers (read: business leaders) immediately start the journey by announcing to the people on the bus where they're going—by setting a new direction or by articulating a fresh corporate vision.

In fact, leaders of companies that go from good to great start not with "where" but with "who." They start by getting the right people on the bus, the wrong people off the bus, and the right people in the right seats. And they stick with that discipline—first the people, then the direction—no matter how dire the circumstances. Take David Maxwell's bus ride. When he became CEO of Fannie Mae in 1981, the company was losing $1 million every business day, with $56 billion worth of mortgage loans underwater. The board desperately wanted to know what Maxwell was going to do to rescue the company.

Maxwell responded to the "what" question the same way that all good-to-great leaders do: He told them, That's the wrong first question. To decide where to drive the bus before you have the right people on the bus, and the wrong people off the bus, is absolutely the wrong approach.

Maxwell told his management team that there would only be seats on the bus for A-level people who were willing to put out A-plus effort. He interviewed every member of the team. He told them all the same thing: It was going to be a tough ride, a very demanding trip. If they didn't want to go, fine; just say so. Now's the time to get off the bus, he said. No questions asked, no recriminations. In all, 14 of 26 executives got off the bus. They were replaced by some of the best, smartest, and hardest-working executives in the world of finance.

With the right people on the bus, in the right seats, Maxwell then turned his full attention to the "what" question. He and his team took Fannie Mae from losing $1 million a day at the start of his tenure to earning $4 million a day at the end. Even after Maxwell left in

1991, his great team continued to drive the flywheel—turn upon turn—and Fannie Mae generated cumulative stock returns nearly eight times better than the general market from 1984 to 1999.

When it comes to getting started, good-to-great leaders understand three simple truths. First, if you begin with "who," you can more easily adapt to a fast-changing world. If people get on your bus because of where they think it's going, you'll be in trouble when you get 10 miles down the road and discover that you need to change direction because the world has changed. But if people board the bus principally because of all the other great people on the bus, you'll be much faster and smarter in responding to changing conditions. Second, if you have the right people on your bus, you don't need to worry about motivating them. The right people are self-motivated: Nothing beats being part of a team that is expected to produce great results. And third, if you have the wrong people on the bus, nothing else matters. You may be headed in the right direction, but you still won't achieve greatness. Great vision with mediocre people still produces mediocre results.

Disciplined Thought: Fox or Hedgehog?

Picture two animals: a fox and a hedgehog. Which are you? An ancient Greek parable distinguishes between foxes, which know many small things, and hedgehogs, which know one big thing. All good-to-great leaders, it turns out, are hedgehogs. They know how to simplify a complex world into a single, organizing idea—the kind of basic principle that unifies, organizes, and guides all decisions. That's not to say hedgehogs are simplistic. Like great thinkers, who take complexities and boil them down into simple, yet profound, ideas (Adam Smith and the invisible hand, Darwin and evolution), leaders of good-to-great companies develop a Hedgehog Concept that is simple but that reflects penetrating insight and deep understanding.

What does it take to come up with a Hedgehog Concept for your company? Start by confronting the brutal facts. One good-to-great CEO began by asking, "Why have we sucked for 100 years?" That's brutal—and it's precisely the type of disciplined question necessary to ignite a transformation. The management climate during a leap from good to great is like a searing scientific debate—with smart, tough-minded people examining hard facts and debating what those facts mean. The point isn't to win the debate but rather to come up with the best answers—and, ultimately, to lock onto a Hedgehog Concept that works.

You'll know that you're getting closer to your Hedgehog Concept when you align three intersecting circles that represent three pivotal questions: What can we be the best in the world at? (And equally important—what can we not be the best at?) What is the economic denominator that best drives our economic engine (profit or cash flow per "x")? And what are our core people deeply passionate about? Answer those three questions honestly, facing the brutal facts without blinking, and you'll begin to see your Hedgehog Concept emerge.

For example, before Wells Fargo understood its Hedgehog Concept, its leaders had tried to make it a global bank: It operated like a mini-Citicorp—and a mediocre one at that. Then the Wells Fargo team asked itself, "What can we potentially do better than any other company?" The brutal fact was that Wells Fargo would never be the best global bank in the world—and so the leadership team pulled the plug on the vast majority of the bank's international operations. When the team asked the question about the bank's economic engine, Wells Fargo's leaders confronted a second brutal fact: In a deregulated world, commercial banking would be a commodity. The essential economic driver would no longer be profit per loan but profit per employee. The bank switched its operations to become a pioneering leader in electronic banking and to open utilitarian branches run by small crews of superb people. Profit per employee skyrocketed. Finally, when it came to passion, members of the Wells Fargo team all agreed: The mindless waste and self-awarded perks of traditional banking culture were revolting. They proudly saw themselves as stoic Spartans in an industry that had been dominated by the wasteful, elitist culture of banking.

The Wells Fargo team eventually translated the three circles into a simple, crystalline Hedgehog Concept: Run a bank like a business, with a focus on the western United States, and consistently increase profit per employee. "Run it like a business" and "run it like you own it" became mantras; simplicity and focus made all the difference. With fanatical adherence to that simple idea, Wells Fargo made the leap from good results to superior results.

In the journey from good to great, defining your Hedgehog Concept is an essential element. But insight and understanding don't happen overnight—or after one off-site. On average, it took four years for the good-to-great companies to crystallize their Hedgehog Concepts. It was an inherently iterative process—consisting of piercing questions, vigorous debate, resolute action, and autopsies without blame—a cycle repeated over and over by the right people, infused with the brutal facts, and guided by the three circles. This is the chicken inside the egg.

Disciplined Action: The "Stop-Doing" List

Take a look at your desk. If you're like most hard-charging leaders, you've got a well-articulated to-do list. Now take another look: Where's your stop-doing list? We've all been told that leaders make things happen—and that's true: Pushing that flywheel takes a lot of concerted effort. But it's also true that good-to-great leaders distinguish themselves by their unyielding discipline to stop doing anything and everything that doesn't fit tightly within their Hedgehog Concept.

When Darwin Smith and his management team crystallized the Hedgehog Concept for Kimberly-Clark, they faced a dilemma. On one hand, they understood that the best path to greatness lay in the consumer business, where the company had demonstrated a best-in-the-world capability in its building of the Kleenex brand. On the other hand, the vast majority of Kimberly-Clark's revenue lay in traditional coated-paper mills, turning out paper for magazines and writing pads—which had been the core business of the company for 100 years. Even the company's namesake town—Kimberly, Wisconsin—was built around a Kimberly-Clark paper mill.

Yet the brutal truth remained: The consumer business was the one arena that best met the three-circle test. If Kimberly-Clark remained principally a paper-mill business, it would retain a secure position as a good company. But its only shot at becoming a great company was to become the best paper-based consumer company—if it could take on such companies as Procter & Gamble and Scott Paper Co. and beat them. That meant it would have to "stop doing" paper mills.

So, in what one director called "the gutsiest decision I've ever seen a CEO make," Darwin Smith sold the mills. He even sold the mill in Kimberly, Wisconsin. Then he threw all the money into a war chest for an epic battle with Procter & Gamble and Scott Paper. Wall Street analysts derided the move, and the business press called it stupid. But Smith did not waver.

Twenty-five years later, Kimberly-Clark emerged from the fray as the number one paper-based consumer-products company in the world, beating P&G in six of eight categories and owning its former archrival Scott Paper outright. For the shareholder, Kimberly-Clark under Darwin Smith beat the market by four times, easily outperforming such great companies as Coca-Cola, General Electric, Hewlett-Packard, and 3M.

In deciding what not to do, Smith gave the flywheel a gigantic push—but it was only one push. After selling the mills, Kimberly-Clark's full transformation required thousands of additional pushes, big and small, accumulated one after another. It took years to gain enough momentum for the press to herald Kimberly-Clark's shift from good to great. One magazine wrote, "When . . . Kimberly-Clark decided to go head to head against P&G, . . . this magazine predicted disaster. What a dumb idea. As it turns out, it wasn't a dumb idea. It was a smart idea." The amount of time between the two articles: 21 years.

Now It Begins

Our study of what it takes to turn good into great required five years—and 10.5 person-years—and amounted to our own flywheel effort. Looking back on our research, what's most striking to me about our findings is the absence of a magic moment in any of the good-to-great companies—or in our own journey to understanding. The real path to greatness, it turns out, requires simplicity and diligence (see the sidebar). It requires clarity, not instant illumination. It demands each of us to focus on what is vital—and to eliminate all the extraneous distractions.

The following information comes from *How the Mighty Fall: And Why Some Companies Never Give In* © 2009 by Jim Collins. Used with permission.

By Applying the Good-to-Great Framework → (Inputs of Greatness)	You Build the Foundations of →	A Great Organization (Outputs of Greatness)
Stage 1: **Disciplined People** Level 5 Leadership First Who, Then What Stage 2: **Disciplined Thought** Confront the Brutal Facts The Hedgehog Concept	→	**Delivers Superior Performance** In business, performance is defined by financial returns and achievement of corporate purpose. In the social sectors, performance is defined by results and efficiency in delivering on the social mission.
Stage 3: **Disciplined Action** Culture of Discipline The Flywheel	→	**Makes a Distinctive Impact** The organization makes such a unique contribution to the communities it touches and does its work with such unadulterated excellence that if it were to disappear, it would leave a hole that could not be easily filled by any other institution on the planet.
Stage 4: **Building Greatness to Last** Clock Building, Not Time Telling Preserve the Core, Stimulate Progress	→	**Achieves Lasting Endurance** The organization can deliver exceptional results over a long period of time, beyond any single leader, great idea, market cycle, or well-funded program. When hit with setbacks, it bounces back even stronger than before.

(continued on next page)

Stage 1: Disciplined People

Level 5 Leadership: Level 5 leaders are ambitious first and foremost for the cause, the organization, the work—not themselves—and they have the fierce resolve to do whatever it takes to make good on that ambition. A level 5 leader displays a paradoxical blend of personal humility and professional will.

First Who, Then What: Those who build great organizations make sure they have the right people on the bus, the wrong people off the bus, and the right people in the key seats *before* they figure out where to drive the bus. They always think *first* about "who" and *then* about what.

Stage 2: Disciplined Thought

Confront the Brutal Facts—the Stockdale Paradox: Retain unwavering faith that you can and will prevail in the end, regardless of the difficulties, *and at the same time* have the discipline to confront the most brutal facts of your current reality, whatever they might be.

The Hedgehog Concept: Greatness comes about by a series of good decisions consistent with a simple, coherent concept—a "Hedgehog Concept." The Hedgehog Concept is an operating model that reflects understanding of three intersecting circles: what you can be the best in the world at, what you are deeply passionate about, and what best drives your economic or resource engine.

Stage 3: Disciplined Action

Culture of Discipline: Disciplined people who engage in disciplined thought and who take disciplined action—operating with freedom within a framework of responsibilities: This is the cornerstone of a culture that creates greatness. People do not have jobs; they have responsibilities.

The Flywheel: There is no single defining action, no grand program, no one killer innovation, no solitary lucky break, no miracle moment. Rather, the process resembles relentlessly pushing a giant heavy flywheel, turn upon turn, building momentum until a point of breakthrough, and beyond.

Stage 4: Building Greatness to Last

Clock Building, Not Time Telling: Truly great organizations prosper through multiple generations of leaders, the exact opposite of being built around a single great leader, great idea, or specific program. Leaders in great organizations build catalytic mechanisms to stimulate progress and do not depend upon having a charismatic personality to get things done; indeed, many have had a "charisma bypass."

Preserve the Core / Stimulate Progress: Enduring great organizations are characterized by a fundamental duality. On the one hand, they have a set of timeless core values and core reasons for being that remain constant over long periods of time. On the other hand, they have a relentless drive for change and progress—a creative compulsion that often manifests in BHAGs (Big Hairy Audacious Goals). Great organizations keep clear the difference between their core values (which never change) and operating strategies and cultural practices (which endlessly adapt to a changing world).

(continued on next page)

> Note: At our website, www.jimcollins.com, we have posted a diagnostic tool for assessing an organization through the lens of these concepts. The diagnostic tool is free for use inside any organization. The principles in Stages 1 through 3 derive from the research for the book *Good to Great* by Jim Collins; the principles in Stage 4 derive from the book *Built to Last* by Jim Collins and Jerry I. Porras.

After five years of research, I'm absolutely convinced that if we just focus our attention on the right things—and stop doing the senseless things that consume so much time and energy—we can create a powerful Flywheel Effect without increasing the number of hours we work.

I'm also convinced that the good-to-great findings apply broadly—not just to CEOs but also to you and me in whatever work we're engaged in, including the work of our own lives. For many people, the first question that occurs is, "But how do I persuade my CEO to get it?" My answer: Don't worry about that. Focus instead on results—on subverting mediocrity by creating a Flywheel Effect within your own span of responsibility. So long as we can choose the people we want to put on our own minibus, each of us can create a pocket of greatness. Each of us can take our own area of work and influence and can concentrate on moving it from good to great. It doesn't really matter whether all the CEOs get it. It only matters that you and I do. Now, it's time to get to work.

Further Reading

Jim Collins, *Good to Great*. New York: HarperBusiness, 2002.
———, *How the Mighty Fall: And Why Some Companies Never Give In*. New York: HarperCollins, 2009.
Jim Collins and Jerry I. Porras, *Built to Last*. New York: HarperBusiness, 1994.

About the Author

Jim Collins is a student and teacher of enduring great companies—how they grow, how they attain superior performance, and how good companies can become great companies. Having invested more than a decade of research on the topic, he has authored or coauthored five books, including the classic *Built to Last*, a fixture on the *BusinessWeek* best-seller list for more than six years. *Good to Great* has sold 3.5 million hardcover copies and has been translated into 35 languages. His most recent book, *How the Mighty Fall: And Why Some Companies Never Give In*, was published in 2009. Driven by a relentless curiosity, Jim began his research and teaching career on the faculty at Stanford Graduate School of Business, where he received the Distinguished Teaching Award in 1992. In 1995, he founded a management laboratory in Boulder, Colorado. He works with senior executives and CEOs at more than a hundred corporations and has worked with social-sector organizations, such as the Johns Hopkins Medical School, the Girl Scouts, the American Association of K-12 School Superintendents, and the U.S. Marine Corps. He is also an avid rock climber.

Copyright © 2001 by Jim Collins. Article first published in *Fast Company,* October 2001.

Unlocking the Mystery of Inspiring Leadership

Jack Zenger, Joe Folkman, and Scott Edinger

In This Chapter

▪ The importance of inspiring and motivating behavior.

▪ Why inspiring and motivating behavior has remained a mystery.

▪ The 10 qualities that set inspiring and motivating leaders apart.

▪ How leaders can make an emotional connection with those they lead.

One of the more common terms we have heard used to describe individuals who are inspiring is "charisma." Though not a perfect match, for a variety of reasons, it is illustrative that charismatic behavior has been recognized as being both extremely important for leaders and yet highly mysterious. Yet despite its importance, little attempt has been made to develop it within leaders. This chapter describes a unique approach to both defining and analyzing it so that its components may be understood and ways provided to develop it. Using an empirical approach, we break down inspiring or charismatic behavior into required attributes, and we explain how inspiring leaders make an emotional connection with their employees.

© 2010 Jack Zenger, Joe Folkman, and Scott Edinger. Used with permission.

Mysteries Block Progress

As a prelude to looking at the mystery of inspiring and motivating behavior, let's look at a former medical mystery, and how it blocked progress in healing. About 5 percent of people will develop a stomach ulcer at some time in their life. For most of the past century, it was assumed that the cause of ulcers was excess acid in the stomach that resulted from stress, an incorrect diet, and mistakes in general lifestyle. These ulcers inflamed the wall of the stomach and sometimes perforated the stomach wall and became bleeding ulcers. Physicians recommended that patients eat bland diets and avoid stress. These recommendations seemed impeccably logical because extreme stress was known to produce a surplus of stomach acid. Some foods were known to either be more acidic or to cause the stomach to produce more acid, and so these were also removed from people's diets. These treatments, however, were largely ineffective—because the basic assumptions about the causes of stomach ulcers were for the most part wrong.

In 1982, two Australian scientists discovered that a bacterium, *helicobacter pylori,* was the cause of more than 90 percent of stomach ulcers. This startling discovery led, of course, to radically different treatments—using antibiotics to kill the bacteria. Without this discovery, we can only assume that physicians would still be prescribing bland diets and stress avoidance for ulcer patients and experiencing minimal healing. Today we seldom hear of people with stomach ulcers.

A Leadership Mystery

With this story of solved mysteries in mind, let's switch to a totally different arena, the study of leadership. Despite all the research that has been done on the nature of leadership, both practitioners and scholars have long acknowledged the existence of a mystery. What's more, we have described this in terms that readily concede that it is something that we simply do not understand.

This mystery is the quality that sets inspiring or charismatic behavior apart from other types of behavior. Throughout history, those people seen as possessing the attribute of charisma have had powerful influence on others because people were attracted to them. And this charisma enabled them to achieve remarkable outcomes. The word "charisma" comes from the Greek word meaning "gift," which conceptually reinforces the notion that this attribute is a unique quality bestowed upon some and not others by an unseen hand. No one knew from whence it came. Because of that perceived reality, the topic of charisma was somewhat out of bounds as far as research and formal development were concerned. The consequence was that unlike other leadership skills—such as leading effective meetings, giving compelling oral presentations, or delegating—no one attempted to teach charisma.

Despite the rather mysterious nature of inspiration or charisma, the fact that it was labeled allowed observers to say things like "Well, the reason she has been so effective in her role as vice president of operations is that she's so inspirational or charismatic." Others hearing this would nod their agreement and concur: "Yes, she's extremely charismatic." Everyone pretended that they understood what was meant. In truth, no one had a clear idea of what the others meant, other than that this person possessed a distinctive quality.

For those involved in leadership development, the questions were even more profound. Not only was there the question of understanding charisma and being able to define it but also, and more important, the question of whether it can be learned or acquired. Do charismatic or inspiring leaders behave only in one way, or does charisma have several "flavors"? These are the questions that piqued our interest, and for which we believe we have found some answers.

Disagreements About Charisma

In fairness, there have been a few attempts to describe or define charisma. Some have argued that charisma has to do with charm and attractiveness. Often this has been equated with being highly extroverted. Thus, the stereotype of the charismatic person has been someone who enters a room with abounding confidence, speaking in a loud voice and commanding everyone's attention. Or it could be the highly ingratiating person who rivets their attention on you and makes you feel as if you are the only person there. Some would equate charisma with the nobility of the cause that a leader pursues. Others have contended that it describes a leader's willingness to take major risks. Still others have identified charisma with a self-sacrificing quality.

Charismatic leaders have often been identified with somewhat unconventional behavior, with proponents of this view arguing that this is what caused them to stand out. Being highly determined was also argued to be a necessary attribute of being charismatic.

Our experience has been that if you ask 20 people to describe "charisma," you will get at least 30 different answers. (And if you keep probing, you could easily reach 40 or 50 answers, because most people invariably come up with more than one. As we have said, there are more than a few disagreements about what it is.)

Why Understanding Charisma Is Important

Let's cut to the chase. Understanding charisma is important for two reasons:

1. Our research confirms that being "inspiring and motivating"—which we're proposing as the best operational definition of charisma that we can find—is the single most important leadership competency.
2. Being "inspiring and motivating" is the leadership competency on which leaders receive the lowest overall scores from their manager, their peers, and those who report to them.

Ponder this for a moment. This most important leadership quality is at the same moment also the one on which leaders get their lowest scores. That isn't a good combination.

In researching this important issue, we first analyzed data on more than 10,000 leaders to determine which of all the leadership competencies were most powerful in predicting the best leaders' effectiveness. We applied four tests:

- We compared the competencies that separated the best from the worst leaders.
- We compared the competencies that separated the best leaders from those who were merely average.
- We looked at the competency that correlated most highly with employee engagement and commitment.
- We asked subordinates what skill they most wanted in their leader.

To our surprise, the answer to all four tests was the same: "Inspires and motivates to high performance." We had not anticipated that four such different tests would lead to exactly the same answer.

Second, when we looked at the overall scores on the competencies for those 12,720 leaders, we also observed that the lowest-ranking competency was "inspires and motivates to high performance." (Note, however, that this was not a low score in absolute terms—in fact, with a composite ranking of 3.51 on a scale of five points, the average here is certainly adequate. It just happened to be the lowest ranked. Yet it is the combination of this stack ranking and our data indicating the critical importance of this competency that was most troubling.) For the data, see figure 18-1.

Deconstructing Inspiration

When the everyday objects around us were more mechanical, it was often fun to take them apart. It becomes clear what makes a mechanical alarm clock work when you take it apart

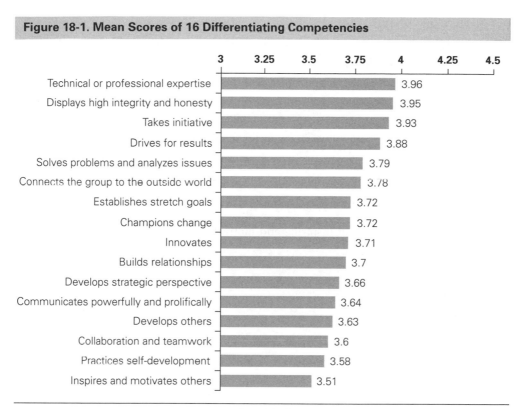

Figure 18-1. Mean Scores of 16 Differentiating Competencies

Competency	Score
Technical or professional expertise	3.96
Displays high integrity and honesty	3.95
Takes initiative	3.93
Drives for results	3.88
Solves problems and analyzes issues	3.79
Connects the group to the outside world	3.78
Establishes stretch goals	3.72
Champions change	3.72
Innovates	3.71
Builds relationships	3.7
Develops strategic perspective	3.66
Communicates powerfully and prolifically	3.64
Develops others	3.63
Collaboration and teamwork	3.6
Practices self-development	3.58
Inspires and motivates others	3.51

Copyright © 2009 by Zenger Folkman. Used with permission.

and reassemble it. Such an analysis is easy when the object is simple and the parts can be disassembled, picked up, and put back together. It also helps if the process of deconstructing doesn't completely destroy the object, once and for all.

The existence of extensive 360-degree feedback data is a marvelous gift, especially when it is accompanied by other information about a leader's impact on subordinates and on organizational performance. It allows the researcher to "look inside" leaders and analyze their perceived behavior in an unobtrusive and nondestructive way.

Here's what we did. We found those leaders who received the highest scores on "inspires and motivates to high performance" from their manager, their peers, and those who report to them. We then analyzed what behaviors differentiated this group of leaders from all the others. Luckily, this process was noninvasive. Better yet, it was based on large bodies of empirical data. No one needed to speculate about what makes people inspiring, provided the questions making up the 360-degree feedback were sufficiently comprehensive and addressed a wide range of important behaviors

We readily acknowledge that, from a research standpoint, it would be nirvana to have a lengthy list of 350 questions that probe every conceivable behavior. But we live in a practical world. Respondents simply won't stand still for exceedingly lengthy questionnaires. If you want high participation and completion rates, you must be reasonable. Our instrument normally has 52 items—each vetted extensively with thousands of leaders as the most predictive items related to a leader's ability to meet organizational objectives. In addition, these are the most robust items in terms of separating the best from the least effective leaders. But we make no pretense at measuring everything.

What Inspiring Leaders Do Differently

We found 10 qualities that set inspiring and motivating leaders apart from all the rest. These 10 fell into three arenas:

- attributes
- behaviors
- emotion.

Let's look briefly at each.

Attributes

The first was a set of attributes, or somewhat broad and general qualities:

- role model
- change champion
- initiative.

It is clear that inspiring and motivating leaders are excellent examples of what they want others to do. How consciously or unconsciously they do this, we don't know. But people watch them 24/7, and there are never "time-outs" or vacations from being the leader.

The other two attributes describe the fact that inspiring leaders are constantly challenging the organization to change. They are a continual driving force to make things happen for the better. Their fingerprints are all over many initiatives. It has long been acknowledged that one of the most distinguishing differences between leadership and management is that managers make things run efficiently but leaders focus more on change. This change may mean moving in a new direction. It may also mean climbing to a new plateau of performance. But leaders are not content with the status quo.

Behaviors

We also found six more discrete, actionable behaviors used by inspiring leaders. The importance of some of these was a bit surprising to us, but none of them come as a huge shock:

- stretch goals
- clear vision and direction
- communication
- developing people
- teamwork
- innovation.

Emotion

The third major finding had to do with the importance of emotion. This had enormously high correlations with inspiring and motivating behavior. The more we analyzed the role of emotion, the more it seemed to be the energy source that makes things move. It turns things on and propels them forward.

An important concept, however, is that the emotion of which we speak is not necessarily emanating from the leader; instead, foremost, it is the emotion that is being evoked within the subordinate. It is also the feeling that is created on the part of the subordinate about the leader or the project on which they are embarked.

Most of us have firsthand experience watching this occur. Imagine yourself in a meeting where there is one extremely negative, dour, or angry participant. This person's behavior changes the meeting's tone and climate, stifling its productivity and creativity, and sucking the energy out of the room. But if this person could somehow be removed from the meeting and replaced with a cheerful, engaged, optimistic, contributing individual, on a psychological level the sun comes out and the climate of the meeting is transformed. The dark clouds disperse, and the meeting takes on a totally different tone. The bottom line is that emotions are contagious, and a leader's emotions are extremely contagious because they are multiplied by his or her power role in the group.

Can Leaders Learn to Make an Emotional Connection?

We've learned that most people believe that the attributes noted above can be learned. Also, most people believe that the specific skills listed above can be acquired. But when it comes to making an emotional connection and arousing emotions in others, there appears to be a widespread belief that these cannot be learned. This may indeed be the reason why inspiring behavior or charisma has been labeled a gift.

If there was only one way for leaders to make this emotional connection, we would be more likely to concede that it can't be learned. But if there are multiple ways, the answer is much more likely to be "yes." This likelihood led us to conduct further research to see if we could better understand the various ways leaders make an emotional connection with their colleagues.

Why We Label Some People as Inspiring

To better understand how inspiring leaders make an emotional connection with their colleagues, we identified the 1,000 leaders who were best at inspiring and motivating others from a database of more than 10,000 leaders. We then did a statistical analysis that helped us identify the different approaches leaders used to inspire. From this analysis, we discovered that leaders use six approaches:

- the enhancers
- the enthusiasts
- the experts
- the visionaries
- the principled
- the drivers.

Some leaders are particularly effective using one of these approaches rather than another one, and, thus, for them, this one approach clearly dominates. More often, however, leaders use several approaches, and these leaders appear to be the most influential ones. They don't do just one thing. Indeed, it is the ability to combine several of these approaches that lifts people to a high level of motivation and performance. Let's look at the key characteristics for each approach.

First, the *enhancers:*

- Often described as sociable and friendly.
- Get team commitment to a difficult goal by using their strong relationships with all team members.
- Like to build supportive relationships.

Second, the *enthusiasts:*

- Often described as passionate about their work.
- Get their teams committed to a difficult goal by sharing their passion and excitement for the task.
- Like getting others excited about a project.

Third, the *experts:*

- Often described as very knowledgeable.
- Get their teams committed to a difficult goal by using their knowledge and expertise.

Fourth, the *visionaries:*

- Are often described as always looking for a better way.
- Get their teams committed to a difficult goal by devising and sharing a strategy for achieving the goal.
- Like coming up with a new strategy for accomplishing a task.

Fifth, the *principled:*

- Are often described as honest and ethical.
- Get their teams committed to a difficult goal by always honoring their commitments.
- Like being able to consistently do the right thing in the right way.
- Like assignments where people honor their commitments and consistently deliver on their promises.

And sixth, the *drivers:*

- Are often described as highly focused on achieving the outcome.
- Get their teams committed to a difficult goal by leading the effort themselves and pushing each member to keep up the pace.
- Enjoy accomplishing something difficult.
- Seek assignments calling for extensive effort that ultimately pays off in success.

Four main conclusions are apparent about these six approaches. The first is the widely different personality styles that are represented. The person who gravitates toward the energetic and enthusiastic approach is clearly different from the visionary, who tends to be more cerebral. The enhancer is at the polar opposite end of a continuum from the person who operates as a driver. Yet each of these approaches can enable a leader to make an emotional connection with those being led.

Second, being inspirational is not confined to one specific pattern of behavior. There is no one single mold for an inspirational leader.

Third, this opens the door for practically everyone to find one or more approaches that he or she can use authentically.

Fourth, the use of several of these approaches by one leader greatly increases the likelihood of him or her being perceived as an inspiring leader. Indeed, we have some strong data to support this conclusion; see figure 18-2. The good news is that nothing in any of the six approaches is out of the realm of being learned and effectively practiced by any leader who seriously wants to be become more inspiring.

Conclusion

Over the past years, but before doing the research presented above, we talked with many leaders about the competency of "inspiring and motivating to high performance." The response essentially was "Well, that's just not me" or "I'm not that kind of person." In hindsight, it is clear that many of these leaders assumed the only way to inspire was to be a highly voluble, energetic enthusiast. What's more, they knew they didn't have that type of personality and were not about to act in such an uncomfortable, phony way. Our recent research clearly dismisses that excuse because it shows that inspiration comes in many forms and

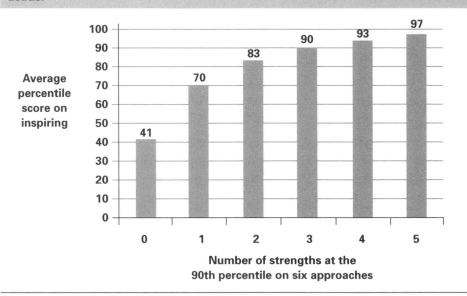

Figure 18-2. The Impact of Multiple Approaches on Being Perceived as an Inspiring Leader

Average percentile score on inspiring

Number of strengths at the 90th percentile on six approaches

Copyright © 2009 by Zenger Folkman. Used with permission.

flavors. Certain leadership actions are highly correlated with being seen as inspirational, and these can be learned. The basic attributes of inspiring leaders can be acquired. There simply are no excuses for leaders not to find genuine ways to inspire their colleagues, who crave this from them.

Further Reading

Kim S. Cameron, *Positive Leadership*. San Francisco: Berrett-Koehler, 2008.

Jay A. Conger and Rabindra N. Kanungo, eds., *Charismatic Leadership in Organizations*. Thousand Oaks, CA: Sage, 1998.

Belle Linda Halpern and Kathy Lubar, *Leadership Presence: Dramatic Techniques to Reach Out, Motivate, and Inspire*. New York: Gotham Books, 2003.

Remus Illies, Timothy Judge, and David Wagner, "Making Sense of Motivational Leadership: The Trail from Transformational Leaders to Motivated Followers," *Journal of Leadership and Organizational Studies*, September 2006.

John H. Zenger and Joseph Folkman, *The Extraordinary Leader: Turning Good Managers into Great Leaders*. New York: McGraw-Hill, 2002.

John H. Zenger, Joseph Folkman, and Scott K. Edinger, *The Inspiring Leader: Unlocking the Secrets of How Extraordinary Leaders Motivate*. New York: McGraw-Hill, 2009.

About the Authors

Jack Zenger is the cofounder and CEO of Zenger Folkman. In 1994, he was inducted into the HRD Hall of Fame. He is the best-selling author or coauthor of eight books on teams, productivity improvement, and leadership, including *Results-Based Leadership* (Harvard Business School Press, 1999), which was voted by the Society for Human Resources Management as the best business book in 2000; *The Extraordinary Leader: Turning Good Managers into Great Leaders* (McGraw-Hill, 2002); *Handbook for Leaders; The Inspiring Leader: Unlocking the Secrets of How Extraordinary Leaders Motivate* (McGraw-Hill, 2009); and, most recently, *The Extraordinary Coach: How the Best Leaders Help Others Grow* (McGraw-Hill, 2010). He has also authored or coauthored more than 50 articles on leadership, productivity, e-learning, training, and measurement.

Joe Folkman is president and cofounder of Zenger Folkman. He holds a doctorate in social and organizational psychology as well as a master's degree in organizational behavior. He has more than 30 years of experience doing consulting work with some of the world's most prestigious and successful organizations. He has extensive expertise in psychometrics, survey research, and managing organizational and individual change. He is a frequent keynote speaker and conference presenter on a variety of topics regarding leadership, feedback, and individual and organizational change. He is the author or coauthor of seven books on feedback that creates change in individuals and organizations.

Scott Edinger is executive vice president of Zenger Folkman, where he consults with *Fortune* 500 companies to initiate and implement large-scale performance improvement and leadership initiatives. Each year, he works with hundreds of leaders to develop leadership talent and address the challenges of organizational change. He is a popular keynote speaker at national conferences and has extensive experience working with some of the most prominent organizations in the world. He is recognized as an expert on helping organizations achieve measurable business results. He is coauthor of *The Inspiring Leader: Unlocking the Secrets of How Extraordinary Leaders Motivate* (McGraw-Hill, 2009).

The Authentic Leader

Bill George

··· **In This Chapter** ·········· ····················

- ▦ The qualities of an authentic, principle-driven leader.

- ▦ The process by which leaders develop their leadership talents.

- ▦ Firsthand accounts of, and lessons from, my own experiences—as well as my contemporaries—as we have explored our own leadership styles.

The world was brought to its knees by the financial collapse of 2008. As politicians and corporate leaders scramble to put the pieces back together, we direly need authentic, principle-driven leaders to lead us back to prosperity. It's precisely this kind of leader—honest, values-centered, purpose-driven, and disciplined—that I describe in this chapter on "the authentic leader."

There is no how-to guide for leadership. Many are born with leadership talents, but authentic leaders must have a passion for leadership and work hard to develop their leadership characteristics to be effective. By citing personal successes and failures across my career, and highlighting examples from many of my contemporaries, I've compiled what

---

© 2010 Bill George. Used with permission.

I'm confident is an insightful look into what is demanded of our leaders today. The demands of true leaders are many, and the needs for true leadership in today's recovering America are real.

Authentic leaders are those rare people who genuinely desire to serve others through their leadership. Because these leaders are more concerned with empowering those around them to make a difference than they are with power, money, or prestige for themselves, they are guided by qualities of the heart as equally as they are by qualities of the mind.

However, authentic leaders are not born this way—many have natural leadership gifts, but they must develop them over time to become outstanding leaders. Nor are authentic leaders above reproach or improvement—they are the first to recognize their shortcomings and work hard to rise above them. But by striving to lead with purpose, meaning, and values, they build enduring relationships with the people whom they lead, and with the other leaders from whom they continually learn. Authentic leaders are consistent and self-disciplined; when their principles are tested, they refuse to compromise, regardless of circumstance. Authentic leaders are dedicated to developing themselves because they know that becoming a leader requires a lifetime of personal growth.

Being Your Own Person

There is no such thing as the "ideal leader." A prospective leader who attempts to emulate all the characteristics of a good leader is doomed to fail. I know because I tried to do so early in my career. It simply doesn't work.

However, there is one essential quality that leaders must possess: They must be themselves, authentic in every regard. The best leaders are autonomous and highly independent. Those who are overly sensitive to others' desires are likely to be whipsawed by competing interests, easily distracted from their chosen course, or incapable of making difficult decisions for fear of offending. When asked for advice on how to be an authentic leader, my advice to the people I mentor is simple: Be yourself.

Of course, this is much easier said than done. Being your own person is most challenging when you feel like everyone else is pressuring you toward a predetermined end, and you are standing alone. In my first semester of business school, we watched the film *The Loneliness of the Long-Distance Runner*. Initially, I did not relate to its message, because I had always surrounded myself with people to avoid being lonely. As I progressed in my career, I learned that coping with the loneliness at the top is crucial so that we are not swayed by the pressure. Being able to stand alone against the majority is essential to being your own person.

Shortly after I joined Medtronic as president, I walked into a meeting where it quickly became evident that a group of my new colleagues had prearranged a strategy to settle a major patent dispute against Siemens on the basis of a "royalty-free" cross-license as a show of good faith. Intuitively, I knew this strategy was doomed to fail, so I stood alone against the entire group and refused to go along. My position may not have made me popular with my new teammates, but it was the right thing to do. We later negotiated a settlement with Siemens for more than $400 million, at the time the second-largest patent settlement ever.

Developing Your Unique Leadership Style

To become authentic, each of us must develop our own leadership style, one that is consistent with our personality and character. Unfortunately, organizational pressures often push us to adhere to a preset normative style. But if you capitulate and conform to a style that is not consistent with who you are, you will never become an authentic leader.

Contrary to what much of the literature says, no one leadership style equates to success. Great world leaders in history—George Washington, Abraham Lincoln, Winston Churchill, Franklin Roosevelt, Margaret Thatcher, Martin Luther King, Jr., Mother Teresa, and John F. Kennedy—all had very different styles, but each was an entirely authentic human being. There is no way any one of us could ever attempt to emulate any one of them without looking foolish.

The same is true for business leaders. Compare the leadership styles of the last three General Electric CEOs: the statesmanship of Reginald Jones, the dynamism of Jack Welch, and the forthrightness of Jeff Immelt. All are highly successful leaders with entirely different leadership styles. Yet GE has rallied around each of them, adapted to their styles, and flourished as a result. What counts is the authenticity of the leader, *not* the style with which he or she leads.

Over time, you will need to hone your style to be effective in leading different types of people and to be able to work in different environments. This is integral to your development as a leader. And to be effective in today's fast-moving, highly competitive globalized environment, leaders also must adapt their styles to fit the immediate situation.

There are times to be inspiring and motivating, and times to be tough and realistic about employee-related and financial decisions. There are times to delegate, and times to become immersed in the details. There are times to communicate public messages, and times to have private conversations. The use of adaptive styles is not inauthentic, and is very different from people who are always playing a role rather than being themselves. Good leaders are able to adapt their styles to the demands of the situation, and to know when and how to deploy which style.

When I first joined Medtronic, I spent a great deal of time learning the business and listening to our customers. I also focused on inspiring employees to fulfill the Medtronic mission of restoring people to full health. At the same time, I saw many ways in which we needed to be more disciplined about decisions and spending, so I was very challenging in budget sessions and put strict controls on head-count additions. At first, some people found this confusing. Eventually, however, they understood my reasons for adapting my style to the situation. They realized that I had to do so to be effective as their leader on the issue, and they eventually came to appreciate my aggressive stance.

Being Aware of Your Weaknesses

Being true to the person you were created to be means accepting your faults as well as using your strengths. Recognizing your shadow side is an essential part of being authentic. The problem comes when we are so eager to win the approval of others that we try to cover our shortcomings and sacrifice our authenticity to gain their respect and admiration.

I, too, have struggled in getting comfortable with my weaknesses—my tendency to intimidate others with an overly challenging style, my impatience, and my occasional lack of tact are all shortcomings I've come to see in myself. Only recently have I realized that my strengths and weaknesses are two sides of the same coin. By challenging others in business meetings, I am able to get quickly to the heart of the issues, but my approach also unnerves and intimidates less confident people. My desire to get things done quickly leads to superior results, but it also exposes my impatience with people who move more slowly. And my penchant for being direct with others ensures that I deliver my message, but it also reveals that I sometimes lack tact. Over time, I have moderated my style and adapted my approach to ensure that people are engaged and empowered, and that their voices are fully heard.

I have always been open to critical feedback, but also quite sensitive to it. For years, I felt I had to be perfect, or at least appear that I was on top of everything. I tried to hide my weaknesses from others, fearing they would reject me if they knew who I really was. Eventually, however, I realized that they could see my weaknesses more clearly than I could. In attempting to cover them up, I was only fooling myself. As I have become more comfortable with myself, I have become more authentic in my interactions with others. It's important that authentic leaders do the same.

The Temptations of Leadership

Former Congressman Amory Houghton, one of the more thoughtful politicians to have worked in the U.S. Congress, tells the story of his predecessor's advice as he was taking over as CEO of Corning Glass: "Think of your decisions being based on two concentric circles. In the outer circle are all the laws, regulations, and ethical standards to which the company must comply. In the inner circle are your core values. Just be darn sure that your decisions as CEO stay within your inner circle" (quoted in George 2003).

We are all painfully aware of corporate leaders who pushed beyond the outer circle and got caught, either by the law or through the financial failures of their companies. More worrisome are the leaders of companies who moved outside their inner circles and engaged in marginal practices, albeit legal ones. Examples include cutting back your company's long-term investments just to make the short-term numbers, bending compensation rules to pay executives in spite of marginal performance, using accounting tricks to meet the quarterly expectations of security analysts, shipping products of marginal quality, compromising security analysts by giving them a cut on investment banking deals, and booking revenues before they are shipped to pump up revenue growth. The list goes on and on, and unfortunately we saw the impact such short-term behavior can have on the world economy in the 2008 financial collapse—we're still feeling its effects today.

All of us who sit in the leader's chair feel the pressure to perform. As CEO, I felt it every day as problems mounted or sales lagged. I knew that the livelihood of tens of thousands of employees, the health of millions of patients, and the financial fortunes of millions of investors rested on my shoulders and those of our executive team. At the same time, I was well aware of the penalties for not performing, even for a single quarter. No CEO wants to appear on CNBC to explain why his company missed its earnings projections, even if it's by a penny.

Little by little, the pressures to succeed can pull us away from our core values, just as we are reinforced by our success in the market. Some people refer to this as "CEO-itis." The irony is that the more successful we become, the more we are tempted to take shortcuts to keep it going. And the rewards—compensation increases, stock option gains, myriad executive perquisites, positive stories in the media, admiring comments from our peers—all reinforce our actions and drive us to keep it going.

Novartis CEO Daniel Vasella once touched on these pressures during an interview with *Fortune* magazine:

> Once you get under the domination of making the quarter—even unwittingly— you start to compromise in the gray areas of your business that cut across the wide swath of terrain between the top and the bottom. Perhaps you'll begin to

sacrifice things that are important and may be vital for your company over the long-term. . . . The culprit that drives this cycle isn't the fear of failure so much as it is the craving for success. For the tyranny of quarterly earnings is a tyranny that is imposed from within. . . . For many of us the idea of being a successful manager is an intoxicating one. It is a pattern of celebration leading to belief, leading to distortion. When you achieve good results, you are typically celebrated, and you begin to believe that the figure at the center of all that champagne toasting is yourself. You are idealized by the outside world, and there is a natural tendency to believe that what is written is true (Vasella and Leaf 2002).

Like Vasella, who is one of the finest and most authentic leaders I know, all leaders must contend with these pressures while continuing to perform, especially when things are going south. The test I used with our team at Medtronic was whether we would feel comfortable having the entire story appear on the front page of *The New York Times*. If we didn't, we went back to the drawing board and reexamined our decision.

Dimensions of Authentic Leaders

Let's examine the essential dimensions of all authentic leaders, the qualities that true leaders must develop. I have determined through many experiences in leading others that authentic leaders demonstrate these five qualities:

1. Understanding purpose.
2. Practicing solid values.
3. Leading with heart.
4. Establishing enduring relationships.
5. Demonstrating self-discipline.

Acquiring these five dimensions of an authentic leader is not a sequential process; rather, leaders are developing them continuously throughout their lives.

Understanding Your Purpose

To become a leader, it is essential that you first answer this question: "Leadership for what purpose?" If you lack purpose and direction in leading, why would anyone want to follow you?

"Alice comes to a fork in the road where she sees a cat in the tree. Alice asks the cat, 'Which road should I take?' 'Do you know where you want to go?' inquires the cat. 'No,' says Alice. To which the cat replies, 'Then any road will get you there.'"

—Lewis Carroll, *Alice in Wonderland*

Many people want to become leaders without giving much thought to their purpose. They are attracted to the power and prestige of leading an organization and the financial rewards that go with it. But without a real sense of purpose, leaders are at the mercy of their egos and are vulnerable to narcissistic impulses. There is no way you can adopt someone else's purpose and still be an authentic leader. You can study that which others pursue and you can work with them toward common purposes, but in the end the purpose for your leadership must be uniquely yours.

To find your purpose, you must first understand yourself, your passions, and your underlying motivations. Then you must seek an environment where there is a fit between the organization's purpose and your own. Your search may take experiences in several organizations before you can find the one that is right for you.

The late Robert Greenleaf, a former AT&T executive, is well known for his concept of leaders as servants of the people. In his book *Servant Leadership*, he advocates service to others as the leader's primary purpose. If people feel you are genuinely interested in serving others, then they will be prepared not just to follow you but also to dedicate themselves to the common cause.

One of the best examples of a leader with purpose was the late David Packard, cofounder of Hewlett-Packard. I met him in early 1969, when he was the new deputy secretary of defense and I was the special assistant to the secretary of the Navy. He had taken a leave from HP to serve his country. He was a big and powerful—yet modest—man, who immediately impressed me with his openness, sincerity, and commitment to making a difference through his work.

He returned to HP a few years later to build it into one of the great companies of its time. Through his dedication to the company's mission, known as "The HP Way," and to excellence in research and development and customer service, he inspired HP's employees to incredible levels of commitment. At his death, he was one of the wealthiest people in the world, yet no one would have ever known it by his spending habits. Most of his money went toward philanthropic projects. Dave Packard was a truly authentic leader, a role model for me and for many in my generation.

Another example can be found in the experience of John Bogle. For 50 years, John Bogle has been a man with a mission: to transform the management of investors' funds. He created the first no-load mutual fund in 1974 and founded Vanguard, the nation's leading purveyor of index funds. Not only has he been a pioneer in financial services, but he has also been the leading advocate for financial funds acting as stewards of their investors' money and long-term interests. His values and his integrity stand in stark relief against those in the financial community who seek to use investment funds for their personal gain.

Practicing Solid Values

Authentic leaders are defined by their values and character, which they shape according to personal beliefs and develop through study, introspection, consultation with others. This is a lifelong experience. These values define their moral compass. They know the "True North" of their compass and have a deep sense of what is right. After all, Ken Lay and Bernie Madoff did not set off seeking shame and disapprobation.

Although the development of fundamental values is crucial, *integrity* is the one value that is required in every authentic leader. Integrity is not just the absence of lying but also the consummate telling of the whole truth—as painful as it may be. Without complete integrity in your interactions, no one can trust you. If they cannot trust you, why would they ever follow you?

I once had a colleague who would never lie to me, but often he shared only positive parts of the story, sheltering me from the ugly side. Finally, I told him that real integrity meant giving me the whole story so that together we could make sound decisions. Rather than thinking less of him, I would have a higher opinion of his courage and integrity.

Most business schools and academic institutions do not teach values as part of leadership development. Some offer ethics courses, often in a theoretical context, but they shy away from the meat and potatoes of the issue. Others assume erroneously that their students already have well-solidified values. What they fail to recognize is the importance of solidifying your values through study and dialogue, and the impact that your environment has in shaping your values.

As Enron was collapsing in the fall of 2001, the *Boston Globe* published an article by a Harvard classmate of Enron CEO Jeff Skilling. The author described how Skilling would argue in class that the role of the business leader was to take advantage of loopholes in regulations and push beyond the laws wherever he could to make money. As Skilling saw the world, it was the job of the regulators to try and catch him. Sound familiar? Twenty-five years later, Skilling's philosophy caught up with him, as the company he led tumbled into bankruptcy (quoted in George 2003).

One of my role models for values-centered leadership is Max DePree, the former CEO of the furniture maker Herman Miller. He is a modest man, guided by a deep concern for serving others, and is true to his values in every aspect of his life. His humanity can be seen through the exemplary way in which his company conducts itself. He describes his philosophy of values-centered leadership in his classic book *Leadership Is an Art*. He also subscribes to Greenleaf's ideas about servant leadership and expands on them by offering his own advice: "The leader's first job is to define reality. The last is to say thank you. In between the leader must become a servant and a debtor."

DePree believes that a corporation should be "a community of people," all of whom have value and share in the fruits of their collective labor. And he practices what he preaches. While he was Herman Miller's CEO, his salary was capped at 20 times that of an hourly worker. In his view, tying the CEO's salary to those of his workers helps cement trust in leadership. Contrast that with today's CEOs, who are earning salaries 400 times that of their hourly workers. As DePree said recently, "When leaders indulge themselves with lavish perks and the trappings of power, they are damaging their standing as leaders" (George 2004).

Leading with Heart

During the last several decades, businesses have evolved from maximizing the physical output of their workers to engaging the minds of their employees. To excel in the 21st century, great companies will go one step further by engaging the hearts of their employees through a sense of purpose. When employees believe their work has a deeper purpose, their results will vastly exceed those who use only their minds and their bodies. This will become the company's competitive advantage.

Sometimes we refer to people as being bighearted. What we really mean is that they are open and willing to share themselves fully with us, and are genuinely interested in us. Leaders who behave this way—like Wal-Mart founder Sam Walton and Metronic founder Earl Bakken—have the ability to ignite the souls of their employees to achieve greatness far beyond what anyone might imagine possible.

One of the most bighearted leaders I know is Marilyn Carlson Nelson, the chair and former CEO of the Carlson Companies, the privately held hospitality and travel services giant. When she became CEO, she inherited a hard-nosed organization that was driven for growth but not known for empathy toward its customers. Shortly after taking the helm, she had an epiphany. She was meeting with the group of MBA students who had been studying the company's culture. In asking the students for feedback, she got a stony silence from the group. Finally, a young woman raised her hand and said, "We hear from employees that Carlson is a sweatshop that doesn't care."

That incident sent Nelson into high gear. She created a motivational program called "Carlson Cares." As the company was preparing for its launch, her staff told her they needed more time to change the culture before introducing the program. She decided that she could not wait and opted to become the company's role model for caring and empathy. She immediately set out to change the environment, using her passion, motivational skills, and sincere interest in her employees and customers. She took the lead on customer sales calls and interacted every day with employees in Carlson's operations. Her positive energy transformed the company's culture, built its customer relationships, accelerated its growth, and strengthened its bottom line.

Establishing Enduring Relationships

The capacity to develop close and enduring relationships is one mark of an authentic leader. Unfortunately, many leaders of major companies believe their jobs are to create the strategy, organizational structure, and organizational processes. Then they simply delegate the tasks to be done, remaining disconnected from the people doing the actual work.

This detached style of leadership will not be successful in the 21st century. Today's employees demand more personal relationships with their leaders before they will give themselves fully to their jobs. They insist on having access to their leaders, knowing that it is in the openness and depth of the relationship with the leader where trust and commitment are built. Jeff Bezos of Amazon.com, Michael Dell of Dell Computers, and Indra Nooyi of PepsiCo are successful because they connect directly with their employees, who respond with a deeper commitment to their work and greater loyalty to the company.

In his book *Eyewitness to Power,* David Gergen writes, "At the heart of leadership is the leader's relationship with followers. People will entrust their hopes and dreams to another person only if they think the other is a reliable vessel." Authentic leaders establish trusting relationships with people throughout the organization as well as in their personal lives—and the rewards of these relationships, both tangible and intangible, are long lasting.

I always tried to establish close relationships with my colleagues, looking to them as a closely knit team whose collective knowledge and wisdom vastly exceeded my own. Many corporate leaders fear these kinds of relationships—as another CEO said to me, "Bill, I don't want to get too close to my subordinates, because someday I may have to terminate them." Actually, the real reason goes much deeper than that. Many leaders—men in particular—fear having their weaknesses and vulnerabilities exposed. So they create distance from employees and an aloofness. Instead of being authentic, they are creating a dispassionate persona they can hide behind.

Demonstrating Self-Discipline

Self-discipline is an essential quality of an authentic leader. Without it, you cannot gain the respect of your followers. It is easy to say that someone has good values but lacks the discipline to convert those values into consistent actions. This is a hollow excuse. None of us is perfect, of course, but authentic leaders must have the self-discipline to do everything

> *"Relationship is the mirror in which we see ourselves as we are."*
> —J. Krishnamurti

they can to demonstrate their values through their actions. When we fall short, it is equally important to admit our mistakes.

Leaders are highly competitive people. They are driven to succeed at whatever they take on. Authentic leaders know that competing requires a consistently high level of self-discipline to be successful. Being very competitive is not a bad thing; in fact, it is an essential quality of successful leaders. But it needs to be channeled through purpose and discipline. Sometimes we mistake competitive people who generate near-term results by improving operational effectiveness for genuine leaders. Achieving operational effectiveness is an essential result for any leader, but it alone does not ensure authenticity or long-term success.

For example, Dick Fuld was a highly competitive and highly motivated leader when he held the reins at Lehman Brothers. But because he could not marry that competitiveness with discipline, he allowed the firm to gorge itself on mortgage-backed securities—and thus, when the financial crisis hit in 2007, Lehman Brothers was left overleveraged and strapped for cash. And eventually, it collapsed.

On the flip side, the most consistent leader I know is Art Collins, my successor as CEO of Medtronic. He is as competitive as any other CEO today, and his self-discipline is equally evident in every interaction. His subordinates never need to worry about what kind of mood he is in, or where he stands on an important issue. Nor does he deviate in his behavior or vacillate in his decisions. He never lets his ego or emotions get in the way of taking the appropriate action. These qualities make working with him easier and more predictable, enabling Medtronic's employees to do their jobs effectively.

Mother Teresa is another compelling example of an authentic leader. Many think of her as simply a nun who reached out to the poor in Calcutta, yet by 1990 she had created an organization of 4,000 missionaries operating in 100 countries. Her organization, Missionaries of Charity, spread to 450 centers around the world. Its mission is "to reach out to the destitute on the streets, offering wholehearted service to the poorest of the poor." Not only did she have a purpose, clear values, and a heart filled with compassion, but she also created intimate relationships with people and exercised self-discipline, all the dimensions of an authentic leader. I doubt that any of us will ever be like Mother Teresa, but her life is indeed an inspiration.

Authentic Leadership

The media often acclaim the "decisive" leader or the "strong" CEO. This superficial view of leadership fails to recognize the complexity of human relationships and the centrality of those relationships to business in the 21st century. It isn't that enterprise resource planning software or Six Sigma don't have a place in today's enterprises—they are critical tools, as are strategy, organizational structure, and organizational process—but these tools are table stakes, and they are imitable. The disconnected manager who delegates tasks or implements operational tools is little more than a technician. The leadership demanded by today's knowledge-based enterprises is more nuanced and more challenging. Yet, the most important for leaders to recognize is that you do not have to be Mother Teresa or Jack Welch or Marilyn Carlson Nelson to lead authentically. You only need to be yourself.

Further Reading

Max Depree, *Leadership Is an Art*. New York: Dell, 1990.

Bill George, *Authentic Leadership: Rediscovering the Secrets to Creating Lasting Value*. San Francisco: Jossey-Bass, 2003.

———, *7 Lessons for Leading in Crisis*. San Francisco: Jossey-Bass, 2009.

David Gergen, *Eyewitness to Power: The Essence of Leadership, Nixon to Clinton*. New York: Simon & Schuster, 2000.

Robert K. Greenleaf, *Servant Leadership: A Journey into the Nature of Legitimate Power and Greatness*. Mahwah, NJ: Paulist Press, 1971.

References

Depree, M. 1990. *Leadership Is an Art*. New York: Dell.

George, B. 2003. *Authentic Leadership: Rediscovering the Secrets to Creating Lasting Value*. San Francisco: Jossey-Bass.

———. 2004. The Journey to Authenticity. *Leader to Leader* 31 (Winter): 29–35.

Gergen, D. 2000. *Eyewitness to Power: The Essence of Leadership, Nixon to Clinton*. New York: Simon & Schuster.

Vasella, D., and C. Leaf. 2002. "Temptation Is All Around Us." Daniel Vasella of Novartis Talks About Making the Numbers, Self-Deception, and the Danger of Craving Success. *Fortune*. November 18.

About the Author

Bill George is a professor of management practice at Harvard Business School, where he has taught leadership since 2004. He is the author of four best-selling books: *7 Lessons for Leading in Crisis, True North, Finding Your True North,* and *Authentic Leadership*. He is the former chairman and CEO of Medtronic. He currently serves as a director of ExxonMobil and Goldman Sachs. He received his BSIE with high honors from the Georgia Institute of Technology and his MBA with high distinction from Harvard University, where he was a Baker Scholar.

 **Chapter 20**

Leading in Turbulent Times

Priscilla Nelson and Ed Cohen

In This Chapter

■ Explore 10 guidelines to help leaders guide people through turbulent times.

■ Personal stories of two employees dealing with turbulent times.

Since we had joined Satyam Computer Services and moved to India in 2005, the company had experienced rapid growth, actually doubling in size by 2007 and on target to again double by 2010. At the end of 2008, Satyam was India's fourth-largest information technology services firm, with 53,000 employees based in 60 countries around the world. But then, on January 7, 2009, we watched Satyam's founder and chairman, Ramalinga Raju, disclose in a statement to the media that he had engaged in actions with respect to the firm's finances that would cause its fall from grace. Those of us who were shareholders saw our investments disappear like a tsunami wave into a pool of financial destruction. And all of us watched in disbelief as the news began to emerge.

In his statement that day, when referring to the widening gap between the real and artificial numbers in the company books, Raju described his situation thus: "It was like riding a tiger,

---

Adapted from book *Riding the Tiger: Learning Strategies for Leaders in Turbulent Times,* published by ASTD Press, 2010.

not knowing how to get off without being eaten." In his resignation letter to the company's board of directors, he stated: "I am now prepared to subject myself to the laws of land and face consequences thereof."

Yet around the world, Satyam's employees were not prepared to subject themselves to the consequences. Tainted, disgraced, beleaguered, scam hit, scandalized, fraudulent, and crisis ridden were just some of the adjectives now used to refer to the once-iconic brand of "India is IT." The scale and impact of Satyam's downfall were put in proper perspective by *The Economist*'s cover story, "India's Enron," and *BusinessWeek*'s cover feature on Raju, headlined "From Icon to I Con."

We feared for our own livelihoods and for the impact the scandal would have on our families; see the sidebar for one employee's experience. Few companies survive such an onslaught, so certainly there could be massive layoffs ahead. The leaders and the culture were not properly prepared for such a crisis. For the leaders of the company's training facility, Satyam Learning World, obviously this presented a major challenge.

As an Indian-headquartered organization, Satyam was entrenched in a hierarchical, largely patriarchal culture. A servant-like attitude was the norm. Decisions were made by the most senior leaders or those with perceived authority due to longevity or seniority with the organization. But since 2005, a sea change had occurred, or so we thought, from this patriarchal structure to a consensus-oriented leadership culture. That is, until communication from Raju diminished in the months before his fateful confession. Employees were lost without direction, and only a few leaders had the courage to step forward. The entire situation was surreal. The media were everywhere. We had instantly gone from hero to zero. And so began the journey toward a new learning strategy for leaders, which included behaviors, competencies, and expectations to control the damage and rebuild as much as possible. We felt that leaders might go on autopilot when it came to managing, and that is exactly what they did. But as Satyam staff members in leadership roles concerned with learning and staff development, we specifically chose to focus on the people and relationship dimensions of the situation.

During turbulent times, leaders must rapidly and proactively convert emotions into actions. Everything speeds up—change, though always constant, is even more prevalent. Emotions, processes, demands, and measures increase as more is expected from everyone. Turbulent times are obviously stressful. Leaders must concurrently take care of themselves and everyone else. This takes time, patience, empathy, and a willingness to shift priorities and engage in constant communication—even what normally might be seen as overcommunication. Leaders should lead "out loud"—be transparent, maintain

A View from Ed

On January 7, 2009, I was on vacation in the states, enjoying a cool evening in Southern California. It was 11 p.m. I was with our cousins and some friends having drinks, dinner, and good laughs. I had decided to completely take the night off, which included not even answering my phone. This turned out to be poor timing. My friend Josh noticed that I had several missed calls—32, to be exact. The phone rang again, and this time I answered. It was my wife, Priscilla: "It's all over the news. Ramalinga Raju has confessed to over-stating the revenues of Satyam since 2001. We are watching it on the news right now. Everyone is in shock; no one knows what to do." I could hear the concern in her voice: "The stock price is diving. Everyone is scared."

I was shocked. I had no words. I needed a few moments to let the news sink in. How was this possible? There had not even been an inkling that this could possibly have happened, and to me, Ramalinga Raju was a leader of the highest integrity.

After completing my call with Priscilla, I checked my phone. There were 13 text messages, all from shocked employees of the company asking me what to do. I logged into email and found hundreds of messages from people who were panicking. I searched the Internet for information. There were already thousands of postings, even though the announcement had only come less than an hour before.

So now what? We were faced with a crisis, the magnitude far greater than anything I had ever experienced. And, I was 10,000 miles away from the center of the crisis, with little information. I phoned my assistant, Vijay Gupta. With his help, less than an hour after Raju's confession, the 300-plus associates of Satyam Learning World were participating in a live web meeting and audio conference. I was still in shock and noticeably shaken by the news. What would we say to the team? Luckily for me, my cousin, Howard Richmond, wrote and flashed notes to guide me throughout the conversation. One such note truly had a profound impact on me and everyone else: "Don't let the news of today undo the successes of yesterday or tomorrow." Without realizing it, I had begun thinking that the past years spent in India working for Satyam were now wasted. Howard's short message restored my sense of accomplishment. So, when we spoke to the Satyam Learning World associates, I shared Howard's words of wisdom and encouragement with them.

We fielded questions and provided as much comfort and advice as we possibly could at that moment. During the next two weeks, we had multiple quick updates throughout the day and a daily call. Even when there wasn't much to report, people still had questions. It was clear they were looking forward to having regular access to their leaders and to each other. They felt comfort in being with each other. Because the team was scattered around the world, we brought them together both physically and virtually. We kept them informed, and all our leaders opened their doors. They each proactively met individually with members of their teams. Each day the leaders came together and we discussed how everyone was doing and our next steps.

their integrity, and be approachable. These are the leaders with whom people want to work, in good times and bad. To successfully lead people through turbulent times, here are 10 daily guidelines for leaders:

1. We will *never* get back to normal.
2. Find ways to take care of each other.
3. React . . . pause . . . respond.
4. Even when you don't believe there is much to say, there is much to say.
5. Now is not the time for hide-and-seek.
6. Maintain integrity and high moral values.
7. Leaders are human, too.
8. Spend time with children.
9. Take care of your emotional, physical, and spiritual well-being.
10. Assess and rebuild trust.

Let's take a look at each.

We Will *Never* Get Back to Normal

We looked up the word "normal" in several dictionaries and found that it means conforming to the norm, to rules, to known standards. Normal? What's normal? The organization we knew before these turbulent times is certainly not the normal to which we wanted to return. Why would anyone even want to return to that "normal"? In that "normal," we were leading a rapidly growing business that was merely a facade to fuel the ambitions of the founder and chairman and a few of his key senior managers. "Normal" thus had two dimensions: (1) the appearance of great success; and (2) deception, with calculated movement to continuously hide the truth.

The word "normal" also means "average." We don't know too many people who want to be called average. The only constant about "normal" is that it is always changing. So, instead of hoping for and trying to get back to normal, move on, seek better ways to do things, and let them become the new normal.

Find Ways to Take Care of Each Other

During turbulent times, leaders need to demonstrate transparency, empathy, patience, and forgiveness. Look for ways to take care of each other. First and foremost, explore your feelings. Find someone with whom you can speak, who will have an objective view and provide you with the empathic listening you need for yourself. At work, don't be afraid to express feelings. And allow others to express their feelings without judgment. Words like hurt, worried, cheated, shock, and disbelief, along with phrases like "How did this happen?" and "Am

I going to lose my job?" will be spoken. *Let them flow.* There is no need to have an answer or even a reply. Now is the time to be a great listener and to demonstrate empathy. Use paraphrasing to let others know you have heard them. People need to verbalize thoughts and feelings to work through them. They want to be heard and need to feel listened to lower their anxiety.

Now is the time to come together in community. Bring everyone together; if an event caused the turbulence, have them talk about where they were when the news first came out. Provide regular updates on what's happening across the organization. Hearing it first from you, as the leader, demonstrates transparency and caring for others. Go out to lunch with colleagues, take a walk together, gather in a conference room to share stories—togetherness is healing.

You can ask people to draw a picture depicting how they are feeling. For example, have everyone draw their river of emotions. Each person draws their own river showing the rough waters, twists, bends, high water, and low water, all depicting their own emotions. Then ask them to draw the river as they would like to see it in the future. Everyone can share their pictures with each other. Without words, all will see they are on similar journeys. When people know they are not alone, they immediately feel better.

React . . . Pause . . . Respond

When a crisis occurs, for safety and expediency, leaders are counted on to react. Adrenaline pushes energy to the parts of the body most required to handle the turbulence. Your mind might be more alert, thinking at a rapid speed, your eyes may dilate so you can see better, and your hearing may sharpen—and all this brings on the "normal" reaction: fight or flight. But if you react in that moment, a normal response, it may or may not be right. So pause. Then reflect, collect as much information as possible, and consider possible benefits and consequences before deciding on your next action.

Moving beyond that, we each face our own turmoil. We each decide how to respond, taking into consideration all factors at that time including our career desires, personal needs, and family situation. No matter how one responds, it will be right for you, as long as it comes from information gathering, integrity, an open heart, and seeking to understand.

Even When You Don't Believe There Is Much to Say, There Is Much to Say

"I don't know what to say." "Everyone is getting information daily from the company." "They can see it on the news." These are some excuses heard from leaders when asked why they are not communicating with their teams. But during turbulent times, there is no such thing as overcommunicating. There is no valid excuse for not communicating. Give regular updates as often as necessary. When the crisis at Satyam began, updates were given every hour. Then we shifted to updates every few hours, and then daily, and then weekly. Never cancel an update. This scares people. Even when there isn't much to report, people appreciate being told what is known again and again. They also appreciate the opportunity to ask questions. They feel connected with regular access to their most senior leaders.

Overcommunication is good communication during turbulent times. You will know that you are communicating enough when people repeat your words to each other and to you. Consistent and continuous messaging prevents the rumor mill from grinding and demonstrates the leader's approachability, transparency, and caring. See the sidebar for how this applied to Satyam's experience.

Now Is Not the Time for Hide-and-Seek

"I have my own stress to deal with." "I have incredibly tight deadlines." "I have no time to hang out and talk to people." These are just a few of the excuses we heard from leaders during Satyam's turbulent time. And though it's true that leaders in such times are tremendously busy working to stabilize their company, that they have many additional requirements, and that they are themselves scared, the need of the hour is the team. When a leader goes into hiding, the people who work for him or her become scared. They question what is happening, and without the leader's presence, they might even make up a story about what is going on. This is how dangerous rumors and urban legends are born.

So *be visible.* Now is not the time to hide away at home or in your office. Open the door, get up from your desk, walk around, and talk with people—let them know you care. During the crisis at Satyam, a colleague sent this quotation (we tried to find out who wrote it but couldn't): "They don't care how much you know until they know how much you care." Listen, empathize, share advice, and provide words of comfort—just be there. You may be injured; we all are. You may have a lot of work to get done; we all do. But as a leader, you must be present to inform, comfort, and provide strength for others.

Maintain Integrity and High Moral Values

During turbulent times, leaders are asked to take steps that they might not feel good about. There may be a pending layoff, a potential sale of the company, or quite possibly something even worse set to happen. But don't let current circumstances influence, broaden, or distort your definition of integrity and other core values. In researching my book *Leadership Without Borders* (Cohen 2007), I conducted a global survey of 250 senior executives who had

A View from Priscilla

The television screen displayed a photo of Ramalinga Raju, Satyam's founder and chairman, on the right and a graph depicting the falling stock price on the left. The value of Satyam's stock plummeted in less than five seconds, drained like an hourglass with the grains of sands pushing to the bottom. I immediately dialed Ed's number. At the time, he was still in California. There was no answer, so I continued trying to call, over and over.

Following the broadcast, two Satyam vice presidents and I called a meeting of those who were in the firm's School of Leadership building. We organized additional meetings in other locations where our learning teams were located. I recall thinking that I didn't know any more than anyone else. I did know that it was important for us to be together as we tried to absorb the shock. But just as a community bands together after a storm or other disasters, we had to count on the human spirit to care for each other. We were all frightened. There was so much we still did not know. How would this affect our jobs? How would our families handle the news? What was to become of Satyam?

I thought back to when my father was in the hospital dying of cancer and I was 3,000 miles away. I wanted constant information, even if there was nothing to report. I wanted to feel connected, and I knew this is what we needed now.

We spoke candidly about our fears and pledged to share information on Satyam's situation as soon as it became available. We also agreed to give regular updates, even if there was nothing to share. We realized how important it was to reach beyond our group, to engage other leaders who would need support to speak with their teams. We went live with these same candid conversations the next day over our company-wide web television station. Every Satyam employee around the world would hear our fears and our stories about how we had communicated with our friends and families (especially those of us with children). This program was made available to all 53,000 employees. We built more programs, reaching out in as many different formats. Whereas, before, a crisis may have caused managers to close their doors, we now recognized the need to use our learning methods, both formal and informal, to include anyone with access to a computer. We became the Satyam Emergency Broadcast Network. We were applauded for our honesty and courage. It was a great and fulfilling experience to be able to mobilize the talents and capabilities of a group of incredibly dedicated professionals to leverage learning and development during this turbulent time.

lived and worked in more than 60 different countries. The results identified 14 core values that are critical for all leaders:

- Conviction: Conveys sincerity and confidence in beliefs and decisions, and a willingness to make and stand by difficult decisions.
- Diversity: Values different perspectives, builds multifaceted diverse teams, seeks to understand what drives and motivates individuals.

- Entrepreneurship: Recognizes opportunities and organizes resources to maximize them.
- Excellence: Strives for excellence, which is not the same as perfection; recognizes that "excellence" may vary from country to country, depending upon the local context.
- Fairness: Makes decisions that are fair, consistent, and equitable.
- Humility: Acts in the knowledge that he or she is not better or more important than others.
- Integrity: Demonstrates honesty and makes ethical decisions.
- Passion: Leads by example and demonstrates a high level of energy and enthusiasm.
- Perseverance: Shows resolve in moving toward the path ahead, with a strong will and the drive to accomplish goals.
- Positive attitude: Maintains a positive attitude and represents decisions and policies in a positive manner.
- Respect: Demonstrates a high regard for others, regardless of their station in life; treats everyone with dignity.
- Service oriented: Provides extraordinary, "extra mile" assistance to everyone, whether internal to the organization or a customer.
- Teamwork: Easily adapts to being a team player and encourages teamwork across the organization.
- Work/life balance: Balances time spent at work with other dimensions of one's family, community, and social life.

Core values represent who you are. Standing by core values in difficult times is the best way to demonstrate the true character of the organization. This means being willing to have difficult conversations and make difficult decisions, and not tolerating a lack of integrity. Let go of people who make such compromises.

Leaders Are Human, Too

During turbulent times, we all go through a lot. We may feel hurt, damaged, and worried—and that's just the tip of the emotional iceberg. Sometimes you will not be at your best, although it is important for you, as the leader, to hold it together as much as possible. Even so, you may still have some bad moments.

The experience of a leader we observed is illustrative. He came to work, carrying his own fears, angry that his company had allowed itself to fall into a severe crisis and not sure how his family would make it through if he lost his job. With all this on his mind, things that would normally not bother him caused an exaggerated reaction. After being confronted late in the day by his assistant, he went home and reflected. Realizing that this behavior was totally out of character, he knew he needed to do something. The next morning, he sent this note to everyone:

> Dear Team,
>
> These are very stressful times we are going through. Yesterday was a particularly bad day for me. I allowed my own fears to interfere with my work and, as many of you know, I lacked patience and displayed a frustrated tone, even shouting at a few people. All of you know this is not my normal behavior. I sincerely apologize to anyone I was harsh with and want everyone to know I am working very hard to be the leader you need me to be.

The response was incredible. The team members, relieved to know that their leader was also going through much of the same pain as they were, not only appreciated the message but also felt closer to their leader for having shown his frailty. At that moment, trust and confidence increased, and what had begun as a very negative experience that could have damaged the leader's standing with his team was transformed into an opportunity to reflect and solidify.

Leaders are human, too. They experience the full range of emotions, just like everyone else. However, many leaders do not feel they should express these emotions openly. We believe the best leaders are willing to express their feelings. So if you experience anger and act out as a result of your turmoil, as soon as you realize it, apologize and move on. Do not beat yourself up. Leaders are human, too.

Spend Time with Children

To some, the idea of spending time with children may seem out of place here. Spend time with children during turbulent times? Wouldn't this be totally inappropriate? Not really, when you think about it. Children do not carry the same burdens as adults; they live in the moment and, especially younger children, are constantly playing. They may sense your sadness or turmoil. They may even ask you about it. But soon they will be running around again, playing their games. Join them, the time will pass, and you will have had a much-needed break. Try it. Take a little time to live "in the moment," as children tend to do—surrender to your playful inner child for an hour or so. This will remind you of the significance of taking time to tune out and not allow business to consume every moment. Work/life balance can still exist, even in turbulent times.

Take Care of Your Emotional, Physical, and Spiritual Well-Being

Your health—including your emotional, physical, and spiritual well-being—is important all the time; it is critical during turbulent times. Don't put any aspect of it on hold. You will feel like ignoring your needs; don't. Calm your mind at night. Get a good night's sleep. If you need to talk with someone, seek out a counselor, a coach, or your best friend. Start or continue an exercise routine. Be more mindful of your diet. And look for the comfort that comes from following your own spiritual path. This is not an easy task for most leaders, who become so consumed in the crisis that they sacrifice everything else.

Assess and Rebuild Trust

Damage control and rebuilding a seriously injured organization require difficult decisions—decisions not everyone will understand. For this reason, leaders must continuously assess and rebuild trust. Can trust be rebuilt? We think the answer is: It depends. People trust the trusted.

There is a saying in Hindi, *Satyameva Jayate,* which means "truth alone triumphs." Be transparent; speak the truth all the time, and trust is renewed each and every day. If you have built a trusting relationship with people before the turbulent times hit, then they will want to give you the benefit of the doubt. Leaders should follow the first nine guidelines presented earlier in this chapter, and also do these things:

- Acknowledge individual and team contributions.
- Sustain and continue to build strong relationships.
- Conduct meetings that skip hierarchical levels to enhance approachability.
- Emphasize collaborative decision making.
- Choose not to collude in the blame game.
- End rumors before they start.
- Help those who become displaced find new positions.
- Learn to detect and "call out" deception. In *Survival of the Savvy: High-Integrity Political Tactics for Career and Company Success,* Marty Seldman and Rick Brandon (2004) provide excellent information on how to detect deception.

The organization can assist leaders so that trust is maintained throughout turbulent times by choosing to quickly

- Sanitize or eliminate the leaders who caused the turbulence (if intentional) or have seriously broken the trust.
- Reinforce or launch core values.
- Hold everyone accountable for "cleaning up the mess" and moving forward.

- Close the communication gaps that have caused breakdowns in trust.
- Provide safe ways for people to express themselves.
- Overcommunicate.
- Conduct regular trust indexing (a one-minute survey asking employees the trust level of their leader, the leader's leader, and the organization's leaders).
- Reward honesty even when it results in negative business outcomes.
- Explain the need for difficult decisions.
- Close out quickly and painlessly those who must be exited (most of the time, a layoff is imminent).

Summary

Encouraging an organization's leaders to follow the 10 guidelines outlined in this chapter, provide consistent communication, and learn to support are the main contributions of its learning strategy during turbulent times. There will be plenty of time later to start again with sales training and business leadership, areas that contribute to the organization's growth.

During turbulent times, leaders must rapidly and proactively convert emotions into actions. Because turbulent times are so stressful, leaders must concurrently take care of themselves and everyone else. This takes time, patience, empathy, and a willingness to shift priorities and engage in constant communication—even what otherwise might seem overcommunication. To successfully lead people through turbulent times, we believe leaders should practice these 10 guidelines each and every day.

To creatively face and move past turbulent times, it is crucial for leaders to develop and communicate a solid plan for the future. They must communicate this plan in simple, straightforward words to all stakeholders. People will feel more confident knowing that there is a plan. And as they pursue this challenging work, leaders should continuously re-mind themselves and their teams of this simple yet profound message, shared by Howard Richmond (www.howardrichmondmd.com): "Don't let the news of today undo the suc-cesses of yesterday or tomorrow."

References

Cohen, Ed. 2007. *Leadership Without Borders: Successful Strategies from World-Class Leaders.* Sin-gapore: John Wiley & Sons.

Seldman, Marty, and Rick Brandon. 2004. *Survival of the Savvy: High-Integrity Political Tactics for Career and Company Success.* New York: Free Press.

About the Authors

Priscilla Nelson is CEO of Nelson Cohen Global Consulting, providing strategic consulting in learning, organization development, and executive coaching for the C-Suite. Her experience in human resources, diversity, organization development, and executive coaching spans three decades. In her global work, she has consulted with such notable organizations as Satyam, Emergent Biosolutions, Glaxo SmithKline, Pfizer Pharmaceuticals, IBM, Guilford Pharmaceuticals, AT&T, Rollins College, Titan Corporation, and the U.S. government. She is an inspiring speaker who has led sessions and given keynotes across the United States, Asia, and Europe. While living in India, she was recognized by India Women in Leadership with the 2008 Women's Choice Award for outstanding leadership, and she received the 2007 IT People Award for global diversity.

Ed Cohen is executive vice president of Nelson Cohen Global Consulting, providing thought leadership and strategic guidance to global companies. He has worked in more than 40 countries with organizations including Booz Allen Hamilton, Satyam, Seer Technologies, National Australia Bank, Larson & Toubro, Farmers Insurance Group, Banco Banesto, and the World Economic Forum. He is the only chief learning officer to have led two companies to the ASTD BEST Award's number one ranking—Booz Allen Hamilton and Satyam Computer Services (the only company outside the United States to achieve this). He is the author of *Leadership Without Borders* (John Wiley & Sons, 2007), which received international accolades.

 **Chapter 21**

Leadership Ethics and Integrity for the 21st Century

Ken Blanchard

After years of studying leadership, I have come to the conclusion that to be an ethical leader is to be a servant leader. We have all witnessed the destructive influence that self-serving leaders have had on people and organizations. And in our interconnected world, the fallout from self-serving leaders affects the global community more than ever before. That is why it is so important that leaders in the 21st century become servant leaders. Leadership based on serving others is inherently grounded in ethics and integrity.

What Is a Servant Leader?

Not everyone understands the concept of "servant leadership." Many think these two words don't go together. How can you lead and serve at the same time? They think servant leadership is either about inmates running the prison or leaders trying to please everyone. But these misconceptions are easily overcome when people understand that servant leadership involves two kinds of leadership: strategic leadership and operational leadership.

© 2010 Ken Blanchard. Used with permission.

Strategic Leadership

Strategic leadership is all about vision and direction. In many ways, it's the *leadership* part of servant leadership. It's all about the "what" of the organization. Why is this important? Because leadership is about going somewhere. In effective organizations, everyone has a compelling vision and a clear sense of where the enterprise is going (Blanchard and Stoner 2003). Clear vision tells people who you are (your purpose), where you're going (your picture of the future), and what will guide your journey (your values). Once a clear vision is set, established goals can be placed in context.

The traditional hierarchical pyramid is well suited for this strategic aspect of leadership. Clear vision and direction start with top management and must be communicated throughout the organization by the leadership. Though top management should involve people in shaping the organization's direction, the ultimate responsibility for strategic leadership remains with the higher-ups and cannot be delegated to others.

Operational Leadership

Once a clear vision is set, operational leadership begins. This is all about the "how" of the organization. In many ways, it's the *servant* part of servant leadership. For this to be done well, leaders should equip people throughout the organization to act as owners of the vision and direction, allowing them to take a proactive role in carrying out the vision and supporting them by removing barriers.

But it's during the operational phase that most organizations get into ethical trouble. Instead of turning the traditional pyramid upside down and serving the people who serve the customers, too often the hierarchy is kept alive and well, with the leaders on top and the people and customers uncared for at the bottom. All the energy in the organization moves up the hierarchy as people try to please their bosses. The bureaucracy rules, and policies and procedures carry the day. People become discouraged and disengaged. The result is an environment that's ripe for self-serving interests and potential corruption. Both the people and the organization run the risk of failing—both morally and financially.

The Right Values Are the Key

So how do you avoid having your people and organization fall victim to unethical self-interest and potential corruption—the leaking away of integrity and profits? It begins with a high purpose and a clear set of operating values, which should be clarified and rank-ordered when the vision and direction of the organization are established.

The terms *values* and *ethics* are not interchangeable. Values are the various beliefs and attitudes that guide behavior. Ethics, on the other hand, has to do with discerning right from wrong and doing what is right. People are free to choose their values, but not all value systems are ethical. For example, an organization that values a strong bottom line regardless of the dishonest marketing practices that are required to make those numbers could not be called ethical.

I believe that we're born with an inherent understanding about the difference between right and wrong. When you watch kids interacting on the playground, you'll sometimes hear them say, "Hey, that's not fair!" Kids know when someone pulls a fast one. Unfortunately, in an ethically compromised environment and under negative influences, people sometimes disable that inner guidance. When their conscience speaks, they push the mute button—especially if the culture puts up with or encourages unethical behavior. Under these circumstances, well-meaning people simply lose their ethical bearings.

Sometimes behaving ethically comes with a high cost. That is why it's so important that leaders give careful consideration to rank-ordered values when they are establishing their organization's vision and direction. Robert Johnson founded Johnson & Johnson for the purpose of alleviating pain and disease. The company's purpose and values, reflected in its credo, continue to guide it. During a 1982 tampering incident that was localized in the Chicago area, Johnson & Johnson made a decision using its rank-ordered values: Focusing first on patients, then on associates, next on the community, and finally on the stockholders, the company quickly recalled all Tylenol capsules throughout the United States. The immediate cost was substantial, but not knowing the extent of the tampering, the company didn't want to risk anyone's safety. In the end, Johnson & Johnson stayed true to its ethical values, recouped its losses, and gained respect (Blanchard and Founding Associates 2007).

The Ethics Check

In 1988, I wrote a book with the late, great Norman Vincent Peale called *The Power of Ethical Management* (Blanchard and Peale 1988). Although the book was written at the close of the 20th century, it is unfortunately more relevant than ever as we embark on a new millennium. In the book, we suggest that people facing an ethical dilemma ask themselves three questions. We called these questions the Ethics Check; see table 21-1.

Question 1: Is It Legal?

The first question is straightforward: Is it legal? The term "legal" doesn't just mean civil or criminal law, it also means an organization's code of ethics or standards of conduct. Many people feel that if your dilemma passes the legality test, you don't have to go on to the other

Table 21-1. The Ethics Check

1. *Is it legal?*
   Will I be violating either civil law or company policy?

2. *Is it balanced?*
   Is it fair to all concerned in the short term as well as the long term? Does it promote win-win relationships?

3. *How will it make me feel about myself?*
   Will it make me proud?
   Would I feel good if my decision was published in the newspaper?
   Would I feel good if my family knew about it?

two questions. But Norman and I advised our readers to answer all the questions before making a final judgment. In many ways, these next two questions are the most important ones to ask.

Question 2: Is It Balanced?

By the second question—Is it balanced?—we mean: Is the decision going to be fair, or will it heavily favor one party over another in the short or long term? Lopsided, win/lose decisions invariably end up as lose/lose situations. If an individual or company makes a decision that benefits one person or company at someone else's real expense—whether it's another employer, a supplier, a customer, or even a competitor—it has a tendency to come back and haunt them.

Question 3: How Will It Make Me Feel About Myself?

The third question gets beyond existing standards and puts the question to that inner guidance I talked about above: How would it make you feel about yourself? Would you like it published in the local newspaper? Would you like your children or grandchildren to know what you did? If you do something that goes against your own innate sense of what's right, you run the risk of eroding your self-esteem. As the famous UCLA basketball coach John Wooden used to say, "There is no pillow as soft as a clear conscience."

Let me give you an example to help you understand the importance of the last two questions. A number of years ago, the head of our accounting department came to my wife, Margie—who was the president of our company at the time—seeking advice about my travel expenses. When I do a speech or consulting for a company, my contract calls for round-trip airfare from San Diego to that city, plus expenses and a fee. On the week in question, I had flown from San Diego to San Francisco on Monday to do a session for a client. On Tuesday,

I'd flown to Chicago to work with a different client. On Wednesday, I'd flown to New York; on Thursday, to Dallas; and on Friday, I'd finished the week in Phoenix—working with a different client each day of the week.

Our accountant said to Margie, "Legally, I could charge all five clients round-trip airfare to their respective cities. What do you think I should do?"

Margie insisted that our accountant ask the next two questions of the Ethics Check:

- *Is it balanced?* Obviously, it wouldn't have been fair to charge each of the five clients for a full round-trip ticket.
- *How will it make me feel about myself?*

The last question really sealed the decision. We wouldn't want it published in the local paper that the Ken Blanchard Companies made extra money by overcharging clients for airfare. So even though it was legal to charge the client full fare, it wasn't ethical.

Acting Ethically Takes Practice: Principles of Ethics

Many people have values—but many fail to live up to them. How do you behave ethically when there are so many pressures not to do so? How do you build up inner strength so you can resist external pressure and consistently do what you know is right in difficult situations? To answer these questions, Norman and I developed the five principles of ethical power; see table 21-2. Practiced regularly, these principles will give you the knowledge you need to better sort out the dilemmas you face. They will also inspire you to act in a way that is ethically consistent with your beliefs.

Principle 1: Purpose

Purpose is the picture you have of yourself—the kind of person you want to be or the kind of life you want to lead. Unlike a goal, which has a beginning and an end, a purpose is ongoing. It gives meaning and definition to our lives. It's the road we choose to travel, whereas a goal is one of the places you intend to visit on that road. Living by your word and contributing to the greater good are examples of purposes.

Principle 2: Pride

The second principle, pride, is important because to hold to your purpose, you must believe in yourself and have faith in your abilities. Ethical behavior is related to self-esteem. People who feel good about themselves have what it takes to withstand outside pressure and do what is right rather than what is merely expedient, popular, or lucrative. Pride doesn't mean a puffed up ego; in fact, it's just the opposite. A healthy sense

Table 21-2. The Five Principles of Ethical Power

1. *Purpose:* I see myself as being an ethically sound person. I let my conscience be my guide. No matter what happens, I am always able to face the mirror, look myself straight in the eye, and feel good about myself.

2. *Pride:* I feel good about myself. I don't need the acceptance of other people to feel important. A balanced self-esteem keeps my ego and my desire to be accepted from influencing my decisions.

3. *Patience:* I believe that things will eventually work out well. I don't need everything to happen right now. I am at peace with what comes my way!

4. *Persistence:* I stick to my purpose, especially when it seems inconvenient to do so. My behavior is consistent with my intentions. As Churchill said, "Never! Never! Never! Never give up!"

5. *Perspective:* I take time to enter each day quietly in a mood of reflection. This helps me to get myself focused and allows me to listen to my inner self and to see things more clearly.

---

of pride is closely related to humility. As Norman and I said in *The Power of Ethical Management,* "People with humility don't think less of themselves; they just think about themselves less."

Principle 3: Patience

Patience is the third principle. Once you have a clear purpose and your ego is under control, patience is necessary for sound ethical behavior. One reason people sometimes get off course is because they lack faith; with a lack of faith, they become impatient. People have faith when they believe in something and base their actions on that belief. When we lack faith, we tend to grab for the here and now. Sometimes people make what they think is a sound decision, but they want immediate reassurance that they did the right thing. They become impatient. Lacking faith in their own judgment, they undo what, in the long run, would have been the best decision.

Principle 4: Persistence

Persistence is the fourth principle. Without it, your attempts to be ethical can fail. Being an ethical person means behaving ethically all the time—not only when it's convenient. In fact, it is especially important to act ethically when it is inconvenient or unpopular to do so. You don't try to do something—you actually do it.

Principle 5: Perspective

Perspective is the capacity to see what is really important in any given situation. When you take time to cultivate perspective, you reflect on your purpose and related goals before making decisions or taking action. If you consistently maintain perspective—the big picture—it will be easier to keep yourself on track and live according to your purpose, values, and ethical beliefs.

Serving Others Makes Ethics Easy

As I stated above, it is the job of leadership to set the vision and direction of the organization by first establishing strong values and an ethical statement of purpose. But the leader's job does not stop there. Equally important is when leaders turn the top-down hierarchy on its head and switch into serving mode. By helping people throughout the organization to implement the vision, servant leaders foster collaboration and trust. Ethical behavior—doing the right thing—is far easier when leaders' egos aren't in the way. The result is a healthy work environment where people don't have to cheat to win.

Ethics and integrity begin at the top, with an organization's leadership, yet everyone must take responsibility. Indeed, we are all leaders in some aspects of our lives. Anytime you are acting in a way that influences the behavior of others, you are engaging in leadership. By using the Ethics Check when faced with ethical dilemmas and by practicing the five principles of ethical power, you can, in the words of an old 20th-century hymn, "brighten the corner where you are" (Ogdon 1913).

Further Reading

Warren Bennis, *On Becoming a Leader*, 4th ed. Philadelphia: Basic Books, 2009.

Ken Blanchard and the Founding Associates and Consulting Partners of the Ken Blanchard Companies, *Leading at a Higher Level: Blanchard on Leadership and Creating High-Performing Organizations*. Upper Saddle River, NJ: Pearson–Prentice Hall, 2007.

Ken Blanchard and Norman Vincent Peale, *The Power of Ethical Management*. New York: William Morrow, 1988.

Ken Blanchard and Jesse Stoner, *Full Steam Ahead! Unleash the Power of Vision in Your Company and Your Life*. San Francisco: Berrett-Koehler, 2003.

Max DePree, *Leadership Is an Art*. New York: Doubleday, 2004.

Peter F. Drucker, *The Effective Executive: The Definitive Guide to Getting the Right Things*. New York: HarperBusiness Essentials, 2006.

James M. Kouzes and Barry Z. Posner, *The Leadership Challenge*, 4th ed. San Francisco: Jossey-Bass, 2007.

Drea Zigarmi, Ken Blanchard, Michael O'Connor, and Carl Edeburn, *The Leader Within: Learning Enough About Yourself to Lead Others*. Upper Saddle River, NJ: Prentice Hall, 2004.

References

Blanchard, Ken, and the Founding Associates and Consulting Partners of the Ken Blanchard Companies. 2007. *Leading at a Higher Level: Blanchard on Leadership and Creating High Performing Organizations.* Upper Saddle River, NJ: Pearson–Prentice Hall.

Blanchard, Ken, and Norman Vincent Peale. 1988. *The Power of Ethical Management.* New York: William Morrow.

Blanchard, Ken, and Jesse Stoner. 2003. *Full Steam Ahead! Unleash the Power of Vision in Your Company and Your Life.* San Francisco: Berrett-Koehler.

Ogdon, Ina Mae Duley. 1913. *Brighten the Corner Where You Are.* Winoa Lake, IN: Rodeheaver Co.

About the Author

Ken Blanchard has had an extraordinary impact on the day-to-day management of millions of people and companies. He is the author of several best-selling books, including the blockbuster international bestseller *The One Minute Manager* and the giant business bestsellers *Leadership and the One Minute Manager, Raving Fans,* and *Gung Ho!* His books have combined sales of nearly 20 million copies in more than 27 languages. In 2005, he was inducted into Amazon's Hall of Fame as number 15 of the top 25 best-selling authors of all time. He is the chief spiritual officer of the Ken Blanchard Companies, an international management training and consulting firm. He is also cofounder of the Lead Like Jesus Ministries. The College of Business at Grand Canyon University bears his name. He and his wife, Margie, live in San Diego.

Chapter 22

Trends Shaping Future Leadership Attributes

Karie Willyerd and Jeanne Meister

> *"The future isn't what it used to be."*
> —Yogi Berra

To understand the future of leadership, we first must understand the business conditions leaders will face and the employees who will make up the workforce of the future. Understanding those conditions allows us to predict the kinds of skills and competencies leaders will need over the next decade. We propose at least three major shifts will create new dynamics and new requirements for the leaders of the future:

- ▦ shifting workforce demographics
- ▦ globalization
- ▦ social technologies.

© 2010 Karie Willyerd and Jeanne Meister. Used with permission.

Shifting Workforce Demographics—Age, Gender, and Ethnicity

In nearly every country in the world, the shifts in demographics are unprecedented in the post-industrial age. In the decade from 2000–2010, the population of Europe declined by 1 percent, and the decline is expected to accelerate over the next 40 years. Germany, Italy, and Spain are all expected to experience population declines ranging from 14 to 25 percent (Delong 2004). In many Asian countries the demographic situation is similar to or more pronounced than that seen in Europe. For example, in Japan the working-age population has already peaked, with 3 million fewer workers in 2010 than in 2005. China will have nearly as many senior citizens aged 65 or older as children aged 15 and younger by the year 2030 (Zakaria 2008).

In the United States, the boom and then bust of birth rates has led to large cohorts of generations, such as baby boomers, and small groups such as Generation X (see figure 22-1). The baby boomers, who have dominated the workforce for nearly two decades, will now take a back seat as the millennial generation roars into the workplace. Generation X, the smallest cohort, will never accede as the largest workforce segment. As baby boomers exit the workforce, an interesting question to ponder is whether the next generation of leaders will come largely from Generation X, who have waited patiently for their turn at the helm, or whether they will be passed over in favor of selecting leaders from the largest segment of the workforce, millennials.

As we move into the future, most workplaces will have five generations working side by side—traditionalists, born before 1946; baby boomers, born between 1946 and 1964; Gen-

Figure 22-1. U.S. Generational Cohorts as of 2008

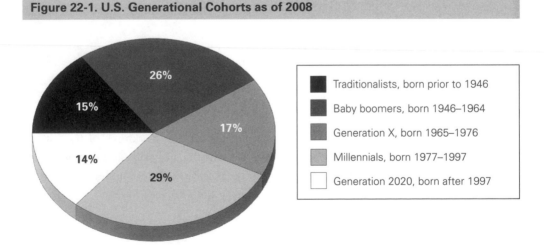

26%

15%

17%

14%

29%

Traditionalists, born prior to 1946

Baby boomers, born 1946–1964

Generation X, born 1965–1976

Millennials, born 1977–1997

Generation 2020, born after 1997

eration X, born between 1965 and 1976; millennials, born between 1977 and 1997; and Generation 2020, born after 1997.

Future leaders are thus likely to face the challenge of leading the most age-diverse workforce in history. Those employees who are in the workforce and healthy at 60, according to the World Health Organization, will on average be physically capable of working until they are 74 if they are male and 77 if they are women (WHO 2004). If baby boomers in the United States now work as long as possible, that means that the leading edge of the boomers may not begin retiring until 2020, while some traditionalists will continue to work into their 80s.

At the other end of the age spectrum, millennials will be entering the workforce in record numbers. While they currently represent 22 percent of all workers, by 2014 they will make up almost 47 percent of the workforce (Tapscott 2009). The post-millennial generation, Generation 2020, will be entering the workforce by 2015, so in just a few years, leaders will face the challenge of managing five generations of workers.

The gender composition will also change, as more women are entering the workforce and staying in it (Rampell 2009). Though women still face other issues when it comes to equal employment, women are now about to surpass men in U.S. payrolls for the first time in history. Women are now half of all U.S. workers, and mothers are the primary breadwinners or co-breadwinners in nearly two-thirds of American families, double the number of households in 1967 when the 1950s and 1960s sitcom *Leave It to Beaver* epitomized the average American family (Shriver and the Center for American Progress 2009).

Ethnicity is also shifting in the United States. From 1980 to 2020, Caucasian workers in the United States will decline from 82 percent to 63 percent. The Latino portion alone will almost triple, from 6 percent to 17 percent, by 2020, and will be almost 30 percent of the U.S population by 2050 (Rodriguez 2008). Thus the face of the new generation of workers will be less and less Caucasian (National Center for Public Policy and Higher Education 2009).

Global Markets and Access to Global Talent

Leaders of the future will encounter a marketplace more globally dispersed than any of their predecessors. The churn in *Fortune* 500 companies is just one example. If a company was on the list in 1980, there was a 56 percent chance that it was still listed in 1994. But for a company listed in 1994, there was only a 30 percent chance of its still being on the list in 2007.

The headquarter locations of the *Financial Times* Global 500 are increasingly moving to Brazil, Russia, India, and China (collectively known as BRIC). Between 2005 and 2008, the U.S.-based global headquarters decreased from 219 to 169, a decline of 23 percent. Japan also lost slots to the tune of 9 percent in the same period. Brazil collected 6 global headquarters, an increase of 120 percent, while Russia grew by 225 percent, India by 160 percent, and China by a staggering 400 percent (*Financial Times* 2008). Thus, future leaders will increasingly be working in companies that are not headquartered in the United States.

The ease of conducting work virtually also increases the likelihood that future leaders will have teams based around the globe. Virtual workplaces have workers organized in global teams who may not report to offices, may not keep set hours, and may be compensated more in cash than in benefits. Akin to transient white-collar workers, they collaborate electronically with participants from three or four continents, through virtual worlds, teleconferencing, instant messaging, posting updates to social networks, or by using document-sharing sites. Savvy recruiting functions are able to find talent from around the world, with no need for expensive relocation. Leaders of the future will not only have to work without being in the same location as their teams, they will also have to work asynchronously. Although it is possible to find one or two hours in a day in which to conduct a call linking continents, anything longer than that becomes an imposition for at least one time zone, so the possibility of synchronous work becomes less and less likely. These shifts in how and where work is done will place new demands on leadership skill sets.

The increased access to global markets will create more interdependence between nation states and large multinational companies, causing a need for integration and collaboration among leaders. This collaboration will extend to how leaders interact with governmental institutions and nongovernmental organizations (NGOs). The global impact of the subprime lending crisis in the United States created a painful awareness of how one country's economic policies and governance can affect other nations. "The CEO of the future is going to have to be somebody who deals well with government," predicts David Gergen, a media and political commentator (quoted in Reingold 2008).

Social Technologies and Mobile Access to the Exploding Information Universe

At the time of writing this chapter, hundreds of millions of people actively construct, maintain, and communicate their identities using Facebook and a host of other networks such as MySpace, Twitter, Friendster, Orkut, LinkedIn, and Bebo (Facebook 2009). Though this number is substantial, what is even more impressive is how fast it is growing. An estimated 250,000 new users each day are creating online profiles and maintaining them on a social network. Just one year ago, Facebook ranked 45th as a destination spot for traditionalists.

Today it ranks 3rd, according to The Nielsen Company (2009). Video and photo sharing sites have also exploded in popularity. In 2009 people in the United States watched more than 7 billion online video streams per month on sites such as YouTube, Metacafe, Vimeo, and Daily Motion. This audience represented almost a twofold increase from the previous year (Swanson 2007). Globally, more than 2.5 trillion text messages were sent in 2008 (Stross 2008).

Along with this unbelievable volume of communication come some standards and expectations of access to information and the expectation of transparent, two-way communication. Anyone who has shopped on eBay or Amazon has been given the opportunity to rate, tag, and comment. Yelp, the website that aggregates user reviews and comments for service providers, is just one example of a philosophy that relies on "the wisdom of the crowds" to contribute and rate anything from restaurants to doctors. In the not-too-distant future, leaders should expect to be evaluated publicly on something like the equivalent of Yelp for bosses. Being open to public feedback will become a requirement for leaders of the future, if this trend continues.

Increasingly, social technologies are penetrating corporate environments as well, with one study showing the top investment for Web 2.0 technologies inside companies is the implementation of social networks.

Leaders must grapple with a host of issues on how to manage all these social technologies and digital content in the workplace as it will affect every part of corporate life. Increasingly, employees are carrying their own social technology connection platforms with them in devices such as laptops, iPods, mobile phones, and slate computers, each one suited to a different aspect of their busy lives. As one Generation X woman said, "I have to keep a list of how to communicate with everyone I know. Brad likes to text and Facebook, but won't answer voicemail. Tori won't even join Facebook but does email and texting. Ida loves everything." Knowing how to communicate with employees is already a challenge and becomes even more so for leaders as the choice of connection platforms increases.

The lines between work time and the rest of life begin to blur as work leaves defined times and spaces. Expectations for leaders to cross the 8-to-5 time barrier will become mandatory to build relationships and trust. At Zappos, an online shoe retailer known for its customer service, managers dedicate 20 percent of their time to after-hours, nonwork activities with their teams, building rapport and trust.

The pace of technology change shows no indication of slowing down. As one article in *The New York Times* declared, the millennials are already old fogies in cyberspace by their 20s, as Generation 2020 emerges with an expectation of books on e-readers, phone calls via Skype, and applications they've used since they were toddlers (Stone 2010). Cody Brown, the 21-year-old founder of kommons and NYU Local posted a guest blog on TechCrunch on April 11, 2010:

> If you, as an author, see the iPad as a place to "publish" your next book, you are completely missing the point. What do you think would have happened if George Orwell had the iPad? Do you think he would have written for print then copy and pasted his story into the iBookstore? If this didn't work out well, do you think he would have complained that there aren't any serious readers anymore? No. He would have looked at the medium, then blown our minds.... I'm 21, I can say with a lot of confidence that the "books" that come to define my generation will be impossible to print. This is great.

The need for leaders to be technology confident and constantly learning will accelerate as we head into a future defined by generations who access information so differently than prior generations.

What the Next Generation Wants from Leaders

Who is being led turns out to be just as important as who is leading. According to recent research, looking at the members of a group is just as important, if not more, than looking at the leader. This is because leadership involves leading from within, fitting into the group, and exerting influence, not imposing views from above (Reicher, Haslam, and Platow 2007).

To understand what people want from their managers, we surveyed 2,200 working professionals from four generations around the world on what they seek from employers, both now and in the future. In a second survey, we queried 300 human resources (HR) executives from around the world about the practices they have in play now, and those they expect to use in the future. One of the items we asked of each of the generations was to rate the leader capabilities that were important to them. We then asked HR executives to rate managers in their companies on each of those same areas. Figure 22-2 shows the preferences of more than 500 millennials from around the globe, who as we've stated will comprise half of the workforce in less than five years. Their preferences are compared with a skill assessment by HR professionals of the managers of their companies.

In some of these items, the gap between what millennials want and what skills managers have is not far apart. However, there are some important variances to note. For the skills that matter most to millennials, the current leadership skill set is far less than effective. Millennials want managers who will help them develop their careers, sponsor them for development, give them straight feedback, and mentor them. They are not the only generation who wants this, but it is more pronounced for millennials. For example, all the generations agreed they wanted a manager who would give them straight feedback, yet this is a skill

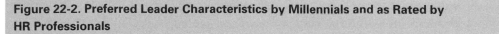

Figure 22-2. Preferred Leader Characteristics by Millennials and as Rated by HR Professionals

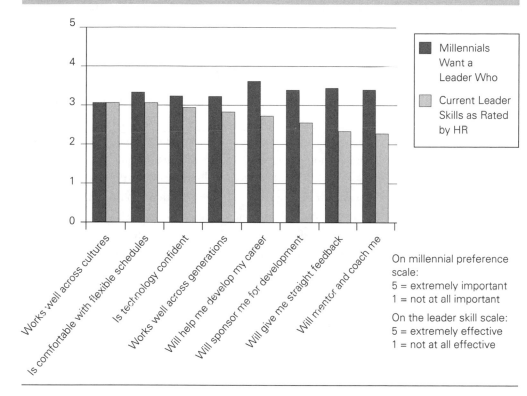

On millennial preference scale:
5 = extremely important
1 = not at all important

On the leader skill scale:
5 = extremely effective
1 = not at all effective

rated as ineffective across a wide swath of organizations. Does this suggest that our current training programs on performance management need to be rethought? Instead, should we be focusing on programs and platforms that give managers the skills to give ongoing, constant, bite-sized direct feedback and skills for crucial confrontations when continuous feedback isn't enough? Is the annual performance review a dinosaur?

Also important to millennials is the need to know that someone is helping them with their careers, their development, and their mentoring and coaching goals. Again, this is rated below average in our current leadership profiles. In an era where anyone can communicate with anyone, anywhere, and at any time, perhaps it is time to rethink what it means to be a leader. If we were to create platforms that unleash the power of peer-to-peer learning, could millennials get their needs fulfilled from anyone in the organization, instead of relying, as is traditionally done, on their managers? Imagine an open mentoring platform that allowed anyone in the organization to volunteer for micro-mentoring engagements that lasted only a few weeks at a time, or allowed managers to buddy up and mentor dozens of employees at a time through an online platform. By having a platform that allows employees to share their knowledge with one another and including rating, tagging, and commenting features, authors are able to get feedback from anyone who views their content. All of these and more are ways we can begin to distribute the traditional role of leadership in ways that enrich both the lives of employees and leaders.

The Emerging Essential Leadership Capabilities

As we have democratized information through the growth of social media tools, our need for bureaucratic hierarchies has been eliminated, and self-governing, involved employees have both the information and power to be involved in the organizational governance process. Hal Varian, Google's chief economist, agrees, "In the old organization, you had to have this whole army of people digesting information to be able to feed it to the decision maker at the top. But that's not the way it works anymore: The information can be available across the ranks, to everyone in the organization. And what you need to ensure is that people have access to the data they need to make their day-to-day decisions. And this can be done much more easily than it could be done in the past. And it really empowers knowledge workers to work more effectively" (Varian 2009).

A few forward-thinking companies have commissioned projects to anticipate what the future of leadership will be in their own organizations, including General Electric and Cisco. Both companies have invested considerable time and effort to define what their leadership capabilities will need to be in the future so that they can begin developing those capabilities now.

We not only reviewed what global shifts were occurring that would affect future leaders, but also talked to some of these companies and thought leaders who want to get ahead of the development curve, and found five leadership areas that seemed to recur. In figure 22-3, we cover five leadership areas that seem to be emerging as requirements for the leader of the future.

Collaborative Mindset

Leaders who have demonstrated a collaborative mindset and who work comfortably in a networked leadership environment will be essential for working in conditions that require cooperating with competitors, working across cultures, and navigating complex markets. Almost any leader rates himself or herself high on collaboration skills, but we believe the collaborative mindset of the future takes this skill set to a whole new level. Allowing decisions to be "hacked," as Gary Hamel, a professor and management expert, promotes, will improve the quality of decisions, but will require leaders who have thick enough skins to endure letting anyone at any level in the organization have a voice.

Figure 22-3. Five Emerging Leadership Requirements

Being This Kind of Leader ...	Requires These Management Behaviors
Collaborative mindset	• Inclusive decision making • Genuine solicitation of feedback
Developer of people	• Mentors and coaches team • Provides straight feedback
Digitally confident	• Uses technology to connect to customers and employees
Global citizen	• Has a diverse mindset • Prioritizes social responsibility
Anticipates and builds for the future	• Builds accountability across levels • Champions innovation

Source: Future Workplace L.L.C. Used with permission.

Recognizing that feedback can come from anywhere, leaders of the future will have to maintain an open mind to sort through inputs from an extraordinary range of voices, from low-level employees to disgruntled customers. Brian Dunn, the CEO of Best Buy, says, "I . . . have a program that searches the Internet anytime somebody mentions Best Buy out there. Sometimes it's really great things, sometimes it's obscenity-laden, but I have a huge appetite for it" (Bryant 2009). As Socrates said, "The only true wisdom is in knowing you know nothing." Leaders who maintain this mindset, and therefore thirst for collaboration and the wisdom of the crowds, will be well served in the future. Of course they will then need to exercise judgment and experience to make decisions, but seeking collaboration first will be essential.

Developer of People

As we showed earlier, the next generation of employees wants leaders who see the development of people as one of their most important goals, including providing honest feedback, career guidance, and learning opportunities. The mass exodus from the workplace of baby boomers will leave a giant talent hole in organizations. The issue is not that there will not be enough people to fill the slots; rather, the right skill sets will not be available to fill critical roles, and organizations will be competing for the same set of people with the scarce skills needed. Consider that by some estimates only 30 percent of the people eligible to apply for entrance into the military qualify or, that in the United States, a student makes a choice to drop out of school every 28 seconds. The competition for scarce skills will be fierce, necessitating an organizational strategy to develop skills inside the organization. This quest for talent will include reaching into middle schools to entice students to pursue careers in fields where there are not enough graduates. Leaders at all levels will have to play a hands-on role in developing the skills they need for their organizations to compete successfully in the marketplace.

Digitally Confident

The leader of the future also will need to be digitally confident and able to speak the language of the newest generation of workers. The structures of management common to most organizations evolved to control and pass information from level to level in the hierarchy. New technologies have not only made that unnecessary but have also freed people from this hierarchy. Leaders will need to embrace these new methods of communication to connect with a virtual workforce scattered around the planet.

Blogging, wikis, virtual meetings, social networks, microblogging, and video sharing are just a few of the tools that leaders will need to use to reach employees with messages of strategy, direction, change, inspiration, and motivation. Just as baby boomers had to learn how to use email instead of copying and routing interoffice mail envelopes, so will the next generation of leaders need to learn to use the new tools of the trade of leadership in an environment of openness and collaboration.

Global Citizen

A fourth facet of the leader of the future is being a global citizen, in the broadest sense. This means being not only a leader who can work well across cultures but also one who realizes the value of working with governments and NGOs in the intertwined dependencies of the future. Likewise, our leadership and management practices must be informed by the ecology of the organizational environment in which employees reside and in which markets change constantly. Millennials have volunteered their time, are environmentally sensitive, and have seen the abuses of unbridled self-interest in leaders. They will expect to work for leaders who build a company that focuses on the triple bottom line—people, planet and profits.

Anticipates and Builds for the Future

Finally, anticipating the future and building the capability to address it is the fifth capability area required for the leader of the future. As Hamel says, "There's little that can be said with certainty about the future except this: sometime over the next decade your company will be challenged to change in a way for which it has no precedent" (Hamel and Breen 2007). Being able to scan the marketplace, search for trends, and build a sustainable company will ensure that short-term success leads to long-term viability. This includes building the skill sets needed to support that future and not counting on layoffs and rehiring to get the skills needed, because demand for talent will be tough for all but the most competitive companies.

Honoring the Past, Anticipating the Future

Leaders are constantly faced with the pressures of living in the present, while keeping an eye to the future to navigate the course. If we are to have any hope of shaping the future, we must begin preparing by anticipating it, building our own skills to face it, and helping others to develop their skills. Our debt to those who entrust us with the leadership of their organizations is to build a sustainable organization and a renewable people capability to compete in the global marketplace. Are you prepared?

References

Brown, C. 2010. Dear Authors, Your Next Book Should Be an App, Not an iBook. Accessed June 11, 2010, at http://techcrunch.com/2010/04/11/dear-authors-your-next-book-should-be-an-app-not-an-ibook/.

Bryant, A. 2009. You Want Insight? Go to the Front Lines. *The New York Times,* August 15. Accessed November 15, 2009, at www.nytimes.com/2009/08/16/business/16corner.html?pagewanted=2&_r=1&sq=You%20Want%20Insights?%20&st=cse&scp=1.

Delong, W. D. 2004. *Lost Knowledge: Confronting the Threat of an Aging Workforce.* New York: Oxford University Press.

Facebook. 2009. Statistics. Accessed May 15, 2009, at www.facebook.com/press/info.php?statistics.

Financial Times. 2008. FT Global, 2008. Accessed December 18, 2008, at www.ft.com/reports/ft5002008.

Hamel, G., with B. Breen. 2007. *The Future of Management.* Boston: Harvard Business School Press.

National Center for Public Policy and Higher Education. 2009. A National Dialogue: The Secretary of Education's Commission on the Future of Higher Education. Accessed November 30, 2009, at http://www2.ed.gov/about/bdscomm/list/hiedfuture/reports/equity.pdf.

Nielsen Company. 2009. Six Million More Seniors Using the Web than Five Years Ago. Accessed July 14, 2010, at http://blog.nielsen.com/nielsenwirc/online_mobile/six-million-more-seniors-using-the-web-than-five-years-ago/.

Rampell, C. 2009. As Layoffs Surge, Women May Pass Men in Job Force. *New York Times,* February 6. Accessed May 14, 2009, at www.nytimes.com/2009/02/06/business/06women.html.

Reicher, S. D., S. A. Haslam, and M. J. Platow. 2007. The New Psychology of Leadership. *Scientific American Mind,* August–September. Accessed December 17, 2009, at www.scientificamerican.com/article.cfm?id=the-new-psychology-of-leadership.

Reingold, J. 2008. Meet Your New Leader. *Fortune,* November 14, 146.

Rodriguez, R. 2008. *Latino Talent: Effective Strategies to Recruit, Retain, and Develop Hispanic Professionals.* Hoboken, NJ: John Wiley & Sons.

Shriver, M., and the Center for American Progress. 2009. The Shriver Report: A Women's Nation Changes Everything. Eds. H. Boushey and A. O'Leary, October 16. Accessed November 26, 2009 at www.americanprogress.org/issues/2009/10/womans_nation.html.

Stone, B. 2010. The Children of Cyberspace: Old Fogies by Their 20s. *The New York Times,* January 10. Accessed April 12, 2010, at www.nytimes.com/2010/01/10/weekinreview/10stone.html.

Stross, R. 2008. What Carriers Aren't Eager to Tell You About Texting. *The New York Times*, December 26. Accessed November 27, 2009, at www.nytimes.com/2008/12/28/business/28digi.html.

Swanson, B. 2007. An Exabyte Here, An Exabyte There.... Accessed June 17, 2009, at www.disco-tech.org/2007/10/an_exabyte_here_an_exabyte_the.php, October 3.

Tapscott, D. 2009. *Grown Up Digital: How the New Generation Is Changing Your World.* New York: McGraw-Hill.

Varian, H. 2009. Hal Varian on How the Web Challenges Mentors. *The McKinsey Quarterly: The Online Journal of McKinsey & Co.,* January. Accessed May 27, 2009, at www.mckinseyquarterly.com/Hal_Varian_on_how_the_Web_challenges_managers_2286.

WHO (World Health Organization). 2004. The World Health Report 2004—Changing History: Annex Table 4. Accessed May 29, 2009, at http://www.who.int/whr/2004/annex/en/index.html.

Zakaria, F. 2008. *The Post-American World.* New York: W.W. Norton & Company.

About the Authors

As the vice president and chief learning officer for Sun Microsystems, **Karie Willyerd** led the top-ranked learning services department in the world, as recognized by ASTD in 2009. She has also been a chief talent officer for a *Fortune* 200 company, head of global leadership development for H.J. Heinz, and head of people development for Lockheed Martin Tactical Aircraft. She is currently the CEO of Jambok, an informal social learning platform. Along with Jeanne Meister, she is the co-author of *The 2020 Workplace: How Innovative Companies Attract, Develop, and Keep Tomorrow's Employees Today* (2010). She lives with her family in Fort Collins, Colorado.

Jeanne Meister is an internationally recognized thought leader, speaker, and author in enterprise learning. Meister was voted by her peers as one of the 20 top influential training professionals in the United States. She is the author of *Corporate Quality Universities* (1993) and *Corporate Universities* (revised 1998), and her research has been profiled in such publications as *The Chronicle of Higher Education, Chief Learning Officer, Fast Company, Harvard Business Review, Workforce Magazine, People and Strategy,* and *The Financial Times.* Along with Karie Willyerd, she is the co-author of *The 2020 Workplace: How Innovative Companies Attract, Develop, and Keep Tomorrow's Employees Today* (2010). She is a cofounder of Future Workplace and frequent blog contributor to *Harvard Business.*

 **Chapter 23**

Derailment: How Successful Leaders Avoid It

William A. Gentry

In This Chapter

- Why derailment is an important topic.
- The history of managerial derailment research.
- The five problem areas of derailed leaders.
- Strategies for avoiding derailment.
- What to do if you have derailed.

We've heard about them, or seen them, or we may have even been one of them. They have initially been given different labels: superstar, can't-miss prospect, golden child, high potential. They had all the promise in the world to succeed at the highest of leadership levels and responsibilities. And sometimes they did in fact succeed. But sometimes these people with high potential flamed out and eventually did not live up to the high expectations others had of them. This chapter looks at the problem areas and behaviors of these once-promising talented managers who started strong but ultimately did not go as far as expected, a phenomenon the literature has labeled "managerial derailment."

The chapter first explains why leaders and organizations should be concerned with the phenomenon of derailment. Next, it details the history of derailment research and how the Center for Creative Leadership identified the five problem areas associated with de-railed leaders:

- problems with interpersonal relationships
- difficulty leading a team
- difficulty changing or adapting
- failure to meet business objectives
- a functional orientation that is too narrow.

The chapter also provides research findings and practical advice on how to minimize the likelihood of derailment and avoid derailment completely. Finally, it outlines strategies to recover from actual derailment.

Ineffective Managers: Are There Really That Many?

We all know managers and leaders who are ineffective. They are portrayed on television shows and in movies. They are real people in the realm of sports or politics. Their travails have been detailed in the media and in books. They may even be in the next cubicle. But are they as prevalent as we think? Table 23-1 shows the estimated ineffective rates of managers in different research studies over recent decades. "Ineffectiveness" in this case is a broad term that encompasses terms such as "disappointment" (for example, Sorcher 1985; White and DeVries 1990), "incompetence" (Millikin-Davies 1992; Shipper and Wilson 1992), "mis-hire" (Smart 2005), and "failure" (Hogan, Curphy, and Hogan 1994; Rogers and Smith 2004). The data suggests that yes, ineffectiveness is prevalent in organizations, with one of every two leaders and managers estimated to be ineffective (that is, a disappointment, incompetent, a mis-hire, or a complete failure) in their current roles.

Given the high prevalence of ineffective managers and leaders, what are the consequences for organizations? What is the cost of ineffective leaders for organizations? In short, managerial ineffectiveness is extremely costly. C-level executives who fail in their jobs and therefore need to be replaced may have buy-out clauses in their contracts or severance packages that can be two to three times their salaries, plus benefits, and they may even be given millions of dollars worth of annual payments (Conger and Nadler 2004). Though not as highly profiled, those lower in the organization such as middle-level managers are also in danger of failing or derailing (Gentry and others 2007; Shipper and Dillard 2000), and replacing these ineffective managers can also be expensive, time consuming, and disruptive because there are so many more managers at these lower levels than C-level executives. Regardless of managerial level, whenever a manager or leader is ineffective and must be replaced, the organization has to spend time and money on recruitment, selection, and onboarding to make a new hire. The total direct and indirect costs can be

Table 23-1. Estimated Ineffective Rates for Managers from Experts' Studies

Study	Estimated Rate (percent)
Bentz (1985b)	50
Charan (2005)	40
Fernandez-Araoz (1999)	40
Hogan, Curphy, and Hogan (1994)	55 (range 50–60)
Hogan and Kaiser (2005)	50
Hogan, Raskin, and Fazzini (1990)	67 (range 60–75)
Lombardo and Eichinger (2005)	50
Millikin-Davies (1992)	50
Rogers and Smith (2004)	50
Sessa and others (1998)	30
Shipper and Wilson (1992)	60
Smart (1999)	50
Smart (2005)	75
Sorcher (1985)	33
White and DeVries (1990)	50
Mean	50
Median	50

Note: "Ineffective" is used here broadly in this context to encompass disappointment, incompetence, mis-hire, and actual failure as used in the actual article cited.

15 to 20 times an executive's salary, upward of millions or maybe billions of dollars spent because of the replacement of one ineffective middle-level leader or C-level executive (Finkelstein 2004; Smart 1999, 2005; Wells 2005). In addition, replacing a failed leader or executive can damage the confidence and psyche of the individual who failed, and it can negatively affect relationships with customers and the morale of co-workers, especially those who worked closely with the failed leader (Finkin 1991; Gillespie and others 2001).

Many of these ineffective managers and executives who eventually failed had all the makings of being the best in their companies early in their careers. But for some reason, these managers got fired, got demoted, or reached a career plateau, and therefore failed to make it as far as others thought they should. This is the phenomenon known as derailment. For more than three decades, researchers have sought to determine the reasons behind managerial derailment.

A Brief Historical Synopsis of 30-Plus Years of Managerial Derailment Research

The impetus of derailment research can be traced back to research at AT&T comparing successful managers who progressed far in their careers with those who never rose through the managerial levels as expected (Bray, Campbell, and Grant 1974; Bray and Howard 1983). These studies showed that unsuccessful managers lacked the leadership, administrative, and career skills that their successful managerial counterparts possessed. This type of research continued with Bentz's (1985a, 1985b) studies at Sears, Roebuck, and Company, where he found several aspects of mental ability, motivation, skills, vocational interests, and personality traits were related to job performance and potential (that is, promotability) and failures. Extending this research, Kotter (1982) concluded that managers who did not succeed at higher levels were a poor fit with the demands of the job, and Gabarro (1987) indicated that executives who failed at higher levels did not have the requisite background to be successful in upper-tier executive positions and had a history of relationship problems with their co-workers. These studies laid the groundwork for studying derailed managers.

Whereas the previous studies concentrated on comparing successful to failed leaders, studies that actually focused on leaders who derailed started at the Center for Creative Leadership in the early 1980s, when McCall and Lombardo (1983) interviewed senior executives from three *Fortune* 500 companies. As part of their research, McCall and Lombardo asked these executives to tell the story of a person who had all the promise to succeed at the highest of levels in an organization but eventually was demoted, fired, plateaued (that is, stopped advancing), or opted for early retirement. These leaders were defined as those who derailed.

At first, McCall and Lombardo (1983) found many similarities between these stories of derailed executives and those of successful executives. Both derailed and successful executives knew the business and were savvy, loyal, driven, and motivated. However, when McCall and Lombardo started to dig deeper into the data, they found clear differences. For instance, derailed managers had a narrow focus about business, whereas successful managers performed well in a variety of assignments. Derailed managers could not handle pressure and stress well and were defensive when it came to their mistakes. Successful executives showed poise under pressure; they admitted and even learned from their mistakes. Derailed managers had relationship problems, whereas successful managers worked well with all sorts of people.

314

From these interviews, McCall and Lombardo (1983) came up with reasons why people derailed. First, their strengths eventually became weaknesses. For example, independence could be a strength early in a career, but as a manager moved higher in the organization and reliance on others became more important, such independence became a weakness. Second, weaknesses early in a career were ignored. Derailed managers may have bullied others through force or intimidation to get things done early in their managerial careers. But as they moved higher in their organizations, their inability to properly manage and influence relationships led to their eventual downfall. Third, the success of derailed managers eventually went to their heads. They never received negative or constructive feedback, and they believed they were invincible. Then one day, they found out they were not invincible, and they could not recover in time. Finally, through no fault of their own, things just happened that made them derail. An economic downturn, a downsizing, a merger or acquisition, bad luck, or something outside their purview led to their eventual failure.

Subsequent derailment studies included a qualitative study of women (Morrison, White, and Van Velsor 1987); quantitative studies (Lombardo and McCauley 1988; Lombardo, Ruderman, and McCauley 1988), which became the impetus for Benchmarks (the Center for Creative Leadership's multisource, or 360-degree, instrument, which includes a section dedicated to problem areas and behaviors associated with derailment; Benchmarks is a registered trademark of the Center for Creative Leadership); and a cross-cultural study on derailment (Leslie and Van Velsor 1996; Van Velsor and Leslie 1995). Across these studies covering two decades, five problem areas of derailed managers kept surfacing.

The Five Problem Areas of Derailed Leaders

The first problem area of derailed leaders was problems with interpersonal relationships. These leaders were described as working in isolation from their co-workers. They were the lone wolves in the organization. They were also described as authoritarian, cold, aloof, arrogant, and insensitive.

The second problem area of derailed leaders that kept surfacing was difficulty leading a team. Often, derailed leaders could not staff effectively and could not form and lead teams successfully. They picked the wrong people to be part of teams; they did not have an eye for talent. Their work teams had high turnover and were ineffective. Also, they failed to handle conflict within their teams.

The third problem area of derailed leaders was that they had difficulty changing or adapting. These derailed leaders could not easily adapt to a boss or superior with a different work or interpersonal style than theirs. Nor could these derailed leaders grow, learn, develop, or think strategically. As these managers rose higher in the ranks, they could not learn new things, they could not change their mindsets, they could not grow and develop new positions, and they could not become agile learners in terms of strategy.

Fourth, these derailed leaders failed to meet business objectives. They were described as poor performers. They were overly ambitious; they had great ideas and laid out ambitious plans, but lacked the follow-through to move their plans toward completion. Simply put, they could not achieve their goals, their numbers, or their obligations to the business.

The fifth and final problem area of derailed leaders was a functional orientation that was too narrow. These leaders were described as ill prepared for promotion. They could not supervise outside their current functions. A classic example was the high-performing, brilliant engineer. His work was so outstanding that he got promoted to management. But all his engineering skills could not compensate for his lack of the relationship orientation needed for management. His engineering orientation was too narrow for the broad management qualities he needed to be successful.

Avoiding Derailment

It is no wonder that one of every two managers is ineffective; many display behaviors in certain problem areas, including problems with interpersonal relationships, difficulty leading a team, difficulty changing or adapting, failure to meet business objectives, and too narrow a functional orientation. If a manager is displaying behaviors in these problem areas, does that mean that he or she is doomed to derailment and ultimate failure? In some cases, yes. Research shows that there are some personality characteristics or profiles that are linked to ineffective managers, managers who show derailment signs, or failed managers (for example, Cangemi, Miller, and Hollopeter 2002; Gentry, Mondore, and Cox 2007; Hogan and Hogan 2001; Moscoso and Salgado 2004). Because personality is usually set by adulthood, the likelihood of a manager's changing his or her personality is rather small at best, and, therefore, some managers may be more likely to derail because of their personalities. This is all the more troubling because a personality trait such as narcissism that has been viewed as a negative trait for leaders to have (Judge, Lepine, and Rich 2006; Paunonen and others 2006) has been found to be linked to leaders that emerge from leaderless groups (Brunell and others 2008). In essence, personality traits such as narcissism may help people emerge as leaders, but could just as easily lead to their ultimate downfall.

Unlike personality, behaviors can change, assuming certain conditions are met. For example, the signs of derailment need to be discovered early. The behaviors that managers need to change must also be clear. In addition, the manager must be focused and motivated to make the changes, and must have support from the organization and/or a development professional. Ultimately, if given enough time, managers showing derailment behaviors can get off the track toward derailment and on a track toward a successful career. What follows is distilled from a host of recent research that has attempted to look into the predictors of derailment to help inform the field and give advice and strategies for managers seeking to avoid derailment.

One practical piece of advice for leaders trying to avoid derailment is to enhance their self-awareness. Leaders must not only understand whether they see themselves the way others see them, but also understand their strengths and weaknesses, and become aware of their work and life circumstances. For instance, many derailed leaders were unaware that they did not fit in well—with the demands of their jobs, their bosses and their managing/leading styles, the people around them, or the directions of their organizations—until it was too late (Leslie and Van Velsor 1996; Lombardo and Eichinger 2005; Lombardo and McCauley 1998). Managers should also take the time to become aware of situations that could trigger derailment, such as work overload, major life or career transitions, or boredom (Dotlich and Cairo 2003). Managers can increase their self-awareness and get off the track toward derailment by

- reflecting on life-shaping moments (Van Velsor, Moxley, and Bunker 2004)
- using executive coaches (Rosinski 2003; Wales 2003)
- using mentors (Couzins and Beagrie 2005)
- taking personality tests (Baillie 2004; Couzins and Beagrie 2005; McCarthy and Garavan 1999)
- journaling (Loo 2002; Van Velsor, Moxley, and Bunker 2004).

Another way to enhance self-awareness is through feedback. Leaders don't always know whether they display derailment behaviors; as recent research has shown, leaders are not in alignment with how others view their derailment tendencies (Gentry and others 2008; Gentry and others 2007). This is especially true for managers at the highest managerial levels (Sala 2003; Gentry and others 2007), who often are out of touch with how they are perceived by others (Goleman, Boyatzis, and McKee 2001), are more arrogant, or may surround themselves with those who are less willing to give truthful, straightforward feedback (Conger and Nadler 2004; Dotlich and Cairo 2003; Kaplan, Drath, and Kofodimos 1987; Kovach 1986; Kramer 2003; Levinson 1994). In short, managers continually believe they are less likely to show derailment signs than their peers, those who report directly to them, and bosses believe.

To avoid derailment, Lombardo and Eichinger (2005) believed, managers must openly receive honest, constructive developmental feedback. By using this feedback from various sources internal and external to the organization, both formally and informally, managers can avoid derailment by developing new strengths, focusing less on the technical matters that got them promoted early in their careers and more on leadership roles that will get them promoted later in their careers, being less controlling of their work and of others and more accepting of ambiguity (which is apparent at higher levels of organizations), being less promotion oriented and more oriented toward problem solving, being less emotionally volatile and more emotionally stable and composed, and becoming more aware of their interpersonal impact on others.

Another important piece of advice is to have a mindset of learning and to be willing to improve. In a study of 173 U.S. college and university administrators, Gentry, Katz, and McFeeters (2009) showed that administrators who understood their strengths and weaknesses and were willing to improve were less likely to display derailment behaviors. Willingness to improve comes with being open to learning new things and having a learning orientation. Managers must try to develop new strengths, learn from their management experiences, handle mistakes and failures by admitting them and learning from them, and become active learners by avoiding past habits to be better equipped to make transitions and deal with novel, challenging situations (Lombardo and Eichinger 2005).

Managers also need to foster relationships and get support from others to lessen others' perceptions that they are displaying behavioral indicators of derailment or to avoid derailment completely. Managers who felt more support from their supervisors and co-workers were less likely to show derailment signs (Gentry, Lambert, and Mondore 2007). A study by Gentry and Shanock (2008) found that positive relationships can lessen the perception of derailment behaviors. Specifically, they found that working effectively with members of upper management and having a good relationship with them helped the managers treat those who reported directly to them in a warm and caring manner, putting them at ease. Ultimately, this led to managers' being seen as less likely to show derailment behaviors. In essence, when managers effectively work with the management team above them and give support to those below them, there are lessened perceptions of derailment behaviors.

Therefore, managers need to try and improve their relationship with members of upper management. They need to meet regularly with upper management and become comfortable and confident around them. They need to get to know those in upper management on a personal level and network with them. Managers need to discover how those in top management think and behave, and attempt and practice influence tactics (that is, managing up) with them. Leaders must also treat their subordinates well, put them at ease, help them, and support them.

Leaders who adopt or enhance certain managerial skills can also be seen as less likely to show derailment signs. For instance, leaders who were more successful at exemplifying the skill of participative management (that is, using effective listening skills and communication to involve others, build a consensus, and influence others in decision making) were rated by their bosses as more successful and less likely to display the characteristics and behaviors associated with derailment (Cox and others 2008). To avoid derailment, managers should therefore try to improve their communication skills, foster collaboration, learn how to build a consensus, and give voice to others in the decision-making process. Also, leaders who are more politically skilled—defined as having "the ability to effectively understand others at work and to use such knowledge to influence others to act in ways that enhance one's personal and/or organizational objectives" (Ferris and others 2005, 127)—are seen as less likely to show derailment signs (Loeb 2008). To avoid derailment, leaders should enhance their political skill by building networks, becoming perceptive observers and discerners of people and situations, practicing influence skills, and acting with true sincerity.

Finally, leaders who are less likely to show derailment signs have a good balance between work and life. Recent research has shown that leaders rated higher in work/life balance were seen as less likely to show derailment behaviors than leaders rated lower in work/life balance (Lyness and Judiesch 2008). This might lend evidence toward the fact that organizations may consider a manager's perception of work/life balance when discussing and planning for career-related decisions and opportunities. Further, it gives credence to the foundation of programs implemented to help managers balance their work and nonwork responsibilities and activities, and thus the results of this research should encourage organizations to help managers lead more balanced lives.

When Derailment Happens: How to Get Back on Track

It is true that despite all these pieces of good advice, managers have derailed, can derail, and continue to derail. But it should also be uplifting to know that derailment does not mean that the manager is beyond hope for the rest of his or her career (Shipper and Dillard 2000). In fact, Kovach (1989) noted that several managers who had derailed in a past situation went on to succeed in a new situation. Therefore, when a manager derails, Kovach believes the manager should take a career slowdown and reflect on who he or she is as a person, including strengths, weaknesses, and key lessons from the experience. More recently, Sonnenfeld and Ward (2008) studied derailed managers and executives who eventually recovered. They found that those who successfully came back from their derailment episode faced up to the issue or mistake, sought new opportunities through their networks and mentors, paid attention to the people involved in the derailment experience (including family and friends), restored their leader image, rebuilt trust and credibility, and started fresh by taking a new leadership role or starting a new venture.

Conclusion

This chapter has attempted to show just how prevalent managerial ineffectiveness can be. Many times, these ineffective managers who eventually failed had all the makings of success, but they eventually derailed because of problems with interpersonal relationships, difficulty leading a team, difficulty changing or adapting, failure to meet business objectives, and too narrow a functional orientation. The odds are that you know a manager with problems like these, or worse, that you may be on a track to becoming one of them or are already there. By knowing the tips and strategies and understanding the advice from this chapter, you may help others take precautionary actions to avert derailment, or get yourself off a track toward derailment and back on a track toward your own career success.

Further Reading

W. A. Gentry and C. T. Chappelow, "Managerial Derailment: Weaknesses That Can Be Fixed," in *The Perils of Accentuating the Positives*, ed. R. B. Kaiser. Tulsa: Hogan Press, 2009.

Jean Brittain Leslie and Ellen Van Velsor, *A Look at Derailment Today: North America and Europe*. Greensboro, NC: Center for Creative Leadership, 1995.

M. M. Lombardo and R. W. Eichinger, *Preventing Derailment: What to Do before It's Too Late*. Greensboro, NC: Center for Creative Leadership, 2005.

Morgan W. McCall Jr. and Michael M. Lombardo, *Off the Track: Why and How Successful Executives Get Derailed*. Greensboro, NC: Center for Creative Leadership, 1983.

References

Baillie, S. 2004. Know Thyself. *Profit* 23: 107–108.

Bentz, V. J. 1985a. Research Findings from Personality Assessment of Executives. In *Personality Assessment in Organizations*, ed. J. H. Bernardin and D. A. Bownas. New York: Praeger.

———. 1985b. *A View of the Top: A Thirty-Year Perspective of Research Devoted to the Discovery, Description and Prediction of Executive Behavior*. Paper presented at annual convention of American Psychological Association, Los Angeles.

Bray, D. W., R. J. Campbell, and D. L. Grant. 1974. *Formative Years in Business*. New York: John Wiley & Sons.

Bray, D. W., and A. Howard. 1983. The AT&T Longitudinal Studies of Managers. In *Longitudinal Studies of Adult Psychological Development*, ed. K. W. Shaie. New York: Guilford Press.

Brunell, A. B., W. A. Gentry, W. K. Campbell, B. J. Hoffman, K. W. Kuhnert, and K. G. DeMarree. 2008. Leader Emergence: The Case of the Narcissistic Leader. *Personality and Social Psychology Bulletin* 34: 1663–1676.

Cangemi, J., R. Miller, and T. Hollopeter. 2002, Winter. When Leadership Fails: Lessons Learned in the '90s and New Directions for 2000 and Beyond. *Organization Development Journal* 20, no. 4: 8–17.

Charan, R. 2005. Ending the CEO Succession Crisis. *Harvard Business Review* 83: 72–81.

Conger, J. A., and D. A. Nadler. 2004. When CEOs Step Up to Fail. *MIT Sloan Management Review* 45, no. 3 (Spring): 50–56.

Couzins, M., and S. Beagrie. 2005. How to . . . Develop Your Self-Awareness. *Personnel Today,* May 17, 31.

Cox, B. D., W. A. Gentry, T. E. Sparks, S. P. Mondore, and K. W. Kuhnert. 2008, April. Participative Management as an Indicator of Managerial Success and Derailment. Poster session presented at Society of Industrial Organizational Psychology conference, San Francisco.

Dotlich, D. L., and P. C. Cairo. 2003. *Why CEOs Fail: The 11 Behaviors That Can Derail Your Climb to the Top—and How to Manage Them.* San Francisco: Jossey-Bass.

Fernandez-Araoz, C. 1999. Hiring without Firing. *Harvard Business Review* 77: 109–120.

Ferris, G. R., D. C. Treadway, R. W. Kolodinsky, W. A. Hochwarter, C. J. Kacmar, C. Douglas, and D. D. Frink. 2005. Development and Validation of the Political Skill Inventory. *Journal of Management* 31: 126–152.

Finkelstein, S. 2004. *Why Smart Executives Fail.* New York: Portfolio.

Finkin, E. F. 1991. Techniques for Making People More Productive. *Journal of Business Strategy* 12 (March–April): 53–56.

Gabarro, J. J. 1987. *The Dynamics of Taking Charge.* Boston: Harvard Business School Press.

Gentry, W. A., P. W. Braddy, J. W. Fleenor, and P. J. Howard. 2008. Self-Observer Rating Discrepancies on the Derailment Behaviors of Hispanic Managers. *Business Journal of Hispanic Research* 2, no. 1: 76–87.

Gentry, W. A., K. M. Hannum, B. Z. Ekelund, and A. de Jong. 2007. A Study of the Discrepancy Between Self- and Observer-Ratings on Managerial Derailment Characteristics of European Managers. *European Journal of Work and Organizational Psychology* 16: 295–325.

Gentry, W. A., R. B. Katz, and B. McFeeters. 2009. The Continual Need for Improvement to Avoid Derailment: A Study of College and University Administrators. *Higher Education Research and Development* 28. 335–348.

Gentry, W. A., T. A. Lambert, and S. P. Mondore. 2007, November. The Influence of Social Support on Managerial Effectiveness: Age as a Moderator. Paper presented at Southern Management Association Meeting, Nashville.

Gentry, W. A., S. P. Mondore, and B. D. Cox. 2007. An Exploratory Study of Managerial Derailment Characteristics and Personality Preferences. *Journal of Management Development* 26: 857–873.

Gentry, W. A., and L. R. Shanock. 2008. Views of Managerial Derailment from Above and Below: The Importance of a Good Relationship with Upper Management and Putting People at Ease. *Journal of Applied Social Psychology* 38: 2469–2494.

Gillespie, N. A., M. Walsh, A. H. Winefield, J. Dua, and C. Stough. 2001. Occupational Stress in Universities: Staff Perceptions of the Causes, Consequences, and Moderators of Stress. *Work and Stress* 15: 53–72.

Goleman, D., R. Boyatzis, and A. McKee. 2001. Primal Leadership: The Hidden Driver of Great Performance. *Harvard Business Review* 79: 42–51.

Hogan, R., G. J. Curphy, and J. Hogan. 1994. What We Know about Leadership: Effectiveness and Personality. *American Psychologist* 49: 493–504.

Hogan, R., and J. Hogan. 2001. Assessing Leadership: A View of the Dark Side. *International Journal of Selection and Assessment* 9: 40–51.

Hogan, R., and R. B. Kaiser. 2005. What We Know about Leadership. *Review of General Psychology* 9: 169–180.

Hogan, R., R. Raskin, and D. Fazzini. 1990. The Dark Side of Charisma. In *Measures of Leadership,* ed. K. E. Clark and M. B. Clark. West Orange, NJ: Leadership Library of America.

Judge, T. A., J. A. LePine, and B. L. Rich. 2006. Loving Yourself Abundantly: Relationship of the Narcissistic Personality to Self- and Other Perceptions of Workplace Deviance, Leadership, and Task and Contextual Performance. *Journal of Applied Psychology* 91: 762–776.

Kaplan, R. E., W. H. Drath, and J. R. Kofodimos. 1987. High Hurdles: The Challenge of Executive Self-Development. *Academy of Management Executive* 1: 195–205.

Kotter, J. P. 1982. *The General Managers.* New York: Free Press.

Kovach, B. E. 1986. The Derailment of Fast-Track Managers. *Organizational Dynamics* 15: 41–48.

———. 1989. Successful Derailment: What Fast-Trackers Can Learn While They're Off the Track. *Organizational Dynamics* 18: 33–47.

Kramer, R. 2003. Recognizing the Symptoms of Reckless Leadership. *Harvard Business Review* 81, no. 10: 65.

Leslie, J. B., and E. Van Velsor. 1996. *A Look at Derailment Today: North America and Europe.* Greensboro, NC: Center for Creative Leadership.

Levinson, H. 1994. Beyond the Selection Failures. *Consulting Psychology Journal* 46: 3–8.

Loeb, M. 2008, January 14. Six Ways to Keep Your Career on Track. *MarketWatch.* http://www.marketwatch.com/story/six-ways-to-keep-your-career-on-track?dist=hplatest.

Lombardo, M. M., and R. W. Eichinger. 2005. *Preventing Derailment: What to Do Before It's Too Late.* Greensboro, NC: Center for Creative Leadership.

Lombardo, M. M., and C. McCauley. 1988. *The Dynamics of Managerial Derailment.* Greensboro, NC: Center for Creative Leadership.

Lombardo, M. M., M. N. Ruderman, and C. D. McCauley. 1988. Explanations of Success and Derailment in Upper-Level Management Positions. *Journal of Business and Psychology* 2: 199–216.

Loo, R. 2002. Journaling: A Learning Tool for Project Management Training and Team-Building. *Project Management Journal* 33: 61–66.

Lyness, K. S., and, M. K. Judiesch. 2008. Can a Manager Have a Life and a Career? International and Multisource Perspectives on Work/Life Balance and Career Advancement Potential. *Journal of Applied Psychology* 93: 789–805.

McCall, M. W., Jr., and M. M. Lombardo. 1983. *Off the Track: Why and How Successful Executives Get Derailed.* Greensboro, NC: Center for Creative Leadership.

McCarthy, A. M., and T. N. Garavan. 1999. Developing Self-Awareness in the Managerial Career Development Process: The Value of 360-Degree Feedback and the MBTI. *Journal of European Industrial Training* 23: 437–445.

Millikin-Davies, M. 1992. An Exploration of Flawed First-Line Supervision. Doctoral dissertation, University of Tulsa.

Morrison, A, M., R. P. White, and E. Van Velsor. 1987. *Breaking the Glass Ceiling: Can Women Reach the Top of America's Largest Corporations?* Reading, MA: Addison-Wesley.

Moscoso, S., and J. F. Salgado, 2004. "Dark Side" Personality Styles as Predictors of Task, Contextual, and Job Performance. *International Journal of Selection and Assessment* 12: 356–362.

Paunonen, S. V., J. Lönnqvist, M. Verkasalo, S. Leikas, and V. Nissinen. 2006. Narcissism and Emergent Leadership in Military Cadets. *Leadership Quarterly* 17: 475–486.

Rogers, R. W., and A. B. Smith. 2004. Spotting Executive Potential and Future Senior Leaders. *Employment Relations Today* 31, no. 1: 51–60.

Rosinski, P. 2003. *Coaching across Cultures: New Tools for Leveraging National, Corporate, and Professional Differences.* London: Nicholas Brealey.

Sala, F. 2003. Executive Blind Spots: Discrepancies between Self- and Other-Ratings. *Consulting Psychology Journal* 55: 222–229.

Sessa, V. I., R. B. Kaiser, J. K. Taylor, and R. J. Campbell. 1998. *Executive Selection: A Research Report on What Works and What Doesn't.* Greensboro, NC: Center for Creative Leadership.

Shipper, F., and J. E. Dillard Jr. 2000. A Study of Impending Derailment and Recovery of Middle Managers across Career Stages. *Human Resource Management* 39: 331–345.

Shipper, F., and C. L. Wilson. 1992. The Impact of Managerial Behaviors on Group Performance, Stress, and Commitment. In *Impact of Leadership*, ed. K. E. Clark, M. B. Clark, and D. P. Campbell. Greensboro, NC: Center for Creative Leadership.

Smart, B. 1999. *Topgrading: How Leading Companies Win by Hiring, Coaching, and Keeping the Best People.* Upper Saddle River, NJ: Prentice Hall.

———. 2005. *Topgrading: How Leading Companies Win by Hiring, Coaching, and Keeping the Best People,* rev. ed. New York: Portfolio.

Sonnenfeld, J., and A. Ward. 2008 . Firing Back: How Great Leaders Rebound after Career Disasters. *Organizational Dynamics* 37: 1–20.

Sorcher, M. 1985. *Predicting Executive Success: What It Takes to Make It into Senior Management.* New York: Wiley.

Van Velsor, E., and Leslie, J. B. 1995. Why Executives Derail: Perspectives across Time and Cultures. *Academy of Management Executive* 9, no. 4: 62–72.

Van Velsor, E., R. S. Moxley, and K. A. Bunker. 2004. The Leader Development Process. In *The Center for Creative Leadership Handbook of Leadership Development*, 2nd edition, ed. C. McCauley and E. Van Velsor. San Francisco: Jossey-Bass and Center for Creative Leadership.

Wales, S. 2003. Why Coaching? *Journal of Change Management* 3: 275–282.

Wells, S. J. 2005. Diving In. *HR Magazine* 50: 54–59.

White, R. P., and D. L. DeVries. 1990. Making the Wrong Choice: Failure in the Selection of Senior-Level Managers. *Issues and Observations* 10, no.1: 1–6.

About the Author

William A. (Bill) Gentry is currently a senior research associate at the Center for Creative Leadership and an adjunct assistant professor in the leadership studies doctoral program at North Carolina A&T State University. He graduated summa cum laude from

Emory University and received his MS and PhD in applied psychology (with a concentration in industrial-organizational psychology) from the University of Georgia. He has published (or has work forthcoming) in the *Journal of Applied Psychology, Journal of Vocational Behavior, Personnel Psychology, Personality and Social Psychology Bulletin, Leadership Quarterly*, and *Journal of Leadership Studies*.

℘ Section IV

Contemporary Leadership Challenges

There is certainly no shortage of leadership challenges today. Indeed, an entire hand-book could have been written based on them. We have elected to include chapters on current challenges for which there are organizational success stories with validated and implementable solutions. So in the next five chapters, you won't be surprised to see the authors exploring these challenges—your organization may be facing them, too:

- How will leaders need to change to lead the workforce of the future?
- How can leaders become more globally savvy?
- How can organizations address the challenges women employees face today?
- What strategies can leaders use to guide, develop, and coach the multiple generations in today's workforce?
- What competencies do leaders need to achieve their organization's diversity vision?

Of course, these topics aren't surprising—it is time that leaders addressed them. But there are also other concerns down the road that need leaders' attention. Where to next? What can the leaders of the next 10 to 20 years expect as they guide the workforce of the future? Events throughout the world during the past couple of years have demonstrated that every successful organization is likely to face challenges that may threaten its survival.

There certainly is no shortage of advice. Turn to the chapters in the first three sections of this handbook, and you will find the authors advising, warning, and pleading for leaders to address key dynamics that affect organizational effectiveness, longevity, and financial performance. So, if leaders have not done so already, they need to immediately tackle the topics explored in this section, so they can move on to the more difficult issues that will soon come their way in this ever-changing, increasingly complex world.

In chapter 24, "Leading the Workforce of the Future," Frances Hesselbein, president and CEO of the Leader to Leader Institute, explains how the competencies and attributes that will be needed to lead the workforce of the future are changing.

In chapter 25, "Globally Savvy Leaders," Stephen Rhinesmith, one of the world's leading experts on global leadership, lays out a nine-step plan a leader can take to become globally savvy. He challenges leaders to rise to a new standard of behavior—to have the empathy, compassion, and capacity to balance achieving financial and organizational objectives with the need to develop collaboration around the world.

In chapter 26, "Women in the Lead," Marian Ruderman, a senior fellow and director at the Center for Creative Leadership, encourages organizations to find ways to strengthen the development of women leaders. She presents a framework that incorporates the unique needs of women and explains how the principles of leadership development can be adapted to meet them.

In chapter 27, "Leading Across Generations," Joanne Sujansky discusses key findings from her recent book *Keeping the Millennials* for addressing the challenge organizations are now facing with four diverse generations in the workplace. She explains how to foster communication, build cross-generational teams, and implement other strategies for working effectively with multiple generations.

In chapter 28, "Leading for Diversity," Kay Iwata, Juan Lopez, and Julie O'Mara—a team of diversity experts with more than 75 years of experience between them—explore the key competencies needed to encourage diversity and inclusion that are summed up by the acronym P-O-W-E-R: proactive advocates of diversity, optimum people developers, willing innovators, exemplary values-based decision makers, and results through people. Leaders who have these competencies are often described as authentic and committed.

 **Chapter 24**

Leading the Workforce of the Future

Frances Hesselbein

In This Chapter

- Crucial characteristics that will be needed by organizations of the future.
- Nine keys to leading the workforce of the future.
- Lessons leaders can learn from the workforce of the future.

I spend a third of my time on college and university campuses, here and abroad, and this is where I find my hope. This is where I get my inspiration. The future generation is vastly different from earlier generations of leaders. The millennials, Gen Y, the echo boomers—whatever you choose to call them—have high expectations, are savvy about technology, value diversity and inclusion, are open-minded and performance driven, are globally aware, and accept their social responsibility—attributes we all admire.

A range of economic and social influences have shaped the attitudes, beliefs, and expectations of this emerging generation. A recent *USA Today* study found that even though jobs are scarce and money is tight, it has not stopped the millennial generation from helping others (Jayson 2010). Young adults who grew up in the shadow of the 9/11 attacks, saw the wreckage of Hurricane Katrina, and have searched for jobs during a recession are volunteering at home and abroad in record numbers. The millennials, the generation that learned to serve in school, as well as to read and write, became the first global Internet explorers as they pioneered social networking for favorite causes at home. Students on campuses here and abroad view community service as part of their DNA. I have a belief, "to serve is to live," which is exemplified by the generation that is currently entering the workforce.

Much has been written, and solid research has been conducted, about today's college and university students. Leadership and civic engagement are indispensable partners for their journey to significance and service. Warren Bennis calls this generation "the Crucible Generation," and recent research tells us that not since the 1930s and 1940s has there been such a powerful generation—seemingly born to serve (Bennis 2009). This causes observers to compare today's university students, and cadets at our military academies, with "the Greatest Generation." Some of us were part of that period, and all of us remember its history. But the characteristics of this generation are not found only in the United States; they are found worldwide.

During a recent trip to Beijing, Nanchang, Shanghai, and Hong Kong to celebrate Peter Drucker's 100th birthday, I met thousands of young members of China's workforce of the future who in many ways were similar to students here in the United States. They all see themselves as part of a global community. They are running on parallel tracks that include the values of respect, inclusion, innovation, and hope for the future—a global workforce of the future. And again, I am inspired.

How can we encourage global collaboration? Because the members of this worldwide Crucible Generation have been students of the history of our society, they can be a powerful force in building and restoring institutions that in the end sustain democracy. In 2009, the University of Pittsburgh launched the Hesselbein Global Academy for Student Leadership and Civic Engagement, and in 2010 will hold a Global Summit comprising 25 students from North American universities and 25 students from around the world. Each year, the same number will attend the conclave. In 2019, all 500 young global leaders of the future will meet, celebrate, and share how they are changing the world.

In addition, U.S. military institutions are also tapping into the workforce of the future. For example, over the next two years I will serve as the chair for the study of leadership at the U.S. Military Academy at West Point, the first woman and the first non–West Point graduate to serve in this position. Approximately every six weeks, I plan to have a great thought leader join me—leaders like Jim Collins, Marshall Goldsmith, Alan Mulally, and Margot Tyler. We will engage in a leadership dialogue with the cadets to share our thoughts and, most important, to tap into their ideas for the future. This promises to be a remarkable leadership learning experience for all of us. It will be a personally meaningful experience for me also, because I am the mother, daughter, sister, and great-great-(many greats) granddaughter of soldiers who have served going back through history—World War I, World War II, the Spanish American War, the Civil War, the War of 1812, and the American Revolution. I feel a reverence and a sense of gratitude for these men and women of my family who have exemplified "the best we can be," as do the cadets of West Point today.

These two personal experiences with students underscore my passionate belief in the quality, potential, and commitment these young members of the workforce of the future will bring to their work, service, and engagement. Their desire for inclusion and to serve is our hope for a better future. "To serve is to live." And again, I am inspired.

These examples demonstrate how two organizations are addressing the leadership development needs of the workforce of the future. What about other organizations and corporations? How can the leaders of today inspire, guide, challenge, and develop future leaders? How can they lead to take advantage of the rich resource we have in the future workforce? I hope that these events at the University of Pittsburgh and West Point will inspire other institutions and corporations to find ways to encourage and support the workforce of the future.

Before we explore how to lead the workforce of the future, let's first consider the organization of the future. What challenges will future organizations face? How might they need to change to be successful? How might their focus change?

Crucial Characteristics of the Organization of the Future

Although none of us can predict with 100 percent accuracy what the organization of the future will look like, a few crucial characteristics of future organizations are currently emerging and will only become stronger:

- Embody collaboration—partnerships—alliances.
- Increase transparency.
- See the world as a community.
- Simplify complexity and change.
- Redefine the work.
- Create a flexible workplace.
- Expand inclusion.

Some of these characteristics are being shaped by the new workforce, and in other cases these characteristics are helping to shape the new workforce. Here are a few of my observations about how organizations of the future will need to include these characteristics.

Embodying Collaboration—Partnerships—Alliances

An organization will only be able to perform globally if there is a strong collaborative effort. The turbulence in the world's economy requires an emphasis on global alliances as well as business-community partnerships and business-to-business relationships promoting collaboration between the corporate and social sectors. In a world trying to do more with less, winning strategies will depend on how well all kinds of organizations can work together for the greater good. Leaders will need to build trust and create relationships to ensure effective collaboration.

Increasing Transparency

As the world continues to become more connected, the actions of organizations will be scrutinized by the media and the public more than ever. Having an effective approach to corporate social responsibility and ethical, principled leadership will continue to be essential. The need to make a profit will be balanced with fair trade, sustainability, corporate social responsibility, and other ethical principles.

Seeing the World as a Community

Organizations will need to be responsive to the communities where they operate, serving and sharing their knowledge and resources. In addition, organizations will see themselves as part of the global community and appreciate that everyone belongs to this community. Organizations have a responsibility to the world community.

Simplifying Complexity and Change

The organization of the future will need to find ways to better address the overwhelming realities of complexity and change. But in this wired world, nothing in the workplace will become simpler or easier. Organizations need to learn to address these realities as a part of their day-to-day operations—not a surprise or inconvenience. Complexity requires simplifying processes and policies. Change is part of the process.

Redefining the Work

An organization will need to step back to examine its work and determine how it can become more agile and responsive to its customers, how it can ensure that the work is more meaningful and motivating for its staff, and how it can eliminate barriers that prevent its people from maximizing their creativity and productivity. Work, learning, collaboration, and having fun need to be bundled together to satisfy both the people of the organization and its customers.

Creating a Flexible Workplace

The 9-to-5 workday is no longer the norm. The office, as the only workplace, has been superseded by telecenters and home offices. Flextime, flexplace, and telework are the reality of today's workforce. Flexibility beyond expectations is the gift that technology has given to every individual and every organization. And when employees do need to come to the office, they require collaborative workspaces and project rooms that can be easily repurposed. Because work and home spill over into each other, the workplace must allow staff to connect with home. In some cases, people may even search for pet-friendly employers.

Expanding Inclusion

The organization's culture, values, and leadership must be committed to inclusion, which will go beyond race and gender. Participation is not just for staff; it will also be for customers who want to be part of the significance, the future. The organization of the future will be more attuned to the needs of its customers. "What does the customer value?" was Peter Drucker's famous and essential question to leaders in all three sectors. The organization of the future will thus respond to the customer's needs.

Nine Keys to Leading the Workforce of the Future

My passionate belief has been, and is today, that leadership is a matter of how to be, not how to do. Yet it is what leaders do that others see and judge, not what leaders are. So what can a leader do? Scanning the checklist I gave in *Hesselbein on Leadership*, I note that all these keys will be important in the future, some more critical than others, and some with a new twist (Hesselbein 2002, 86–90):

1. Define a clear vision that has its foundation in the organization's values.
2. Give regular feedback.
3. Provide meaningful work.
4. Recognize the importance of teamwork and inclusion.
5. Provide opportunities to lead sooner.
6. Balance communication methods.
7. Inspire commitment and keep millennials engaged.
8. Make work enjoyable.
9. Find ways for millennials to serve society.

These nine keys are what I believe to be critical for leaders in meeting the challenges and providing opportunities for the workforce of the future, which includes staff from four generational groups: traditionalists, baby boomers, Generation X, and the millennials. Because most leaders have figured out how to work with the earlier generations, these keys focus mostly on emerging leaders, the leaders of the future.

In general, the leaders of the organizations and workforce of the future will need to challenge the gospel of the status quo, of past practices, and thus maintain only relevant strategies. Let's briefly consider each of the nine keys.

Defining a Clear Vision with Its Foundation in the Organization's Values

Most leaders are far more comfortable with defining, executing, and measuring today's efforts than grappling with tomorrow's needs. Too often, the vision is a mere projection of more of today than of something truly different for tomorrow. It is this lack of prospecting that has caused some leading organizations to decline over the past few years. Leaders plan strategically, taking into account all the possibilities. Start with a solid set of values that lend integrity to the vision, and define a vision that will inspire all your people.

Giving Regular Feedback

Leaders can't provide too much feedback. And it does need to be provided often. It must be honest and candid. The workforce of the future has a constant need for feedback, and this feedback provides them with the inspiration and motivation for growth and development. Praise, acknowledgment, and recognition, along with course correction and suggestions for other options, are part of the feedback people need.

Providing Meaningful Work

The members of the workforce of the future grew up in a fast-moving world. They have their fingers on the pulse of changing technology. They multitask and enjoy a challenge. They need projects that utilize their knowledge and skills, that can connect with their philosophical and deeper interests. They contact people around the world and depend on the Internet to deliver vast amounts of data about any topic. They are interested in learning and developing in their jobs, and moving into new and challenging opportunities. They will leave when they think the job has become meaningless or that they are no longer learning and growing.

Recognizing the Importance of Teamwork and Inclusion

The millennial generation is considered the most open generation of all. For them, inclusion and diversity are a way of life, and they see themselves as part of a global community to which everyone belongs. They want to be connected with teams at work and with customers. They are good at leveraging the efforts of others to achieve results and sharing rewards. If they are new to the workforce, it is important that they be encouraged to become involved in teams where their contribution will be recognized and valued.

Providing Opportunities to Lead Sooner

Providing opportunities to lead sooner is one thing the U.S. military does very well. For example, Warren Bennis was only 19 years of age when he led his first U.S. Army platoon in World War II in Germany. This experience showed him how critical it was to rely on his platoon members. Thrust into the situation, he learned that he needed to trust them to help him be their leader. Look for projects and assignments where millennials have a chance to lead.

Balancing Communication Methods

Text messaging is a main communication vehicle for millennials. Instant messages can take the place of phone calls, and email can take the place of face-to-face visits. Because person-to-person conversation may be a struggle, leaders must create opportunities for millennials to develop their networking and speaking skills. And when leaders listen intently to the staff they are guiding, the benefits are immeasurable. They learn about the staff's needs and expertise, can identify better ways to work, and in so doing demonstrate that they care about the staff and their ideas. This helps build trust.

Inspiring Commitment and Keeping Millennials Engaged

Ensure that millennials have reasons to continue with your organization. They will stay longer when they know the organization is invested in their careers and leadership development. Promoting from within is a signal that the organization values developing its own people. When asked "Who does the best job of developing leaders?" Peter Drucker replied "The U.S. Army. They develop their leaders from within." Ensure that the organization's leaders are open and accessible to its millennials. This helps them see how they are part of the organization. They value the authenticity and transparency, which keep them engaged.

Making Work Enjoyable

Find ways to have fun in the workplace. This is not a new concept, but the people entering the workforce today take it to new levels. They look for excuses for celebrations. They expect to find fun and excitement along the way, in the doing, along with positive relationships and inclusion.

Finding Ways for Millennials to Serve Society

For millennials, being true to themselves equates with being personally and socially responsible. They advocate reducing, reusing, recycling, repurposing, rescuing, and remembering.

So enable them to reduce their carbon footprint; reuse wrapping paper, clothes, and goods that are no longer useful to others; recycle paper, plastic, and aluminum cans; repurpose everything from pill bottles to entire rooms; rescue cats and dogs from shelters; and remember those around the world who need their support, their concern. Leaders must find ways to support this deeply felt need to help others. This is the generation for whom "to serve is to live."

Summing Up

What about building trust? Isn't building trust on everyone's "good leader list"? As I noted at the start of this section, leadership is much less about what you *do* and much more about who you *are*. If a leader, thus, "does" these nine imperatives, the "how to be" leader will emerge as he or she builds trust with the workforce of the future.

Lessons from the Workforce of the Future

Organizations and leaders can learn every day. Today's leaders have as much to learn from the workforce of the future as they can learn from us. Here's a sampling of lessons today's leaders can learn from the workforce of the future.

Building Relationships

The millennials develop friendships and maintain relationships. They stay connected to friends, relatives, and colleagues—many on a daily basis. These relationships encourage collaboration and teamwork on the job. Relationships make improving communication and building trust easier. Leadership skills are developed by working with people. Get out of the office and find out who is working for you—and with you. Remember management by walking around? That's the bud of building relationships. People follow leaders they know, like, and trust.

Balancing Work and Life

The millennials have it right. And if most of us are honest with ourselves, we too wish for less work and more play in our lives. Can you honestly say that if everything were equal, you'd choose to work 60 or 70 hours every week at a stressful job? Wouldn't you like to find more time for your friends and family, and for taking care of yourself? It's called "work/life balance."

Giving Back

The millennials have a strong sense of service to their fellow humans and other creatures, the community, and the world. Many organizations require their leaders to find ways to give back to the community—more and more known as simply practicing corporate social responsibility. This is good for the world, good for the company, good for the staff, and good for the soul. Again, "to serve is to live."

Celebrating Technology

The millennials, or the Crucible Generation, grew up with a Game Boy in one hand and a cell phone in the other. Thus, the leaders of successful organizations appreciate why networking on Facebook, podcasting, blogging, and sending tweets on Twitter are a significant part of the lives of young leaders. And as new technology emerges, these leaders make it their own.

Last Thoughts

I make time to meet with young leaders who want to come to my office just to talk or to connect. And sometime later, they introduce me as their "mentor." I'm not that, in the strictest sense, but we are "fellow travelers," sharing the journey. Mentoring is a leadership privilege, and it is circular. They learn from me; I learn from them. I hope this chapter provides you with ideas for how you too can become a fellow traveler, sharing the exciting journey to the future. To provoke more thoughts, see the sidebar.

The emerging leaders I encounter are sending a powerful message of leadership, of building trust, of ethics in action, of the power of diversity and inclusion, of the importance of courage, of celebrating the intellect, of leading from the front into an uncertain future, and of service. In response, my message to them is: "We look to you to take the lead into the future, as an inspiring example of the power of learning, a model of ethical global citizenship. To serve is to live."

Recently, some university students and cadets at West Point asked me, "Why are you always so positive?" And "What makes you so positive?" My reply: "It is your generation that gives me hope for the future."

For some time, I have been talking and writing about this generation—the Crucible Generation. They are volunteering, making enormous contributions, both in the United States and abroad. I have found them different from previous age cohorts. And recently, solid research has been telling us that this present generation is more like the generation of the 1930s and 1940s that we now call the Greatest Generation.

Today's generation gives me hope, enormous energy, and inspires me to do what I am called to do. "To serve is to live" is the language of this workforce of the future.

Thought-Provoking Questions for Every Leader to Consider

Use these questions based on this chapter to create an internal examination of your current strengths and shortcomings as a leader of the workforce of the future:

1. How many lives have I changed because I took an interest in someone at work?
2. How well do I treat people as individuals, respecting their culture?
3. How many hours do I work each week, and how does that influence my attitude toward others who do not work the same number of hours?
4. Do I truly connect with people at work, or merely communicate?
5. How well have I mastered Facebook, LinkedIn, blogging, Twitter, and other social networking sites and services to benefit the organization?
6. What aspects of social learning can be leveraged to gather and dispense knowledge?
7. How often do I use instant messaging?
8. Do all my people know how important they are to the organization?
9. How can my organization ensure that everyone influences and embraces change?
10. How much fun do we have at work?
11. How open and transparent am I?
12. How much passion do I bring to work?
13. How do I encourage authenticity throughout the organization?
14. How would I rate my authenticity? How would others rate it?
15. How accessible am I to everyone in the organization?
16. How can we better tap into the learning and knowledge that occur across the organization?
17. How convinced am I that the organization is prepared for the future?
18. How can the organization build social responsibility into individual development plans?
19. What is the organization doing to support the community? The world?
20. Every day is a gift; what have I given today?
21. To serve is to live; how have I served today?

How do you feel about your answers? What might you do differently as a result of your self-examination? How could you garner information about these questions from your workforce of the future?

Further Reading

Jim Collins, *Good to Great and the Social Sectors: A Monograph to Accompany Good to Great.* New York: HarperCollins, 2005.

———, *How the Mighty Fall: And Why Some Companies Never Give In.* New York: HarperCollins, 2009.

Peter F. Drucker, *The Effective Executive: The Definitive Guide to Getting the Right Things.* New York: HarperPaperbacks, 2006.

Frances Hesselbein and Marshall Goldsmith, *Leader of the Future 2*. San Francisco: Jossey-Bass, 2006.

————, *Organization of the Future 2*. San Francisco: Jossey-Bass, 2009.

Rosabeth Moss Kanter, *Supercorp: How Vanguard Companies Create Innovation, Profits, and Social Good*. New York: Crown Business, 2009.

Eric Shinseki and Frances Hesselbein, *Be°Know°Do: Leadership the Army Way*. San Francisco: Jossey-Bass, 2004.

References

Bennis, W. 2009. Another Greatest Generation Is on the Way. *Forbes,* April 1.

Hesselbein, F. 2002. *Hesselbein on Leadership*. San Francisco: Jossey-Bass.

Jayson, S. 2010. Study: Millennial Generation: More Education, Less Employed. *USA Today,* February 23.

About the Author

Frances Hesselbein is the president and CEO of the Leader to Leader Institute (formerly the Peter F. Drucker Foundation for Nonprofit Management), and its founding president. She was awarded the Presidential Medal of Freedom, the United States' highest civilian honor, in 1998. She serves on numerous nonprofit and private-sector corporate boards and is the recipient of 20 honorary doctoral degrees. She has been appointed to the Class of 1951 Chair for the Study of Leadership at the U.S. Military Academy at West Point, and in 2009 the University of Pittsburgh introduced the Hesselbein Global Academy for Student Leadership and Civic Engagement, whose aim is to produce experience and ethical leaders who will address the most critical national and international issues, and advance positive social and economic initiatives throughout the world. She has been honored with a Lifetime Award for her work as a former CEO of the Girl Scouts of the USA. She was awarded the John F. Kennedy Memorial Fellowship by Fulbright New Zealand and was the first recipient of the Dwight D. Eisenhower National Security Award in 2003. She is editor in chief of the award-winning quarterly journal *Leader to Leader,* and is the author or editor of 27 books in 30 languages.

∽ **Chapter 25**

Globally Savvy Leaders

Stephen H. Rhinesmith

In This Chapter

- What a "whole" leader looks like, and how using head, heart, and guts skills are necessary to meet the challenges of a complex, diverse, and uncertain world.

- Why a globally savvy leader must be a whole leader—a leader who is balanced in head, heart, and guts.

- Nine steps a leader can take to become a globally savvy leader.

- What a globally responsible leader looks like, and some of the emerging principles one must have to be a globally responsible leader.

The need for leaders who are comfortable dealing on a global level has never been greater, but the demand still exceeds the supply. In an increasingly complex, diverse, and uncertain world, leaders will have to use their head, heart, and guts in new ways to become globally savvy leaders. They'll be challenged to rise to a new standard of leadership behavior during the years ahead, and they will be required to focus on the right issues and have the empathy, compassion, and capacity to achieve their financial and organizational objectives with the delicate balance needed for the world to develop in a collaborative and sustainable manner.

When Ian Cook became CEO of Colgate-Palmolive, he stepped into a role previously held by Reuben Mark, who had led the company during two decades of nearly unparalleled growth. Rather than leading in the same way, however, Cook recognized the new challenges of today's global marketplace. He recognized that to maintain financial strength, ability to execute, and strong values, Colgate would have to find a blend of skills between the old model and the new requirements of the marketplace. As Cook has proceeded, he has been careful to analyze but not paralyze his company, and Colgate continues to grow—even during the recession of 2008 and 2009.

The late Anita Roddick, founder of the Body Shop, worked to advance social rights through a strong niche market. The company has provided onsite child care at its British location; campaigned against the scientific testing on animals; and been on the cutting edge of diversity issues. Roddick even wrote a book titled *A Revolution in Kindness* and founded the Social Adventure Network, a coalition of companies focused on "making business kinder." Though her heart and compassion drove these initiatives, her passion for social causes would have gone unnoticed if her company had not been successful. But she balanced her compassion with intellect and risk taking to create a strong business as well.

In 1997, Steve Jobs returned to his position as CEO of Apple and shocked both the company and the world when he announced in his first speech that Apple would have to reach outside the company to other partners for help in innovation. He gave his people permission to find innovative ideas from anywhere outside the corporate culture, and in the process, took Apple from a sheltered technology organization to a global empire. As a result of this "open innovation," Apple now has more than 200,000 companies worldwide creating Apple-compatible products. Jobs took a big risk that paid off.

Although it's encouraging to read about the successes of a Cook, Roddick, or Jobs, the truth is that for every successful, globally savvy leader, there are dozens more who lack the skills to become the globally savvy leaders their companies need. The supply of these leaders is growing, but demand is moving at exponential speed. And the fastest growth of supply is in countries outside the traditional U.S. and European markets. Large populations of graduate students and young professionals in China, India, and other emerging countries are investing time, money, and attention developing the multilingual skills and the global cultural and business acumen that will allow them to operate effectively in a highly interdependent world.

What does it take to be an effective global leader in today's fast-moving and complex business environment? And how can all leaders prepare to compete in a globalized economy with leaders who are more globally savvy every day? Let's look at nine steps that leaders can take to become globally savvy:

- Develop a global mindset.
- Drive for the broader picture.
- Balance paradoxes.
- Develop cultural self-awareness.
- Develop cultural empathy.
- Lead and develop globally diverse talent.
- Clarify important values.
- Balance money and meaning.
- Become a globally responsible leader.

The rest of this chapter considers these steps within the framework of a model delineated below, organized within the realities of head, heart, and guts.

Whole Leadership

A few years ago my colleagues Peter Cairo and David Dotlich and I wrote a book in which we presented a perspective on leadership based on more than 50 years of collective coaching and training of leaders throughout the world. We called it *Head, Heart and Guts: How the World's Best Companies Develop Complete Leaders.*

The formula is very simple, but it translates well across many cultures and levels of leadership around the world. We have found that the truly effective leaders with whom we have worked have some combination of the following:

- *Head:* They use their intellect to analyze business issues and develop a business vision, purpose, and strategy that allow their companies to be successful in a highly competitive and complex global marketplace.
- *Heart:* They use their emotional intelligence to understand global markets, a diverse workforce, and increasingly demanding stakeholders who present concerns about everything from child labor to carbon footprints to sustainable development.
- *Guts:* They make tough choices based on clear values and use their intuition and experience to guide them in balancing the competing interests of an uncertain world.

We call these leaders "whole leaders." Partial leaders can be successful, but usually only under limited circumstances. Head-dominant leaders can dominate strategy. Heart-dominant leaders can generate the loyalty of workforces around the world. And guts-dominant leaders may be able to make bold moves based on clear beliefs. But when the business agenda changes, which it inevitably does, these partial leaders stumble if they are unable to use other skills to respond to new leadership demands.

Global Complexity, Diversity, and Uncertainty

The last 20 years have brought great evolutions in the world, making it vastly more complex, diverse, and uncertain than the world the leaders of the past had to face.

The world is growing more and more complex. The last 20 years have seen the emergence of China as a major economic power, India's rise as an unparalleled service provider, and Russia beginning to reassert itself as a major political, military, and economic power. Other countries continue to develop new competitive companies on a global scale. The global banking crisis and subsequent recession have rendered business models obsolete in many industries, and leaders throughout the world are grappling with the need for continued growth in revenues and profits while simultaneously facing a shortage of new products and services and the need to reduce costs and gain greater efficiencies along the supply chain. We have seen the banking, automotive, airline, and pharmaceutical industries caught in the throes of new market and global dynamics in ways that leaders and analysts are only beginning to understand. And the business environment and businesses themselves have become so complex that without a good intellect it is practically impossible to be a successful leader.

The world is also becoming more and more diverse. There has been an explosion of cultural and generational diversity among consumers and workers. Oversight by regulatory agencies demanding attention to many new special interests has increased dramatically. And a wide range of regional and global interest groups have emerged demanding responsiveness to their concerns. As a result, leaders today must be able to identify with multiple perspectives while maintaining a focused agenda to sort through the demands being made on them. Being responsive to the forces of a diverse world while guiding an organization through increasingly competitive business shoals requires sensitivity on the one hand and resolute determination on the other—a balance not often found in most leaders.

And finally, the world is becoming more and more uncertain. Many leaders are facing greater uncertainty than ever as the challenges they confront often cannot be solved but must be balanced as unending dilemmas and paradoxes needing constant monitoring and attention. Balancing global needs for integration and coordination to gain economies of scale with local interests for customization and tailoring products to local interests and tastes is just one of a multitude of issues with which a global manager must continually deal. In such cases, vision, values, judgment, and experience become key factors in enabling leaders to find a path in uncertain times.

The Globally Savvy Leader

These two trends—the need for leaders with head, heart, and guts; and the need to deal with an increasingly complex, diverse, and uncertain world—can be organized in a model for the globally savvy leader, as represented in figure 25-1. Globally savvy leaders use their head, heart, and guts to deal with this more complex, diverse, and uncertain world. A leader today must have adequate cerebral intelligence to manage the challenges of a complex world; adequate emotional intelligence to respond to the diverse demands of global consumers, workforces, and stakeholders; and the foundational moral intelligence that allows him or her to make their way through the vagaries of choices that depend on a higher vision and purpose that provides light at the end of some very dark tunnels.

Although it is true that these challenges can be met by leaders who have these three characteristics, it is not quite this simple. A whole leader in the end must use all three components of leadership—head, heart, and guts—to deal with each of the global challenges—complexity, diversity, and uncertainty. For the purposes of this brief discussion, however, let's focus on the use of head for complexity, heart for diversity, and guts for uncertainty. (A fuller examination of how head, heart, and guts each applies to these challenges is developed in *Leading in Times of Crisis: Navigating Complexity, Diversity and Uncertainty to Save Your Business* [Dotlich, Cairo, and Rhinesmith 2009].) Let's look at each of these in more detail.

Figure 25-1. Becoming a Globally Savvy Leader

Use your head to manage complexity.

- Develop a global mindset.
- Drive for the broader picture.
- Balance paradoxes.

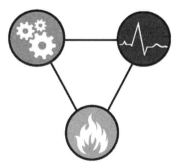

Demonstrate heart to manage diversity.

- Develop cultural self-awareness.
- Develop cultural empathy.
- Lead and develop globally diverse talent.

Act with guts to manage uncertainty.

- Clarify important values.
- Balance money and meaning.
- Become a globally responsible leader.

A Head to Manage Global Complexity

Senior leaders today face an unprecedented number of complex global issues that they must understand, with which they must identify, and to which they must respond. But for many leaders this is uncharted territory. Though having been raised in one country with skills honed on a domestic landscape, many leaders now find themselves facing global competitors, suppliers, regulators, and customers with a dizzying array of concerns and needs. The capacity to respond to this globally complex and interdependent set of variables requires leaders who have a strong intellect and a broad understanding of global social, political, and economic dynamics.

Developing a Global Mindset

The truly savvy global leader today must begin by developing a global mindset. It is estimated that substantially less than 10 percent of adults in the developed world have reached a level of personal development wherein they have a genuinely global outlook. Recent research by Mansour Javidan and others at the Thunderbird School in the well-known GLOBE (Global Leadership and Organizational Behavior Effectiveness) project have provided detailed analysis of a global mindset. They have found that a global mindset requires what they call "intellectual, psychological and social capital." The first of these, intellectual capital, "is all about having knowledge and cognitive ability to deal with complexity, because the global world of business is more complex than the national world of business," says Javidan. This requirement to understand complex global social, economic, and political dynamics and their interaction is key for globally savvy leaders, who must develop strategies that anticipate global trends and reflect a close-up familiarity with different countries. They must develop products and services that will be accepted in wide-ranging markets around the world. And they must analyze the comparative advantages that can be gained in the complex supply chains needed to deliver the best quality to the most profitable market at the lowest cost under constantly changing market and competitive conditions.

Adrian Slywotzsky, a colleague of mine at Oliver Wyman, has written extensively about value migration and its effect on business strategy and organizational design. His basic hypothesis is that as consumer definition of value migrates from quality, to quality plus cost, to quality plus cost plus timely delivery, for example, an organization's design and business strategy must constantly be updated. The complexity that this introduces into global organizations requires leaders who not only understand complex markets but are also able to manage complex organizational designs, systems, and processes to deliver efficient and effective products and services on a global scale.

Driving for the Broader Picture

I have often said that none of us was born global. We were all born local, but those of us who have lived globally can be characterized by a desire to drive for the bigger, broader picture and to understand the context of management challenges as well as the content.

Our organization did a study several years ago of CEO success and failure. We discovered that CEOs who focused on content—that is, being the smartest person in the room with all the answers—failed at a rate three times higher than those CEOs who focused on context—that is, understanding the broader picture and then utilizing the resources in the room to address areas where they did not have specific knowledge or expertise. Understanding the world with a global perspective is a lifelong journey. Global leadership learning never ends, because each year global leaders are faced with changing market conditions, business capacity, and personal conditions that mean that approaches to leadership that worked last year probably will not work this year, and definitely will not work as well in five years. If one is not a lifelong learner, one can never be a globally savvy leader.

Lifelong learning doesn't have to be difficult. For many leaders, developing this perspective can be as simple as asking questions or admitting that more information should be gathered. Bill Weldon, the CEO of Johnson & Johnson, regularly invites feedback by asking his executives "How can I be more effective?" He's also not afraid to say "I don't know" when people ask what should be done. Mark Parker, the CEO of Nike, will often say publicly "I'm still learning." These attitudes foster an environment of curiosity, openness, and willingness to discover that helps create a global perspective.

Balancing Paradoxes

Probably the best example of the complexity that leaders face in global organizations today is the challenge of managing global/local paradoxes. Paradox or dilemma management has become a basic skill of all effective global leaders. Paradox management requires the balancing of conflicting demands—what Joseph Badarocco at Harvard Business School has called choosing between right and right. He maintains that it is comparatively easy to choose between right and wrong, but choosing between right and right requires leaders to know who they are, what they are trying to achieve, and what they have the courage to be known for. This is one reason why global leadership training focuses more on the development of a whole leader with extensive self-awareness than merely on an executive who is knowledgeable about strategy, finance, or organization.

Balancing global and local interests requires a deep understanding of local interests on the ground and around the world. This means that a globally savvy leader must travel. It's that plain and simple—and complex, because such a leader must not only travel but must also learn—and learn fast. He or she must have in place the analytical and conceptual frameworks that allow taking in enormous amounts of information around the world and seeing emerging patterns that can provide insights into how resources will be allocated and where competitive advantage can be gained. You cannot successfully manage a global organization in 45 countries if you have only been to 20 of them.

One study done at the Massachusetts Institute of Technology some years ago discovered that the single most important factor affecting a local organization's willingness to accept the decision of global headquarters was a belief that the leaders making the decision at the global level understood the local conditions in their country. This is not going to happen if leaders do not travel. And this does not even begin to address the interpersonal aspects of trust that need to be developed in most relationship-oriented countries of the world.

Leaders who successfully balance the competing demands of global needs for efficiency and consistency and local needs for differentiation and customization must develop a point of view on a wide range of complex problems. A leadership point of view must be understandable, easily communicable across many cultures, and expressed in ways that are authentic and believable. To achieve this, a leader must be transparent in his or her decision-making process. Transparency in decision making and leadership communication consists of four basic steps:

1. Clearly state the problem or dilemma that one is trying to manage.
2. Describe all alternative solutions that have been offered by various constituents with a stake in the outcome of the decision.
3. Lay out the criteria used in making the final decision.
4. Describe how the problem will be solved or the dilemma will be managed by the choice that has been made.

Those familiar with paradox management will understand that the fourth step refers to the fact that only problems can be solved. Dilemmas or paradoxes cannot. They must be managed over time through a process of balance and understanding of the inevitability of both sides' needs being met. Think of work/family balance as an example. One does not solve the work/family dilemma by choosing one side or the other (at least not if one wants to live with both parts in one's life). Instead, work and family are balanced through an oscillating process that seeks to optimize the needs of both demands over time.

These three skills—developing a global mindset, driving for the broader picture, and balancing paradoxes—are basic for the globally savvy leader in dealing with complexity.

A Heart to Manage Global Diversity

There is perhaps no better example of the challenges of global diversity than the Disney experience in Paris, Tokyo, and Hong Kong. Disney has always stood for happiness, family, service, and fun in its theme parks in the United States. It has developed a wholesome image and an "efficiency with a smile" reputation that has seldom been matched in the entertainment industry. Disney assumed that global expansion would be reasonably easy because a large proportion of the people who visited its theme parks in the United States came from overseas.

But international tourists and local consumers are two different things. In Paris, the French interpreted the new Euro-Disneyland as American imperialism. In contrast, the Japanese and Chinese had no problem with the theme parks themselves, but very different ways of managing their employees and marketing the experiences. Although Disney has survived the challenges of its global expansion, it has learned a great deal about managing global diversity, and in the process has discovered that customs, beliefs, values, and perceptions make an enormous difference in experiencing "family entertainment."

Disney's global expansion reflects a lack of what I call "global emotional intelligence." Daniel Goleman (1995) described emotional intelligence as the need for (1) self-awareness, (2) self-regulation, (3) empathy, and (4) social skills. I have extended each of these components to (1) cultural self-awareness, (2) cultural adjustment, (3) cross-cultural empathy, and (4) cross-cultural leadership.

Developing Cultural Self-Awareness

Cultural self-awareness is very simply the awareness of what it is to be from the country you are from. This includes an understanding of the characteristics, values, and behaviors peculiar to your country, and especially those that may prove helpful or pose problems in working with people from other countries. Cultural self-awareness includes an understanding of the values and prejudices you carry with you. These values and prejudices are not necessarily right or wrong, but they can create difficulties when you operate in radically different cultures.

Cultural self-awareness is hard to develop without spending some time outside your own country. Many companies have learned that until leaders are sent on overseas assignments, it is difficult for them to understand the merits and difficulties of transferring knowledge and skills across borders, cultures, and values. Overseas assignments also help managers better understand different worldviews and appreciate their impact on marketing, advertising, human resource management, product development, strategic planning, and many leadership activities critical for success in a global world.

Jack Welch, the former CEO of General Electric, recognized the need for a deeper understanding of cultural differences. In a speech to GE employees in 2001, he said, "The Jack Welch of the future cannot be me. I spent my entire career in the United States. The next head of General Electric will be somebody who spent time in Bombay, in Hong Kong, in Buenos Aires. We have to send our best and brightest overseas and make sure they have the training that will allow them to be the global leaders who will make GE flourish in the future."

Developing Cultural Empathy and Adjustment

To effectively manage in other countries, leaders need "cultural empathy," or the ability to "place themselves in another person's shoes." But while "cultural empathy" is useful as a general concept, it isn't quite enough when working in different countries around the world. Companies and leaders must be willing to make necessary adjustments that will allow them to hold true to core company values while enabling them to adjust to local environments and remain attractive to the local populations.

McDonald's has achieved a good balance between core values and local traditions as it has expanded worldwide. The company has developed common standards for food preparation, purchasing, and customer service, but it still allows local franchises to establish different menus, product promotions, and pricing.

Arun Sarin, CEO of the Britain-based Vodafone, sums up cultural empathy as it is practiced at Vodafone this way: "Less than 5 percent of our operating profits come from the U.K. We've had to fundamentally redesign this company as a global company. In Germany, we feel German. In Italy, we feel Italian. In Spain, we feel Spanish. In India, we feel Indian. Here, we feel British. But there are [still] common values and common skills we look for." Vodafone has 60,000 employees across 25 countries.

Without empathy *and* the willingness to adjust expectations, it is impossible to truly understand people, to gain their trust, or to provide products and services that respond to their needs. Empathy is also required to understand the strategies of competitors, to negotiate with governments, and to be credible to the people with whom you work day by day.

Leading and Developing Diverse Talent

Cross-cultural leadership, the final challenge of cross-cultural effectiveness, requires the ability to understand and manage diverse talent. Leaders must use their "heart" skills to understand and manage the diversity of talent in an increasingly global organization.

At Novartis, CEO Daniel Vasella, MD, wanted to implement assessment and performance rating tools that would help create a performance culture worldwide. Yet such an ambitious plan meant that he and his leaders would have to confront not only various cultural challenges to the "pay-for-performance" standard but also roadblocks in nations with a history of high inflation or strong union representation. In Turkey, for instance, the company demonstrated to the unions that not only were base salaries already high compared with international competition, but also that employees would have the potential to earn greater wages if allowed to work under the pay-for-performance system. In 2007, the company successfully negotiated with the union to install the pay-for-performance system among all its unionized employees in Turkey.

Even attracting top talent can present challenges. For example, to attract and keep top talent in the United States, Nike demonstrates the career benefits of being at Nike and gives employees rewards and personally challenging career paths. In China, however, recruitment has proved more challenging. Many times, career decisions are a family issue in China, and the decision to join a company is made by the family, not the individual. For Nike, talent strategy in China must rest on a recognition of the importance of family in Chinese culture and how the family influences an individual employee's career.

These three skills—developing cultural self-awareness, developing cultural empathy, and leading and developing diverse talent—are all basic for the globally savvy leader in dealing with diversity.

The Guts to Manage Global Uncertainty

Uncertain times place enormous demands on leaders. It is clear by now, however, that when the world has become so complex that it cannot be understood through analysis and so diverse that all the needs and demands of various stakeholders cannot be met, then some other criteria, other than head and heart, must be used to make decisions and find a way forward. Thus, managing uncertainty through guts is a process whereby leaders learn to understand their values, develop a vision that is based on these values, and create an agenda that is ultimately resonant with broader, globally responsible goals. I call this moral intelligence.

Clarifying Important Values

In January 2009, at the nadir of the global economic recession, I was invited to speak about leadership to the 150 Young Global Leaders at the World Economic Forum in Davos, Switzerland. The World Economic Forum has become the annual gathering of world leaders across many sectors and continents to discuss the state of the world and how people can work cooperatively to meet the challenges of a changing world.

The Young Global Leaders Program was developed some years ago for a select group of the world's leaders under the age of 40 who have had distinguished accomplishments in their fields of endeavor. It is a wide mixture of artists, politicians, royalty, entrepreneurs, business people, leaders of nongovernmental organizations, and others from around the world who come together to share their views on a wide range of global topics. I was asked to speak about leadership and the need for whole global leaders.

After my lunchtime remarks, I spent the rest of the day with the group as they discussed what they felt had led to the economic crisis and the best path forward. There were many ideas discussed and debated, but there emerged a general consensus that the global economic crisis had at some level been created by leaders who had lost their way on values. They felt the current leadership had failed to achieve an intergenerational perspective with a sense of long-term responsibility and commitment to the greater global community. In other words, the global economic system had lost its way due to a lack of moral intelligence on the part of thousands of leaders around the globe who had focused on short-term personal monetary objectives over longer-term global community needs. There was a feeling in the room that it was their generation's responsibility to clarify the important values for leadership in an ecologically fragile and economically interdependent world, and that as leaders, they were obligated to speak out about the need to rebalance the priorities that many global leaders had failed to observe.

Balancing Money and Meaning

At the same time, there was a sense that leaders at all levels of all society had lost touch with the fact that people go to work for meaning more than for money. These leaders shared a belief that for the world to regain its economic balance, it needed to regain its moral balance—a feat that would require leadership to focus once again on those issues that are preeminent for the world's ability to sustain itself not only in the present but also in the future.

Although the room at the World Economic Forum in Davos was filled with a healthy number of millionaires, and even some billionaires, there was an acknowledgment that the global wage structure had gotten out of balance and that the multiples of salary distance between the highest- and lowest-paid workers in organizations in many parts of the world had exceeded any reasonable number. This disparity, combined with a global economic recession, was leading to rising tensions between a super-rich class and a middle class losing its grip on its ability to continue living in a manner that it had achieved with a lot of work, sweat, and tears. The implications of this kind of gap, exacerbated by the poverty of spirit and soul into which it forced people, were felt to be not only politically unsustainable but also at some level immoral.

The need for moral intelligence in the world has been great at many times during history. But today anyone in a position of global leadership needs to be prepared to consider fundamental questions of human collaboration and coexistence, not only for the world today but also for the world of tomorrow.

Becoming a Globally Responsible Leader

In 2004, senior representatives from companies, business schools, and centers for leadership learning formed the Globally Responsible Leadership Initiative as a partnership to define what globally responsive leaders should do (see Globally Responsible Leadership Initiative 2005). They concluded that globally responsible leaders at all organizational levels face four key challenges:

1. They should think and act in a global context.
2. They should broaden their corporate purpose to reflect accountability to society around the globe.
3. They should put ethics at the center of their thoughts, words, and deeds.
4. They should transform their business education to give corporate global responsibility the centrality it deserves.

They described this leadership as globally responsible leadership—"the global exercise of ethical, values-based leadership in pursuit of economic and societal progress and sustainable development." They continued: "It is based on a fundamental understanding of the interconnectedness of the world and recognition of the need for economic, societal and environmental advancement. It also requires the vision and courage to place decision-making and management practices in a global context. . . . Decisions made by globally responsible leaders rely both on their awareness of principles and regulations and on the development of their inner dimension and their personal conscience" (Globally Responsible Leadership Initiative 2005).

This group of leaders recognized that there was no world consensus on what was globally responsible leadership, but they also acknowledged that progress was being made. They wrote that "decisions regarding what [is] globally responsible and 'right' are continuously evolving. There may be no single solution. In such cases, a core aspect of decision making is the degree to which an individual leader has developed his or her own level of consciousness and awareness of both the external global context and the inner dimensions of themselves. This is the starting point that defines the extent to which they are able to determine, with others, the right action in a global setting" (Globally Responsible Leadership Initiative 2005).

They also noted that there was general agreement among those attending the meeting that there were emerging principles for what constituted globally responsible behavior. These principles included

- *Fairness:* justice, fair play, and evenhandedness
- *Freedom:* the right of free expression and accountability

- *Honesty:* integrity, truthfulness, openness, keeping promises
- *Humanity:* recognition of mutual dependence, care for the needy
- *Solidarity:* care for the environment, responsible use of power
- *Tolerance:* respect for what is different
- *Transparency:* open communication and proactive dialogues
- *Sustainable development:* meeting the needs of the present without compromising the ability of future generations to meet their own needs.

The world is moving toward some common standards for ethical behavior. A sampling of 52 different international agreements include the Organization for Economic Cooperation and Development's Guidelines for Multinational Enterprises and its Principles of Corporate Governance, the International Chamber of Commerce's Business Charter for Sustainable Development, and the International Labor Organization's declaration on Fundamental Principles and Rights at Work.

These three skills—clarifying important values, balancing money and meaning, and becoming a globally responsible leader—are all basic for the globally savvy leader in dealing with uncertainty.

Conclusion

Globally savvy leaders will be challenged to rise to a new standard of leadership behavior during the years ahead. With growing complexity, diversity, and uncertainty, only these leaders will be able to respond effectively to the needs of the world. By using their head, heart, and guts, they will, it is hoped, be able to focus on the right issues and have the empathy, compassion, and capacity to achieve their financial and organizational objectives with the delicate balance needed for the world to develop in a collaborative and sustainable manner.

Further Reading

David Dotlich, Peter Cairo, and Stephen Rhinesmith, *Head, Heart and Guts: How the World's Best Companies Develop Complete Leaders.* San Francisco: Jossey-Bass, 2006.
———, *Leading in Times of Crisis: Navigating Complexity, Diversity and Uncertainty to Save Your Business.* San Francisco: Jossey-Bass, 2009.

References

Dotlich, D., P. Cairo, and S. Rhinesmith. 2006. *Head, Heart and Guts: How the World's Best Companies Develop Complete Leaders.* San Francisco: Jossey-Bass.

———. 2009. *Leading in Times of Crisis: Navigating Complexity, Diversity and Uncertainty to Save Your Business.* San Francisco: Jossey-Bass.

Globally Responsible Leadership Initiative. 2005. *A Call for Engagement, 2005.* http://www.grli.org/index.php/component/docman/doc_download/10-grli-call-for-engagement-2005-in-english.

Goleman, D. 1995. *Emotional Intelligence.* New York: Bantam Books.

House, R., M. Javidan, P. Hanges, and P. Dorfman. 2002. Understanding Cultures and Implicit Leadership Theories across the Globe: An Introduction to Project GLOBE. *Journal of World Business* 37, no. 1: 3–10.

Rhinesmith, Stephen. 2003. Global Leadership and Global Emotional Intelligence. In *The Many Facets of Leadership,* ed. Marshall Goldsmith, Vijay Govindarajan, Beverly Kaye, and Albert Vicere. Upper Saddle River, NJ: Financial Times / Prentice Hall.

———. 2005. Learning to Live with Paradox: A Manager's Guide to the Survival of the Most Cooperative. *Mercer Management Journal,* no. 20.

About the Author

Stephen H. Rhinesmith, PhD, is a senior advisor to Oliver Wyman and a founder of Oliver Wyman Leadership Development. He is the founder of Stephen Rhinesmith, Inc., holds a professorship at the Asian Business School, Tianjin University of Finance and Economics and a director of the Nasbitt China Institute where he is conducting research on Chinese leadership mindsets and skills. He is one of the world's leading experts on global leadership and has taught global leadership for Samsung, Mitsubishi, Novartis, Ford, Bank of America, Merck, Avon, Burberry, Grupo Santander, and Saudi Aramco. He is the author or coauthor of 4 books and 30 articles on leadership development and brings to his consulting practice 20 years of senior international management experience. He also served for 10 years as a senior leadership consultant to the World Bank and was U.S. President Ronald Reagan's coordinator for U.S.-Soviet exchanges, with the rank of ambassador.

Chapter 26

Women in the Lead

Marian N. Ruderman

In This Chapter

- The context, choices, and challenges women leaders face in organizations.

- Five themes influencing the development of women leaders.

- Principles of development: assessment, challenge, support, and reward.

- Actions organizations can take to develop women leaders.

Although there have always been women in positions of leadership, the trend has accelerated in recent times. Between 1972 and 2002, the proportion of women employed as managers in the United States grew substantially, from 19.7 to 45.9 percent (*Monthly Labor Review* 2003). Although the U.S. Census Bureau (2007) has modified the "managerial" classification over the years, the data indicate that as of 2006, women made up 50.6 percent of managers and professionals. Overall, women's progress in the last 30 years has been substantial; they have made significant inroads into leadership positions.

As the participation of women in the workplace increases, organizations are asking if they are developing the talent of women leaders effectively. The question is a good one, because until recently leader development was a one-size-fits-all proposition. Women in positions of leadership were expected to act and develop just like men. Yet, although there may be universal principles of leader development, there are also specific nuances and differences that vary with the circumstances, with gender being a significant contextual factor.

This chapter focuses on the unique needs of women leaders by providing a framework for understanding the context and developmental pressures women face. Following a discussion of the framework, the chapter looks at how the basic principles of leader development can be adapted for greater effectiveness for women leaders. Finally, the chapter discusses the costs of underestimating the talents of women.

The Context for Development

The challenges women leaders face are both the same and different as those men face. Like their male counterparts, they must focus on developing as leaders while moving the business forward in the face of threats from the environment. However, for women, this takes place in an environment that isn't fully accepting of all that women have to offer. Even with all the progress women have made, there are still subtle and not-so-subtle differences in the workplace that pose a different landscape for both acting and growing as a leader. For example, let's look at three main differences.

First, women must contend with prejudice and discrimination. Volumes have been written on the ways prejudice has blocked the opportunities of women in organizations and has contributed to a gender pay gap (Blau and Kahn 2006).

Second, prejudice and discrimination create different opportunities for men and women. Thus women have less access to the types of positions that provide opportunities for growth, learning, and exposure to senior executives.

Third, women must navigate organizational cultures that tend to have been shaped by men and as such reinforce men's norms and values. It's not that there is anything inherently wrong with this. The problem is that male values permeate most organizations, making it difficult for women to feel included and excel.

In summing up the differential treatment of women and men, Eagly and Carli (2007) describe the career advancement of women as traveling through a labyrinth where opportunities for direct movement are not apparent but the goal is held out as attainable.

Five Themes Influencing Development

Growth and learning do not happen in a vacuum. To further understand the degree to which common and well-regarded leadership development strategies serve the needs of women leaders, it is important to understand the forces shaping the careers of women leaders. In the book *Standing at the Crossroads: Next Steps for High-Achieving Women,* Ruderman and Ohlott (2002) identified five themes influencing the development of women leaders:

- authenticity
- connection
- agency
- wholeness
- self-clarity.

These themes represent values that tend to be important to women. Similar forces also shape the careers of men, but with different weights and emphases. Let's look briefly at each theme.

Authenticity refers to the degree to which daily actions reflect deeply held values and beliefs. Someone who is authentic has a good understanding of his or her own priorities and emotions and the relationship of these values to everyday behavior. Authenticity is an important influence on development, because adults learn more effectively when they can act in accordance with their own values. Authenticity is of particular relevance to women, because organizations are often structured so that male values and preferences predominate. This clash of subtle preferences can make it more challenging for female leaders to learn and grow.

For example, many women have a relational approach to leadership, emphasizing relationships and the mutual growth from these relationships (Fletcher 1999; Eagly and Johnson 1990). This approach may be at odds with a more macho organization favoring a command-and-control style of leadership. Women who regard a relational approach as their basic modus operandi may find working in more traditional hierarchical and authoritative organizations inauthentic. Authenticity can be a factor for reasons other than gender-related issues. Organizations can change in response to external events, such as the economy or government regulation, and organizations that once felt welcoming and hospitable may become less so. Difficulty being authentic in a large organization is often a reason why women leave corporations and start their own businesses (Scherer, Brodzinski, and Wiebe 1990).

Connection refers to the need to be attached or close to other human beings, whether family, friends, a community, or co-workers. Psychologists refer to this desire to belong to others as one of two fundamental human motives (the other being agency; see below). Traditionally, connection has been seen as the strength of women in society. It is incredibly important to the development of women leaders; several psychologists see the drive for connection and relationships as the central organizing force in women's lives (Jordan and others 1991; Miller and Stiver 1997). This stands in contrast to male-oriented theories of development, which emphasize independence and autonomy at the expense of relationships. Women leaders in organizations may have concerns about the not-getting-rich-enough opportunities for connection in their organizations or working in environments that deemphasize the importance of feelings of attachment, belonging, and empowerment in favor of independence and action. Development is rougher if a primary source of meaning is undervalued by the organization.

Agency is the other fundamental motivating force for humans. Agency refers to the desire to control one's own destiny and act on one's behalf. It literally means to be "an agent" on one's environment. Traditionally, agentic behavior has been seen as reflecting masculine qualities. Positions of leadership certainly require a high level of agentic behavior. However, sometimes when women employ the behavior of agency (for example, assertiveness, self-promotion, and questioning the actions of others), they are seen as coming on too strong. Morrison, White, and Van Velsor (1987) have pointed that there is a "narrow band" of acceptable behavior for women. Women who engage in agentic behavior can be seen as coming on too strong because they are acting counter to stereotype. Women who don't sufficiently engage in agentic behavior are seen as being too weak. The bandwidth for acceptable action is rather narrow and limits the steps women can take without violating gender stereotypes. Eagly and Carli (2007) have described the challenge of managing agency in relation to connection as a double bind: Women who are too agentic are criticized for lacking empathy, and women who are focused on connection are described as too soft.

According to Miller and Stiver (1997), the key to effectiveness for both genders is to be agentic without sacrificing the quality of connections. Effective behavior in organizations requires both acknowledging interdependence with others and acting on one's own behalf.

The development of women leaders is also influenced by a desire to feel *whole* or complete as a human being. According to Still (1993), a driving life force for women is the need to integrate various life roles. Women (as well as men) want a life that encompasses multiple roles—roles that allow for the expression of both connection and agency. The demands of the business world and the insensitivity of the business world to caregiving and relational needs make this hard to achieve. Women leaders strive to fulfill both professional and personal desires. The prevailing norms of organizations are obviously to prioritize professional needs, which makes it difficult to address needs in the private sphere of life. Although organizations deter women from having a whole life, wholeness is beneficial for both the organization and the individual (Ruderman and others 2002). Organizations struggle with how to help managers manage the border between work and personal life. Leaders (both male and female) must struggle to develop within an organizational context that hasn't quite figured out how to encourage leaders to have a whole life. Organizations still have vestiges of the days when men were breadwinners and women were homemakers.

A final theme in the development of women has to do with the desire for *self-clarity*. Women have a need to understand themselves within the context of the world in which they operate. They want to know more than just how others see their strengths and weaknesses. They want to understand themselves against the backdrop of an organization that may treat men and women differently. Because stereotypes influence perceptions of behavior, it may be difficult for a woman to get an effective reading from others as to how others see her. This is especially true in an organization where women are scarce and stereotypes are prevalent. It can also be more difficult for women to get instrumental feedback in male-dominated parts of organizations because gender role issues can get in the way of honest feedback. Learning and growth can be compromised because misperceptions cloud the environment.

Together, these five themes form the landscape in which women leaders develop. Understanding the suitability of common leader development strategies requires consideration of these themes. The development of leaders is not context-free. These forces influence how the primary strategies of leader development—assessment, challenge, and support (Van Velsor and McCauley 2004) should be enacted. Women are now a force in the managerial ranks. Advancement to the executive level requires leader development practices that take the nuanced environment of women leaders into account. The next section examines three primary drivers of leader development in light of the forces framing the lives of women leaders.

Drivers of Leader Development

Assessment is a major driver of leader development. Assessment can take many forms:

- It can be informally delivered in the course of work.
- It can be a formal 360-degree evaluation.
- It can be an annual performance evaluation.
- It can consist of reports from consultants, customer satisfaction survey data, or even comments from family.

Assessment is important because it provides feedback as to what a leader is doing well, or not so well. It both clarifies what leaders need to learn to be more effective and can provide the motivation to learn.

When considering assessment in light of gender differences, there are three main issues to consider. The first issue has to do with the suitability of formal assessment procedures. Many organizations purchase off-the-shelf assessments. A key consideration in using these is to examine the validity of the assessment for use with both genders. If leaders are going to act on the information from the assessment, it is critical that its validity be established for the population using it. In terms of gender, this means that formal assessments must have evidence for validity from both men and women. One concern is that some instruments have been validated with primarily male leaders.

A second issue has to do with content of the assessment. Developmental assessments can clarify areas that leaders can explore to promote their growth. This means that assessments should be relevant to development. Obviously, most performance-related and organization-specific assessments are highly relevant to development. However, there is likely to be other content that is relevant as well. For example, a self-assessment (see figure 26-1) on the five themes influencing the development of women leaders is useful for planning developmental actions. Understanding the differential salience of the themes can help in developmental goal setting and career planning.

Another content-related area might be an assessment looking at management of the boundary between work and personal life. Women in managerial roles are often derailed in their careers because of shifting priorities between different life roles (Eagly and Carli 2007). There are many different ways in which women (and men) attend to this boundary. Feedback on preferred styles and the impact of those styles on stakeholders could be very useful in clarifying self-understanding and establishing goals.

A third assessment-related issue has to do with the quality of informal feedback to women. Large numbers of women report being on a lonely journey in the upper echelons of organizations. Isolation can be a consequence of being outnumbered. Informal assessment can be limited if women leaders don't have access to the same networks of colleagues as men. The differences are subtle and can put women in the position of getting less or a different quality of feedback than their male counterparts. People take into account their own comfort level when providing feedback and are less likely to reach out to those to whom they may feel dissimilar.

Challenge is another powerful driver of development. Challenge can come in many forms; for example, it can take the shape of a high-stakes assignment, significant questions from a coach, or a training activity. Challenge provides both the motivation and the opportunity to learn.

Challenging jobs promote growth for leaders around the globe. Through studies conducted in different countries and at different times, challenging assignments have been identified as the tour de force of development (Yip and Wilson 2010). There are, however, some noticeable differences in how challenges occur for men and women. Significantly, women don't always get the same access to challenging assignments as men. Generally, compared

Figure 26-1. Sample Checklist and Scoring Sheet: Clarifying Your Goals for Development—a Tool for Leaders

The following is a list of possible goals for development. Skim the entire list and select the 15 items that seem most relevant to you. Place a check mark next to those items.

- ☐ 1. Dropping the mask I've been putting on at work.
- ☐ 2. Learning from experience, including mistakes.
- ☐ 3. Placing greater importance on friendships.
- ☐ 4. Being more honest with myself.
- ☐ 5. Learning to say "no."
- ☐ 6. Taking a calculated risk.
- ☐ 7. Taking more time for myself.
- ☐ 8. Understanding my organization and how I fit in.
- ☐ 9. Overcoming barriers in my way.
- ☐ 10. Finding what's missing in my life.
- ☐ 11. Further developing my networks.
- ☐ 12. Getting "unstuck."
- ☐ 13. Finding a mentor or mentors.
- ☐ 14. Clarifying my values and needs.
- ☐ 15. Having good sounding boards.
- ☐ 16. Taking charge of my life.
- ☐ 17. Feeling more whole.
- ☐ 18. Attaining greater self-understanding.
- ☐ 19. Being part of a congenial group.
- ☐ 20. Using my power more effectively.
- ☐ 21. Finding more time for my loved ones.
- ☐ 22. Developing my own definition of success.
- ☐ 23. Developing my relationships with co-workers.
- ☐ 24. Identifying patterns in my life.
- ☐ 25. Attaining at least one closer and deeper relationship.
- ☐ 26. Using feedback more effectively.
- ☐ 27. Not taking difficult work situations so personally.
- ☐ 28. Being more effective while remaining true to my values.
- ☐ 29. Becoming more influential.
- ☐ 30. Accepting inevitable conflicts in my life.
- ☐ 31. Making my dreams a reality.
- ☐ 32. Trusting my own judgment.
- ☐ 33. Freeing myself from the tyranny of perfection.
- ☐ 34. Finding my own leadership style.
- ☐ 35. Being a better advocate for myself.

(continued on next page)

Figure 26-1. Sample Checklist and Scoring Sheet: Clarifying Your Goals for Development—a Tool for Leaders (continued)

Scoring Sheet

Transfer your check marks to the appropriate lines below. Note that items are not in numerical order. Total the number of check marks in each section to obtain your score on each theme. Scores can range from 0 to 7. The higher your score, the more prominent that theme is in your developmental goals. You may see a couple of themes emerge clearly, or you may find relevance to your goals spread across the themes.

Authenticity		Self-Clarity	
1.	_____	2.	_____
4.	_____	8.	_____
22.	_____	14.	_____
28.	_____	18.	_____
31.	_____	24.	_____
32.	_____	26.	_____
34.	_____	27.	_____
Total	_____	**Total**	_____

Connection		Wholeness	
3.	_____	5.	_____
11.	_____	7.	_____
13.	_____	10.	_____
15.	_____	17.	_____
19.	_____	21.	_____
23.	_____	30.	_____
25.	_____	33.	_____
Total	_____	**Total**	_____

Agency	
6.	_____
9.	_____
12.	_____
16.	_____
20.	_____
29.	_____
35.	_____
Total	_____

with men at the same level of management, women experience their jobs as less visible and as having less of an impact on the organization (Ohlott, Ruderman, and McCauley 1994; Lyness and Thompson 1997). Men and women may be promoted to the same level in organizations, but this data suggests that men are offered more challenging learning opportunities. Even when women and men have the same title, they may have different exposure to developmental challenges.

In addition to the subtle difference in the quality of challenges men and women experience, women also face additional challenges. These challenges could stem from the stereotypes of women in organizations; the experience of isolation; and the "second shift" of work women must often face after a day at the office, requiring them to take primary responsibility for the home (Hochschild 1989). Bell and Nkomo (2001) have pointed that these extra demands can be especially significant for African American women leaders who have additional role-modeling responsibilities toward the African American community or are asked by the organization to be a spokesperson for diversity initiatives.

Organizations serious about the development of women leaders can find meaningful job assignments a potent force. However, using job challenges to encourage development is not a simple and straightforward activity. It can be difficult to find the right level of challenge for any individual. Ryan and Haslam (2004) point out that women sometimes get too much challenge and are put into precarious positions with the qualities of a glass cliff. They may be given risky assignments that others don't want to take. Other organizations, however, may err on the side of too little challenge. Fearing that women may fail, executives may be more cautious about promoting them (Ruderman, Ohlott, and Kram 1995) and provide them with promotions of smaller scope. If organizations want to use challenge for development for both men and women, it is important that they look at how they use job challenges and assess the distribution of key assignments across gender. Using a systematic approach to understanding and classifying assignment-based challenges can be useful. McCauley (2006) offers excellent ideas about development in workplace assignments.

Organizations can amplify the impact of challenge as a developmental lever by providing support to the managers who take on key challenges. There are many forms of support that can help leaders develop effectively. Support is a key ingredient in any recipe for development. Support can come from mentors, sponsors, bosses, peers, coaches, friends, networks, and families. Supportive others can provide advice, affirmation, information, feedback, perspective, stress relief, and fun. Supportive alliances can help leaders draw wisdom from challenging situations and can help leaders figure out how to address evaluative information. Support both works directly toward development and indirectly by lubricating the impact of assessment and challenge.

Gender can have an impact on supportive processes in that there may be fewer sources of support for women than men in organizations. For example, because there are fewer women in the executive suite than men, there are fewer role models available for aspiring female executives. Role models can provide a source of tacit information about how to behave in an organization. They influence the socialization process. To the extent that they are less available, it makes it difficult for women to get this type of information.

Gender also introduces some problematic dynamics into the availability of mentoring relationships for women. Mentoring provides mentees with power and resources. Although men and women report similar rates of having mentors, they report different types of experiences, especially with male mentors. Given that most executive positions are still held by men, cross-gender mentoring relationships are important for women. However, people in these relationships must deal with the extra stress of worrying that others may misconstrue the relationship as sexual, adding a different dynamic to the relationship.

Like role models and mentoring relationships, network relationships can be beneficial for leader development. Networks can provide support for managers who share similar issues and challenges and provide a channel for information and advice. Critical organizational information can often be shared informally through networks. A developmental consideration, however, is that women often report feeling excluded from informal networks. According to Catalyst (2004), 46 percent of women but only 18 percent of men feel excluded from informal networks. This lack of access restricts the information and opportunities available to women.

There are numerous steps that women can take to increase their access to supportive relationships. There are a large number of women's networking organizations available extraorganizationally through professional and regional women's associations. Although these networks can't provide organization-specific information, they can be an invaluable source of advice, encouragement, and role models more generally. Many organizations also offer formal mentoring programs as a way of supplementing informal mentoring relationships. These relationships can provide many forms of support, and the formal nature legitimizes the relationship in the eyes of others. Further, there is also value in women becoming mentors. Serving in a mentoring relationship provides many important benefits (Kram and Hall 1996; Gentry, Weber and Sadri 2008) to the mentor and helps to address needs for connection to others. Finally, formal coaching is another interaction that can help women develop. The one-to-one nature of coaching allows the unique needs of the individual to be taken into account.

Assessment, challenge, and support are the cornerstones of development practices in general. They are powerful with many different populations in different countries. At this point in time, however, it is important that leadership developers with a unique interest in women leaders consider a fourth driver of development: rewards. Rewards in organizations come in many forms—promotions, wages, praise, titles, and the like. It is basic psychology that rewards can have an impact on learning because they reinforce new or learned behaviors. The many comparisons of men and women show that even when men and women have equivalent positions, women still lag men in terms of rewards (Blau and Kahn 2006). Because rewards of all sorts make people feel good by enhancing esteem, it is important that those concerned pay attention to this differential. This may not be a problem in all organizations, but all organizations should be on the lookout for it. Differences in wages, benefits, titles, and the like can dramatically influence the development process by introducing gender disparities into the reinforcement process.

What Organizations Should Do

The principles of assessment, challenge, and support promote and sustain the development of both men and women. The reality is that most tools of development have been tailored to the needs of men given the historical dominance of men in organizations. This means that tools based on these principles need some fine-tuning and adjustment to better address the needs of women leaders. The content, form, and availability of these forces require attention. There is subtle and unconscious discrimination. Companies can address this by modifying developmental practices based on these principles to ensure that they are accessible to all and appropriately applied. Some basic steps include

- Provide structured assessment tools that include content relevant to the developmental concerns of women and that have validity evidence.
- Help decision makers understand and create appropriately challenging assignments for all employees.
- Educate all in leadership positions on how to initiate and develop relationships with people who are different from themselves. Utilize a variety of types of developmental relationships. Don't simply rely on informal mentoring.
- Create networks for women so as to deal with isolation and to create opportunities for informal assessment.
- Be vigilant about addressing discriminatory practices.

In today's competitive environment, organizations can't really afford to overlook the impact of gender. Making the best use of the workforce requires understanding that people are different. Standard developmental processes don't work the same way for everyone. Gender dynamics influence the availability and quality of many career-shaping experiences. Disregarding gender in leader development means that organizations could lose out on fundamental sources of talent. Catalyst (2007), a nonprofit advocacy organization for women, has documented that organizations with greater numbers of women in senior management and board roles actually perform better financially than those with fewer women. With today's proliferating global competition and rapidly changing world, organizations cannot afford to overlook ways to enhance the development of women leaders. In the coming years, women are poised to make important contributions; education and experience levels have increased. Widening the pool of candidates is the best way for organizations to increase their competitive stance.

Further Reading

Alice Hendrickson Eagly and Linda Lorene Carli, *Through the Labyrinth: The Truth about How Women Become Leaders.* Boston: Harvard Business School Press, 2007.

Cynthia D. McCauley, *Developmental Assignments: Creating Learning Opportunities without Changing Jobs.* Greensboro, NC: Center for Creative Leadership, 2006.

Marian N. Ruderman and Patricia J. Ohlott, *Standing at the Crossroads: Next Steps for High-Achieving Women.* San Francisco: Jossey-Bass, 2002.

Claire Shipman and Katty Kay, *Womenomics: Write Your Own Rules for Success.* New York: HarperCollins, 2009.

References

Bell, E. L., and S. M. Nkomo. 2001. *Our Separate Ways: Black and White Women and the Struggle for Professional Identity.* Boston: Harvard Business School Press.

Blau, F. D., and L. M. Kahn. 2006. The U.S. Gender Pay Gap in the 1990s: Slowing Convergence. *Industrial and Labor Relations Review* 60, no 1: 45–66.

Catalyst. 2004. Women and Men in U.S. Corporate Leadership: Same Workplace, Different Realities? New York: Catalyst. http://www.catalyst.org/publication/145/women-and-men-in-us-corporate-leadership-same-workplace-different-realities.

———. 2007. The Bottom Line: Corporate Performance and Women's Representation on Boards. New York: Catalyst. http://www.catalyst.org/file/139/bottom percent20line percent202.pdf.

Eagly, A. H., and L. L. Carli. 2007. *Through the Labyrinth: The Truth about How Women Become Leaders.* Boston: Harvard Business School Press.

Eagly, A. H., and B. Johnson. 1990. Gender and Leadership Style: A Meta-Analysis. *Psychological Bulletin* 108, no. 2: 233–236.

Fletcher, J. K. 1999. *Disappearing Acts: Gender, Power and Relational Practice at Work.* Cambridge, MA: MIT Press.

Gentry, W. A., T. J. Weber, and G. Sadri. 2008. Examining Career-Related Mentoring and Managerial Performance across Cultures: A Multilevel Analysis. *Journal of Vocational Behavior* 72, no. 20: 241–253.

Hochschild, A., with A. Machung. 1989. *The Second Shift.* New York: Avon Books.

Jordan, J., A. G. Kaplan, J. B. Miller, I. P. Stiver, and J. L. Surrey. 1991. *Women's Growth in Connection: Writings from the Stone Center.* New York: Guilford Press.

Kram, K. E., and D. T. Hall. 1996. Mentoring in a Context of Diversity and Turbulence. In *Managing Diversity: Human Resource Strategies for Transforming the Workplace,* ed. E. E. Kossek and S. Lobel. Cambridge, MA: Blackwell.

Lyness, K. S., and D. E. Thompson. 1997. Above the Glass Ceiling? A Comparison of Matched Samples of Female and Male Executives. *Journal of Applied Psychology* 82: 359–375.

McCauley, C. D. 2006. *Developmental Assignments: Creating Learning Opportunities without Changing Jobs.* Greensboro, NC: Center for Creative Leadership.

Miller, J. B., and I. P. Stiver. 1997. *The Healing Connection: How Women Form Relationships in Therapy and in Life.* Boston: Beacon Press.

Monthly Labor Review. 2003. Women at Work: A Visual Essay. October, 45–50.

Morrison, A. M., R. P. White, and E. Van Velsor. 1987. *Breaking the Glass Ceiling.* Reading, MA: Addison-Wesley.

Ohlott, P. J., M. N. Ruderman, and C. D. McCauley. 1994. Gender Differences in Managers' Developmental Job Experiences. *Academy of Management Journal* 37, no. 1: 46–68.

Ruderman, M. N., and P. J. Ohlott. 2002. *Standing at the Crossroads: Next Steps for High-Achieving Women.* San Francisco: Jossey-Bass.

Ruderman, M. N., P. J. Ohlott, and K. E. Kram. 1995. Promotion Decisions as a Diversity Practice. *Journal of Management Development* 4, no. 2: 6–23.

Ruderman, M. N., P. J. Ohlott, K. Panzer, and S. N. King. 2002. Benefits of Multiple Roles for Managerial Women. *Academy of Management Journal* 45, no. 2: 369–386.

Ryan, M., and A. Haslam. 2004. The Glass Cliff: Evidence That Women Are Over-Represented in Precarious Leadership Positions. *British Journal of Management* 15: 1–10.

Scherer, R. F., J. D. Brodzinski, and F. A. Wiebe. 1990. Entrepreneur Career Selection and Gender: A Socialization Approach. *Journal of Small Business Management* 28, no. 2: 37–45.

Still, L. B. 1993. *Where to from Here? The Managerial Woman in Transition.* Sydney: Business and Professional Publishing.

U.S. Census Bureau. 2007. *Statistical Abstract of the United States: 2008,* 127th ed. Washington, DC: U.S. Government Printing Office.

Van Velsor, E., and C. D. McCauley. 2004. Introduction: Our View of Leadership Development. In *The Center for Creative Leadership Handbook of Leadership Development,* ed. C. D. McCauley and E. Van Velsor. San Francisco: Jossey-Bass.

Yip, J., and M. Wilson. 2010. Learning from Experience. In *The Center for Creative Leadership Handbook of Leadership Development,* ed. E. Van Velsor, C. D. McCauley, and M. N. Ruderman. San Francisco: Jossey-Bass.

About the Author

Marian N. Ruderman is a senior fellow and director of research for the Americas, Europe, the Middle East, and Africa at the Center for Creative Leadership. She has coauthored dozens of articles and book chapters on leadership. Her work has been published in the *Journal of Applied Psychology* and *Academy of Management Journal,* among many others. In addition, the popular press has reported widely on her work. Her books include *Standing at the Crossroads: Next Steps for High-Achieving Women* (coauthored with Patricia Ohlott); *Diversity in Work Teams: Research Paradigms for a Changing Workplace* (coedited with Susan Jackson); and *The Center for Creative Leadership Handbook of Leadership Development*, 3rd edition (coedited with Ellen Van Velsor and Cynthia McCauley).

⤲ **Chapter 27**

Leading Across Generations

Joanne G. Sujansky

--------------------------------- **In This Chapter** ---------------------------------

▪ Recognize and address the distinctive needs of each generation.

▪ Foster effective communication across generations.

▪ Employ strategies for leading, developing, and coaching multiple generations.

▪ Resolve conflict and build cross-generational teams.

For the first time in history, there are four generations sharing the workplace. These age groups—the matures (sometimes called traditionalists), baby boomers, Generation Xers, and millennials—each bring different experiences, talents, and viewpoints to the job. As a result, the task of leading a multigenerational workforce is rapidly becoming a challenge for leaders around the world. However, armed with an understanding of these differences and equipped with strategies for dealing with the unique needs of each generation, a savvy leader can forge an effective and dynamic team of employees.

A Team in Turmoil

A critical deadline was looming at Claremore Laboratories, and Cal Woodson was becoming worried. As vice president and director of business development, he was responsible for overall account management, and one of the company's most important clients was expecting the delivery of a new product line within two weeks. But after making the rounds of various departments, it was becoming clear to Cal that they were in danger of missing that delivery date.

Claremore Laboratories produces and packages private label nutritional supplements. Its typical clients are medical professionals (such as chiropractors), clinics, natural pharmacies, nutritionists, and other practitioners that provide customers with vitamins and nutritionals. Claremore was one of the leaders in its field because it provided a complete range of client services, from research and development through packaging and marketing.

The management of the privately held firm also took pride in outstanding customer service, which had garnered the 20-year-old company numerous industry awards. Cal knew that his bosses wouldn't be happy if his team missed this particular deadline. He even feared that his job could be in jeopardy.

Fortunately, there was still time enough to make the deadline, provided every department pulled together. Cal started making the rounds and speaking with the heads of each department. But everywhere he went, it seemed the story was the same. Each department supervisor complained that it was *another* department, which simply didn't understand his or her problems, that was causing the holdup.

Nicole, who was in her mid-20s, was the supervisor of the graphics department. Her staff designed the custom labels and packages for the new product line, but she complained to Cal that they couldn't very well execute a set of designs without specifications for containers and labels, which came from the purchasing department. Like her staff, she could be counted on to punch out promptly at the end of the eight-hour shift Monday through Friday.

The director of the purchasing department was a 37-year-old veteran employee who worked his way up through the ranks. He explained to Cal that they were still shopping for the best prices on blank containers, boxes, and other packaging components. Recent increases in raw materials costs had cut into company profits, and his number one goal for the year was to find ways to lower the cost of materials. In fact, his performance review depended upon it.

The 64-year-old head of the legal department, Monica, along with her experienced staff of two, were responsible for legally verifying all product claims, disclaimers, and warnings on labels and packaging. She complained to Cal that she and her staff were overwhelmed with new product lines for numerous clients and were proceeding as fast as humanly possible. After all, a careless mistake or oversight could prove to be disaster for Claremore Laboratories.

Thom was a 48-year-old dynamo who ran the sales department. His problem, which he patiently explained to Cal, was that he had to coordinate all proofs for product packaging, labeling, and marketing through the client for final approval. He was frustrated that proofs and comps were slow to come in from the graphics and legal departments, making it difficult to get feedback from the client. He was particularly upset with the graphics department, which he perceived as a bunch of kids with little to no work ethic. The customer was "king" in his book, and his staff did whatever it took to keep customers happy.

When Cal got back to his office and reflected on the problems that were plaguing his project, he began to feel as though he was in the middle of a nightmare. Not only was there little coordination among these departments, it was almost as if they were speaking different languages. If nothing else, Cal realized that the department heads were operating with seemingly different perceptions and priorities. How could he break the bottleneck and get the project moving smoothly to completion on time?

Cal's problems aren't unique. As mentioned above, for the first time ever in history, there are four generations crowding the workplace. Their differing experiences, unique talents, and distinctive viewpoints make managing a multigenerational workforce the challenge of our era.

A multigenerational workforce is composed, by definition, of individuals who are at varying career stages. With one generation preparing to exit the world of work and another generation just entering it, the middle generations are juggling issues with job stability, career growth, and work/life balance.

For leaders, it may seem like a potential quagmire filled with traps and dilemmas. But in reality, it's an opportunity to build a dynamic team of workers that brings an unparalleled breadth of experience and talents to the workplace.

To use a sports analogy, it's much like coaching a team that's a blend of talented rookies, reliable superstars, and wise veterans. The coaches who can coax the best performances from these teammates stand the best chances of coaching a winner. But first we need to understand some of the differences and strengths of the team.

Crossing the Generational Divide

The totality of our experiences as human beings is what shapes us as individuals. Factors such as our gender, socioeconomic level, ethnicity, and education all play a part in how we see and relate to the world around us. But one of the most distinguishing factors that shape our perceptions (and behaviors) is connected to *when* we were born and grew up.

These experiences that we shared with our peers while growing up in a particular era—historical, cultural, and social—have shaped our viewpoints and perceptions in ways both subtle and profound. The author of the seminal work in this area, Morris Massey, wrote, "What you are is where you were when." He contrasted the differences between generations by focusing on the significant emotional events that influenced them during their "coming of age years" (Massey 1979).

It's important to at least touch on the broader distinguishing characteristics of the cultural differences among the four generations now in the workplace. This will give us a better handle on how to manage the four generations. And these generations—matures, boomers, Generation Xers, and millennials (also called Generation Y)—can each pose different challenges for those charged with leading and managing them.

The mature, or silent, generation, born between 1925 and 1945, displays a loyalty to the company that places duty before pleasure. These are the folks who survived the Great Depression and fought World War II. They are often seen as traditionalists for whom nothing is impossible. They would prefer to retire after 35 years of service with the same organization.

Baby boomers, born between 1946 and 1964, have been described as workaholics who have a love/hate relationship with authority. They have been known for being both idealistic and optimistic, particularly with their goal of changing the world of work. They exhibited endurance for long hours at work. Many expected to retire from the organization that first hired them.

Gen Xers, the MTV generation, came into the world between 1965 and 1979. They often demonstrate independence and a strong orientation toward results but are also sometimes known for their skepticism. They are above all pragmatic workers who like to get things done.

The millennials (or Generation Y) were born between 1980 and 1999. They grew up in a time of economic expansion and unprecedented prosperity and, until recently, they have not experienced a downturn. This generation has perhaps seen more "where were you" events at an earlier age than most members of previous generations, such as the Oklahoma City bombing, the Columbine shootings, and the September 11, 2001, terrorist attacks. Exposure to these events through 24-hour media has brought the world to them instantaneously. This is a techno-savvy generation for whom multitasking is second nature. They are supremely confident and possess high expectations for their own success.

Without overgeneralizing, it's easy to see why individuals from different generations might approach a task or a problem with contrasting perceptions and expectations. The savvy leader must take these differences into consideration when developing strategies to lead and manage a workforce composed of four different generations.

The Leadership Juggling Act

As leaders, we can't afford to forget that we are invariably leading individuals, not archetypes. Our employees, no matter what their generation, still possess unique talents, individual needs, and varying weaknesses.

Though it's important to consider how their generation may be influencing their thoughts and actions, we need to remember that they're not all cut from the same generational cloth. We also need to take into consideration their individual career aspirations, intelligence, training, skills, and desires.

To lead a multigenerational workforce, traditional and widely accepted theories of motivation and performance management have as much relevance as our understanding of an individual's history. Besides, good management is simply good management, whether your employees are matures, boomers, Gen Xers, or millennials. If anything, our reflecting on generational differences underscores just how important sound management techniques are to our organizational success. And the payoff for building a diverse team is always the same: shared success along with personal satisfaction, whether that satisfaction belongs to the leader, the employee or, ideally, both.

Generations in the Workplace

What does each of the generations expect from a job? How do they characteristically adapt themselves to the organization? What motivates them? What frustrates them? These are just a few of the questions that can tell us a lot about how to lead across different generations.

With the growing presence of millennials in the worldwide workplace—by 2014, there will be more than 58 million millennials employed in various U.S. organizations alone—many of the differences and contrasts between them and previous generations are becoming more apparent.

The World War II generation, the matures, grew up in an era when authority was respected. The boss was "the boss," and he (for it was usually a he) was seldom questioned. As employees, the matures are thought of as hard working, dependable, and loyal. For them the workplace should be well structured, with clear rules for all.

The generation that followed, the baby boomers, came of age in an era of social unrest and are often thought of as challenging authority, although most weren't involved in marches or protests. But upon entering the workplace, the boomers did indeed challenge many of the rules and looked for new ways to get things done. This generation saw employment as an opportunity for self-fulfillment and accomplishment. They expected to play a meaningful role in the workplace, and they worked long and hard to attain this role.

The first group of boomer offspring was the Gen Xers. They came along at a time when the economy was expanding and grew up in an era that saw the beginnings of the technology boom. But they arrived in the workplace during an economic downturn and saw many of their parents lose jobs and careers to downsizing and restructuring. Instead of following the all-or-nothing approach to career management, they sought to achieve a greater work/life balance. Some have seen in this generation a tendency toward cynicism, but they are in reality just pragmatic.

The second group of boomer offspring—the millennials—has its own workplace expectations. (Remember, boomers spanned a lot of childbearing years.) Millennials, too, saw many of their parents lose jobs and, like the Gen Xers before them, had to deal with an escalating divorce rate. But they received lots of positive feedback from their parents and teachers. They're goal-focused, anxious to learn, and skilled at collaboration. As they enter the workforce, they'll be seeking opportunities commensurate with their image of themselves (economic opportunities notwithstanding).

Leaders need to begin adapting their techniques and approaches to managing each generation somewhat differently when it comes to learning, development and coaching, communication, and feedback and team building.

Learning, Development, and Coaching Across the Generations

One of the most critical tasks for every manager is to make sure that his or her employees are appropriately trained and developed for their current and future roles. Effective learning and development also requires that managers coach employees to keep improving their performance, which is really the principle means by which most organizations achieve their goals. But over the years, the methods and strategies managers have used to train and coach their people have been evolving.

The concept of training and coaching employees for improved performance became popular around the World War II era. The need for systematic skills training became obvious as thousands of new employees (including women) began joining the workforce for the first time. That's when the role of supervisor began to evolve from the concept of "boss" to teacher. But, over the years, it also became apparent that to be effective, supervisors had to tailor their training to the unique needs of each individual. Thus the supervisor's role has evolved to that of coach.

Today, with multiple generations working side by side, it's more critical than ever for leaders to tailor their approach to the unique needs of each individual:

- *Matures:* Members of this generation are obviously experienced and may only require training in new procedures or technologies. Traditionally, this group tends to see the value of learning and development in terms of how it benefits the organization, so supervisors should explain to matures how learning new skills contributes to the success of the company.

- *Boomers:* By the time they began joining the workforce in the late 1960s, formalized training had become commonplace. Boomers tend to see training and development as good for organizational goals but also critical to their career advancement.

- *Gen Xers:* Technology was becoming widespread when Gen Xers began entering the workforce, so their familiarity with computers and cell phones gave them a bit of a head start. Gen Xers tend to see training first as a means for enhancing their skills and marketability, in addition to the benefits it provides to the organization.

- *Millennials:* The members of the youngest generation are new to organizational life, so they may not know what they don't know. But with their high confidence level and technological savvy, they should be able to learn quickly. Like the generation before them, they will most likely see training as a way to enhance their inevitable career advancement but may also need to be shown how their growth fits into the corporate mission. Their technological savvy presents great "reverse mentoring" opportunities for millennials to coach other generations on technological advances in addition to their being mentored by more tenured managers in leadership development.

The millennial generation may also challenge leaders in one other way. Corporate learning and development professionals have always been on the leading edge of educational technology, including multimedia, e-learning, avatars, wikis, and Internet-based conferencing. But millennial employees will no doubt push the technological envelope even further. They're so quick to adapt to new technologies that they've been driving the fastest-growing technologies on the web—social networking. Facebook, MySpace, Twitter, and other social networking innovations are already being integrated into business operations by today's more leading-edge organizations, so leaders looking to expand their employees' skills and knowledge need to leverage these tools.

However, training alone isn't usually sufficient to help individuals and organizations achieve their goals. Leaders also need to give feedback that can help employees overcome deficiencies, minimize mistakes, and generally improve performance. Individuals may be motivated by many different needs, but the common denominator across the generations is success. Show your employees how they can become more successful and they will become highly motivated. The only differences between the generations may be in how each group tends to define success.

Despite some of the differences in how you may approach each generation to provide coaching and feedback, the fundamentals of giving feedback always remain the same:

- *Set clear, measurable, achievable goals:* To improve performance, you must make sure the employee understands exactly what needs to be done, and you need to set a target date for accomplishment. At the same time, be sure to set a concrete standard for how you both will agree that the goals have been achieved (measurement).

- *Connect your goals to your organization's mission:* The members of each generation are exactly alike in one important way: They each need to see how their efforts contribute to the big picture. It's surprising how easily people can lose sight of your common goals and the organization's mission. When they understand their role in the organization's success, it raises their accountability.

- *Provide recognition and reinforcement on met goals:* Never assume your employees understand when they've been successful. Even if they know they've succeeded, they still need to hear it from you.

- *Provide corrective feedback on missed goals and problem behaviors:* No one likes to be the bearer of bad news, but when your employees fall short on performance, it's your job to let them know that. This is the secret to turning problems into good performance. It starts with well-thought-out feedback.

- *Set expectations for continuing success:* The best way for your employees to keep improving is to understand that you and the organization are expecting improvement. Set the standards for them and they will keep striving to improve. But allow them to believe that no one cares (or is even noticing) and they will slip.

Recognize that while the strategies are consistent across generations, your attention and personal touch are the lubrication that makes coaching roll smoothly.

Communicating Across the Generations

When guiding multiple generations, leaders must be prepared to raise communication to an art form. Good communication is an almost universal standard for all organizations and spans the generational divides. Employees at every level and from each generation need to understand the "big picture." They want to know what the organizational mission is and how they are expected to contribute to it. This need is the same, no matter where they sit in the organization.

However, one thing that clearly distinguishes the experience of one generation from that of another is the type of communication they had available to them when they first entered the workforce.

In the case of matures, they came of age in an era where the tools of communication were pretty much relegated to the telephone and written communications, such as letters and memos. When you wanted something to be made official, you told someone to "put it in writing."

But a revolution in organizational communication arose not long after the boomers started taking their places at work. The advent of email communication meant the inevitable demise of paper communications, both inside and outside the company. Written communication was now as instant as speaking on the phone. At the same time, the advent of voicemail meant that phone messages could be stored, replayed, and eventually time-shifted.

Generation X, possessing a higher comfort level with technology, took to email and voicemail even more quickly than their parents. But the advent of cell phones and portable computers also meant they were no longer tied to the office. Their "desk" was wherever there was an electrical outlet or a car lighter.

But millennials, even more than their older siblings, have grown up with technology. They've come to prefer instantaneous communication technologies, such as text messaging and Twitter. They even use social networking sites such as Facebook as a means of real-time communication.

So, over the past half century or so, office communications have become both more immediate and less personal. This technological trade-off means that many members of later generations have less patience with traditional communications, preferring more immediate contact. At this juncture, it's too soon to say how these technologies will change how managers communicate with employees. Organizations are already experimenting with using Twitter as a tool to communicate with customers and build brand loyalty. How long will it be before organizations regularly use these technologies for employee recruitment, onboarding, and many other tasks?

Clearly managers can take advantage of these technologies to keep everyone on the same page. However, there will still be an ongoing need for face-to-face communication, including meetings, to solve problems, share the organizational vision, and explain how it relates to each individual. However, we should mention briefly that your face-to-face communication may need to be framed somewhat differently for members of each generation:

- To communicate effectively with matures, you may need to frame feedback or inquiries with something like "Your experience is an important asset for the organization. To help your team succeed . . ."
- With boomers, the more effective approach may be to suggest "I value your work and I need your help to . . ."

- Xers may prefer to hear "We need your best thinking on this project . . ."
- Millennials may respond well to something like "This is a chance for you to work with our best staff . . ."

Always remember that the big mistake is engaging in less rather than more communication. Failure to communicate costs corporations money because the mistakes, reworking, and time lost caused by miscommunication all lead to dollars lost.

Managing Intergenerational Conflict

No matter how carefully a leader tries to lead a multigenerational team, conflicts are inevitably bound to arise. Sometimes conflict arises out of simple personality differences. Sometimes it can stem from differences in expectations or perceptions.

Economic conditions can also cause cross-generational conflict. When jobs and careers are jeopardized, that uncertainty can lead employees to identify more with their generation and blame other generations for workplace problems and issues. When cutbacks do occur, if they must, few people want to be among the first to go, and the most recent employees may have a hard time seeing why their numbers should be the first called.

But it's more common for conflicts to arise among the four generations because of differences in values, ambitions, views, mindsets, and demographics. For example, some sources of on-the-job conflict may include

- communication preferences
- definition of the workday
- flexible scheduling
- promotional opportunities
- work/life balance.

To resolve intergenerational conflict, leaders should strive to do these things:

- *Keep discussions focused on the facts:* The source of the conflict should be dissected, not the nature of the personalities or generations involved.
- *Find points of common agreement:* Shared goals and problems are the best basis for getting conflicting parties to pull together.
- *Be specific about the organization's needs and goals:* The big picture never gets old, primarily because people tend to lose sight of it so easily. Remind the parties how they fit into the big picture and how their efforts contribute to organizational goals.
- *Acknowledge diverse viewpoints:* Opinions may not always be shared, but they need to be respected. When you acknowledge the validity of each party's

viewpoint, you make it easier for them to shift position, or at least to agree to compromise.

- ■ *Solicit changes that all parties can agree to (no matter how small):* Small concessions are often the building blocks of larger agreements.

Resolving conflicts across the generations may require more patience than average (and more flexibility), but it's well worth the extra effort. Despite obvious differences in background and orientation, multiple generations can function together very effectively in the workplace.

Building a Generationally Diverse Team

There really isn't a special secret to building a team comprising members from different generations. The same requirements for effective teamwork still apply, whether the team is homogeneous or heterogeneous. Teams must recognize common goals, develop a practical approach to solving common problems, and understand how to take advantage of differences.

Homogeneous teams may be faster to come up with solutions because of their tendency to think and work alike. But heterogeneous teams are better positioned to come up with complex and highly creative solutions because of the synergy that grows out of differences. In this sense, a team composed of matures, boomers, Xers, and millennials may have a harder time getting started but could really be impressive at the end of the day. To build effective cross-generational teams, leaders need to

- ■ Clearly define all members' roles and expectations.
- ■ Take into account the background, experience, and skill sets of each member when assigning roles and tasks.
- ■ Clarify productive styles of confrontation and ways to resolve conflict for team members.
- ■ Promote shared leadership.
- ■ Clarify the meaning of consensus.
- ■ Guide the team toward a consensus on the team's mission and goals.
- ■ Establish benchmarks for success.
- ■ Celebrate team victories.

A well-functioning team isn't necessarily built on generational differences and similarities. You may well find more general agreement among team members that you expected. But don't be afraid to challenge the members of your team to move out of their comfort zones and challenge new ways of thinking to help the team succeed.

Preparing for Leadership Transitions

More and more members of the mature generation will be heading into retirement within the next few years, even at the most senior levels of organizations. In addition, the leading edge of the baby boomer generation is rapidly reaching retirement age (though we'll have to see whether they can afford to retire—or even want to).

These shifts will affect not merely the generations in question, but will also reach down into the lower levels of your organization to also affect Gen Xers and millennials. The time to begin succession planning and the transition of leadership from one generation to the next is now. The oldest members of Generation X are quickly reaching the usual age of ascendancy in business.

At the same time that the members of Generation X are preparing for promotion to higher management levels, the millennials are arriving with a very high set of expectations. Whether you think it's appropriate or not, they won't be waiting long to ask for job advancement and promotion opportunities. But this isn't really surprising.

One of the biggest complaints about millennials is that they possess a sense of entitlement (if not actual arrogance). We have to remember that this generation, far more than that of their predecessors, grew up in an atmosphere of positive feedback, rewards, recognition, and praise. They were told all through their childhoods that they were talented and "special," and likewise they've been taught to expect a lot of themselves.

In contrast, the members of each preceding generation grew up in a competitive atmosphere where they were expected to start on the bottom rung and work their way up the ladder. Training was somewhat rare, and more often than not the matures, boomers, and Xers were expected to sink or swim.

So when millennials show up in your organization asking when they can expect to be promoted, you shouldn't be surprised. You also shouldn't be discouraging.

Very real labor shortages are expected due to Boomer retirement and a smaller Gen X labor pool. Your job will be to make sure that your current Gen Xers and Millennials are ready to climb up to that next rung of the ladder.

Within your organization, you're going to have to look at the managers and supervisors you presently have in key positions and determine whether you have the bench strength to fill those spots when vacancies occur. In the meantime, here are several strategies you can begin to employ to prepare your managerial staff for greater responsibilities:

- *Take advantage of your matures and boomers before it's too late:* Schedule cross-training and job enrichment opportunities for younger employees that include matures and boomers. Create learning opportunities, such as mentorships, that can facilitate the transfer of practical knowledge.

- *Assess your employees:* Use objective assessment tools that identify top performers in your organization and base hiring, development, and promotional decisions on assessment results.

- *Be creative about promotions:* If actual management promotions are scarce for your senior employees, consider giving them team leadership opportunities.

- *Begin to groom your Xers:* Look for both in-company and outside classes on management skills. Assign special projects to provide development opportunities.

- *Create career paths for your younger employees:* Develop a formal career path for your Millennials. Show them the stepping-stones leading to introductory and higher management opportunities. Provide them with ongoing orientation to the organization and try to give them communication and entry-level training opportunities.

- *Conduct regular developmental reviews for each individual:* Set goals and benchmarks, and track progress together. Clarify how accomplishing their personal goals can contribute to the organization as a whole, creating a path for their future.

By taking these kinds of steps now, you can ensure that your organization will have the requisite management depth to provide staffing and meet future challenges.

A Final Word—or "Leading Across the Generalizations"

On the basis of the reactions to the book I recently coauthored—*Keeping the Millennials: Why Companies Are Losing Billions in Turnover to This Generation and What to Do About It*—not everyone typifies the same generational traits. Leaders need to remember that their employees are individuals first and members of a generation second. Not all generational characteristics apply to every employee of a certain age. Boomers and matures, to take another case, also share many common characteristics because they lived extensively through the same time period.

And now we find that in addition to showing many similarities to their boomer parents, many millennials also share a common affection for technology with Gen Xers.

Always recognize that understanding more about your employees will make you more effective as a leader. Use generational influences and tendencies as a means to gaining insight to employee needs, and take time to discover the unique strengths, talents, and contributions that each employee brings to your organization.

Further Reading

Warren Bennis, *Geeks and Geezers: How Era, Values, and Defining Moments Shape Leaders.* Boston: Harvard Business Press, 2002.

Marshall Goldsmith, *Succession: Are You Ready? (Memo to the CEO).* Boston: Harvard Business School Press, 2009.

Neil Howe and William Strause, *Generations: The History of America's Future, 1584 to 2069.* New York: HarperCollins, 1992.

James Kouzes and Barry Posner, *The Leadership Challenge.* San Francisco: John Wiley & Sons, 2008.

Morris Massey, *The People Puzzle: Understanding Yourself and Others.* Reston, VA: Reston Press, 1979.

Joanne Sujansky and Jan Ferri-Reed, *Keeping the Millennials: Why Companies Are Losing Billions in Turnover to This Generation and What to Do About It.* Hoboken, NJ: John Wiley & Sons, 2009.

Reference

Massey, Morris. 1979. *The People Puzzle: Understanding Yourself and Others.* Reston, VA: Reston Press.

About the Author

Joanne G. Sujansky died shortly after completing this chapter at the end of 2009. She was a certified speaking professional, and the founder and CEO of KEYGroup. She worked with leaders to create exciting workplaces to attract, retain, and get the most from their talent. As a consultant and speaker with more than 25 years of experience, her many clients included American Express, GlaxoSmithKline, and the Mayo Clinic. She was called upon by such publications as *Time, Forbes,* and *USA Today* to provide leadership expertise. She was the author of 12 books and the coauthor of the best-selling book *Keeping the Millennials: Why Companies Are Losing Billions in Turnover to This Generation and What to Do About It* (John Wiley & Sons, 2009). She will be missed by her colleagues and clients.

❧ **Chapter 28**

Leading for Diversity

Kay Iwata, Juan T. Lopez, and Julie O'Mara

In This Chapter

- Diversity leaders have a mindset of diversity and inclusion effectiveness.

- Diversity leaders drive their team, organization, and/or community in a planned, strategic course of action.

- Diversity leaders excel at all five diversity P-O-W-E-R competencies.

- Diversity leaders hold themselves and others accountable for achieving the diversity vision.

What is the biggest challenge in effectively leading a diverse workforce? This was a question asked in a study done by Kay Iwata and published in *The POWER of Diversity: 5 Essential Competencies for Leading a Diverse Workforce* (Iwata 2004). The answer given in the book: Overcoming the perspective that diversity is primarily about race, quotas, or equal opportunity legal compliance. Respondents noted that many people have "dug in" ideas and do not view diversity as a business opportunity but as a human resources or legal initiative. They said the first step is to help people understand the broader sense of what diversity is all about.

© 2010 Kay Iwata, Juan T. Lopez, and Julie O'Mara. Used with permission.

Effective leaders of diversity understand that diversity and inclusion represent more than a focus on human resources initiatives. They know that their role is to expand the organization's approach in both mindset and action. It is something many take to heart.

The beauty of leadership is that it allows for an ever-changing study of humanity. There are limitless books and studies on the qualities of an effective leader and what he or she does that stands out as remarkable. In truth, we often find that leadership evolves with consciousness. Each century has authentic leaders, identified because of their unique, relevant, and timely practices. As we enter the 21st century, there is a new leadership consciousness emerging that is intricately tied to diversity and inclusion.

The effective leader understands the critical importance of diversity and inclusion. Effective leaders have a mindset that is ingrained into their way of being. This clarity of vision enables them to see the big picture—organizational success—as well as the complexities of the organizational life shaped by beliefs, norms, values, and practices.

Diversity is multidimensional, and knowing how all the dimensions relate is a must. The leaders who have these abilities "show up in a different way." They are often described as authentic and committed. They do this by consistently demonstrating the P-O-W-E-R competencies:

- P—Proactive advocates of diversity
- O—Optimum people developers
- W—Willing innovators
- E—Exemplary values-based decision makers
- R—Results through people.

The P-O-W-E-R Competencies

The following is a brief description of the P-O-W-E-R competencies in action and what you can do to increase your own level of competency. You will notice that these competencies and their behaviors do blend with and support one another. This allows you to leverage your time and energy because many behaviors and actions will have an impact across several competencies at the same time (figure 28-1).

P—Proactive Advocates of Diversity

"What really shifted my belief system was the difference one leader's expectations made on the performance of a peer. It took him from the 'dunce' on the team to a top performer. His capability was always there, I just didn't see it." What stands out with the competency of proactive advocates of diversity is the strong extrinsic and intrinsic value that leaders

Figure 28-1. P-O-W-E-R Competencies

Proactive advocates of diversity
- Champion behaviors, practices, and strategies that leverage the competitive advantage of diversity.
- True believers in the value of diversity both from an intrinsic and business perspective.
- Role models' inclusion.

Optimum people developers
- Encourage, motivate, and empower a broad spectrum of individuals.
- Recognize and leverage the unique skill sets and talents.
- Active listeners.
- Keen relationship builders.
- Match talent to task.

Willing innovators
- Intellectual and emotional curiosity.
- Openness to new and different people and ideas.
- Willingness to take calculated risks.
- Listen to and include a wide variety of perspectives.
- Encourage new ways of doing things.

Exemplary values-based decision makers
- Guided by their integrity and courage.
- Consistently do the right thing.
- Known for their honesty, and have high credibility.
- Hold firm to their principles.

Results through people achievers
- Focus on "getting things done."
- Set clear expectations.
- Provide relevant, consistent feedback.
- Hold themselves as well as others accountable.
- Provide sincere recognition for a job well done.

Source: © 2007 K. Iwata Associates, Inc. All rights reserved. Used with permission.

have for diversity and inclusion. They clearly get the business case and communicate it frequently. In addition, they have a strong personal value of diversity and inclusion based on their life experiences. This is a powerful combination. They consistently advocate for practices that enhance diversity and inclusion. Their decision-making processes reflect the importance of diversity as key consideration. There is no hesitation in challenging inappropriate behaviors.

To strengthen this competency, there must be a willingness to "lean into discomfort" on business and personal levels and put yourself out there in challenging situations where you are the only one or one of few. Also, you need to be able to focus on listening with a willingness to be influenced even when you have to override a strong inclination to be right and have all the answers. Finally, ask yourself tough questions about your unearned privileges (these are those "perks" that are the result of the luck of the draw but do benefit you in significant ways), and how they affect your ability to be a leader in a diverse environment.

O—Optimum People Developers

"My manager saw a bigger picture for me than I saw for myself." The competency of optimum people developers resides in the belief that leaders are only as successful as the people they lead. There is a sincere interest in seeing others excel. They recognize that what is required to be successful is basically the same for everyone. Lowering standards is not an option. What makes them unique is that they also recognize that for those perceived as "different," there are additional barriers to overcome. They work with these employees to eliminate or at least mitigate the influence these barriers have on access to development and opportunities. To do this effectively, you first must invest the time to really know your employees. Matching good talent to task will increase effectiveness. Weave employee development and coaching into every opportunity that arises. Challenge co-workers when you see barriers surfacing based on unconscious bias and stereotyping.

W—Willing Innovators

"I can't get to innovation if I don't have and fully leverage diversity." A key characteristic driving the competency of willing innovators is high intellectual and emotional curiosity. This creates the motivation to seek different perspectives and ideas, to be open to change, to take "off-the-wall" ideas seriously, to challenge the status quo, and to take risks. They believe in "failing forward." To get to innovation, seek those different from you in ways that are obvious and not so obvious. Don't fall into the "comfort of similarities" trap. Encourage vigorous, civil dissent. Provide different ways to foster input and participation. For example, try dyad dialogues first or have written ideas submitted before a meeting for those who may not be so verbally inclined. Finally, recognize and address what may be an additional barrier for those underrepresented in the organization. This can be the pressure of avoiding failure, because their failures tend to stand out more and it increases pressure for them to prove their value.

E—Exemplary Values-Based Decision Makers

"Being in integrity is what you do when no one else is looking." The leaders and managers we interviewed in particular rated the competency of exemplary values-based decision

makers the most important. Courage and integrity are the focal points. It isn't about doing special things for certain employees. Rather, it's about what should be done that is often avoided when diversity tensions appear. It's confronting and addressing the tough issues that affect a respectful, productive workplace for all employees. The specific behaviors that matter most are

- Speak up for what is right, even when the stakes are personally high for you.
- Give honest constructive feedback to all employees.
- Keep employees informed so they are not blindsided.
- Own your own biases and work to eliminate them.
- Be your word.
- If conditions change, clearly communicate and renegotiate previous agreements.

R—Results Through People Achievers

"Diversity can make a good result great!" Results are a given in terms of a requirement. Leaders who demonstrate the competency of results through people achievers believe that the "secret in the sauce" to extraordinary results is people. The diversity-competent leader knows how to work across lines of difference, develop people, leverage the diversity each member brings, and build a cohesive team to get great results. This provides a greater sustainability of these outcomes. When leaders respect and fully utilize the diversity each employee brings to the team, they get that extra discretionary effort that really puts them over the top. To get those superior results requires knowing your employees in terms of their talents, interests, concerns, and challenges. Blend their talents and interests with a focus on team building and inclusion, especially as new members join. Keep them mission and vision focused. Provide clear expectations and feedback on achieving those expectations. Have tangible measures of progress, and hold yourself and others accountable. It is important to use differences to expand the ways and means of how goals are met.

Tying P-O-W-E-R to Behavior and Beliefs

One inescapable theme that threads it way through all the P-O-W-E-R competencies is the importance of the deeply held beliefs these leaders have about diversity and inclusion. No longer can we say, "It's not about what you believe, rather how you behave." It does matter what leaders believe. It drives their authenticity and commitment. Later in this chapter, we share a diversity paradigm tool that supports leaders in getting in touch with their own paradigm about diversity and inclusion.

Within the diversity field, there are many definitions of diversity and inclusion work. We view diversity work as actions that make it possible for different perspectives, styles, experiences, skills, conditions, and backgrounds of people and systems to work together to achieve a common vision. As our colleague Roosevelt Thomas said in his landmark diversity book *Beyond Race and Gender* (Thomas 1992), diversity is much broader than a focus on getting people of various dimensions of identity to respect each other. Diversity encompasses many dimensions, and they are central to one's identity. Race and gender are elements of this work, but not the total focus.

Employees want to feel included, able to bring their whole self to the organization. They want to know what the strategic plan is and how they can help the business enterprise, and they believe their talent and collaboration will help the organization accomplish the common goal. To build on this spirit of engagement, the effective leader must guide, share information, and honor diversity and flexibility, recognizing that individual contributors bring a wealth of talent and that most want to realize their full potential.

In this chapter, we examine the leader and what he or she does systemically that demonstrates outstanding practices at the individual, group, organization, and community levels.

Diversity Leaders Have a Mindset of Diversity and Inclusion Effectiveness

The Diversity and Inclusion—Changing the Leadership Mindset Model captures the shift from an old paradigm of organizational management to one that is more contemporary (figure 28-2). The old paradigm treated people as androids. The intention was not to dehumanize people so much as it was to control their output in a mechanized fashion, allowing for a predictable estimate of cost to the bottom line. As such, people were an expense, and the most effective way to curb their cost to the organization's bottom line was to amortize them like equipment.

In the 1960s, leaders were forced to change their perspective on human capital. This period was the "perfect storm." Social norms were changing with respect to the employment contract, millions of baby boomers were questioning leaders on the purpose of the Vietnam War and its cost to humanity, the struggle for civil rights and equality for racial and ethnic minorities was rattling the foundations of institutions, and the feminist movement was challenging the right of males to be the only models of leadership. These changing values had an impact on organizations and forced them to reexamine their cultures. This convergence of events laid the groundwork for diverse people, along the dimensions of gender, race, and ethnicity, who were entering organizations in much larger numbers. Additionally, the Hudson Institute, a conservative think tank, published a study that projected the diversity of the workforce in the United States by the year 2000 (Johnston and Packer 1987). Diversity was here to stay, and the critical question was how to effectively lead and include people to ensure organizational success.

Figure 28-2. The Diversity and Inclusion—Changing the Leadership Mindset Model

From	To
People as an expense ⟶	People as an asset
Managing others ⟶	Leading others
Directing ⟶	Guiding
Competing ⟶	Collaborating
Relying on rules ⟶	Focusing on outcomes
Rigidity/sameness ⟶	Diversity/flexibility
Using hierarchy ⟶	Using network
Stability/passivity ⟶	Innovative risk taking
Isolation ⟶	Inclusion
Secrecy ⟶	Sharing information

Source: Adapted from *The Changing Management Mindset* by D. Jamieson and J. O'Mara. Copyright © 2009 Juan T. Lopez and Julie O'Mara. All rights reserved. Used with permission.

As the composition of the workforce changed, the need to increase the capability to manage diversity became apparent. Treating people rigidly and uniformly undermined individual contributions. The inability of managers to value employees whose differences cut across race, gender, and ethnicity led to major complaints, often ending with the federal courts deciding the remedy that dictated how managers had to fairly evaluate the performance of employees who were culturally different from them, and forcing cultural change.

People are not all the same. We do not come from a single culture and have not been socialized with the same values with respect to work, communication, power, competition, and a host of other important areas. Organizational leaders grasped this reality; it was reinforced by costly lawsuits. The Diversity and Inclusion—Changing the Leadership Mindset Model is a natural shift from one state of consciousness—often identified as "old school"—to a more contemporary state that reflects the fact that people expect to be individualized and treated with dignity and respect.

When employees are hired and start their jobs, what they need from the organization varies from person to person. Effective leaders of diversity and inclusion understand this dynamic and incorporate it into practice. Furthermore, they know that employees do their best work in the service of others when they feel valued and respected.

Randy Snowden, director of Napa County Health and Human Services, summarizes the need for commitment: "Rather than simply wait and see what the native yeast is going to do and what kind of bread we're going to be baking, why don't we instead make up our own recipe? Agree on relationships and processes and consistently work toward those. We have a long-standing culture of wanting to serve the community, and diversity is very fertile ground in which to cultivate it" (Charles and Deanne 2009).

The Diversity and Inclusion—Changing the Leadership Mindset Model (see figure 28-2) represents a huge shift from viewing people as an expense to seeing them as an asset. If organizations treat people as an expense, they can develop a "throwaway" mindset. Who among us is willing to give to the organization all that it demands with no reciprocal benefit beyond our paycheck?

Most of us want more. We want to feel like our actions contribute to the goals of the organization. We seek a sense of meaning to our involvement. This need has been a constant variable in our work for the last three decades, with people in private and public organizations alike. We have found employees on the graveyard shift of manufacturing production lines as well as frontline sales clerks in large retail businesses clamoring for diversity inclusion, wanting their voices to be heard and their contributions respected. A quotation illustrates our point. A young Latina employee said, "I'm in a lower-level, entry position, and some managers interpret this to mean I'm a lower-class person so it is easy to ignore me." The perspective of employees at all levels of the organization has evolved so that what they desire in organizational viability is no different from that of the senior manager.

The effective leader of diversity and inclusion efforts has a tremendous responsibility. To be successful, one must be authentic; faking diversity management is practically impossible. Sooner or later, behavior (body language) or words will reveal a person's real beliefs. In our coaching of senior managers, we have found many examples of something that was said or done that derailed the leader. We live in a time where the need for authenticity is demanded, and congruent actions are scrutinized frequently.

Kay Iwata's model, the Three Levels of Learning, illustrates how the right mindset is central to being an effective diversity leader. The Three Levels of Learning Model was the outcome of Kay's original research, which was published in *The POWER of Diversity: 5 Essential Competencies for Leading a Diverse Workforce* (2004). The study used expert opinions to develop competencies, followed by in-depth interviews with a diverse (by race, gender, level, experience, and type and size of organization) group of 135 leaders who had been identified as effective leaders of a diverse workforce. The interviews were then analyzed, and the levels of learning and the five P-O-W-E-R competencies (figure 28-3) were among the useful tools and processes created from the information.

Figure 28-3. The Three Levels of Learning

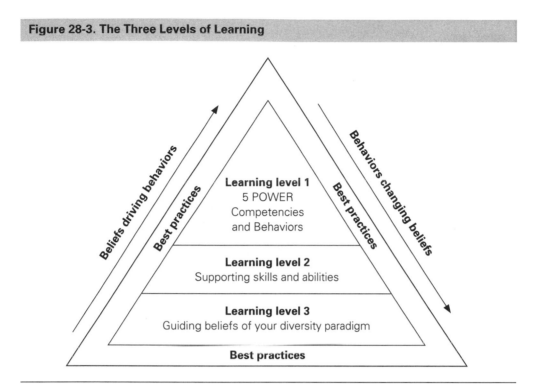

Source: Copyright © 2009 K. Iwata Associates, Inc. All rights reserved. Used with permission.

The study indicated that developing diversity competency required three levels of learning. Level 1, at the top, consists of the P-O-W-E-R competencies and their supporting behaviors. But Iwata found that to consistently demonstrate these competencies and behaviors, leaders and managers needed a set of underlying skills, depicted in level 2. As she probed even deeper, she came to realize that effective leaders held certain beliefs about diversity that were at the core of how they behaved, and she represented these in level 3. Leaders do behave in accordance with what they believe.

Yet, for many years, the discussion of beliefs was rarely broached. Diversity training focused on behaviors. In essence, the thinking was that the individual leader could believe the way he or she wanted to because the crucial determination of competency was behavior.

The leaders and managers in Iwata's study said this does not work. Those leaders studied made it absolutely clear; you cannot be effective if your beliefs create doubt in the importance of diversity. Simply stated, when things get tough, people resort to what they believe, and those beliefs will drive behavior.

Iwata's diversity paradigm further illustrates the impact of a leader minimizing diversity/ inclusion beliefs. It shows how "rigidity/sameness," as identified in the Diversity and Inclusion—Changing the Leadership Mindset Model (figure 28-2), can devalue the individual and create organizational tension, whereas the process of leveraging diversity/inclusion beliefs takes into account the importance of diversity and flexibility by recognizing that each person has a right to succeed, based on his or her talent and ability. The model also recognizes that people in organizations make mistakes and are imperfect; therefore, systems need to be in place to ensure a healthy environment for diversity and inclusion (figure 28-4).

Diversity Leaders Drive Their Team, Organization, and/or Community in a Planned, Strategic Course of Action

In the answer to the opening question of this chapter, Iwata stated that many people do not see diversity as a business opportunity and that people must have a broader understanding of diversity. Once they grasp that broader sense of what diversity and inclusion are about, they must take action. They must also know how to plan and implement a strategic course of action that drives toward a vision, and be able to sustain a long-term, ongoing process of individual and organization development and change. This is not easy work for the unskilled.

Some leaders will be more hands-on than others—the implementation of a diversity and inclusion strategic plan will be dependent on the leader's level and style, and the size of the organization. But all leaders must know enough about what it takes to make change happen to be able to direct and drive it and sustain momentum. They will need to staff the diversity and inclusion strategic effort with professionals who think strategically and systemically and have the skills and knowledge to execute the needed change.

There are many good change models and organization development process models available, as well as diversity and inclusion tools. An Internet search identified hundreds. Three that are specific to diversity include the Diversity 9-S Framework for Organizational Change by Ed Hubbard, Global Diversity and Inclusion Benchmarks by Julie O'Mara and Alan Richter (available free at www.qedconsulting.com and at www.omaraassoc.com), and O'Mara's Diversity Futures Model.

Leaders need to ensure that the principles of an effective diversity and inclusion change effort are integral to whatever change process is used. Some of these principles include collaboration, being values driven and business smart, high integrity, significant involvement of key stakeholders, a cross-level and cross-functional approach, and ongoing communication. Other principles vary with the size and business function of the organization.

Figure 28-4. Diversity Paradigm

A set of beliefs and values that drive attitudes and behavior toward diversity.

Minimizing Diversity/Inclusion Beliefs	Leveraging Diversity/Inclusion Beliefs
To be successful, people need to conform to the norms of the dominant group. "When in Rome do as the Romans do."	To be successful, people need to conform to certain norms as they relate to requirements but not to all the norms of the dominant group.
The cream always rises to the top.	Merit doesn't mean you will succeed.
The past is the past and people need to stop using it as an excuse.	The past is the past but accrued benefits and losses as a result of the past are still being experienced today.
People are really all the same.	People have many things in common but also have important differences.
The ultimate goal of diversity is to have more women and people of color represented in upper management.	The ultimate goal of diversity is to have a workplace that fully utilizes the diverse talents of all employees.
Stereotyping is not a behavioral issue in my organization.	Stereotyping still creates barriers for people in my organization.
In terms of roles and responsibilities, what really matters is how well I perform on the technical aspects of my job.	How well I develop, motivate, and fully utilize people is critical to my success.
The key to success with diversity is recruitment.	The key to success with diversity is culture change.
There is no business case for diversity, but it is the right thing to do.	There is a business case for diversity, and it is the right thing to do.
We have a level playing field.	The playing field is not level.

Source: Copyright © 2007 K. Iwata Associates, Inc. All rights reserved.

The leader must ensure that the process of diversity and inclusion is not shortsighted. Although a key intervention may be the training and development of employees, many organizational leaders mistakenly see training and development as the complete or primary intervention when it is only one intervention among many. Important elements and steps of a diversity and inclusion change process are similar to most organization development interventions:

- planning to plan/contracting
- data collection

- data analysis, which in diversity work is best accomplished through a process that involves a cross-section of employees and other key stakeholders
- gap analysis, which is the agreement of the current state and the desired future state
- determination of actions needed to close the gaps
- implementation and measurement
- continuous sensing and reassessment.

Diversity Leaders Excel at All Five Diversity P-O-W-E-R Competencies

Some people believe that a leader who is effective in general will also be an effective leader of diversity and inclusion efforts. But there is more to it than that. The competencies that diversity leaders need have been explained definitively by Iwata's research, as identified in figure 28-1.

One of the most significant contributions to the field of diversity and inclusion from this research was the recognition of the importance of a leader having a personal belief system and diversity paradigm that results in diversity being leveraged (see figures 28-2 and 28-4). Previously, it was advocated that, no matter what a leader's personal beliefs were about diversity and inclusion, he or she would still be able to lead by focusing only on role-modeling appropriate behaviors. Although organizations can only hold employees accountable for their behavior and achievement of performance goals, leaders will be most effective if their belief systems are in alignment with diversity and inclusion principles.

One way leaders can get insight into their diversity competence is to ask for feedback from others. Iwata's 360-degree feedback tool on the P-O-W-E-R competencies has helped many leaders increase their diversity competence and their commitment to diversity and inclusion. George Chavel, the president and CEO of Sodexo, Inc., was quoted in the September 2008 issue of *Diversity Inc.* as saying: "I found myself really learning more about my personal journey on diversity and inclusion. Not only things that I could apply to my business applications, but to my personal life as well with my kids and with my family" (Visconti 2008).

Diversity Leaders Hold Themselves and Others Accountable for Achieving the Diversity Vision

Each of us has had the distinct pleasure of working with CEOs and nongovernmental organization leaders whose beliefs about diversity and inclusion fundamentally changed how the organization operated. These leaders were effective because they understood that success was not only based on a clear vision and strategic plan. It also included detailed metrics that held members of the organization accountable for performance from the front line to the boardroom.

There is a Hopi saying: "Tradition gets in the way of progress, and progress gets in the way of tradition." An organization changes slowly, and its traditions can thwart the need for innovation. As we have discussed in this chapter, beliefs, norms, values, and practices are deeply held. Many employees in organizations have had to learn new customs to survive and succeed. Traditions represent more than "just a way of doing business"—they speak to inclusion within a community that also provides for your welfare.

Introducing change is a big task. Making changes is terrifying for many. The effective diversity leader understands how humans react to change. He or she also recognizes that people are more inclined to change when they see how the change converges with their self-interest. This is not intended to be a mercenary statement. People do change, and they change more easily when there is a benefit from doing so.

The effective diversity leader has the vision to see the organization as a system that has many moving parts. At individual and team levels, people make it happen, so leaders must put the right people in place and hold them accountable for making the right decisions and creating an environment that includes a healthy diversity mixture, incorporating thought and cultural competency skills.

A client of ours has been instrumental in building a powerful case for diversity and inclusion. Over the past eight years, this company has remained in the top 20 corporations benchmarked by others. How has its commitment to diversity and inclusion been sustained? It started with the CEO, who believes so strongly in diversity that he inspired others to follow suit.

This company's employees required some time to get past their skepticism. The prevailing thought was that if an organization pursued diversity, it was avoiding a lawsuit, at worst, or seeking to enhance its public relations, at best. This opinion of diversity was common for many organizations, and many articles were written that also questioned the veracity of diversity. It took time for people to realize that respecting individual diversity helps an organization recognize the value of its employees and, ultimately, its stakeholders.

In this case, the effective leader established a compelling case for diversity being great for the bottom line, while creating a brand image in communities of color and enriching employees who could become the next wave of leaders. In a busy organization where people have multiple jobs, keeping diversity at the forefront of business requires accountability. This CEO assigned the responsibility to a senior vice president who reported to him, essentially giving him the task of keeping the CEO, his executive team, and the organization on track. The CEO also held the members of the executive team accountable for their actions and ensured that each reported on his or her progress, by tying it to their bonus.

Additionally, a diversity team was established, made up of employees representing all sectors of the business both in the United States and globally. This team was asked to keep the CEO challenged and hold him accountable for diversity and inclusion. He personally reviewed the team's work and responded to questions about the effectiveness of his leadership of diversity and the senior management team's accountability for its diversity leadership and role modeling.

Conclusion

The authors of this chapter have dedicated their lives to the emerging field of study of diversity and inclusion. As pioneers, we have been involved in diversity work since its inception. We have worked with top 50 corporations, government organizations, and others that have been benchmarked for diversity and inclusion success. In our work with the leaders of these highly touted organizations, we have witnessed their ability to transform their cultures for the benefit of employees and customers.

It is not easy work. Holding individuals accountable has required courage, and, by holding themselves accountable first, leaders have exemplified committed leadership. Competency and authenticity make for a leadership in which we can all believe.

Further Reading

Edward E. Hubbard, *Measuring Diversity Results,* vol. 1. Petaluma, CA: Global Insights Publishing, 1997.

Kay Iwata, *The POWER of Diversity: 5 Essential Competencies for Leading a Diverse Workforce.* Petaluma, CA: Global Insights Publishing, 2004.

David Jamieson and Julie O'Mara, *Managing Workforce 2000: Gaining the Diversity Advantage.* San Francisco: Jossey-Bass, 1991.

Frederick A. Miller and Judith H. Katz, *The Inclusion Breakthrough: Unleashing the Real Power of Diversity.* San Francisco: Berrett-Koehler, 2002.

Sondra Thiederman, *Making Diversity Work: 7 Steps for Defeating Bias in the Workplace.* Chicago: Dearborn Trade Publishing, 2003.

R. Roosevelt Thomas Jr., *Building a House for Diversity: How a Fable about a Giraffe and an Elephant Offers New Strategies for Today's Workforce.* New York: AMACOM, 1999.

References

Charles, Janna, and Barbara Deanne. 2009. A How To Guide for Developing a Diversity Initiative: Case Study of Napa County HHSA. Available at www.diversitycentral.com.

Iwata, K. 2004. *The POWER of Diversity: 5 Essential Competencies for Leading a Diverse Workforce.* Petaluma, CA: Global Insights Publishing.

Johnston, W. B., and A. E. Packer. 1987. *Workforce 2000: Word and Workers for the 21st Century.* Indianapolis, IN: The Hudson Institute.

Thomas, R. 1992. *Beyond Race and Gender: Unleashing the Power of Your Total Work Force by Managing Diversity.* New York: AMACOM.

Visconti, L. 2008. Sodexo's CEO George Chavel: Taking a Diversity Leader to a Whole New Level. *DiversityInc Magazine,* September 22–31. http://www.diversityinc-digital.com/diversityincmedia/200809#pg24.

About the Authors

Kay Iwata has built a reputation in the diversity field as a consultant with a strong inclination toward practical application. The applications are supported by a solid foundation of conceptual clarity and understanding. The focus of her first book is no surprise. *The POWER of Diversity: 5 Essential Competencies for Leading a Diverse Workforce* is based upon a first-of-its-kind field study to understand the "how to" of diversity competence for managers and leaders. She has effectively translated the lessons from the study into realistic workplace applications. This content has been successfully used by several major organizations to increase their diversity competence.

Juan T. Lopez is president of Amistad Associates, a consulting practice that focuses on strategic planning, organizational innovation, and leadership and diversity excellence. He is a cofounder of Llead, a senior Latino leadership program. He and his colleagues are currently writing a book on their research based on 15 years of training and coaching. He has developed a global accelerated leadership program for men of color and multicultural men and is a cofounder of Diversity 2000, a think tank now entering its 17th year.

Julie O'Mara is president of O'Mara and Associates, an organization development consulting firm that serves clients in several sectors. She specializes in leadership and strategic diversity processes. A former national president of ASTD, she has received several awards for her leadership and diversity work. She is coauthor of the bestseller *Managing Workforce 2000: Gaining the Diversity Advantage* (Jossey-Bass); author of *Diversity Activities and Training Designs* (Pfeiffer); and coauthor of *Global Diversity and Inclusion Benchmarks.*

✺ Section V

Broadening the Leadership Discussion

The vision for this handbook is to include several chapters that take our readers outside the normal paradigms of corporate leadership—beyond the typical boundaries of how to lead, whom to lead, and what to lead. Thus, this section reflects our search for ideas that might stretch our thinking and explores leadership from a potpourri of perspectives.

We hope the wisdom expressed in the five chapters of this section gives you pause to think. There are thousands of books about leadership. Indeed, this handbook presents chapters by several of the top authors in the field. Yet at the same time, those of us who are concerned about leadership development and leadership in the future would do well to focus our attention on areas other than the corporate halls of business.

An effective creativity technique used to see problems or issues from different perspectives is to ask "How would _____ view this problem?" For example, we could ask "What leadership lessons can we learn about . . .

- charisma from the Dalai Lama in the foothills of the Himalayas?"
- talent management from a preschool class?"
- enabling others to act from staff at a top-notch nursing home?"
- building trust from firefighters, the most trusted occupation?"

You could pose dozens of other questions. But the idea is to look at leadership from another perspective.

In the next five chapters, the authors challenge us to consider what can be learned from the military about development, from public-sector leadership challenges, and from adolescents in Ghana. They also dare us to answer questions such as: Should we begin to give employees opportunities to lead earlier in their careers? How can we support leadership skills training in primary and secondary schools in all the countries of the world? What can private industry learn from the challenges of the public sector? What kind of a world should leaders be prepared for in 2020? What can we learn from the difficulties of Chinese leaders? As you ponder these kinds of thought-provoking questions, read the chapters in this section realizing that while this is the end of the handbook, it is just the beginning for your learning.

In chapter 29, "Why Leadership Development Should Go to School," Lyndon Rego, Steadman Harrison, and David Altman explore the need for educational systems worldwide to create an added emphasis on leadership skills, creativity, emotional intelligence, and other personal skill development that extends beyond academics and technical knowledge.

In chapter 30, "Growing Tomorrow's Leaders for the Worlds of 2020," Lawrena Colombo and John Verderese envision the varied worlds of 2020 that leaders will face and suggest ideas for how to successfully prepare leaders at various stages of their careers and with diverse perspectives to meet the challenges of the future.

In chapter 31, "A Military View of Leadership in the Private Sector," John Lockard, a retired three-star admiral, compares leadership in the private sector with that in military organizations and offers ideas for consideration. He also delineates his nine essentials for leadership based on his experience in the military and the private sector.

In chapter 32, "Leading in the Public Sector," Will Brown presents practical ideas for how to ensure effective leadership in the public sector (or any other organization that relies on political savvy). He states that it begins with understanding the people and the organization.

In chapter 33, "Chinese 'Sheng Yi': Reinterpreting Challenges for Leaders," Cheng Zhu presents some of the major challenges that Chinese CEOs in private industry face because of inadequate legal, political, and cultural support.

Chapter 29

Why Leadership Development Should Go to School

Lyndon Rego, Steadman D. Harrison III, and David G. Altman

In This Chapter

- How developing leadership skills early can make a difference.

- The Center for Creative Leadership's role in bringing leadership into schools.

- Examples of activities used to teach leadership in schools.

The president of the Center for Creative Leadership (CCL), John Ryan (a former chancellor and retired Navy admiral), observed that leadership is not something to which many mainstream college students aspire. In his years as president of several universities and then as chancellor in the State University of New York system, he was known to ask incoming freshman students at orientation the question, "How many of you are here to learn to be a leader?" He usually found that fewer than one-third of the students would raise their hand, and many of these would do so only after they looked around to make sure that someone else had raised their hand. In contrast, when he was superintendent (that is, president) of the U.S. Naval Academy and posed this same question to freshman midshipmen, every student would immediately raise their hand and some even raised both hands.

This is mirrored by another account by the late Gordon MacKenzie of Hallmark Cards, who wrote that when he went into first grade classes and asked students how many were artists, every child would stick up their hand enthusiastically. The number willing to be identified as artists shrunk to half by second grade, and by sixth grade, only a child or two would acknowledge being an artist. MacKenzie (1996) noted that schools are somehow banishing the creativity that children innately possess.

As staff members of CCL, an organization focused on creative leadership, we have also heard a regret expressed by many of the 40-something participants who attend our leadership development programs around the globe. We hear them sigh that they wished they'd had this experience 20 years earlier, when it would have made a greater difference in their lives. Curiously, in our work with youth, we've also heard a 15-year-old student reflect at the conclusion of a leadership program, "I can't tell you how many things I would have done differently if I had only had this training back in junior high school."

This gap in leadership development among young people is something we've heard bemoaned by employers in the developing world who are frustrated by the limited capabilities of many graduates of the education system. For instance, a senior executive at a software company in India stated that even prominent management schools aren't equipping students with adequate self-awareness and clarity about what they want from a career and life. A managing director of an Indian steel company echoed this sentiment, saying that students need to spend much more time reflecting in an organized way on their thinking processes, aspirations, and strengths, because these are the keys for personal and professional growth (Altman, Rego, and Harrison 2009).

A feature in *BusinessWeek* notes that employers also want creativity: "The driving forces of innovation and globalization are pushing companies to revamp their managerial ranks and hire people with new skills. . . . And in an era of constant change, they want people who are comfortable with complexity and uncertainty. Schools that teach design thinking, with its emphasis on maximizing possibilities rather than managing for efficiency, are in high demand" (Woyke and Atal 2007).

All this reveals a need for educational systems worldwide to create an added emphasis on leadership skills, creativity, emotional intelligence—or however we label this sphere of development that extends beyond academics and technical knowledge. In this chapter, we explore why leadership development (our label for this area of development) is essential to young people, and how CCL and other kindred organizations are working to make it part of what young people study in school.

A Look at the Literature

The literature on the value of leadership development is broad and deep. Here, we focus on a slice of the literature that maintains that creative leadership skills can be developed. This perspective has grown in acceptance in recent years, though there are still some believers in the philosophy that leaders are born and not made or that there are innately creative and noncreative people. Over the years, psychology has expanded its focus from a predominantly problem-based orientation to one that covers topics such as wellness and resilience (Rappaport 1977; Rudkin 2003). Indeed, the subfield of "positive psychology," with a focus on the strengths that help humans thrive in life, has established a foothold and considerable interest among scholars and practitioners (Seligman 1998).

As we began working with young people in developing countries and teenagers in the United States from disadvantaged communities, we were continually impressed with their ability to take on tough odds. It became clear that if we didn't move beyond societal stereotypes or victim blaming about the long odds that these individuals faced in attempts to be successful as leaders or as important contributors to robust community life, our efforts would be for naught. Indeed, some have argued that youth development—and the subsequent political engagement and empowerment it engenders—is central to building a more humane, democratic, and just world (Ryan 1971; Ginwright and James 2002).

A large literature in social psychology on attribution theory is relevant to this discussion. There is considerable evidence that when attributions are made about behavior, we are more likely to attribute behavior to dispositions (for example, a trait or personal quality of an individual) than to the environment in which the behavior occurs (Ross and Nisbett 1991). In our work with young people, we have tried to make situational attributions more than dispositional attributions. Where others might look at the challenges young people in developing countries face as a reflection on their own inabilities to "pull themselves up by their bootstraps," we instead tried to understand how the context in which these young people lived affected their behavior (Trickett 2009). This minor shift in our thinking had a major effect on our work. Where others might have found it easy to write off these "disadvantaged" young people as unworthy of attention or engagement, we decided to take a strengths-based approach informed by the tradition of positive psychology. As such, in these young people with whom we worked, we saw strengths rather than deficits. Where others might be focusing on "fixing" these young people through problem-based interventions, we focused instead on unleashing their potential. Where others might have seen the environment in which young people lived as squalid, we focused on the many indigenous resources that could be tapped if we were more creative and persistent in considering the possibilities.

We were also influenced by the body of research on the "self-fulfilling prophecy" (Smith and Mackie 2007; Rappaport 1977; Rosenthal and Jacobson 1968). Numerous studies have found that expectations significantly affect behavior. That is, when we have certain expectations about the qualities and skills of another person, we explicitly and implicitly find ways to reinforce the behaviors of others in ways that ultimately prove that our expectations were correct. Hence, our expectations and perceptions of others may create corresponding behaviors in others and thus become a self-fulfilling prophecy. In a classic experiment conducted several decades ago, Rosenthal and Jacobson found that when teachers were informed of which students were (supposedly) about to "bloom" academically (or were "gifted" in today's lexicon), the students labeled as "bloomers" had greater gains on end-of-year IQ and performance tests and were rated by teachers more favorably than students not labeled as "bloomers." In this and other studies, teachers' high expectations for certain students had a significant effect on the students' actual achievements, even when the students were randomly assigned a "bloomer" or "not bloomer" label. In our own work, we made the assumption that every young person had gifts, regardless of his or her socioeconomic status, family situation, or the home or community in which he or she lived. We engaged with these young people with the expectation that they could develop their leadership skills. Moreover, we conveyed to them the importance of having what Carol Dweck (2006) has labeled a growth mindset, or the belief that one's skills and effectiveness are not predetermined by traits such as intelligence but rather are developed by cultivation, practice, effort, feedback, and time.

Likewise, we were influenced by Albert Bandura's (1997, 2001) work on self-efficacy, or the beliefs people have about the relationship between their behavior and outcomes. Bandura (2001) has found that to successfully navigate the vicissitudes of life, individuals must have self-awareness of their capabilities, an ability to estimate the probable causes and effects of actions they take, an understanding of the context in which they operate, and an ability to regulate their behavior. He has also written about collective efficacy, or the confidence that a group of people have in their ability to achieve a desired outcome. Because efficacy influences whether individuals or groups are optimistic, take on challenges, persevere against challenges, or expend energy on a task, it stands to reason that increasing perceptions of efficacy through educational and behavioral interventions and through the adoption of a growth mindset was a keen focus of our leadership development activities with young people. The perspective we took is also consistent with key tenets in the literature on youth development. For example, the five key elements of youth development programs—the five Cs—have been identified as competence, confidence, connections, character, and caring (Roth and Brooks-Gunn 2003). As noted throughout this chapter, each of these Cs has been at the root of our work on youth leadership development.

Thus, our perspective on reaching out to underserved young people is influenced by our commitment to unleashing the capabilities of indigenous resources. In summarizing the essence of human motivation, Smith and Mackie (2007, 17) suggest that three principles dominate: "As they construct reality and influence and are influenced by others, people have three basic motives: to strive for mastery, to seek connectedness with others, and to value themselves and others connected to them." These three principles certainly resonate with our philosophical and tactical approach. We made an explicit choice to look carefully for resources in individuals and communities rather than for deficits that needed to be fixed.

As we reflect on our experiences to date, we think it is important to make the distinction between capacity and capability. In simple terms, *capacity* refers to the reservoir of potential knowledge and skills at one's disposal. Rather than being fixed, capacity is dynamic and can be increased through education, learning, and practice. In contrast, *capability* refers to the skill sets that are available to an individual, team, or organization. Using simple arithmetic as an analogy, capacity is the denominator (that is, the theoretical maximum possible resources and skills that can be brought to bear) and capability is the numerator (that is, the resources that are actually brought to bear). Our goal, then, was to work with the existing capacity of young people and the contexts in which they live, with a constant eye toward increasing their capacity and capability. This was done by employing principles related to a growth mindset, improving self-efficacy and collective efficacy, tapping these young people's strengths and resilient behaviors, and setting a high bar with respect to our and their expectations for leadership development.

Developing Leadership Skills Early

The need to develop leadership skills early has been picked up by many community organizations, like the YMCA, Boy Scouts and Girl Scouts, Outward Bound, and Rotary and Kiwanis. These programs are valuable for those who have the opportunity to participate in them. But as an optional, extracurricular activity, these social programs do not reach many children who would greatly benefit from them if they were offered as part of the basic construct of education at school. Though a large number of schools offer leadership development only outside the classroom or to those students who are high academic achievers, some schools have begun to incorporate it in significant, substantive, and inclusive ways into their curricula. Let's look at four varied examples: the Riverside School, the African Leadership Academy, Northwest Guilford High School, and the Halogen Foundation Singapore.

The Riverside School

The Riverside School in Ahmedabad, India, was founded by Kiran bir Sethi in 2001 (www .schoolriverside.com). Kiran has created a school focused on student well-being where all processes and practices are designed to make young people "more competent and less helpless." The Riverside School is building in its students the depth of emotional intelligence and leadership skills that many individuals only acquire through years of life and work experience. Furthermore, the school demonstrates that developing intrapersonal and interpersonal skills elevates academic performance.

At Riverside, the approach to education reflects Carol Dweck's research that effectiveness is developed through cultivation, practice, effort, feedback, and time. The school takes the children through key stages of becoming aware of the world around them; then acquiring and honing skills and strategies to become empowered to lead the change through self-management; and aquiring an ability to work with others, appreciate differences, and realize as well as exercise their potential. Ultimately, the program at Riverside helps children "be the change" and gain confidence that they can shape their lives and the world around them through their actions. The end goal is to make children visible and active members of their communities, so that they understand and fulfill their future role as citizens.

While visiting the Riverside School, we found kindergarten children weaving stories from pictures they had seen in school. Middle school students spoke eloquently about the value of self-awareness and explained the nuances of Riverside pedagogy. The walls were covered with documentation designed to indicate the relevance of their work, the relationships they forged to get there, and the rigor with which they honed their skills.

This belief in the potential of children to be agents of change is important in a country with one of the world's largest and youngest populations. Kiran observes that the Riverside School stands in contrast to the prevalent approaches to education in India, where children, depending on their economic status, can be either pushed very hard to achieve academically or opt out of school to help earn a living to support their families. Kiran's efforts via the Riverside School espouse the idea that there's "a protagonist in every child," and her outreach efforts extend to schools around the country through sharing of the curriculum, contests for social action, and programs that enable children at large to express their creativity and their potential. Despite Riverside's focus on a broader array of competencies, in a nationwide assessment test, its students have outperformed the top schools in India in the core competencies of language, mathematics, and science—proving that they do well when they feel good (personal communication; www.schoolriverside.com).

The African Leadership Academy

In the fall of 2007, our team was introduced to the inspirational vision of Chris Bradford, an American social entrepreneur with a heart for Africa's future leaders. Chris and Fred Swaniker cofounded the African Leadership Academy (ALA) in Johannesburg (www.africanleadershipacademy.org). The school, with students representing nearly every country across Africa, began teaching its first classes in September 2008. The curriculum builds knowledge and skills in the areas of entrepreneurship, pan-African culture, and leadership development. The ALA model weaves in coaching, mentoring, and action learning projects. Students must implement their culminating project in the community, and through their work in these small group projects they learn to appreciate difference and diversity.

With the choice for the school name and their tag line, "Developing the next generation of African leaders," their founding team made a point to emphasize the importance of leadership as well as academic excellence. They identify leadership development as one of the five distinctive elements of their school:

> Leadership will be formally taught in the Academy's curriculum with the goal of instilling a robust system of values in our students. Students will discover the traits of highly effective African leaders from case studies about leaders like Ellen Johnson-Sirleaf or Desmond Tutu. The Academy's "Leadership Perspectives" speaker series will bring distinguished leaders from across the continent to share their experiences with students. Each student will also receive individual leadership coaching from his or her personal mentor, a mid-career professional who embodies the Academy values. Students will engage in various exercises and experiences designed to develop their interpersonal skills. And in their final year on campus, each student will be required to plan and execute a Culminating Project that has a lasting positive impact on an African community (African Leadership Academy 2010).

ALA's students come from a diverse array of cultural backgrounds and have important lessons to teach one another. At ALA, they have the opportunity to share their experiences and discuss what they are learning and why it is important to them. From our work with orphaned youth in Uganda, we shared with ALA the critical role that the perspective that is taken can have in the lives of young people. By helping students understand multiple aspects of their own identities, they grow in their self-awareness as well as their understanding of how others around them see the world. We have seen the power that this self-knowledge provides. This ability to understand and lead self provides a path forward through the constant challenges and changes that these young people will face in a world that is growing in its complexity.

ALA has gained international attention because of its unique approach. It is expected that the very best universities in the world will actively recruit from this academy where African culture is taught and celebrated and nearly every country in Africa is represented. We expect to see many of these students taking the lead in meeting the challenges that Africa faces.

Northwest Guilford High School

The staff of the Center for Creative Leadership found an advocate and partner for studying and implementing youth leadership in the Greensboro, North Carolina, high schools when we began working with Brent Irwin, a guidance counselor and teacher in the school system. Brent observed, "Regardless of the career direction students are heading, having a solid foundation in leadership training is essential to their success." He emphasized that every high school needs to provide leadership development hand in hand with other traditional subjects of study. Knowledge of and the skills needed for leadership, he believes, are just as essential for future success as the knowledge of mathematics and history and economics. He says that the study of leadership should be inseparable—that is, woven into the fabric of academic studies. His passion for leadership development led to the implementation of a leadership service club at the school where he teaches, Northwest Guilford High School (NGHS) in Greensboro, and in the last year, NGHS has seen the enrollment of its leadership classes double in size.

CCL was invited to host a series of sessions at NGHS, where Brent engaged students in relation to perceptions of leadership; more than 300 students participated. CCL's facilitators used a tool we created, called Leader Sort, to explore perceptions of who is a leader. Leader Sort consists of a deck of cards featuring pictures of people ranging from well-known political, entertainment, and media figures to anonymous characters (such as a woman with a T-shirt that states "Soccer Mom"). The students were asked to rank order the deck from those most leaderlike to least leaderlike. The CCL research team was surprised to discover that the "Soccer Mom" made the top of most students' Leader Sort decks. In fact, mother figures consistently ranked alongside Gandhi and Martin Luther King, Jr. as people who represented the greatest leaders to these students. Popular people such as Bill Gates made the middle of their card sort—not because of financial success at Microsoft but because of the philanthropic work of the Bill and Melinda Gates Foundation. We heard that students perceive their parents as the most influential leaders they know. Students almost universally stated that influence and confidence are the most important characteristics they can develop to help them with future success.

In a debrief, many students reflected that the most powerful lesson they learned through the use of Leader Sort was that anyone can play the role of leader—including themselves. Students voiced an interest in increasing their self-confidence and their learning and listening skills, and in becoming more decisive. They expressed a desire to learn more about "how to inspire others." They said that they learn important skills—such as getting the job done, dedication, persistence, and being team players—from family and from life experience and not from school.

Our use of the Leader Sort card decks and other CCL interactive tools helped draw out students who were perceived as reserved or disinterested in their traditional classroom studies. At the close of these CCL focus group sessions at NGHS, teachers reported that they were surprised to observe certain students speaking up who had previously been noted for a lack of participation, interest, and engagement. As Brent put it, "When the students were using the facilitation tools from CCL, I saw them engaging in discussion at a level beyond what I normally see. In terms of the depth of content, their personal investment, and their overall enthusiasm, it was encouraging to see the students so actively involved and enjoying the learning process."

CCL's decision to create youth leadership toolkits to enable schools to offer leadership development experiences was significantly influenced by these initial inquiries. Even in a short exercise such as this one, it is clear that young people can quickly start to become more mindful of what effective leadership looks like and how it connects with their own aspirations for personal growth. It is our hope that these tools will make it easier for schools to incorporate leadership development into their existing coursework (also see more on this in the section below on curriculum and tools).

The Halogen Foundation

The Halogen Foundation Singapore is a nonprofit organization that is a catalyst for getting leadership development into Singapore schools (www.halogen.sg). Halogen's team is dedicated to making high-quality leadership education available and accessible to all young people. Halogen espouses the belief that every young person represents an outstanding leader in the making. In keeping with this philosophy, Halogen has worked to develop more than 40,000 young people through a combination of events, workshops, camps, and school-based engagements. In these events, Halogen brings together inspiration and challenge, encouraging young people to act in the service of their dreams and for the common good. A key event, One Degree Asia, symbolizes how small changes can make a big difference in time. This echoes Halogen's message that leadership development should focus on the young, for they have the most potential to give over the course of their lives. As Martin Tan, Halogen's founder and executive director, explained, a critical age at which to inspire young people is as young as 11 years—when critical images of self are shaped.

In bringing leadership development to schools, Halogen offers that "leadership development must be holistic, integrated with the formal education system and continually improved upon in order for it to be of impact and value to youths." Halogen works with teachers to enable educators to not only impart knowledge but also affect lives as developers of people. Halogen folds in content, training methodologies, and tools from CCL and other providers and adapts these to be youth friendly. Adapting this knowledge so that it is more accessible and engaging for young people is essential. At the same time, Halogen demonstrates that young people can absorb sophisticated leadership lessons about creativity, conflict, and mentoring.

In Singapore's affluent and achievement-oriented schools, Halogen finds a fertile ground to operate. But its aspirations extend beyond, to reach hundreds of thousands of youth in

Southeast Asia for whom notions of leadership and empowerment may be less familiar but are no less essential.

Summing Up

These brief case examples illustrate the potential of young people to develop leadership skills and how leadership development can enhance student achievement and success. So what will help more schools get on board?

Broadening the Base: CCL's Overall Role

As a leadership development organization, CCL's efforts center on what it can do to help those who wish to bring leadership development into schools. Leadership development is something that most teachers haven't had and may be hard pressed to offer their students. CCL's staff believes that there are two important enablers for it and the field to focus on. One is to make evidence-based curricula and tools available for use by schools. The other entails developing facilitation skills for teachers.

Curriculum and Tools

CCL is working on developing an inexpensive, flexible youth leadership toolkit that can be used by schools and youth leadership trainers around the world. Currently, the toolkit encompasses 20 modules that are designed to be adaptable for use in a number of ways, from an hour-long session to a series of leadership workshops, to extended service-learning programs. CCL is also working on a social innovation curriculum to equip young people with the leadership and innovation tools needed to enact change.

Leadership development can perhaps be most easily incorporated into schools when it isn't a completely new and standalone effort. Many schools today include projects that require teamwork and engagement with external organizations or populations. There are also an increasing number of service learning projects meant to help students exercise their passion for community service and apply what they have learned in school to real-life work. What is missing in many of these programs is the opportunity to help students develop their emotional intelligence—to use their experience to reflect on their behaviors and emotions, observe group dynamics, build interpersonal skills such as providing feedback, and better understand their gifts and challenges. The toolkits and curriculum that CCL is developing offer frameworks and exercises that can be used to address this gap.

It is possible to envision the youth leadership toolkit—or a stream of such products—making their way into schools around the world, touching both elite schools and the millions of modest schools in developing countries. Furthermore, this would likely create an explosion of new and innovative content as teachers adapt, create, and share the new tools and techniques they have created for development.

Teachers as Facilitators

The secret to leadership development is that it is not about teaching as much as it is about creating the space for individuals to learn about themselves and others. If leadership as a practice is to be incorporated into classrooms for younger students, it must be delivered by teachers willing to move into facilitator roles and away from lecturing. Teachers observing the leadership modules and the use of leadership tools presented by CCL staff for younger people frequently recognize the increased attention and participation of students who have previously had a reputation for "tuning out" or "having little to contribute." At CCL, the staff believes that by creating a safe learning environment, participants are able to actively shape and internalize their own learning.

CCL's use of the Socratic method, whereby participants are asked questions and learning comes from reflection and dialogue, closely mirrors the successful education models enacted by Marva Collins during her 30 years of teaching (1975–2008) at Chicago's Westside Preparatory School (Collins 2009). She used the Socratic method with students living in an impoverished environment where many young people were considered "learning disabled" or "unteachable." By encouraging these students to talk about the content that was read out loud and helping them see meaning by discussing and writing about why the subject matter was important to them, her classroom succeeded in teaching young people who had been dismissed and underserved. She was able to accomplish what others thought was impossible by moving into facilitating learning rather than teaching more and more facts. In essence, she was able to discover and unlock the human potential that had been hidden within each underprivileged student. In her words, "There is a brilliant child locked inside every student" (thinkexist.com).

As with Marva Collins's efforts, we have seen the impact that simple tools and guided reflection can have in transforming the lives of young people, especially those less privileged or prioritized. For instance, Boomerang, a YMCA program in North Carolina that works with children thrown out of school for misconduct (Geffner 2008), uses an empowerment technique it calls the Tree of Life to help these children find what's good in their lives and extend it to create the future they desire for themselves. This technique uses the metaphor of a tree to help young people map their roots—the strengths and resources that keep them grounded and nourished. They then trace their aspirations and hopes in the form of branches that extend outward and upward. The trunk of the tree links the roots and branches and forms the path to the future that the youth are challenged to create. Finally, the youth are asked to identify what can threaten their tree and what they can do to ward off these threats.

We took this technique to Ghana, where we shared it with Cheri Baker, a Peace Corps volunteer stationed in an isolated rural village without running water or electricity. Cheri used the Tree of Life to help a group of young girls map their aspirations (branches) and their strengths (roots) and to think about how their strengths are a pathway (the trunk of the tree) to enable them to achieve their hopes for the future. The tree took shape on a chalkboard as the girls traced the contours of their lives and dreams. "Desire and support, a nurse in the village, parents, books to learn" wrote the girls for their roots. A profusion of branches cascaded out—"tailor shop, teacher, big house, a husband who is a great parent." The trunk of the tree represented lessons that perhaps are universal—"finish school, stay away from boys, be happy, work hard, focus, and consult respected people for advice." Asked to identify what could threaten their tree, they marked the hard everyday realities that could snatch away their dreams—"prostitution, HIV/AIDS, and unplanned pregnancy" (http://leadbeyond.net/?p=421).

These examples make clear what is at stake in the developing world for young children whose lives depend more on individual will than entitlement. In a compelling report titled *Grit: The Skills for Success and How They Are Grown* (Young Foundation 2009), there is a call to action about the importance of this kind of development for young people: "When we deny children and young people the kind of educational ecology in which they can 'grow' their capabilities, we are also denying them their freedom."

A Call to Action

We cannot make a call to action more evocatively than that made above in the quotation from *Grit*, but we echo its message for the well-being of children, their future employers, and society at large. If the purpose of school is to prepare young people for work and life, leadership development can help them do better in school and prepare them to be more effective in working with others once they arrive in the workforce. If we wait until the workforce is in its 40s before offering it formal leadership development opportunities, which is now largely the case among U.S. companies, we will have missed important opportunities to strengthen the pipeline of emerging leaders and the greater impact they can have as young people. By increasing the sense of confidence, empowerment, and purpose that young people acquire early in life, we will enable them to become more prepared to take on the mantle of leadership and serve as active members of society earlier in life.

For the readers of this chapter, likely those in human resources and training roles, we ask that you consider what you can do to enable, recognize, and reward schools that invest in leadership development. We know that the pull of employers in favor of the development of these skills will matter a great deal. There is much at stake here to improve the human condition using the lever of leadership development. A world where everyone has access to leadership development will likely become more collaborative, creative, resilient, and resourceful.

Further Reading

David Altman, Lyndon Rego, and Steadman Harrison, "Democratizing Leader Development," in *The Center for Creative Leadership Handbook of Leadership Development*, 3rd edition, ed. Ellen Van Velsor, Cynthia McCauley, and Marian Ruderman. San Francisco: Jossey-Bass, 2010.

S. M. Datur, D. A. Garvin, and C. A. Knoop, *The Center for Creative Leadership.* Harvard Business School Case Study N9-308-013. Cambridge, MA: Harvard Business School, 2008.

Christopher Gergen and Gregg Vanourek, *Life Entrepreneurs: Ordinary People Creating Extraordinary Lives.* San Francisco: Jossey-Bass, 2008.

Center for Creative Leadership, "Young People Are Leaders, Too," *Making a Difference,* www.ccl .org/leadership/pdf/news/newsletters/mad0909.pdf.

R. W. Larson, Toward a Psychology of Positive Youth Development. *American Psychologist* 55, no. 1: 170–183, 2000.

Leadership Beyond Boundaries blog, www.leadbeyond.org.

Lyndon Rego, David Altman, and Steadman Harrison, *And Leadership Development for All: Self-Management and Leadership Development.* Northampton, MA: Edward Elgar, forthcoming.

Sandy Speicher, "IDEO's Ten Tips for Creating a 21st-Century Classroom Experience," *Metropolis,* http://www.metropolismag.com/story/20090218/ideos-ten-tips-for-creating-a-21st-century -classroom-experience.

References

African Leadership Academy. 2010. Our Five Distinctive Elements. http://www.africanleadership academy.org/site/about/five_distinctive_elements.

Altman, D., L. Rego, and S. Harrison. 2009. *Democratizing Leader Development: The Center for Creative Leadership Handbook of Leadership Development,* 3rd ed. San Francisco: Jossey-Bass.

Bandura, A. 1997. *Self-Efficacy. The Exercise of Control.* New York: W. H. Freeman.

———. 2001. Social Cognitive Theory: An Agentic Perspective. *Annual Review of Psychology* 52: 1–26.

Collins, Marva. 2009. Bibliography. www.marvacollins.com/biography.html.

Dweck, C. S. 2006. *Mindset: The New Psychology of Success.* New York: Ballantine Books.

Geffner, I. 2008. Inspiring Program Helps Suspended Students. *Carrboro* [NC] *Citizen,* February 21. www.carrborocitizen.com/main/2008/02/21/inspiring-program-helps-suspended-students/.

Ginright, S., and T. James. 2002. From Assets to Agents of Change: Social Justice, Organizing and Youth Development. *New Directions for Youth Development* 96.

MacKenzie, G. 1996. *Orbiting the Giant Hairball: A Corporate Fool's Guide to Surviving with Grace.* New York: Penguin.

Rappaport, J. 1977. *Community Psychology: Values, Research and Action.* New York: Holt, Rinehart & Winston.

Rosenthal, R., and L. F. Jacobson. 1968. Teacher Expectations for the Disadvantaged. *Scientific American* 218, no. 4: 3–7.

Roth, J. L., and J. Brooks-Gunn. 2003. Youth Development Programs: Risk, Prevention and Policy. *Journal of Adolescent Health* 32: 170–182.

Ross, L., and R. E. Nisbett. 1991. *The Person and the Situation: Perspectives of Social Psychology.* New York: McGraw-Hill.

Rudkin, J. K. 2003. *Community Psychology: Guiding Principles and Orienting Concepts.* Upper Saddle River, NJ: Prentice Hall.

Ryan, W. 1971. *Blaming the Victim.* New York: Vintage Books.

Seligman, M. E. P. 1998. *Learned Optimism: How to Change Your Mind and Your Life.* New York: Pocket Books.

Smith, E. R., and D. M. Mackie. 2007. *Social Psychology,* 3rd ed. New York: Psychology Press.

Trickett, E. J. 2009. Community Psychology: Individuals and Interventions in Community Context. *Annual Review of Psychology* 60: 395–419.

Young Foundation. 2009. *Grit: The Skills for Success and How They Are Grown.* London: Young Foundation. www.youngfoundation.org/files/images/publications/GRIT.pdf.

Woyke, E., and M. Atal. 2007. The Talent Hunt: Design Programs Are Shaping a New Generation of Creative Managers. *BusinessWeek,* October 4, 54–59. http://www.businessweek.com/innovate/content/oct2007/id2007104_575219.htm.

About the Authors

Lyndon Rego is the director of the Innovation Incubator at the Center for Creative Leadership. He focuses on innovation that addresses key leadership challenges and expands the boundaries of leadership development through new programs, tools, and delivery platforms. Via the Leadership Beyond Boundaries effort, he has helped CCL extend leadership development to a range of underserved populations, encompassing developing countries, social-sector organizations, and youth. He has an MBA from the University of North Carolina–Chapel Hill and an MA in communication from the University of North Dakota. He writes and speaks on issues at the intersection of social innovation, complexity, and leadership.

Steadman D. Harrison III is the senior innovation associate for the Center for Creative Leadership. His work at CCL focuses on organizational innovation, particularly extending leadership development to new populations and through new platforms. Recent initiatives have included a focus on emerging markets, nonprofits, and young leaders. As a key member of the Research Innovation and Product Development Group, he serves as an innovation catalyst to help design, deliver, and test new and sustainable models for leadership development that are inclusive, accessible, and affordable. He holds a BA in psychology from the University of North Carolina–Chapel Hill and an MA/MTS from the Houston Graduate School of Theology.

David G. Altman, PhD, is executive vice president of research, innovation, and product development at the Center for Creative Leadership. Previously, he spent 19 years in academia, 10 years as an associate professor and professor of public health sciences and of pediatrics at Wake Forest University School of Medicine and 10 years as a senior research scientist (and postdoctoral fellow and research associate) at the Stanford University Center for Research in Disease Prevention. He received his MA and PhD in social ecology from the University of California, Irvine, and his BA in psychology from the University of California, Santa Barbara.

Chapter 30

Growing Tomorrow's Leaders for the Worlds of 2020

Lawrena Colombo and John Verderese

In This Chapter

- Leadership development programs are most effective when linked with an organization's strategy and its long-term scenario planning.

- There are opportunities at various stages of a person's career to develop global leadership competencies.

- Innovative leadership development programs such as global immersion are most successful when they have a high degree of executive advocacy and involvement.

- The leaders of tomorrow must be prepared to operate in a global, interconnected world and must be comfortable reinventing themselves, given the pace of change.

Thousands of applications have already been developed for the iPhone. That's a startling number, considering that this device did not exist until 2007. In today's ever-changing and evolving world, some might consider the thought of developing global business leaders to be like trying to create an application for the next revolutionary generation of mobile

---

© 2010 PricewaterhouseCoopers. Used with permission.

handheld devices. How can we prepare for what we do not know? After all, 20 years ago, when today's global leaders may have been in their formative years, had anyone really predicted the rise of globalism, the flattening of the world, and the speed at which information traverses the globe?

All this change calls into question whether the traditional leadership model of the global organization still even applies. Are global leaders really those who have been groomed over the long term, or are they simply those who have demonstrated the adaptability and tenacity to thrive to become the accidental leaders who succeed today, and, if so, is that individual success sustainable? Twenty years ago, leaders may have been prepared for a multinational world, but they must now function in a *globally* interconnected world.

So, with this in mind, can we really prepare individuals in our organizations to be global leaders, and if so, at what point, and how good of a crystal ball do we all need? Though some organizations may be content to think they are aptly developing their future global leaders, they may have forgotten to ask a very important question: "Preparing them for what?" To answer this question, it is important to do some scenario planning for what the future may look like, to prepare individuals for the kinds of scenarios that we may face, and at the same time, to give them the skills and experiences they will need to adapt to the ever-changing world.

At the end of 2007, PricewaterhouseCoopers (PwC) published its first report on the future of people management. It predicted that the growing talent crisis, demographic shifts, advances in technology, and rise of sustainability issues on the corporate agenda would dramatically change organizational models and the way in which companies manage their operations and people. The report, *Managing Tomorrow's People: The Future of Work to 2020,* produced with the help of the James Martin Institute for Science and Civilization at the Said Business School, Oxford, explored three scenarios or worlds which might coexist in 2020.

The Three Worlds of 2020

According to these three scenarios, in 2020, there might be three worlds—orange, green, and blue (figure 30-1). In the Orange World, businesses are fragmented, and so-called companies are usually small, lean, nimble, and reliant on an extensive network of suppliers. They have multiple clients and contracts and access a globally diverse workforce called team workers on a supply-and-demand basis. Communication networks are enabled by continual technological advancement and innovation. Loose collaborative cloud networks come and go, project by project. Employees in the Orange World are technology savvy and networked to communities of other employees with similar skills.

Figure 30-1. 2020: Where Three Worlds Coexist

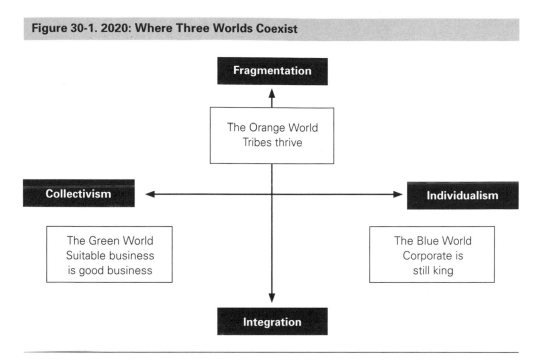

In the Green World, companies have a powerful social conscience intrinsic to the brand and a green, or environmental, sense of responsibility. The focus is on sustainable and ethical business practices and a strong drive to minimize and mitigate risky practices. This responsibility ethos is enforced by governments and regulators and is more prevalent in certain industries such as energy, automobiles, and financial services. Green World employees engage with the company brand because it reflects their own values. They are recognized for good corporate behavior, not just business results.

In 2020, Blue World companies embody big company capitalism, and individual preferences override a belief in collective social responsibility. Blue World companies have invested in size, technology, the talent pipeline, strong leadership (as traditionally defined), and sophisticated metrics. They have highly energized and committed workforces that are well trained, skilled, and operate globally. Work may be pressurized and fast-paced, but employees enjoy a wide range of benefits that help them sustain busy lifestyles and lock them into the organization. For those who perform well, the rewards can be very high.

How close any or all three of these scenarios are to reality will only be known in 2020, but as far as they are related to growing global leaders, the point is clear. The leader of tomorrow needs to grow for the world *not* as we know it today but for what we think it will be in the future. Yet at the same time, even with the best succession planning, some leaders will be thrust upon the scene who will need to be grown rapidly for the world we live in today. The world, our organizations, and our workforces are changing so rapidly that when it comes to developing global leaders, we need a collective mindset that it's never too early and never too late.

The Modalities of Leadership Development

Regardless of which color world a leader is destined for, traditional methods of leadership development can only go so far. They may develop good managers, but they will not develop visionary individuals who inspire others, collaborate across organizational and continental boundaries, and produce the kinds of individuals who can lead in a dynamic global world. Though a 2020 leader may thrive in his or her *own* colored world, he or she must also be able to work across organizational boundaries and operate in the other worlds.

Traditional leadership development includes such modalities as assessments, rotational assignments, attendance at leading business school programs, and traditional coaching and mentoring. But those leaders who seek to thrive in the Orange, Green, and Blue worlds are likely to require more of a special type of experience, a flagship immersion program, which traditionally has lagged the others (figure 30-2).

A flagship immersion program creates an experience in which selected individuals participate in a program considered in some ways as a rite of passage for high-potential or pivotal talent—see the sidebar. Though there is a long-held belief that adults learn best in a safe, low-risk environment such as a classroom or even a retreat, an interactive and truly global experience sidesteps this thinking and exposes the leader to settings and situations that introduce a healthy level of risk, adventure, and excitement.

Leveraging Global Experience into Trust-Based Relationships

International immersion is a key common element of both programs described in the sidebar, Genesis Park and Project Ulysses. As global leaders increasingly interact in the Blue, Orange, and Green worlds, global experiences will become an increasingly necessary core competency. "It doesn't necessarily matter *where* someone has had a global immersion experience or whether it happens to have been in the same place as someone with whom you are developing a global relationship," says PwC's global clients and markets leader, Don Almeida. "The fact that someone has had had a game-changing global experience becomes a shared rite of passage and a common bond with other global leaders, whether they be clients, colleagues, or other stakeholders such as attorneys, investment bankers, and the like.

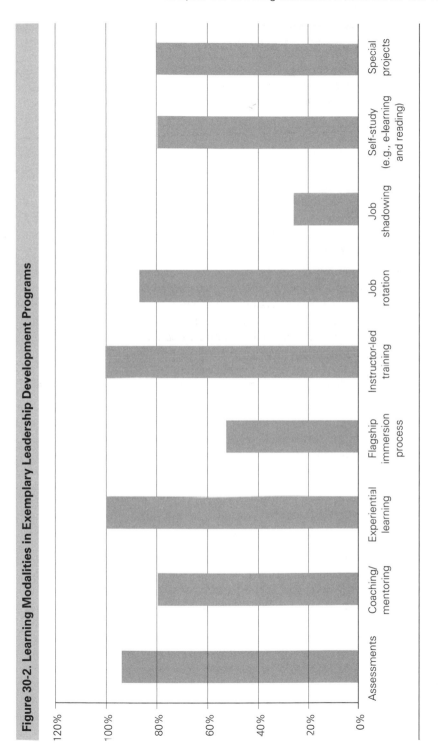

Figure 30-2. Learning Modalities in Exemplary Leadership Development Programs

It's Never Too Early, Never Too Late

PricewaterhouseCoopers believes that when it comes to developing global leaders, "it's never too early, never too late," and as such includes in its suite of leadership development opportunities two unique programs, Genesis Park and Project Ulysses.

Genesis Park brings together high-performing staff members from around the world who have demonstrated clear leadership potential and immerses them in an intense 16-week residency program, during which participants are freed of all client obligations. Genesis Park participants have demonstrated a willingness, eagerness, and ability to grasp and analyze business concepts, explore market and industry trends, approach challenges creatively, and effectively articulate their thinking. "The Park," as it has come to be known, is designed to take a globally diverse group of promising leaders (who have not yet reached the partner/principal level) and develop them into business leaders capable of creating differentiating value for PwC and its clients.

Genesis Park teams are often called upon by PwC to research complex business issues and make recommendations to leadership. "I am constantly amazed by the depth and breadth of problem solving these teams have brought to the many leading-edge business issues I have put on their plate," says PwC's global advisory leader, Juan Pujadas. "But even more amazing is how quickly, as a result of a structured onboarding experience, a group of individuals who do not know each other become a cohesive, high-performing team and, rather than trying to set their cultural, language, and ethnic backgrounds aside, they instead leverage their differences to bring unique perspectives that solve a problem better—and faster."

Candidates for participation in Genesis Park require sponsorship, most typically by a senior partner from the candidate's home office, and there is an active alumni network that helps maintain ongoing professional and personal contact among Genesis Park graduates—and because the participants are from all over the world, a robust global network flourishes. Upon returning to their home firm, Genesis Park graduates are ready to take on important new roles for clients, manage teams, and develop new business opportunities. Their experience at Genesis Park is often viewed by others as a metamorphosis, and these individuals quickly get a reputation for thinking and doing "beyond their tenure."

Achieving a career milestone of being admitted as a partner or principal at PwC is not considered an end state bur rather a platform for continuing growth. Following the tenet that "it's never too late," individuals at the partner level are selected to attend the Ulysses Program. Ulysses is designed to build a global network of responsible leaders who are committed to developing quality, trust-based relationships with a diverse range of stakeholders; leaders who understand the responsibilities of *their* partnership and their responsibilities as individuals to integrate stakeholder collaboration into the role of high-performing business to create sustainable success for communities and markets across the world. The program comprises five learning modules and is distinguished by an eight-week project assignment where multicultural teams work in developing countries in collaboration with social and nongovernmental organizations.

An example of a project was for Aravind Eye Care, based in India. Aravind is the world's largest provider of eye care services, performing 250,000 surgeries a year. The long-term aim of the organization is to perform 1 million surgeries a year by 2015. To help them achieve this goal, the Ulysses team was asked to design a strategic road map for Aravind so it would be able to form partnerships with other eye care organizations in the poor regions of India. Implicit in this task was the creation of marketing strategies for identifying partners and the development of monitoring processes to evaluate any new operations.

Ulysses was designed as an innovative response to the core challenges that businesses face in an increasingly interconnected global world, and thus it seeks to empower global leaders to achieve the following:

- *Trust-based stakeholder relationships:* to build a global network of leaders who understand the importance of values in developing trust-based relationships with a diverse range of stakeholders and who can create a sustainable brand that is differentiated by the quality of those relationships with clients, colleagues, and the broader international community.
- *Sustainable business practices:* to help developing global leaders understand the changing role of business in influencing the economic, political, social, and environmental well-being of communities and markets around the globe, and the responsibility of organizations and individuals to work in collaboration with a broader group of stakeholders to achieve sustainable success through responsible worldwide business practices.
- *Responsible leadership model:* to develop a model of leadership that will enable the next generation to lead responsibly within a globally networked world, and to position this responsible leadership model as a foundational organizational element.

Rich Baird, a former PwC global human capital leader and a Ulysses champion, says that "Ulysses builds responsible leaders with heightened self-awareness, cross-cultural teaming, and by providing opportunities to make the world a better place. The program is truly unique and enhances the participants' understanding of their place in a global society and the importance of building networks with similarly focused, visionary leaders."

Source: Interviews with authors.

However for United States–based leaders, immersion in other traditional Western locations will increasingly become less relevant and career defining as the truly game-changing experiences will stretch individuals in terms of learning non-Western culture, customs, and language" (from interview with authors).

Keys to Success

These are just two distinctive offerings in the range of traditional leadership development programs and opportunities at PwC, but "what makes them unique and sustainable," says

Karen VanderLinde, PwC's global leader of people and change, "is that they are aligned with PwC's strategy and have executive commitment that not only survives but *thrives* with executive leadership changes. Genesis Park is a frequent stop for partners who assume significant leadership roles in our firm, and once they see the talent at their disposal, they are quick to put one of their teams to work on a challenging issue" (from interview with authors).

Executive commitment isn't measured by investment dollars alone, but also, and more important, by the amount of executive time dedicated and the extent to which an organization's top executives *have the feel* of these programs. The more nontraditional the program, the more chance naysayers in the organization, often those charged with managing the bottom line, may try to cancel them, particularly in lean times. It is important to know that the more innovative and game-changing a leadership program is, the more advocacy and active involvement it needs from senior executives. Leaders at the top must encourage those at lower levels to attend and sponsor, and they themselves must lead by example by allowing their own protégées to attend these types of programs.

So whether an organization is headed for the Blue, Green, or Orange world—or some other color still to be determined—it is important to continually invest in leadership development and make it as innovative and game-changing for the organization and individual as possible. And remember, when it comes to developing highly talented people into global leaders, it's never too early and never too late.

Further Reading

Marc Effron, Shelli Greenslade, and Michelle Salob, "Growing Great Leaders: Does It Really Matter?" *Human Resource Planning Journal,* vol. 28, no. 3 (September 2005): 18–23.

Thomas Maak and Nicola M. Pless, *Responsible Leadership.* New York: Routledge, 2006.

Mark E. Mendenhall, Gunter K. Stahl, and Torsten M. Kuhlmann, eds., *Developing Global Business Leaders: Policies, Processes and Innovation.* Westport, CT: Quorum Books, 2000.

About the Authors

Lawrena Colombo is a partner in PricewaterhouseCoopers' advisory people and change practice and specializes in change management, communications, and learning and development. She consults with many global clients to optimize their business results by aligning their people strategies. Her career has included working and living abroad as well as having global human capital responsibility for a practice of more than 10,000 professionals. She is a member of ASTD, the Society for Human Resources Management, and the Human Capital Institute. She formerly served as the U.S. and global human capital leader for PricewaterhouseCoopers' tax practice.

John Verderese is a managing director in PricewaterhouseCoopers' advisory people and change practice. He specializes in talent management, including leadership development, talent assessment, diversity and inclusion, and flexible workplace arrangements. He formerly served as PricewaterhouseCoopers' human capital leader for its U.S. advisory practice. In this role, he was responsible for all aspects of talent management, development, compensation, and benefits for advisory partners and principals and advisory professional staff in the United States. During his tenure in that role, PricewaterhouseCoopers received numerous accolades, including being named to *Fortune*'s 100 best companies to work for and Diversity Inc.'s top 10. He is a member of the Society for Human Resources Management.

A Military View of Leadership in the Private Sector

John Lockard

In This Chapter

- A comparison of leadership in the private sector and in military organizations.

- Nine essentials for good leadership in any organization.

After a very satisfying 36-year military career, I had the good fortune of joining the private sector in a senior executive leadership position. I had really never taken the time to think about leadership outside the service until I started to prepare for transition to a second career. It was at that point that I started to relate my experience in military service to potential strengths that would be valued in the private sector.

Leadership Basics

It was easy to draw parallels with my technical skills in engineering and program management, but it was a completely different matter when it came to leadership. During my service years, I had the opportunity to grow as a leader, starting with a formal introduction to the basics of leadership from the very beginning during officer training to leading my first small team of 19 military aircraft maintenance technicians in my first operational flying squadron

---

© 2010 John Lockard. Used with permission.

to my final position as the top executive in charge of a large 27,000-person organization with global presence. I knew the introductory leadership training was common for each of us. It was easy to align each person with the vision and mission, as each could see where he or she fit and what his or her potential contribution meant to the success of the entire team or organization. We were all there to support each other as we worked for a common goal. The results of individual leadership skills, both positive and negative, were seen relatively quickly. Individual and team motivations were fairly easy to measure, if one took the time to define and quantify them using the universal language that was part of the military lingo for mission accomplishment. Military organizations were well understood; where you fit and your role were easy to define. Outcomes were obviously apparent and there for all to see. Accomplishment was easy to measure in generally well-defined segments that all related to the mission.

Providing a Common Foundation

When I looked at private industry, the common fundamentals that were shared as part of military training for individuals and teams were not there. The entry-level training for those joining industry was focused on technical knowledge and individual accomplishment. There is commonality with the military in that individuals are generally taught the fundamental skills peculiar to a company or group by the bosses, but a common foundation of language and understanding is missing.

Like the military, where individuals in the private sector fit in the organization is also fairly easy to see, but my observations are that the organizations are not consistent from one job or unit to the next, and individual alignment with the goals of the larger organization is much more complex. Team accomplishment and motivation are often more difficult as a result of organizational complexity. Individual accomplishment is harder to relate to the larger outcome of the team or unit because daily feedback in relation to goals is more difficult to measure.

More often than not, people are rewarded for individual accomplishment rather than team results. This makes alignment with team goals more difficult. Additionally, in the private sector people normally have to wait until much later in their career before they are put in charge of a team when compared with the military. This makes it harder to build leadership skills and grow as a leader in the professional formative years. This does not, however, preclude individuals from learning from their surroundings and being guided by the examples set by those in charge. Learning what works for you is just delayed a bit.

Expanding Opportunities to Grow and Learn

During my military service years, I was able to observe many different leadership styles as I moved from assignment to assignment. Each new assignment built on the last one as responsibility increased with each step. I made mental notes along the way of those leadership traits or attributes that were, in my view, most effective for creating the desired outcomes. These were attributes that I wanted to include in my leadership approach or style as I sought to improve my personal effectiveness as a leader. I also noted those leadership attributes or styles that didn't achieve the desired effect relative to outcomes, whether it involved mission accomplishment or individual and team achievement. I wanted to make sure that none of these negative leadership behaviors or motivators became part of my personal leadership toolkit.

In a military career, individuals are generally given a broader exposure to leadership styles because they move more often from assignment to assignment and from one environment to the next. The same can be said for formal leadership training, because of the military focus on continuous education as service members move up the career ladder. Military professionals are generally provided with opportunities to attend service schools, where they spend several months with peers in a formal academic atmosphere to share experiences. These professional education opportunities almost always have a segment that focuses on leadership. Simply put, the military has a continuous focus on leadership, which has a direct correlation to mission accomplishment.

In the military, each individual is graded on personal leadership skills in regular performance evaluations. Additionally, individuals are provided with frequent feedback on their accomplishments as a leader as well as their contributions to the organization's goals. In my experience, industry is more focused on technical performance and on the bottom line. Unfortunately, more often than not, the balance has shifted in the direction of short-duration financial performance. Clearly, quarterly performance is important, but it must be kept in proper balance with the longer-term goals. Good leaders in industry achieve the proper balance of long-term mission accomplishment as related to a strategic objectives and financial results, both short and long term.

The Essentials of Good Leadership

Over the years, I have solidified a set of fundamental leadership traits or principles that I think are common to those I classify as great leaders. I think most of us are able to think of a few great leaders from our own experience or education that have been defined as such by what they were able to accomplish. It is useful to address a few of the fundamental leadership attributes that the military and the private-sector environment have in common. I think of these attributes as enduring and not limited in application. Common to all is that they are essential to gaining and maintaining trust.

Know Yourself

We all have individual strengths and weaknesses. The natural tendency is to use the strengths to get ahead and hide the weaknesses because we perceive they make us vulnerable. As we grow in our professional lives, we are in a continuous learning environment, and most of us are able to improve our weak spots as our knowledge grows. Knowing this is the case, we are able to become more complete in our understanding, but we are never totally free of a few of those troublesome areas in our knowledge set. Though improving our weaknesses is important, knowing what they are is critical. If we know them and are candid with ourselves, we can look for ways to offset their effect on our performance. One of the better ways to compensate is to find members of our team who complement the weak spots while we endeavor to improve over time. Good leaders don't have to do it all by themselves.

The people with whom we work will observe our every action. The higher in the organization we rise, the more we are watched. They will know us more completely than we think. Clearly, our strengths are evident, but it is a natural tendency to look for the weak spots. If there is an appearance of a cover-up, it eats at that essential element of trust. Being open and secure in who we are is far more powerful in developing and maintaining trust.

Before I leave this topic of knowing yourself, it is important to talk about another aspect of this attribute. As I mentioned above, we all grow and change over time. We gain knowledge with experience. These are the things that help get us ahead. We achieve higher responsibility as a leader as a result. Unfortunately, I have observed too many leaders who have a sense that new assignments require different behavior. This is not true when it comes to leadership. We must be mindful of changing behaviors as we move to ever higher leadership roles. A general tendency is that we receive less and less personal feedback on how we are perceived by those we lead. It becomes easy to make gradual changes in our behavior without recognizing it. It is likely that if we do not continuously check for drift away from our core values we will not see it, but our people surely do. The media is filled with examples of high-level executives who have lost touch with themselves and lose touch with the organization or get in personal trouble as a result. If we continuously take stock of ourselves and seek candid feedback, we will stay grounded in our core values and trust will be maintained.

Know Your People and Take Care of Them

Good leaders must relate to people. They must be trusted to act in the best interest of the individual and the organization. In short, the people you lead must trust you. Trust is gained on a personal basis. It is between two individuals. Although, in large organizations, it is not possible to know each individual, we still must gain their trust if we are going to be an effective leader.

A certain amount of respect will be gained by the fact that each of us goes through some sort of vetting process as we are selected for new positions of leadership. As an aside, this is why an open and consistent promotion process is so important to an organization. The people in the organization must believe the process is fair and that the most deserving candidates are selected. If they respect the process, they will respect those selected to lead. Respect opens the door for building trust. But it does not relieve a good leader of the requirement to demonstrate concern for the individual.

A good leader will go out of his or her way to connect with people. He or she will look for opportunities to have short conversations with people as part of the daily routine. The conversations can be about work-related topics or non-probing discussions unrelated to work. The main objective is to show your concern for individuals, and in doing so to demonstrate that individuals are valued. Often these discussions lead to uncovering individual concerns or organizational issues. The important thing for a leader to do is listen and respond, even if it means explaining why an issue or concern may not be valid when it is put into a larger context. It is important to follow up with a response or action that demonstrates the input was valued. The more these exchanges occur with the people in the organization, the faster word will spread about your concern for people. Trust builds quickly in an atmosphere where people feel valued.

Create a Vision Others See with Passion to Go There with You

Part of being a leader is the ability to establish a vision for the organization. Though there are many visionaries out there, the thing that sets a good leader apart from a pure visionary is the capability to communicate a vision in a manner that enables others to clearly see the destination. More important, it must be portrayed so others can identify with it, creating a desire to go there with the rest of the team. All see the positive potential of the outcome in relation to individual value—how it is good for the organization and for the individuals who are part of it. They are able to see what is in it for them. Again, they feel valued.

Communicate Effectively—Both Ways

Effective communication is at the heart of everything a good leader does. This means open and honest communication is both ways, from the leader to the follower and vice versa. It is easy to see that a good leader must be able to communicate messages that are well understood. Equally, if not more important, great leaders must never lose sight of the need to listen well. Without effective two-way communication, trust is likely to be difficult to gain or to erode quickly once established.

Set the Example—Never Forgetting What Got You Here

All too often, people for some reason believe it is necessary to change their behavior when they take a position of higher responsibility. For various reasons, there is a perception that the new position needs something different. In fact, what the new position needs is exactly the attributes that were manifested in your selection process. People are selected for new positions of leadership because of their demonstrated skills and the belief in their potential to grow with more responsibility. There is generally no need for radical change in leadership behavior. We only need to learn as we grow and complement what we have demonstrated with what we learn. This is particularly important when setting the example as a leader. Build on your strengths as a leader, mindful that others are watching, including those who helped you along the way. Never forget those who helped you get where you are, because none of us does it alone. This is a critical element of maintaining trust as a person moves up the leadership ladder.

Align Expectations and Set Boundaries

A good leader focuses on removing uncertainty. People need to know what is expected of them. They need to know where they fit and understand their role with clarity. Great leaders achieve maximum results through effective delegation. They use the power of individuals working together as teams. Each member complements the combined knowledge of the team and aligns with a common goal in highly effective teams. The team is empowered as a unit to achieve the expected outcome. The limits of the delegation are understood by all through clearly articulated boundaries that define the limits of action. The strength of the delegation is maintained by open and effective communication, which provides all with the confidence that the alignment is sound and the boundaries are being respected and have not been exceeded.

Play the Hand You Are Dealt

Often there is a tendency by leaders to move people off the team to improve overall performance. There are times when this is needed, but if done too often, it leaves people with uncertainty about who will be next. It can rapidly erode trust. Good leaders know their people and have the instinct to move people to positions on the team that allow them to use their strengths to complement the team's performance. By demonstrating understanding of individual capabilities and a willingness to position teammates in areas where each can contribute, a leader can foster cohesion among the team members and encourage personal growth with well-placed personal coaching.

Be Inclusive, But Decisive When It Is Time for Action

The best ideas surface when the entire team feels empowered to contribute. It is especially powerful when all recognize that their ideas are valued. Establishing an atmosphere of inclusion opens the gate for innovation and diversity of thought. A good leader fosters engagement and contribution by the entire team. This does not mean that collaboration is endless.

A good leader never loses sight of when it is time for a decision, and he or she is timely in stopping debate with a firm decision when it is time to move forward. When people feel their inputs have been heard and considered, they feel valued and find it easier to align with the decision—even when it might be counter to their input.

Don't Be Dissuaded by Risk—Manage It

A leader is always confronted with risk. It can come in all forms—technical, financial, schedule, personnel resources, and others. A good leader will search out the risks so they can be managed. This is where independent views, outside inputs, and team communications are extremely valuable. The more time spent identifying possible risk, the greater the opportunity to develop risk mitigation plans. These plans provide the team with confidence to deal with the unknowns that are sure to surface along the way. Confidence comes from understanding, and trust comes from the willingness to share in open communication, as all are allowed to contribute with the knowledge they bring to develop solutions for the team. It creates an environment where risks are understood and surprises are less frequent as a result.

Summary

The fundamentals of leadership apply in all workplace environments:

- Know yourself.
- Know your people and take care of them.
- Create a vision others can see with passion to go there with you.
- Communicate effectively—both ways.
- Set the example—never forgetting what got you here.
- Align expectations and set boundaries.
- Play the hand you are dealt.
- Be inclusive, but decisive when it is time for action.
- Don't be dissuaded by risk—manage it.

Great leaders use the essential elements of leadership to gain the trust of their people. They build an environment that values the positive and establishes a foundation of open and honest communication. They motivate individuals and teams to align and execute to achieve success. They remove uncertainty at every opportunity. They focus on producing outcomes that all value, individually and collectively. Great leaders are mindful of the example they set and thrive on what others are able to accomplish by helping them succeed.

About the Author

John Lockard is chief operating officer and deputy to the president and CEO of Boeing Integrated Defense Systems, a $32 billion, 70,000-person business unit. Lockard joined Boeing in 2000 after retiring as a vice admiral with 36 years of distinguished service in the U.S. Navy. While in the Navy, he served in numerous operational assignments, including combat operations flying from Navy carriers. He attended the Naval War College, commanded two aviation squadrons, was the executive officer of an aircraft carrier, and served as the Navy F/A-18 program manager before being selected for flag rank in 1991. He held several flag rank assignments before assuming command of the Naval Air Systems Command in 1995. He is a highly decorated veteran and holds a bachelor's degree in aeronautical engineering from the Naval Postgraduate School. He is chairman of the Board of Directors of the Navy Federal Credit Union, the world's largest credit union, with more than $40 billion in assets. In 2007, the Navy League of the United States presented him with one of its highest honors, the Admiral Arleigh Burke Leadership Award.

 **Chapter 31**

Leading in the Public Sector

Will Brown

In This Chapter

- How to ensure effective leadership in the public sector by understanding the people and the organization.

- How to recognize and use the power leaders already have.

- Effective meeting management by getting people out of the room.

- How to implement the elevator diplomacy concept.

- How to make decisions easier for senior leaders.

Leaders must be effective, for if they are not they cannot call themselves leaders. This is true in the public sector as well as in private industry or any other organization. In fact, given the potential burden of red tape and bureaucracy, effectiveness becomes even more critical in the public sector. The key to effectiveness is in understanding the organization and the people with whom you work. Only by really understanding can leaders maximize their contribution to their organizations. This chapter addresses four elements that help all leaders, but in particular public sector leaders, to be more effective. You will recognize that the four elements are all tinged with internal politics—a critical element in public sector organizations. These four elements are using power you already have, ensuring effective meetings by getting people out of the room, practicing elevator diplomacy, and making decisions easier for senior leaders.

Webster's dictionary defines leadership as "leading others along a way, guiding." To me, the one word that pinpoints the major element of leadership is "influence." The literature on leadership supports this concept:

- "Leadership is the process of persuasion or example by which an individual induces a group to pursue objectives" (Gardner 1990, 1).
- "I define leadership as leaders inducing followers to act for certain goals that represent the values and motivations—the wants and needs, the aspirations and expectations—of both leaders and followers" (Burns 1978, 19).
- "The one who knows the right thing but cannot achieve it fails because he is ineffectual. The great leader needs. . .the capacity to achieve" (Nixon 1982, 5).

The unique operating environment of the federal workplace and the skills necessary to enable leaders to emerge and create opportunities for success is critical to effectively run the United States. This chapter focuses on leaders just below the top levels of the organization (middle leaders). In many cases these individuals possess an unrealized influence in organizations, but too often spend time seeking power they already possess. They are positioned within the organization to be the best at facilitating the business of the organization. The ability to operate in that role depends on having the requisite skills to be effective in wielding leadership or influence. This chapter provides insight in how to achieve that objective.

The Federal Workforce

Individuals come to work for the United States' federal government for a variety of reasons. The most prevalent are stability, patriotism, location or salary, and interesting work. These factors are important because they provide insight into the things that motivate federal workers and provide opportunities to influence them. Stereotypical federal workers are seen as less motivated and less talented than their private sector counterparts. Neither of these stereotypes is true in the aggregate. Having been part of the federal workforce for more than 35 years, I have recognized that the reality is that this workforce is full of some of the most talented, motivated, and dedicated individuals in the country. They come and continue to work for the federal government because they want and believe they can make a difference. Understanding that must be the basis for any idea about leadership in the federal sector.

However, leadership in the federal environment has its own unique set of concerns. The organizational design of many federal agencies creates an inherently bureaucratic environment that, in and of itself, manifests a resistance to change and efficiency. Furthermore, the rotational nature of leaders of defense and other federal organizations creates the potential tendency to wait out militarily and politically appointed leadership. A senior general officer once stated that "a staff exists to protect the organization from the boss." We need to turn this idea around to a staff exists to assist the boss in helping and leading the organization.

Using the Power You Have

One of the biggest fallacies of middle leaders is seeking power they already possess. This may take the form of asking the boss if they can do something or calling a meeting to make a decision that is clearly the middle leader's to make. What often happens in these situations is that an activity fails to move forward while a leader seeks the authority to decide. Leaders must achieve a level of confidence in their own authority and ability. They must avoid substituting a lack of authority for lack of resolve or lack of adequate research and deliberation. This is critical because so many initiatives fail as a result of unwillingness to make decisions that are theirs to make. This often leads taxpayers to believe the federal government is inefficient and ineffective.

Failure to move forward may occur as people pass through middle management to senior management to executive levels. They may have achieved the success they sought, but they have not adjusted their thinking to their new-found authority. Leaders must understand why they fail to make a decision and instead seek authority that they already possess. Over time, leaders learn that few decisions in life cannot be fixed or revisited. Leaders are much better off deciding and moving ahead instead of agonizing over their decisions. The absence of decisions leads to an unsure workforce, miscommunication, the need for more meetings, and other undesirable and wasteful activities. My point is not arbitrary decision making. On the contrary, it is ensuring leaders gather the right information and discuss with the appropriate individuals so they are comfortable making decisions within their authority. Leaders should operate at the outer edge of their authority.

This condition requires extreme confidence in the things that leaders take on. The more prepared leaders are for the decisions they face, the more inclined they will be to exercise authority without seeking approval. They need to ensure they know all the elements involved in issues that they have to make decisions about. They can do this by obtaining as much input as possible from the people involved, including their recommendations. Effective leaders resolve to make the best decisions they can with the information available, leaving the option of modifying the decision if additional information becomes available in a reasonable time frame.

Effective leaders know that they will almost never have all the information they desire. Making a decision without total information is always better than continuing to avoid making the decision. Furthermore, effective leaders do not abdicate their decision-making authority in the absence of exact information. Asking a senior leader to make a decision with the same information you have because you are reluctant to exercise authority does not result in better decisions. And it most certainly does not result in better leadership.

Getting People Out of the Room

We have all participated in meetings with an unclear purpose or that have reached a point of impasse and lack a clear way forward. This happens for a variety of reasons, including not having a clear intent when the meeting was called, not knowing what was desired from the meeting, not having the right individuals in the meeting, and having participants who are more concerned with their personal agendas than resolving an issue. The result is senior people who do not have a way of getting out of the meeting—and the room.

A useful skill in this situation is the ability to see clearly what is happening and offer a means for people to exit the meeting. All too often people do not listen in meetings and as a result miss opportunities to resolve the issues at hand. Mechanisms for compromise are offered, but missed. Look for these opportunities by listening. Resist the urge to talk. Limiting your conversation during meetings, unless you really have something pertinent to say increases the probability of being listened to when you do talk. People will listen to a person with an established reputation for offering sound recommendations. The importance of reputation in organizations suggests considering carefully before offering solutions to issues.

Sometimes important proposals are introduced at meetings and on-the-spot decisions are requested. A better option is to meet individually with decision makers to explain the issues in depth. This strategy will likely be more effective. Leaders do not like to appear uninformed about a topic. Offering a private meeting often enables them to get up to speed and beyond their current objections.

Another option is to suggest that a decision be modified to increase its acceptability to those who are at present neutral to the idea. You might offer a small test or limited pilot program. If successful it could be expanded. If not, it could be discontinued at minimum cost. The key is to listen and be alert to opportunities for compromise and a means of getting people out of the meeting room, so final conversations and negotiations can be completed.

In the federal government situations often arise in which people sit on opposite "sides of the aisle"—even outside Congress. Efficient leaders avoid the tendency to dismiss people from the "other side" as they comment during meetings. This may happen when participants are set in their opinions or not looking for input from other attendees, but instead wait to offer their individual input. These individuals usually miss the points on which they may connect with others. An effective leader attempts to identify and build a potential coalition of participants who are able to carry the idea through.

Look for ways to get people out of the room to establish the agreements that already exist, but may not be recognized by all.

Elevator Diplomacy

In some cases, despite your best efforts, an ill-timed or ill-conceived meeting is unsalvageable and results in either a bad decision or no decision—a situation that should not be allowed to continue. This is where the issue of leadership moves closer to an art than a science. Leaders' power does not come from the ability to force people to comply with their wishes, but from the ability to get people to voluntarily agree to comply. I call this "elevator diplomacy" because it often involves shuttling up and down between the organization's offices on different floors to negotiate a more acceptable solution to an issue. This may not be an assigned responsibility, but a leader may undertake it because an issue needs to move forward, or because a decision has been made that is not in the best interest of the organization and requires remedy.

This responsibility often does not come with "real authority" on the issue at hand. The ability to resolve the situation revolves around the use of "personal power"—the power granted to leaders because of who they are and what they can do and not because of their position in the organization. In this case, influence and political skills can have important benefits. To be effective, leaders need to understand the competing issues and the options that represent a win-win for the individuals involved. Leaders must also operate as trusted agents—individuals who look at the overall best interests of the organization and highlight the benefits to those involved. The ability to present and provide implicit promises or understandings between parties greatly assists in the resolution process. Once this role is assumed and acted on successfully, the "authority" ceded to personnel operating as elevator diplomats tends to increase. What happens over time is that problems that have customarily languished as irresolvable will migrate to these individuals to take on and resolve.

Clearly leaders with this kind of informal authority cannot succeed in every case, but they start with a higher probability of success because people expect them to be able to find solutions to issues. That expectation alone will empower them in a way no other part of the organization is empowered. This is a learned skill set, which is acquired over time and through repeated attempts. Effective organizations recognize leaders who possess these skills and continue to allow them to work across lines in the organization for overall mission enhancement.

Making Decisions Easier for Senior Leadership—Managing Your Bosses

Academic discussions often treat the process of decision making as a purely intellectual exercise. However, leaders need to ensure they consider everything their leaders have to consider before approving or accepting recommendations. The idea of "managing your boss" may seem inappropriate to some. But it is necessary in many cases because of time or other limitations. Effective leaders put themselves in senior leaders' shoes and try to imagine the input required to increase the boss's comfort level with any decisions. Making a deliberate effort to think of issues surrounding recommendations is proof that consideration has been given to what is important. When asking senior leaders to make decisions, make the process as easy as possible for them. Effective leadership is marked by a detailed knowledge of the organization's decision and incentive system. Knowing the factors within the organization that will support and that will oppose the proposal is critical information for the decision maker.

Leaders will be more successful in this process when they consider participation and ownership. Leaders are rarely successful when they merely present a finished plan for senior leadership to approve, without having given the various elements of the organization an opportunity to participate in plan development. People support what they create. Do not create organizational disagreements or problems for your boss by asking for approval on an issue that creates negative feedback. In some cases, regardless of the feedback, the right thing to do is to approve the plan. But bosses should be aware of potential resistance before they approve a decision. Failing to make them aware of issues you are aware of will complicate your ability to get them to approve issues in the future. Decision makers often rely on people with established reputations for providing sound advice. They must be provided with the appropriate incentive to make the required decisions when needed. This means working within the architecture of the organization to get things approved and implemented. Doing the coordination required to make the decision easier upfront empowers the decision maker to be comfortable in making a decision because he or she sees it as involving limited risk or unknowns.

In the federal government, there is a saying, "Would you like to see this on the front page of *The Washington Post*?" When leaders help their senior leaders make decisions that are well thought out, good for the organization, a good use of taxpayer money, and the right thing to do, the answer can be a resounding yes.

Summary

The behavior and individual leadership skills described can be developed and learned—in fact, *should* be developed and learned to create more effective leaders in any organization.

Ensuring leaders feel empowered to use power they have, finding ways out of difficult meetings, fostering solutions via elevator diplomacy, and moving decisions and actions forward by making it easy for senior leaders to reach a decision are behaviors that aid in getting the business of the department or organization accomplished. Effective leadership within organizations requires a true understanding of the organization and how it works, which begins with understanding the people in positions within it. This combination of knowing the people and the organization is powerful and can be used to forecast how people in the organization are likely to respond to ideas, solutions, or change. A strategy can then be designed that will maximize the likelihood of achieving success.

Effective leaders are necessary in every organization. At the federal government level, effective leaders touch all of us. As taxpayers we want our government to make well informed decisions, based on accurate and valuable data. We want to see government agencies make the right decisions for the country and take efficient action toward results. Being an efficient government does not have to be a dream. It starts with effective leaders.

Further Reading

The Arbinger Institute, *Leadership and Self-Deception. Getting Out of the Box.* San Francisco: Berrett-Koehler Publishers, 2000.

David Cottrell, *Monday Morning Leadership: 8 Mentoring Sessions You Can't Afford to Miss.* Dallas, TX: Cornerstone Leadership Institute, 2003.

David W. Delong, *Lost Knowledge: Confronting the Threat of an Aging Workforce.* New York: Oxford University Press, 2004.

Stewart Liff, *Managing Government Employees.* New York: AMACOM, 2007.

Stewart Liff, *The Complete Guide to Hiring and Firing Government Employees.* New York: AMACOM, 2010.

Gordon Mackenzie, *Orbiting the Giant Hair Ball: A Corporate Fool's Guide to Surviving With Grace.* New York: Viking Penguin, 1998.

Margaret J. Wheatley, *Leadership and the New Science.* San Francisco: Berrett-Koehler Publishers, 1992.

References

Burns, J. M. 1978. *Leadership.* New York: Harper & Row.

Gardner, J. W. 1990. *On Leadership.* New York: The Free Press.

Nixon, R. M. 1982. *Leaders.* New York: Warner Books.

About the Author

Will Brown has spent most of his professional career working for the U.S. Department of Defense. He served as an officer in the U.S. Navy and currently serves as a civilian leader for the Office of Naval Research (ONR). As a role model and mentor to those who work for and with him, Brown demonstrates leadership skills that help him and others to navigate the federal government workplace. While in the Navy, Captain Brown's awards included the Legion of Merit, the Meritorious Service Medal, the Navy Commendation Medal, the Navy Achievement Medal, the Sea Service Ribbon, Battle "E" Ribbon, and others. Brown currently serves as the ONR Deputy of Business Operations and Services, which oversees all supporting departments, including information, human resources, acquisition, counsel, logistics, communications, legislative affairs, and others. As ONR's talent manager, he has initiated ONR's Leadership Development Program, Mentoring Program, Academy of Learning, and other employee development opportunities.

Chapter 33

Chinese "Sheng Yi": Reinterpreting Challenges for Leaders

Cheng Zhu

In This Chapter

- How exemplary Chinese CEOs describe their leadership journey.

- How top Chinese CEOs reinterpret crucible events for development.

- A summary of key cultural, philosophical, and ideological influences on Chinese CEOs' mindsets.

> *"It was the best of times, it was the worst of times."*
>
> —Charles Dickens, *A Tale of Two Cities*
>
> *"Just as water retains no constant shape, in war there are no constant conditions. He who can modify his tactics according to the enemy's situations shall be victorious and may be called the Divine Commander."*
>
> —Sun Zi, *The Art of War*, 6: 32–33

Sheng yi (生意) is the two-character Chinese word for "business." As a noun, *Sheng* means "life," "birth," or "growth"; and as a verb, it means to "generate" or "produce." *Yi* refers to meanings, ideas, or intentions. *Sheng yi* can be translated literally as "the meaning of life" or "to create meaning." In contrast to the sense of "care, anxiety, occupied, work, and occupation" originally associated with the English word "business" (*Online Etymology Dictionary* 2009), the Chinese etymology for "business" connotes a philosophical approach to construing and conducting business.

To understand Chinese business leaders' developmental journey, I interviewed 15 exemplary Chinese CEOs of top-ranking private enterprises in China (quotes throughout this chapter derive from these interviews). A salient pattern emerged from the CEOs' stories: Challenging events can powerfully trigger and accelerate leadership development. More important, I found that the secret to the leaders' success lies not simply in their courage to endure a large dose of pain and stress during crucible events but also in their ability to reinterpret challenges and regain a balanced sense of which changes to embrace and which to resist. This chapter presents how, through constant reframing, the "worst of times" can in effect become the "best of times," as the leaders invent new meanings themselves, transcend their early life enculturation, and break down barriers of preconceived cultural prejudices and practices. Consequently, their self-transformation enhances their companies' capacity to adapt and to achieve exponential growth.

Challenging or Crucible Events as Triggers for Leadership Development

China has experienced unprecedented economic transformation during the past three decades. A fundamental shift in ownership sources has led to a "relative decline of the state-owned sector" and a rise in the "foreign-owned sector, private enterprise, and hybrid public or private forms" (Hassard, Morris, and Sheehan 2004, 314). Private enterprises are not only booming but constantly outperform state-owned enterprises (SOEs) in various aspects, including product quality, delivery, and customer responsiveness (Wilkinson, Millington, and Eberhardt 2006). Since China's entrance into the World Trade Organization in 2001, many private enterprises have been actively repositioning themselves and growing leaders who can think globally and act locally.

Accompanying these economic changes, the Chinese legal system, government regulations, and cultural mentality are in constant flux. The most daunting challenges facing the Chinese CEOs of private enterprises involve dealing with the conflicts between change and continuity. To capture the intensity of the work to overcome these difficult challenges, they use a Chinese idiomatic expression: "Confront a man with the danger of death, and he will fight to live" (*Zhi si di er hou sheng;* 置死地而后生). This chapter describes the major challenges associated with the inadequate legal, political, and cultural support for the Chinese CEOs of private enterprises.

Evolving Challenges

There are two main evolving challenges for China's government and the Chinese CEOs of private enterprises: instituting a new legal system for the private sector and privatizing SOEs. Let's briefly consider each one.

The Challenge of Instituting a New Legal System for the Private Sector

China's imperfect legal system and shifting regulatory political environment have posed constant obstacles in recent years. Between 1978 and 1997, the Chinese Constitution changed statements about private enterprises three times—from "we allow the non-state-owned enterprises to exist," to "the private sector can supplement the state-owned and collective sectors," to "private enterprises are an important component of the national economy." Domestic private enterprises had become the second-largest contributor to national economic growth, after SOEs, in the late 1990s, leading to a further constitutional amendment in 1999. This amendment formally recognized the mixed structure of the national economy as consisting of SOEs, collective enterprises, and private enterprises, which precipitated the growth of domestic private enterprises by freeing them from the shadows (Gregory and Tenev 2001). In 2000, the government added a new sentence to official documents, stating that "the government and the entire nation should stay on course and relentlessly support private enterprises." The rising importance of private enterprises has had a profound influence on Chinese employees' perception of government and corporate accountability, because SOE workers and government employees used to receive cradle-to-grave social welfare (Saich 2008).

While private enterprises are proliferating, many laws and regulations necessary for a free market economy are not in place. Chinese business leaders must perform a delicate dance to meet the demands of economic growth and simultaneously operate within an immature free market economy. Several CEOs acknowledge that the Chinese public has a desire for the rule of law, is open to change, and values the best technology and experts, but that it might take a generation to train judges and lawyers to reinforce the law. They observe that, as a consequence, government officials make decisions in lieu of judges. The CEOs must be artful in cultivating the relationships between private enterprises and government. They caution about the importance of drawing the line, but they also admit the dilemma: "On the one hand, you know you should stay within the line; on the other, you don't know where the line is until you have crossed it. Sometimes you just have to have tragedy ahead of time in order to succeed." In the sidebar, case 1, one CEO tells his story of handling the challenge of dealing with novel tasks without any precedents or clear guidance from law and policy.

Case 1: New Demand for a Mature Legal Structure

Zhang is the CEO of a chain of highly successful Chinese supermarkets. He started his company in the rural areas in the Middle South, and now his chain stores cover most of Southern China and major cities across the nation. Although his company grew explosively in the past five years, he faced fierce competition from Wal-Mart and other Western multinationals enjoying more favorable policies drafted by local governments. In the past several years, local government officials have been evaluated based on their economic achievements (that is, the amount of foreign investment they attracted to the local area). Zhang is the first private entrepreneur in China who personally funded legal scholars and lawyers to research the laws conducive to the private sector's growth. On the basis of this research, involving 100 experts, he presented a white paper to the central government in which he proposed a policy change to create a fair, competitive environment for both Chinese entrepreneurs and foreign businessmen. The government ignored his proposal in the ensuing two years. His political friends tried to sway him, arguing that businessmen should not meddle with laws and policies and that one individual's initiative cannot change the entire legal landscape. Later, upon his persistence, the government acknowledged the legal deficiencies, but it did not undertake any measures to improve the situation. Zhang has continued to lead his research team in writing articles and requesting meetings with policy makers. In the past year, these efforts finally have obtained buy-in from the central government, spurring the establishment of a special committee to consider how government could make the needed changes and enact them into law.

The Challenge of Privatizing SOEs

Merging with SOEs and privatizing them presents another challenge of striking a delicate balance between exercising discipline in professional business practice while respecting the local culture, which has a strong influence on employees' interactions in organizations. One CEO characterizes this practice using a Chinese idiom—"respecting the rules of the village" (*ru xiang sui su;* 入乡随俗). He illustrates his point with an example: "You cannot get any business done if you are talking about business only in the offices of the local businesspeople. You have to take them out for lunch or dinner and get to know them." This idea resonates with Gardner's (2004) advice in *Changing Minds* to convey a message in a variety of ways and arrange different experiences for the listener. It is easier to convince people in situations where the usual assumptions and resistances may be waiting (Gardner 2004).

Negative Elements of Cultural Assumptions and Practices

The alternating cultural emphasis on change and stability in China presents myriad obstacles to private enterprises' sustainability. The CEOs in my interviews identified several major negative elements of the traditional Chinese culture: overdoing the Middle Way;

stereotypes of private enterprises; and the competing interests of companies, families, and competitors.

Overdoing the Middle Way

Several CEOs are concerned that the general public's interpretations of the Confucian notion of the Middle Way (*zhong yong;* 中庸) debilitate people's capacity to be creative and exercise initiatives. Abundant Chinese idioms reflect the Middle Way mentality: "The bird that takes the lead gets shot" (*qiang da chu tou niao;* 枪打出头鸟) and "A famed person and a fattened pig are alike in danger" (*ren pa chu ming, zhu pa zhuang;* 人怕出名，猪怕壮). They observed that many of their counterparts failed to foster higher aspirations after attaining considerable success, which led them to divide their enterprises into several smaller ones. They suspect that the Middle Way mentality has limited the mindsets of many successful Chinese private enterprises and hindered them from developing into multinational conglomerates.

The tradition of the Middle Way induces high concern for *guanxi* (关系). The concept of *guanxi* is multifaceted. It encompasses not only the American concepts of networking, building trust, and maintaining relationship, but also the notion of exploiting various political, economic, and social affiliations in a positive or unethical manner to advance personal interests. A few CEOs report that they feel the obligation of offering face to the other party or extending social favors to the other party, which might not be in the best interests of their companies. Overdoing the Middle Way might mislead one into shouldering undue responsibilities for others' emotions or ignoring ethical principles and laws. The American business leaders interviewed in Gardner, Csikszentmihalyi, and Damon's (2001) *Good Work* project identified the skill of balancing professionalism and empathy as a common leadership challenge. Similarly, the Chinese CEOs struggle to maintain a culturally defined morality and a modern managerial sense of professional excellence.

Eliminating Stereotypes of Private Enterprises

A number of mainstream Confucian teachings tend to exhort people to "value righteousness than profit" (*zhongyi qingli;* 重义轻利) and even juxtapose "righteousness" and "profits." Such attitudes have influenced many Chinese to avoid explicit conversations about profits and self-interests. For example, *The Confucian Analects,* a classic Chinese canon for character education, prescribes two qualitatively different mindsets of a gentleman and a petty man: "The gentleman knows righteousness, while the petty man understands profits" (*junzi yu yu yi, xiaoren yu yu li;* 君子喻于义，小人喻于利).

The Confucian tradition of "patronizing agriculture while repressing commerce" (*zhongnong yishang;* 重农抑商) has shaped the policy of the natural economy in ancient China that favored farmers and confined merchants in Chinese feudal dynasties. The negative effects of the remnants of the tradition still emerge in the early years of many private enterprises' development. When many of the CEOs started their businesses in rural areas three decades ago, they had to put in extra effort to reverse the cultural stereotypes or social stigma associated with private enterprises. They self-regulated their personal lifestyles to create a positive image and gain public trust.

Balancing the Interests of Companies, Families, and Competitors

Another dilemma facing the Chinese CEOs is that they not only need to be forward-looking but also must take great care to respect the work of the older generation and not to upset the delicate balance between past and future. They acknowledge that, despite their meteoric rise and legendary financial success, they still have a long way to go to achieve international acclaim. They must be mindful of complacency, and urge the older generation to incorporate a global perspective on the community and to learn to engage the global audience. On these issues, see cases 2 and 3.

Case 2: Conflict of Interests Between Family Members and the Company

Liu is the CEO of a private enterprise that is ranked among the top three enterprises in China's manufacturing industry. He established the company as a family business 15 years ago. For about eight years, many of his family members were in top management positions and held shares in the company. In 2001, he implemented a company-wide reform that expanded the availability of the stock options to more employees rather than restricting them to family members. He believed that this would provide employees with a sense of ownership and encourage them to make more contributions. He also asked older family members to relinquish their management positions because he sensed their inability to adapt and change.

Liu encountered strong opposition during the initial stage of the reform, for none of the older family members wanted to leave the company. To address his family members' negative emotions, he organized study groups and follow-up one-to-one sessions on a regular basis, in which he educated his family members on his vision for developing the enterprise in a new direction. He also engaged in a series of conversations with his father, the firm's chairman, to persuade him to retire, even though he avoided confronting his father's bad temper and had limited communication with his father in his teenage years. Eventually, his father agreed to retire, and Liu reassigned the older family members to less prominent positions, so he could carry out the reform successfully.

Case 3: Conflicts of Interests with Competing Organizations

Jiang is the CEO of a top-ranking textile company in China. He noted the dilemma of trying to behave both ethically and competitively, an issue shared by the rest of the CEOs. Pressured by fierce competition, one of his competing companies bribed certain authorities and government officials to gain economic favors. Jiang consulted with his executive team and company lawyers, weighed the consequences of offering bribes, and eventually resolved not to emulate the competitor's unethical and unlawful behaviors, even though abiding by the yet-to-be improved economic regulations meant incurring short-term financial losses. Furthermore, rather than taking countermoves to regain an edge on the competition, Jiang actively engaged in building affiliations with his competitors. When his own company did not have enough labor power or time to fill customers' orders, he would even give these orders to his competitors in the same region. He says,

> Many of my friends thought that I was committing career suicide by introducing my clients to my competitors. But I think the goodwill will pay off eventually. We need to change the regional culture into a collaborative one. It is not enough for my own company to be famous for textiles. We need to make our entire region famous for textile production, so that whenever people think of purchasing textiles, they will think of coming to our region, and then they will know that our company is the best one in the region. Then my company can attract contracts not just from the rest of China but also from around the globe.

Difficulties Faced by Other Companies

A number of CEOs mentioned that they advanced their leadership ability by developing a habit of imagining imminent crises for the companies to work out how to circumvent them. See case 4 for an example.

Self-Reflection as a Learning Tool for Shifting Perspectives

A few CEOs stress the importance of practicing self-reflection in understanding their surrounding situations. They consider it a useful tool that helps them shift perspectives, to change their views of paradoxical situations or dilemmas, and eventually to find creative ways to turn sometimes undesirable factors into favorable ones for their business. One CEO gives his own interesting interpretation of the dragon symbol:

> In Western culture, a dragon is a monster and symbolizes evil and violence. It is something to be attacked or shunned. In China, on the contrary, the dragon

---

Case 4: An Imagined Crisis

Bao is the chairman of a top-ranked fund-management company. He exhibits a keen awareness of potential future crises coupled with a stable, peaceful, and contented present-centered mindset. He frequently reads newspaper articles about other companies' setbacks and historical and business cases of high-profile leaders who had been successful but failed to create enduring success. He considers those leaders' cases as lessons of "winners' curses." He regularly imagines crises for his company, even though his company ranks among the top three in the industry and continues to develop without any signs of loss in the immediate future. As he puts it,

> It is highly important to have a peaceful and stable mindset and a sense of crisis. When the TV Weather Channel broadcasts that it is going to be sunny today, I always ask myself, "Am I mentally prepared if a terrible storm arrives five minutes later?" Every day I spend 70 percent of my time planning for the future.

As he transports himself into an imaginary crisis situation and imagines himself handling every difficult task in the turmoil, Bao increases his ability to identify the weak links within his company, invent the best solutions, and prevent problems beforehand.

---

embodies justice, harmony, and high power and is a symbol that Chinese emperors like to wear on their clothes. Like Westerners, the ancient Chinese leaders understood that the dragon had destructive power, but they also saw that it could bring rainfall, which is important for the country's agricultural production. So instead of slaying or avoiding the dragon, they hugged it and wore it and made the maximum use of its constructive and positive power to get its protection and support. Effective business leaders should adopt this kind of practice.

A parallel to this approach of turning unfavorable factors to one's aid can also be found in the Chinese approach to meditation, a type of self-reflection. Many Western religious practices and Indian meditations teach people to try to forget about the external material world and to ignore outside influences. In contrast, the practitioners of Chinese Zen Buddhist meditation strive to forget about internal lusts and to work with the aid of external influences, so that the mind can both assert itself and perform in harmony within the material world.

It is worth noting the composition of the Chinese character for self-reflection, *wu* or *wu xing* (悟 or 悟性; savvy). Most Chinese linguistic characters consist of two parts: a radical that usually reflects the semantic class of the character, and a phonetic that typically cues its pronunciation. In the case of the Chinese character for *wu* (悟), its left part is a radical that means "heart," and its right part is a phonetic, which not only indicates its pronunciation but also happens to be a standalone character meaning "I" (*wu;* 吾) in classical and poetic terms. Chinese scholars argue that this otherwise phonetic contributes its meaning to the sense of the composite character, so that *wu* (悟) indicates that understanding one's own heart must be of primary importance in learning. This idea resonates with Socrates' saying "Know thyself."

Discussions: Reframing Conflicts and Reinterpreting Chinese Cultural Beliefs

From the perspective of Kegan's (1982, 1994) theory of constructive-developmental psychology, the drastically changing social, political, and economic landscape of China poses a developmental demand that calls for a qualitatively different way of thinking for CEOs. This new way of thinking involves a higher level of epistemological and cognitive complexity to account for and incorporate the new and different challenges. Kegan (1984) argues that three gradually evolving meaning systems (self-reading, self-authoring, and self-revising) throughout adulthood influence people's relationship with leadership and their leadership behaviors. For example, leaders with a self-reading/socialized mind tend to rely on the views of important others as the only source of understanding themselves, and they might feel at a loss when confronted with conflicting images about themselves from different external guides. Leaders with a self-authoring mind depend on themselves, not others, in making meaning of and prioritizing multiple demands or views. Leaders with a self-revising mind incorporate both their own and others' perspectives to find personal direction and meaning and have the ability to complexify their self-images and revise their definitions of themselves.

The contemporary environment serves as a catalyst for disrupting the equilibrium of the Chinese CEOs' existing developmental positions and propelling them to move toward the next developmental level. In the terms of Kegan's (1982, 1994) theory, the CEOs make two types of transitions that correspond to the developmental movement from "socialized mind" to "self-authoring mind," and from "self-authoring mind" to an indication of "self-revising mind."

From Socialized Mind to Self-Authoring Mind

In case 1, Zhang's advocacy for a change in the law governing private businesses might appear self-serving. Some of his close political allies even perceived his move as a personal assault and worried about their own annual performance appraisals because they were evaluated, by and large, on the basis of their ability to attract foreign funds to the local area. But Zhang does not let the judgments of his political friends define what he should do as the CEO of a private enterprise. With a self-authoring mindset, he creates precedents and gives a good example for other entrepreneurs of how to improve the market economy system and how to create a level playing field for all businesses in China. He is also changing the political culture and the way local political leaders measure their own leadership success.

In case 2, Liu has arrived at a critical juncture in his leadership development. He is struggling with the accustomed beliefs that he can read himself in the views of others—of his father and his relatives. On the one hand, his loved ones have instilled in him the value of upholding the Confucian ideal of filial piety (revere and care for parents). On the other hand, he envisions running his company with modern managerial procedures and standards. He must reevaluate his relationship with his cherished belief in the Confucian values and with his idealized vision for his company. As he tries to understand himself and his company through the judgments of his loved ones and through his own views, he encounters a wilderness of confusion between self-reading and self-authoring. The sweeping changes in the environment call for a paradigm shift in how he defines and evaluates himself as a leader. He has gradually come to understand that his previously held cultural beliefs are not wrong but are simply incomplete. He creates a new self-concept by using the lever of "representational redescription," one of the seven mind-changing levers proposed in Gardner's (2004) book *Changing Minds*. Just because Confucian teachings of filial piety came earlier in Liu's life does not make those beliefs better or worse than his more recent beliefs about how modern family businesses should best operate in a market economy. It is simply not useful or even appropriate to apply the concept of filial piety at this particular developmental stage of his company.

Liu's ability to resolve this conflict demonstrates that he is able to redefine his sense of purpose on his own rather than relying on previously internalized Confucian values to dictate his actions. This is not a superficial change in leadership style but rather a profound transformation in the way he understands himself and his relationships with his family members, and how he leads his company. He changes the assumptions subconsciously ingrained in him by the Confucian tradition—the assumptions he has taken for granted about himself and his relationship with his family members. Though much of his development as CEO of the company entails many skills specific to his leadership position (for example, communicating with various members of his company, or recruiting supporters for his vision of a modern family business), his most significant and qualitatively different change as a leader lies in his ability to change his underlying beliefs about himself and his relationship with family members. He is able to separate himself from the webs of cultural beliefs and reconstruct interconnected, underlying assumptions that delineate his capacity to acquire new leadership behavior.

In case 3, Jiang had internal struggles about what moves to make in response to his competitors' unethical behaviors. He performed a thought experiment, basing his decisions on (1) the judgments of important others (that is, executive team); and (2) his internalized, conventional perception of competitors as foes, a view that encourages him to garner all profit-making opportunities for his own company. He then moved his eyes from the prize in the short term to the prize in the long term and adopted a new model of understanding his company's position not simply in relation to the rest of the competitors in the region and the nation but, more important, to others in the world. This cognitive shift in perspective empowered him to gain a heightened sense of freedom of action, a stronger sense of integrity, and the will to reverse his competitive tendency, and further led him to share opportunities with or give more opportunities to his competitors. This could potentially create a larger pie for both him and his competitors. He shows the ability to not only make use of input from outside sources (that is, the opinions of his top management members about winning and losing) but also to take the conventional perspective of competition into account in the formation of a more complex ability to self-determine the right course of action. His self-authoring mind enables him to remain ethical toward and even collaborative with his unethical competitor.

The CEOs in the first three cases presented above demonstrate a move toward a self-authoring mind. They are comfortable with unlearning old habits and with improvisation. Zhang is not only able to appreciate his political friends' perspectives and care about their personal concerns, but he is also able to feel free to disagree with their views on the leadership of private enterprises. He is actively shaping the environment by directing government officials to respect the Constitution and the law. Liu respects the popular Confucian ideal of filial piety, but he does not unconditionally accept every practice that the culture teaches, and he rejects its blind application in the managerial arena. He redefines how to preserve traditional culture and values by experimenting with a new way of integrating more rational and scientific managerial methods in leading his organization. Jiang has eliminated his fears of being labeled a weak or an unwise competitor through the lens of conventional wisdom, and he is able to embrace the uncertainty inherent in his collaborative gestures toward his competitors.

In sum, these CEOs redefine and gain a clearer understanding of their own fundamental values, instead of adopting the values of important others or acting indiscriminately on the basis of ingrained cultural and conventional beliefs. On the one hand, these leaders are not embedded in the conformity that traditional Chinese culture tends to induce. They are able to overcome their own enculturation and to recognize which aspects of their personal value systems are a result of their uncritically examined previous experiences. On the other hand, they are not just blindly accepting Western managerial practice as a whole. They are integrating the suitable part of Western management rather than swapping out Chinese culture for Western culture. Most important, they are working to construct *third* cultures in their organizations and in the larger environment, introducing new ways of organizing thoughts and making sense of economic, legal, cultural, and social factors. And this effort of cultural reconstruction eventually helps to transform conflicts into harmony and brings about effective leadership behaviors congruent with the new cultures.

The Indication of a Self-Revising Mind

In case 4, Bao, a highly successful CEO in his early 50s, first impressed me as an "insecure overachiever." However, I quickly noted his most important quality. His sense of imminent crisis does not set off a vicious cycle of worrying. Instead, he maintains a very stable emotional state, which helps him perform daily tasks in an automatic manner, routinize complicated leadership tasks, and maintain consistency. In this way, he is able to release a considerable amount of energy and focus more on long-term planning. Even though outsiders might perceive him as busy and restless for success, he is calm and peaceful in his mind and heart.

Bao's seemingly contradictory traits indicate that he is at the developmental stage of a "self-revising mind." Without relying on immediate situational prompts, he is internally determined, and he can trigger his own development by envisioning obstacles to his future success, thereby maintaining short-term profits as well as attaining long-term goals. This developmental level of leadership—the level of being able to self-regulate one's behavior and to automatically revise one's cognitive framework—cannot be attained simply by improving specific skills or changing styles of leadership behavior. Skills and behaviors can only be enacted within the framework of assumptions about the self (Kegan 1982, 1994). If Bao's framework had only included one of the two elements—either the current success or the invisible future crisis—his leadership capacities and skills would have been limited to attending to only one side of the conflict. It was only after he completed the intellectually and emotionally challenging task of reconstructing his web of competing beliefs about how to manage the success and failure of his company that he was able to transform the conflict and thereby eliminate the self-formed crucible. This ability to rewrite the "book on himself" has empowered him to overcome his "immunity to change" (Kegan and Lahey 2009) and implement a lasting change effect.

The above analysis demonstrates that cognitive complexity is associated with leadership effectiveness and is a critical component of promoting leaders' development. The CEOs in the first three cases presented above are capable of higher-order thinking (that is, level-four thinking), and the one in case 4 shows an indication of level-five thinking. The rest of the CEOs in my interviews seem to be on their way to developing a high level of cognitive complexity. This finding is in line with the notion of the highest level of consciousness—the ideal state of leadership in Daoism. In the words of Daoism, the greatest leaders embody both the opposites—Yin and Yang—and lead in a fluid and dynamic way. This finding also agrees with U.S. scholars' view that cognitive complexity is characteristic of effective leadership (Eigel and Kuhnert 2005; Kegan 1984). Thus, highly effective leaders have the capacity to author or revise their individual leadership identity and engage in dialectical thinking.

Summary

Challenging, disorienting, and disruptive events tend to initiate the Chinese CEOs' development. The high level of cognitive complexity at which individual CEOs interpret the negative experiences can then accelerate their development. One CEO uses a holistic approach to address organizational imbalances. He alludes to traditional Chinese medicine's holistic view of disease. A traditional Chinese doctor does not usually treat the infectious organism but identifies a certain type of imbalance within the human body and addresses its underlying causes. This traditional Chinese wisdom resembles Peter Senge's (2006) view of a corporation as a system within a system within a system: "The same is true for organizations. We cannot always solve departmental problems routinely because most of the time those problems are signaling a larger organizational or environmental malady."

The traditional Chinese diagnosis process serves as a suitable metaphor for the external and psychological transformations that the CEOs experienced. They changed from "ruling the game" to "gaming the rules"; that is, they changed from understanding the rules of leading their companies and playing effectively within their boundaries to fundamentally revamping the rules for the larger system. In the process of their diagnosis, they broke the boundaries previously defined by borrowed ideologies and values, or they made those boundaries more open and fluid.

The Chinese CEOs share several characteristics of authentic and transformational leadership in that they take the cultural context forward without losing their former learning. In other words, they maintain a clear understanding of their family upbringing, educational background, and cultural beliefs in the respective contexts of these influences, and simultaneously they move into a new territory, integrating Chinese and Western cultural essences and practices. As the CEOs experience conflicts, the meanings of the conflicts evolve in a way amenable to enhancing their effectiveness. They abandon the old and familiar ways of understanding the conflicts. They take responsibility for development through the power of reinterpreting challenges and *sheng yi*—making new meanings.

Suggestions for Readers

Table 33-1 describes types of cultural, philosophical, and ideological influences on Chinese CEOs' thinking. Several major leadership thoughts and practices in China and the United States are juxtaposed for comparison.

Figure 33-1. Cultural, Philosophical, and Ideological Influences on Chinese CEOs' Thinking

Aspect	Confucianism	Bing Jia	Daoism	Legalism	Communism	Quantitative Studies
Assumptions	One can cultivate the innate goodness of human beings.	One can achieve maximum results with minimal time and at least cost.	One can balance Yin and Yang (the opposite governing forces in the universe) to achieve social harmony.	"Individuals are evil, and human interactions are focused on exchange relationships."	All historical growth, change, and development results from the struggle of opposites, especially the class struggle.	Survey results can be extrapolated to the sample population—middle-level Chinese business leaders.
Key principles about leadership competencies	Emphasis on the morality of leaders. Leaders should be a role model for establishing moral order. Humaneness (which involves sympathy and empathy). "Ritualism" (in which leaders "comply with established social norms" and serve as a "model for the populace"). Sense of righteousness and propriety, wisdom.	The best strategy is to win wars without engaging in physical battle (that is, to foil an adversary's plot). Self-image, purpose, continuous effort, responsibility, knowledge, achievement orientation, and loyalty.	Emphasis on authenticity of leaders. "Leaders should shun glory and wealth in order to keep the spirit free." The "doctrine of inaction" discourages leaders from intervening in daily leadership activities. Leaders create a self-leading and self-sustaining organizational culture.	Emphasis on wisdom and its combination with cunning. Leaders should follow three principles: law, tactic, and legitimacy. That is, leaders should use penal law, political technique, and authority to maintain control. Political strategist, art of rulership, and enlightened despotism behind realpolitik.	Leaders should know and use followers appropriately, and gain their trust and confidence. There is an emphasis on pragmatism and efficiency (for example, Deng's quotes: "Do not argue"; "Cat theory"; "Practice is the sole criterion for testing truth"). Be creative, upright, and self-disciplined, and have qualities of revolutionaries, youth, knowledge, and expertise.	Effective leaders are morally sound, attend to organizational performance, and care about subordinates. Efficient in attaining goals. Have interpersonal competence (which encompasses American perceptions of leaders' sensitivity, attractiveness, charisma, and versatility. Participative leadership is viewed less positively in China than the United States.

Aspect	Confucianism	Bing Jia	Daoism	Legalism	Communism	Quantitative Studies
Key ideas about leadership development	Leadership development is a lifelong process. Wisdom and maturity develop at a later age. Daily self-reflections as means to continuous improvement. *Zhong Yong*, or Golden Way: non-extreme ways of leading with morality, wisdom, and mental cultivation.	Leaders should frequently practice the principles from *The Art of War* to foster a good habit of thinking and acting. Proverb: "The more you sweat in peacetime, the less you bleed in war."	Leaders should develop the ability to use a transcendental way of approaching seemingly antithetical views.	Leaders should learn political technique.	Leaders should have the courage to emancipate their minds. Leaders should be creative. Leaders should think dialectically, have a long-term vision and a big picture view.	Not applicable
Similar Western theories or practices	Transformational leadership	Results-based leadership	Authentic leadership	"Self-authoring" leaders through the lens of Kegan's (1984) constructive-developmental theory	Not applicable	Multiple Intelligences (Gardner 1999) and leadership. Transformational and value-based leadership. Charismatic leadership.

Source: Author's compilation.

457

You can find practical resources listed in the further reading section below. For example, the "Four Column Exercise" (Kegan and Lahey 2009) is a powerful learning technology that can accelerate your personal leadership development and help you discover your own "competing commitments" and constraining assumptions and overcome "immunity to change." You can expect to enhance your learning agility and achieve breakthrough leadership results by applying the seven "levers" for changing minds (Gardner 2004). By reframing tough challenges and questioning unexamined assumptions, leaders are able to shift energy from grieving over pain and loss to rescripting new meanings and to searching for opportunities to turn lemons into lemonade. To use the words of Sun Zi and Charles Dickens, you shape the "water" (the conditions for your actions) and turn the "worst of times" into the "best of times."

Further Reading

Howard Gardner, *Changing Minds: The Art and Science of Changing Our Own and Other People's Minds.* Boston: Harvard Business School Press, 2004.

———, *Five Minds for the Future.* Boston: Harvard Business School Press, 2007.

Daniel Goleman, Richard E. Boyatzis, and Annie McKee, *Primal Leadership: Learning to Lead with Emotional Intelligence.* Boston: Harvard Business School Press, 2004.

Harvard Business School Press, *Harvard Business Review on Doing Business in China.* Boston: Harvard Business School Press, 2004.

Ronald A. Heifetz, Marty Linsky, and Alexander Grashow, *The Practice of Adaptive Leadership: Tools and Tactics for Changing Your Organization and the World.* Boston: Harvard Business School Press, 2009.

Robert Kegan, *How the Way We Talk Can Change the Way We Work: Seven Languages of Transformation.* San Francisco: Jossey-Bass, 2000.

Robert Kegan and Lisa Laskow Lahey, *Immunity to Change: How to Overcome It and Unlock the Potential in Yourself.* Boston: Harvard Business School Press, 2009.

Anthony Saich, *Providing Public Goods in Transitional China.* New York: Palgrave Macmillan, 2008.

References

Eigel, Keith M., and Karl W. Kuhnert. 2005. Authentic Development: Leadership Development Level and Executive Effectiveness. In *Authentic Leadership Theory and Practice: Origins, Effects and Development,* ed. W. L. Gardner, B. J. Avolio, and F. O. Walumbwa. Boston: Elsevier.

Gardner, Howard. 1999. *Intelligence Reframed: Multiple Intelligences for the 21st Century.* New York: Basic Books.

———. 2004. *Changing Minds: The Art and Science of Changing Our Own and Other People's Minds.* Boston: Harvard Business School Press.

Gardner, Howard, Mihaly Csikszentmihalyi, and William Damon. 2001. *Good Work: When Excellence and Ethics Meet.* New York: Basic Books.

Gregory, Neil, and Stoya Tenev. 2001. China's Home-Grown Entrepreneurs. *China Business Review,* January 15, available at www.chinabusinessreview.com.

Hassard, John, Jonathan Morris, and Jackie Sheehan, 2004. The "Third Way": The Future of Work and Organization in a "Corporatized" Chinese Economy. *International Journal of Human Resource Management* 15, no. 2: 314–330.

Kegan, Robert. 1982. *The Evolving Self: Problem and Process in Human Development.* Cambridge, MA: Harvard University Press.

———. 1984. Adult Leadership and Adult Development: A Constructionist View. In *Leadership: Multidisciplinary Perspectives,* ed. B. Kellerman. Englewood Cliffs, NJ: Prentice-Hall.

———. 1994. *In Over Our Heads: The Mental Demands of Modern Life.* Cambridge, MA: Harvard University Press.

Kegan, Robert, and Lisa Laskow Lahey. 2009. *Immunity to Change: How to Overcome It and Unlock the Potential in Yourself.* Boston: Harvard Business School Press.

Online Etymology Dictionary. www.etymonline.com.

Saich, Anthony. 2008. *Providing Public Goods in Transitional China.* New York: Palgrave Macmillan.

Senge, Peter. 2006. *The Fifth Discipline: The Art and Practice of the Learning Organization.* New York: Doubleday/Currency.

Wilkinson, Barry, Andrew Millington, and Markus Eberhardt. 2006. On the Performance of Chinese State-Owned and Private Enterprises: The View from Foreign-Invested Enterprises. *Journal of General Management* 32, no. 1: 65–80.

About the Author

Cheng Zhu is a senior faculty member at the Center for Creative Leadership, where she trains the Leadership Development Program, the Innovation Leadership Program, and the Foundations of Leadership, and also designs and delivers custom programs that incorporate blended learning solutions to provide psychological assessments, feedback, and coaching experiences to help senior executives lead change effectively. Her areas of expertise include adult learning, cross-cultural leadership, cross-border negotiation and conflict resolution, and developmental and positive psychology. She previously worked as a research associate at Harvard Business School and as a research assistant at the John F. Kennedy School of Government's Center for Public Leadership at Harvard. During her service as president of the Harvard Graduate Council and president of the Student Government Association for the Harvard Graduate School of Education, she twice received the Outstanding Service Award from the Harvard provost and the school's dean. She received a BA from Beijing University and a master's and doctorate from Harvard.

List and Descriptions of the Tools on the Website

Contributors to *The ASTD Leadership Handbook* provided tools to help you implement the leadership concepts you read about in the book. The tools are available for downloading at a companion website: www.astd.org/LeadershipHandbook. As long as you maintain the copyright information and the "used with permission" designation on the tool, you will be able to use it for your daily work.

Tool 2-1. The Five Practices and 10 Commitments of Leadership

James M. Kouzes and Barry Z. Posner

A list of 10 leadership commitments associated with the five practices of leadership.

Tool 3-1. Is Your Team Dysfunctional?

Patrick M. Lencioni

A straightforward diagnostic tool to help you evaluate your team's susceptibility to the five dysfunctions.

Tool 4-1. Strategic Planning Analysis Questionnaire

Leonard D. Goodstein

A questionnaire intended to help understand the role of strategic planning in an organization.

Tool 5-1. Checklist of Poor Personal Communication

Dianna Booher

An individual checklist of symptoms of ineffective communication.

Tool 6-1. Influence Scenario Exercise

Gary Yukl

An exercise designed to help you think about effective ways to use proactive influence tactics with subordinates and peers.

Tool 7-1. John Kotter's Eight-Stage Process

John Kotter

An eight-step process to ensure an orderly change that considers all steps in the change process.

Tool 8-1. Checklist for Managing Talent

Kevin Oakes, Holly Tompson, and Lorrie Lykins

A checklist to compare your organization's practices with the best practices of leading talent management companies.

Tool 8-2. Checklist of Common Talent Management and Financial Measurements

Kevin Oakes, Holly Tompson, and Lorrie Lykins

A list of common measures that companies use to analyze their talent management practices.

Tool 9-1. The Virtuous Cycle of Attributes and Results

Dave Ulrich and Norm Smallwood

A chart for comparing various leaders' perspectives.

Tool 10-1. Who's the Jerk at Work?

Beverly Kaye and Sharon Jordan-Evans

A self-assessment for measuring your negative leadership behavior.

Tool 11-1. Decreasing Rank Orders of Learning Activities by Leader Level

Tacy M. Byham and William C. Byham

A table for considering the type of training that is most effective for different levels of supervisors.

Tool 12-1. Competency Engagement Checklist

Mark David Jones

A checklist for integrating leadership competencies into your organization's operation for best-in-industry results.

Tool 13-1. Checklist for Avoiding Common Problems with Using 360-Degree Feedback

Craig Chappelow

A checklist to help your organization avoid common problems associated with 360-degree feedback assessments.

Tool 14-1. Decision Tool for Identifying Ways in Which Leaders Can Serve as Mentors and Teachers

Edward Betof

A checklist to help guide your thinking about the best ways that leaders can serve as mentors and teachers in your organization.

Tool 15-1. Developmental Assignment Plan Template

Ellen Van Velsor

A planning sheet to help map out a strategy for development opportunities.

Tool 15-2. Questions to Ask to Facilitate Learning from a Developmental Assignment

Ellen Van Velsor

A list of questions to assess personal competencies and reveal potential learning.

Tool 15-3. Enhancing Learning on the Job

Ellen Van Velsor

A checklist to determine how best to enhance individual learning in organizations.

Tool 16-1. Sample Minisurvey

Marshall Goldsmith

A sample minisurvey to be used as a guide for creating your own questions for coaching leaders.

Tool 17-1. What Inspiring Leaders Do Differently

Jack Zenger, Joe Folkman, and Scott Edinger

A list of the 10 behaviors that set inspiring and motivating leaders apart from the rest.

Tool 18-1. Leaders' Personal Beliefs

Bill George

A list of thought-provoking questions to explore your own personal beliefs or those of other leaders.

Tool 19-1. Trust Index

Priscilla Nelson and Ed Cohen
A tool to self-assess leadership traits.

Tool 20-1. The Ethics Check

Ken Blanchard
A checklist to test the ethics of decision making.

Tool 21-1. Trends Shaping Future Leadership Attributes

Karie Willyerd and Jeanne Meister
A diagnostic tool to help you align future business conditions with leadership skills and competencies.

Tool 22-1. Checklist for Avoiding Leader Derailment

William A. Gentry
A checklist to identify steps to avoid leader derailment.

Tool 24-1. Nine Steps to Becoming a Globally Savvy Leader

Stephen H. Rhinesmith
A step-by-step process for becoming a globally savvy leader.

Tool 25-1. Clarifying Your Goals for Development: Tool for Leaders

Marian N. Ruderman
A way to assess which of the five themes that affect the development of women are most prevalent.

Tool 26-1. Guidelines for Positive Feedback

Joanne G. Sujansky
A set of four guidelines for providing positive feedback that works.

Tool 26-2. Cross-Generational Model for Giving Corrective Feedback

Joanne G. Sujansky
A model for providing results-oriented and constructive feedback.

Tool 27-1. Diversity Paradigm Tool

Kay Iwata, Juan T. Lopez, and Julie O'Mara
A self-assessment tool to gain insight into personal diversity attitudes to increase your diversity competence.

Tool 28-1. Tree of Life

Lyndon Rego, Steadman D. Harrison III, and David G. Altman

A self-empowerment exercise to help individuals or groups explore how they can achieve their desired future using their skills and resources.

Tool 29-1. 10 Diagnostic Questions for a Successful Immersion Program

Lawrena Colombo and John Verderese

Ten diagnostic questions that reveal the critical aspects of developing a successful leadership immersion program.

Tool 30-1. Essentials for Good Leadership

John Lockard

A checklist of essential leadership qualities for any organization.

Tool 31-2. Political Savvy Skills for Effective Leadership in the Federal Government

Will Brown

A list to help define four key behaviors that ensure mid- to upper-level leaders are effective in the federal government, or any organization where political savvy is required.

Tool 32-3. Cultural, Philosophical, and Ideological Influences on Chinese CEOs' Thinking

Cheng Zhu

A chart for comparing the philosophy and ideology of major Chinese thought systems.

ASTD Leadership Handbook Contact Information

Altman, David G.
Center for Creative Leadership
One Leadership Place
Post Office Box 26300
Greensboro, NC 27438
altmand@ccl.org

Betof, Edward
32 Poplar Drive
Richboro, PA 18954
ebetof@wharton.upenn.edu

Biech, Elaine
ebb associates inc
Box 8249
Norfolk, VA 23503
ebboffice@aol.com

Blanchard, Ken
Blanchard International
125 State Place
Escondido, CA 92029
kenblanchard@kenblanchard
   .com

Booher, Dianna
Booher Consultants, Inc.
2051 Hughes Road
Grapevine, TX 76051
dianna.booher@booher.com

Brown, Will
Office of Naval Research
Code 00BD
875 North Randolph St., Rm 921
Arlington, VA 22203
brownw@onr.navy.mil

Byham, William C.
DDI
1225 Washington Pike
Bridgeville, PA 15017
bill.byham@ddiworld.com

Byham, Tacy M.
DDI
1225 Washington Pike
Bridgeville, PA 15017
tacy.byham@ddiworld.com

Chappelow, Craig
Center for Creative Leadership
One Leadership Place
Post Office Box 26300
Greensboro, NC 27438
chappelow@ccl.org

Cohen, Ed
Nelson Cohen Global
   Consulting
502 Neptune Avenue
Encinitas, CA 92024
ed@nelsoncohen.com

Colombo, Lawrena
PricewaterhouseCoopers
1800 Tysons Boulevard
McLean, VA 22102
lawrena.colombo@us.pwc.com

Edinger, Scott
Zenger Folkman
610 Technology Ave, Bldg B
Orem, UT 84097

Folkman, Joe
Zenger Folkman
610 Technology Ave, Bldg B
Orem, UT 84097

Gentry, William A.
Center for Creative Leadership
One Leadership Place
Post Office Box 26300
Greensboro, NC 27438
gentryb@ccl.org

George, Bill
1818 Oliver Ave S.
Minneapolis, MN 55405
bgeorge@hbs.edu;
bill@bpgeorge.com

Goldsmith, Marshall
Goldsmith Partners LLC
PO Box 9735
16770 Via de los Rosales
Rancho Santa Fe, CA 92067
marshall@marshallgoldsmith
.com

Goodstein, Leonard D.
4815 Foxhall Cres., NW
Washington DC, 20007
lendg@aol.com

Harrison, Steadman
Center for Creative Leadership
One Leadership Place
Post Office Box 26300
Greensboro, NC 27438
harrisons@ccl.org

Hesselbein, Frances
Leader to Leader Institute
320 Park Avenue, 3rd Floor
New York, NY 10022
frances@leadertoleader.org

Iwata, Kay
K. Iwata Associates, Inc.
32466 Monterey Drive
Union City, CA 94587
info@kiwata.com

Jones, Mark David
Small World Alliance
165 Costa Loop
Auburndale, FL 33823
mdjones@worldclass
benchmarking.com

Jordan-Evans, Sharon
Jordan-Evans Group
565 Chiswick Way
Cambria, CA 93428
sharon@jeg.org

Kaye, Beverly
Career Systems International
3545 Alana Drive
Sherman Oaks, CA 91403
beverly.kaye@careersystemsintl
.com

Kotter, John P.
Harvard Business School
Cambridge Office
975 Memorial Drive #207
Cambridge, MA 02138
jkotter@hbs.edu

Kouzes, James M.
117 Casa Vieja Place
Orinda, CA 94536
jim@kouzes.com

Lencioni, Patrick M.
The Table Group
3640 Mt. Diablo Blvd, Suite 202
Lafayette, CA 94549
tracy@tablegroup.com

Lockard, John
The Boeing Company
1215 S. Clark St., Ste 100
MC 793C-G010
Arlington, VA 22202
john.a.lockard@boeing.com

Lopez, Juan T.
Amistad Associates
6610 Barbara Drive
Sebastopol, Ca 95472
amistadasc@aol.com

Lykins, Lorrie
8950 Ninth Street N, Suite 115
St. Petersburg, FL 33702
lorrielykins@i4cp.com

McCauley, Cynthia D.
Center for Creative Leadership
One Leadership Place
Post Office Box 26300
Greensboro, NC 27438
mccauley@ccl.org

Meister, Jeanne
Future Workplace
1501 Broadway, Suite 800
New York, NY 10036
jeanne@futureworkplace.com

Nelson, Priscilla
Nelson Cohen Global
Consulting
502 Neptune Avenue
Encinitas, CA 92024
pris@nelsoncohen.com

Oakes, Kevin
411 First Ave South, Suite 402
Seattle, WA 98104
kevin.oakes@i4cp.com

O'Mara, Julie
O'Mara and Associates
2124 Water Rail Avenue
North Las Vegas, NV 89084
julie@omaraassoc.com

Posner, Barry Z.
15419 Banyan Lane
Monte Serano, CA 95030
bposner@scu.edu

Rego, Lyndon
Center for Creative Leadership
One Leadership Place
Post Office Box 26300
Greensboro, NC 27438
regol@ccl.org

Rhinesmith, Stephen H.
Stephen Rhinesmith, Inc.
P.O. Box 748
Chatham, MA 02633
SHRGlobal@Stephen
Rhinesmith.com

Ruderman, Marian H.
Center for Creative Leadership
One Leadership Place
Post Office Box 26300
Greensboro, NC 27438
ruderman@ccl.org

Smallwood, Norm
RBL Group
3521 N. University Ave, Ste 100
Provo, UT 84604
nsmallwood@rbl.net

**Sujansky, Joanne G.
 (Deceased)**
KEYGroup
1800 Sainte Claire Plaza
Pittsburgh, PA 15241
jsujansky@keygroupconsulting
 .com
www.joannesujansky.com

Tompson, Holly
411 First Ave South, Suite 402
Seattle, WA 98104

Ulrich, Dave
RBL Group
3521 N. University Ave, Ste 100
Provo, UT 84604
dou@umich.edu

Van Velsor, Ellen
Center for Creative Leadership
One Leadership Place
Post Office Box 26300
Greensboro, NC 27438
vanvelsor@ccl.org

Verderese, John
PricewaterhouseCoopers
1800 Tysons Boulevard
McLean, VA 22102
john.t.verderese@us.pwc.com

Willyerd, Karie
1220 Forest Hills Lane
Fort Collins, CO 80524
karie@jambok.com

Yukl, Gary
University at Albany, State
1400 Washington Ave
Albany, NY 12222
g.yukl@albany.edu

Zenger, Jack
Zenger Folkman
610 Technology Ave, Bldg B
Orem, UT 84097
jzenger@zfco.com

Zhu, Cheng
Center for Creative Leadership
One Leadership Place
Post Office Box 26300
Greensboro, NC 27438
cheng_zhu@post.harvard.edu
zhuc@ccl.org

✺ About the Editor

Elaine Biech is president and managing principal of ebb associates inc, an organization and leadership development firm that helps organizations work through large-scale change. She has been in the training and consulting field for thirty years working with private industry, government, and non-profit organizations.

Biech specializes in helping people work as teams to maximize their effectiveness. Customizing all of her work for individual clients, she conducts strategic planning sessions and implements corporate-wide systems such as quality improvement, change management, reengineering of business processes, and mentoring programs. She facilitates topics such as coaching today's employee, fostering creativity, customer service, creating leadership development programs, time management, speaking skills, coaching, consulting skills, training competence, conducting productive meetings, managing corporate-wide change, handling the difficult employee, organizational communication, conflict resolution, and effective listening. She is particularly adept at turning dysfunctional teams into productive teams.

She has developed media presentations and training materials and has presented at dozens of national and international conferences. Known as the trainer's trainer, she custom designs training programs for managers, leaders, trainers, and consultants. Biech has been featured in dozens of publications, including *The Wall Street Journal, Harvard Management Update, The Washington Post,* and *Fortune* magazine.

As a management and executive consultant, trainer, and designer, she has provided services to Outback Steakhouse, FAA, Land O'Lakes, McDonald's, Lands' End, General Casualty Insurance, Chrysler, Johnson Wax, PricewaterhouseCoopers, American Family Insurance, Marathon Oil, Hershey Chocolate, Federal Reserve Bank, the U.S. Navy, NASA, Newport News Shipbuilding, Kohler Company, ASTD, American Red Cross, the Association of Independent Certified Public Accountants, the University of Wisconsin, the College of William and Mary, ODU, and hundreds of other public and private sector organizations to prepare them for the challenges of the new millennium.

She is the author and editor of more than fifty books, including *A Coach's Guide to Developing Exemplary Leaders,* 2010; *The ASTD Leadership Handbook*, 2010; *The Leadership Challenge Activities Book*, 2010; *ASTD's Ultimate Train the Trainer,* 2009; *10 Steps to Successful Training,* 2009; *The Consultant's Quick Start Guide,* 2nd edition, 2009; *The ASTD Handbook for Workplace Learning Professionals,* 2008; *Trainer's Warehouse Book of Games,* 2008; *The Business of Consulting,* 2nd edition, 2007; *Thriving Through Change: A Leader's Practical Guide to Change Mastery,* 2007; *Successful Team-Building Tools,* 2nd edition, 2007; *90 World-Class Activities by 90 World-Class Trainers,* 2007 (named a Training Review Best Training Product of 2007); nine-volume set of *The ASTD Learning System,* 2006; *12 Habits of Successful Trainers,* ASTD *Infoline,* 2005; *The ASTD Infoline Dictionary of Basic Trainer Terms,* 2005; *Training for Dummies,* 2005; *Marketing Your Consulting Services,* 2003; *The Consultant's Legal Guide,* 2000; *Interpersonal Skills: Understanding Your Impact on Others,* 1996; *Building High Performance,* 1998; *The Pfeiffer Annual for Consultants* and *The Pfeiffer Annual for Trainers,* 1998–2011; *The ASTD Sourcebook: Creativity and Innovation—Widen Your Spectrum,* 1996; *The HR Handbook,* 1996; *Ten Mistakes CEOs Make About Training,* 1995; *TQM for Training,* 1994; *Diagnostic Tools for Total Quality,* ASTD *Infoline,* 1991; *Managing Teamwork,* 1994; *Process Improvement: Achieving Quality Together,* 1994; *Business Communications,* 1992; *Delegating For Results,* 1992; *Increased Productivity Through Effective Meetings,* 1987; and *Stress Management, Building Healthy Families,* 1984. Her books have been translated into Chinese, German, and Dutch.

Biech has her BS from the University of Wisconsin-Superior in Business and Education Consulting, and her MS in Human Resource Development. She is active at the national level of ASTD, is a life-time member, served on the 1990 National Conference Design Committee, was a member of the National ASTD Board of Directors, and served as the Society's Secretary from 1991–1994, initiated and chaired Consultant's Day for seven years, and was the International Conference Design Chair in 2000. In addition to her work with ASTD, she has served on the Independent Consultants Association's (ICA) Advisory Committee and on the Instructional Systems Association (ISA) board of directors.

Biech is the recipient of the 1992 National ASTD Torch Award, the 2004 ASTD Volunteer-Staff Partnership Award, and the 2006 ASTD Gordon M. Bliss Memorial Award. She was selected for the 1995 Wisconsin Women Entrepreneur's Mentor Award. In 2001, she received ISA's highest award, The ISA Spirit Award. She has been the consulting editor for the prestigious Training and Consulting Annuals published by Jossey-Bass/Pfeiffer for the past 12 years.

THE ASTD MISSION:

Through exceptional learning and performance, we create a world that works better.

The American Society for Training & Development provides world-class professional development opportunities, content, networking, and resources for workplace learning and performance professionals.

Dedicated to helping members increase their relevance, enhance their skills, and align learning to business results, ASTD sets the standard for best practices within the profession.

The society is recognized for shaping global discussions on workforce development and providing the tools to demonstrate the impact of learning on the organizational bottom line. ASTD represents the profession's interests to corporate executives, policy makers, academic leaders, small business owners, and consultants through world-class content, convening opportunities, professional development, and awards and recognition.

Resources
- *T+D (Training + Development)* Magazine
- ASTD Press
- Industry Newsletters
- Research and Benchmarking
- Representation to Policy Makers

Professional Development
- Certificate Programs
- Conferences and Workshops
- Online Learning
- CPLP™ Certification through the ASTD Certification Institute
- Career Center and Job Bank

Networking
- Local Chapters
- Online Communities
- ASTD Connect
- Benchmarking Forum
- Learning Executives Network

Awards and Best Practices
- ASTD Best Awards
- Excellence in Practice Awards
- E-Learning Courseware Certification (ECC) through the ASTD Certification Institute

Learn more about ASTD at www.astd.org.
1.800.628.2783 (U.S.) or 1.703.683.8100
customercare@astd.org

080615.31410

About Berrett-Koehler Publishers

Berrett-Koehler is an independent publisher dedicated to an ambitious mission: Creating a World That Works for All.

We believe that to truly create a better world, action is needed at all levels—individual, organizational, and societal. At the individual level, our publications help people align their lives with their values and with their aspirations for a better world. At the organizational level, our publications promote progressive leadership and management practices, socially responsible approaches to business, and humane and effective organizations. At the societal level, our publications advance social and economic justice, shared prosperity, sustainability, and new solutions to national and global issues.

Visit our website

Go to www.bkconnection.com to read exclusive excerpts of new books, get special discounts, see videos of our authors, read their blogs, find out about author appearances and other BK events, browse our complete catalog, and more!

Get the *BK Communiqué,* our free eNewsletter

News about Berrett-Koehler, yes—new book announcements, special offers, author interviews. But also news by Berrett-Koehler authors, employees, and fellow travelers. Tales of the book trade. Links to our favorite websites and videos—informative, amusing, sometimes inexplicable. Trivia questions—win a free book! Letters to the editor. And much more!

See a sample issue: www.bkconnection.com/BKCommunique.

Berrett–Koehler Publishers, Inc.
San Francisco. *www.bkconnection.com*

❧ Index